Fruits Basket

Volume 6

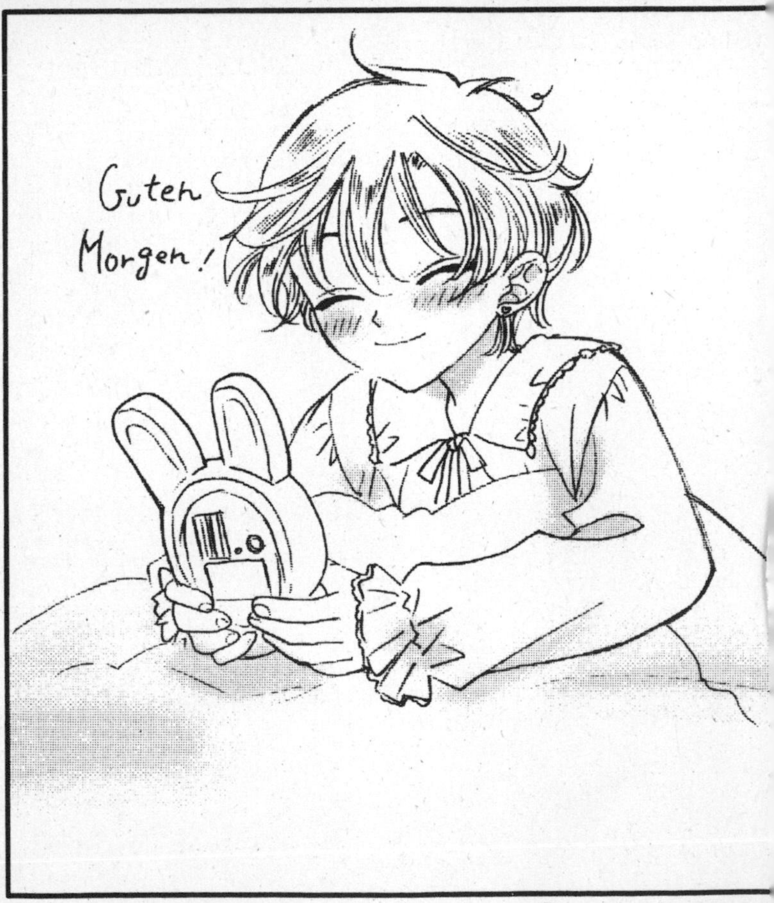
Guten Morgen!

Natsuki Taka

Fruits Basket Vol. 6
Created by Natsuki Takaya

Translation - Alethea Nibley and Athena Nibley
Additional Translation - Alexis Kirsch
Contributing Writer - Adam Arnold
Copy Editor - Lillian Diaz-Przybyl
Retouch and Lettering - Deron Bennett
Production Artists - Yoohae Yang, James Dashiell
Cover Design - Aaron Suhr

Editor - Jake Forbes
Digital Imaging Manager - Chris Buford
Pre-Press Manager - Antonio DePietro
Production Managers - Jennifer Miller and Mutsumi Miyazaki
Art Director - Matt Alford
Managing Editor - Jill Freshney
VP of Production - Ron Klamert
President and C.O.O. - John Parker
Publisher and C.E.O. - Stuart Levy

A  Manga

TOKYOPOP Inc.
5900 Wilshire Blvd. Suite 2000
Los Angeles, CA 90036

E-mail: info@TOKYOPOP.com
Come visit us online at www.TOKYOPOP.com

ISBN: 1-59182-608-X

First TOKYOPOP printing: December 2004
20 19 18 17 16 15 14 13
Printed in the USA

Fruits Basket

Volume 6

By
Natsuki Takaya

HAMBURG // LONDON // LOS ANGELES // TOKYO

Fruits Basket™

Table of Contents

STORY SO FAR...

Hello, I'm Tohru Honda and I have com to know a terrible secret. After the dea of my mother, I was living by myself in tent, when the Sohma family took me in. I soon learned that the Sohma family lives with a curse! Each family member is possessed by the vengeful spirit of an animal from the Chinese Zodiac. Whenever one of them become weak or is hugged by a member of the opposite sex, they change into their Zodiac animal!

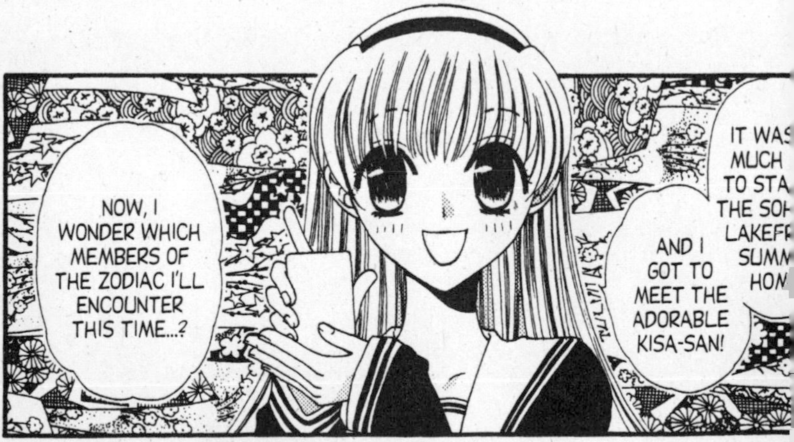
IT WAS MUCH TO STA THE SOH LAKEFR SUMM HOM
AND I GOT TO MEET THE ADORABLE KISA-SAN!
NOW, I WONDER WHICH MEMBERS OF THE ZODIAC I'LL ENCOUNTER THIS TIME...?

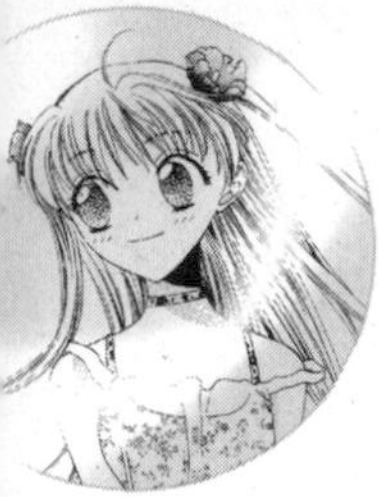

Tohru Honda

The ever-optimistic hero of our story. An orphan, she now lives in Shigure's house, along with Yuki and Kyo, and is the only person outside of the family who knows the Sohma family's curse.

Yuki Sohma, the Rat

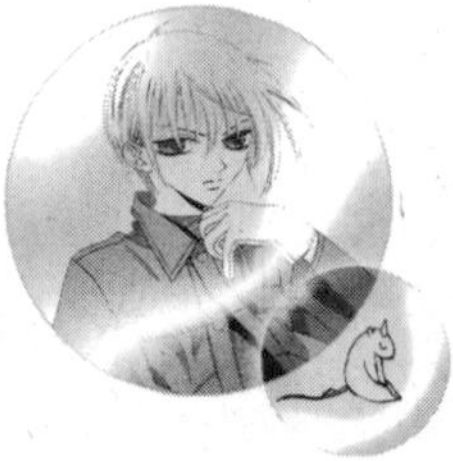

Soft-spoken. Self-esteem issues. At school he's called "Prince Yuki."

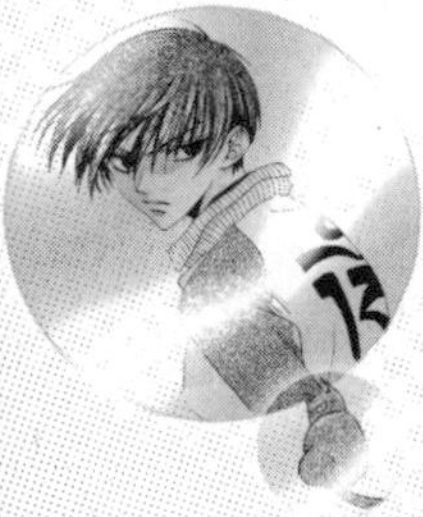

Kyo Sohma, the Cat

The Cat who was left out of the Zodiac. Hates Yuki, leeks and Miso. But mostly Yuki.

Mabudachi Trio

Shigure Sohma, the Dog

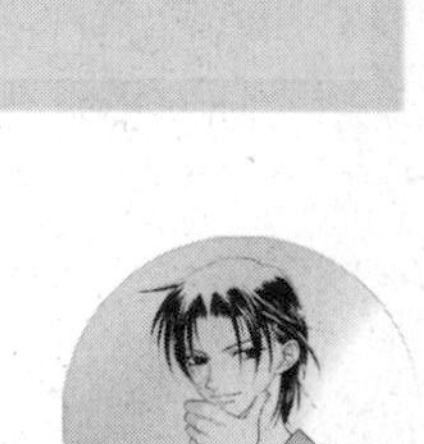

Enigmatic, mischievous and a little perverted. A popular novelist.

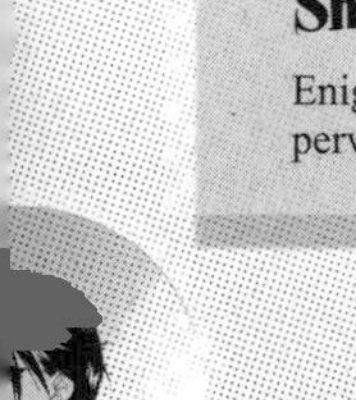

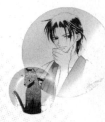

Hatori Sohma, the Dragon

Family doctor to the Sohmas. Only thing he can't cure is his broken heart.

Ayame Sohma, the Snake

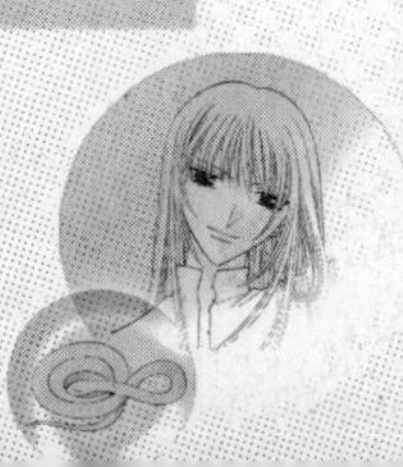

Yuki's older brother. A proud and playful drama queen…er, king. Runs a costume shop.

Fruits Basket Characters

Kagura Sohma, the Boar

Bashful, yet headstrong. Determined to marry Kyo, even if it kills him.

Momiji Sohma, the Rabbit

Half-German. He's older than he looks.
Mother rejected him because of the Sohma curse.

Hatsuharu Sohma, the Ox

The nicest of guys, except when he goes "Black."
Then you'd better watch out.

Akito Sohma

The head of the Sohma clan. A dark figure of many secrets.
Treated with fear and reverence.

Tohru's Best Friends

Saki Hanajima

"Hana-chan." Can sense people's "waves." Goth demeanor scares her classmates.

Arisa Uotani

"Uo-chan." A tough-talking "Yankee" who looks out for her friends.

Kisa Sohma, the Tiger

Kisa became shy and self-conscious due to constant teasing by her classmates. Yuki, who has similar insecurities, feels particularly close to Kisa.

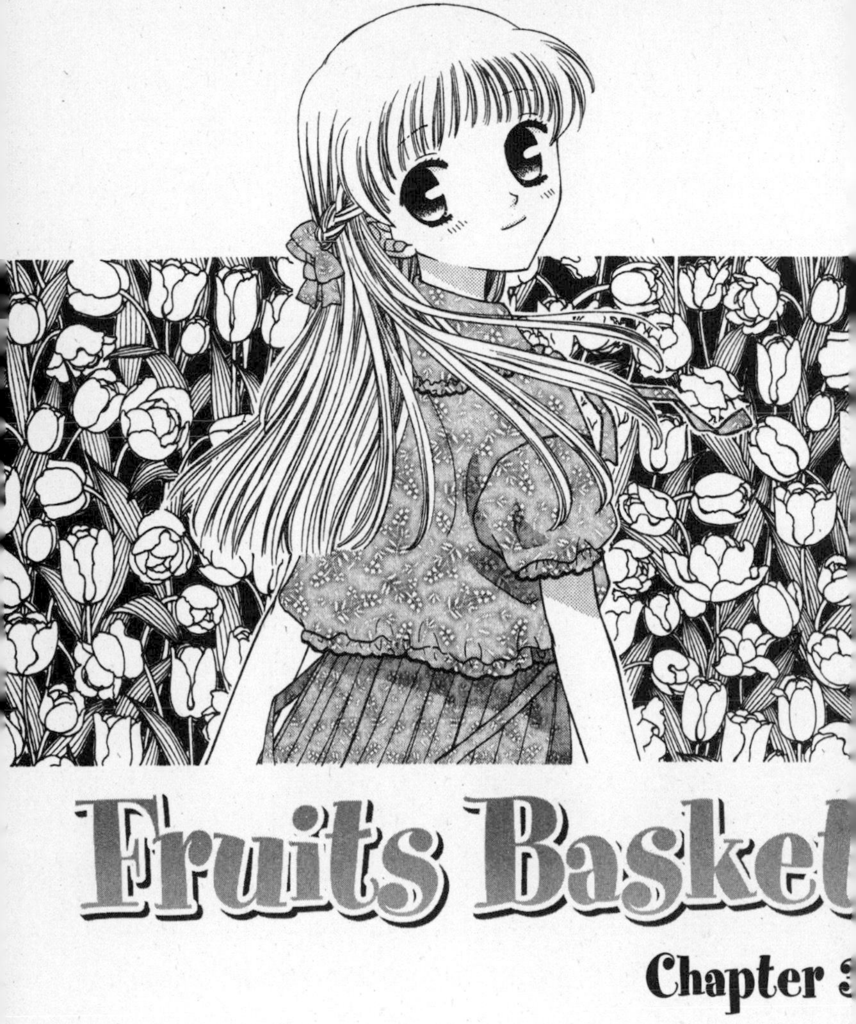

Fruits Basket

Chapter 3

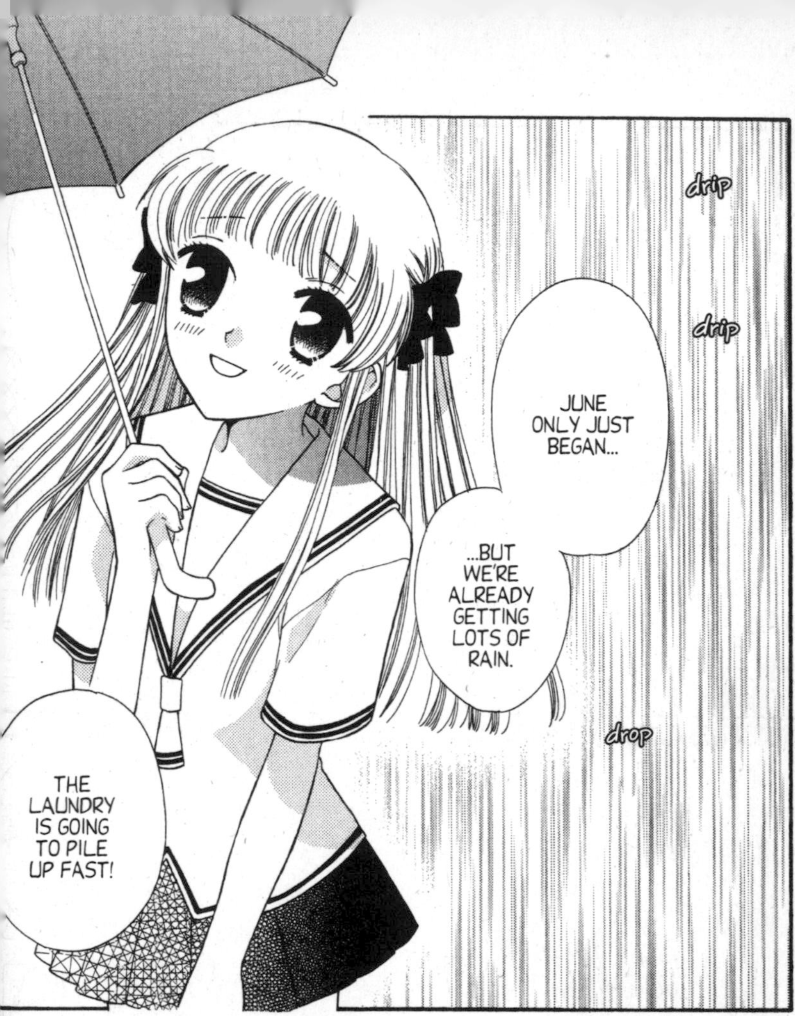
drip
JUNE ONLY JUST BEGAN...
drip
...BUT WE'RE ALREADY GETTING LOTS OF RAIN.
drop
THE LAUNDRY IS GOING TO PILE UP FAST!

ULTRA SPECIAL BLAH BLAH BLAH 1

I've been going through some hard times lately.
And on top of that, I had a fever of over 105°.
It's like Punch, Punch, Kick!
By the way, I tend to get sick on rainy days.

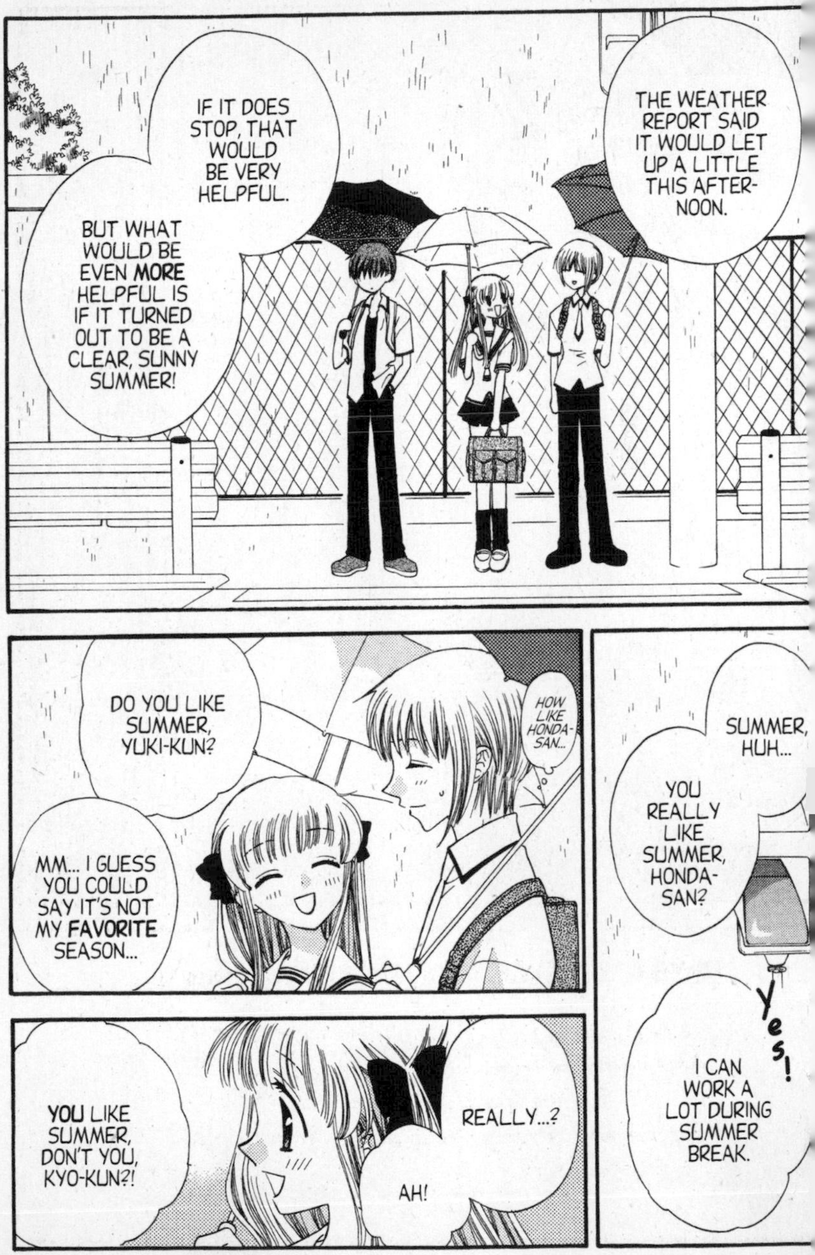
THE WEATHER REPORT SAID IT WOULD LET UP A LITTLE THIS AFTER-NOON.
IF IT DOES STOP, THAT WOULD BE VERY HELPFUL.
BUT WHAT WOULD BE EVEN **MORE** HELPFUL IS IF IT TURNED OUT TO BE A CLEAR, SUNNY SUMMER!
SUMMER, HUH...
YOU REALLY LIKE SUMMER, HONDA-SAN?
Yes!
I CAN WORK A LOT DURING SUMMER BREAK.
HOW LIKE HONDA-SAN...
DO YOU LIKE SUMMER, YUKI-KUN?
MM... I GUESS YOU COULD SAY IT'S NOT MY **FAVORITE** SEASON...
REALLY...?
AH!
YOU LIKE SUMMER, DON'T YOU, KYO-KUN?!

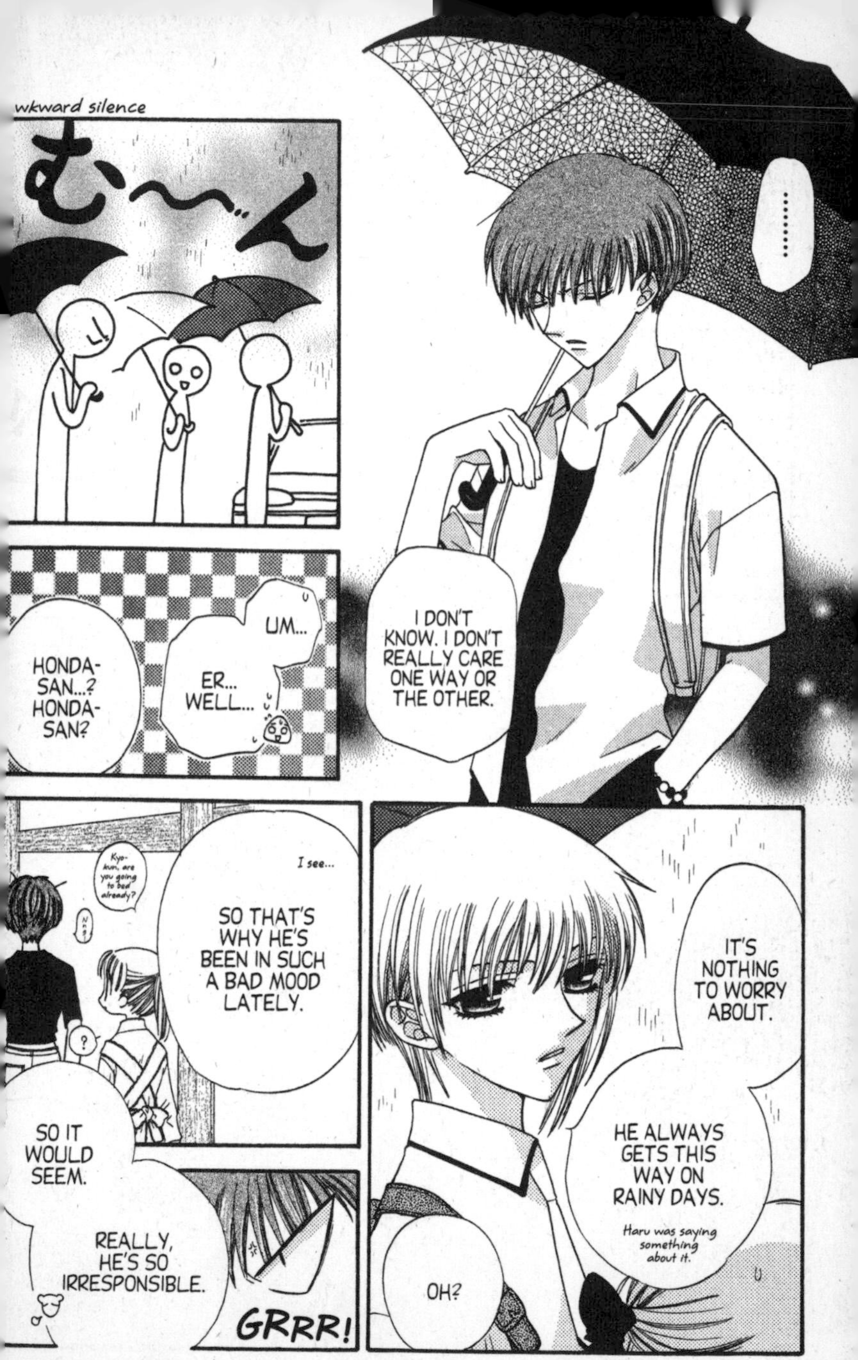
......
I DON'T KNOW. I DON'T REALLY CARE ONE WAY OR THE OTHER.
wkward silence
むーん
HONDA-SAN...? HONDA-SAN?
UM...
ER... WELL...
IT'S NOTHING TO WORRY ABOUT.
HE ALWAYS GETS THIS WAY ON RAINY DAYS.
Haru was saying something about it.
OH?
I see...
SO THAT'S WHY HE'S BEEN IN SUCH A BAD MOOD LATELY.
Kyo-kun, are you going to bed already?
Nng
?
SO IT WOULD SEEM.
REALLY, HE'S SO IRRESPONSIBLE.
GRRR!

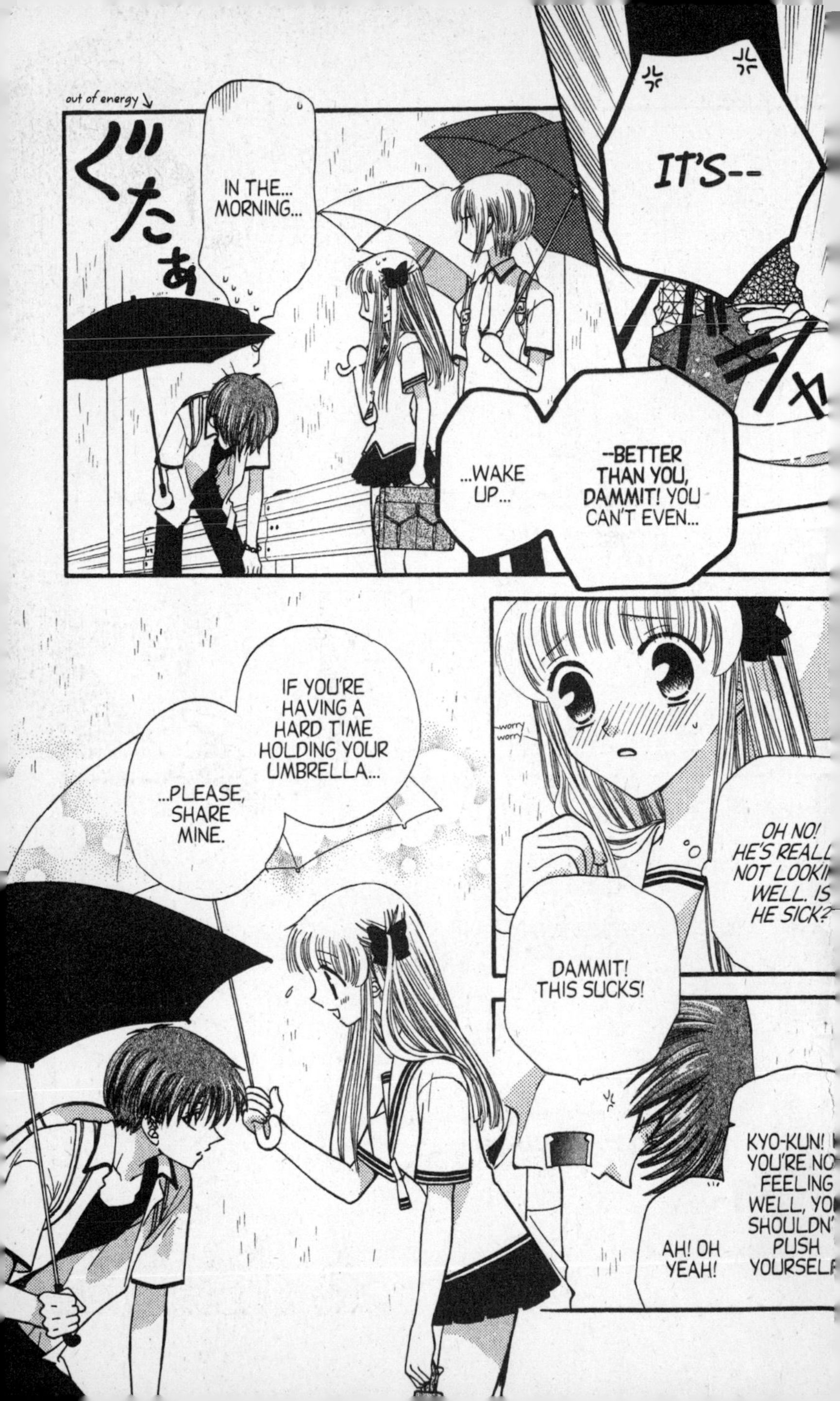
IT'S--
--BETTER THAN YOU, DAMMIT! YOU CAN'T EVEN...
...WAKE UP...
IN THE... MORNING...
out of energy
ぐたぁ
worry worry
OH NO! HE'S REALL NOT LOOKI WELL. IS HE SICK?
KYO-KUN! YOU'RE NO FEELING WELL, YO SHOULDN' PUSH YOURSEL
DAMMIT! THIS SUCKS!
AH! OH YEAH!
IF YOU'RE HAVING A HARD TIME HOLDING YOUR UMBRELLA...
...PLEASE, SHARE MINE.

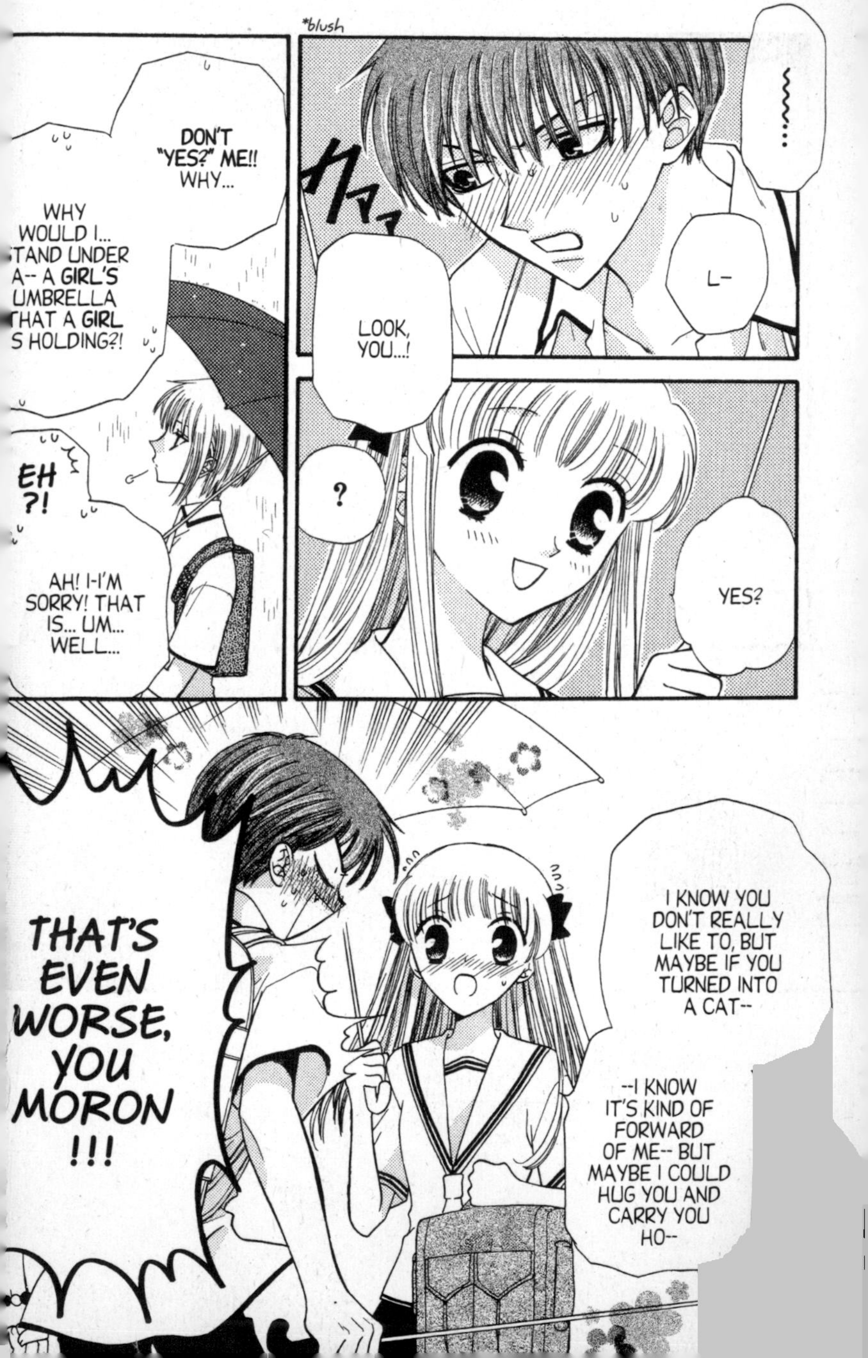
*blush
......
L-
LOOK, YOU...!
?
YES?
DON'T "YES?" ME!! WHY...
WHY WOULD I... STAND UNDER A-- A GIRL'S UMBRELLA THAT A GIRL S HOLDING?!
EH?!
AH! I-I'M SORRY! THAT IS... UM... WELL...
I KNOW YOU DON'T REALLY LIKE TO, BUT MAYBE IF YOU TURNED INTO A CAT--
--I KNOW IT'S KIND OF FORWARD OF ME-- BUT MAYBE I COULD HUG YOU AND CARRY YOU HO--
THAT'S EVEN WORSE, YOU MORON!!!

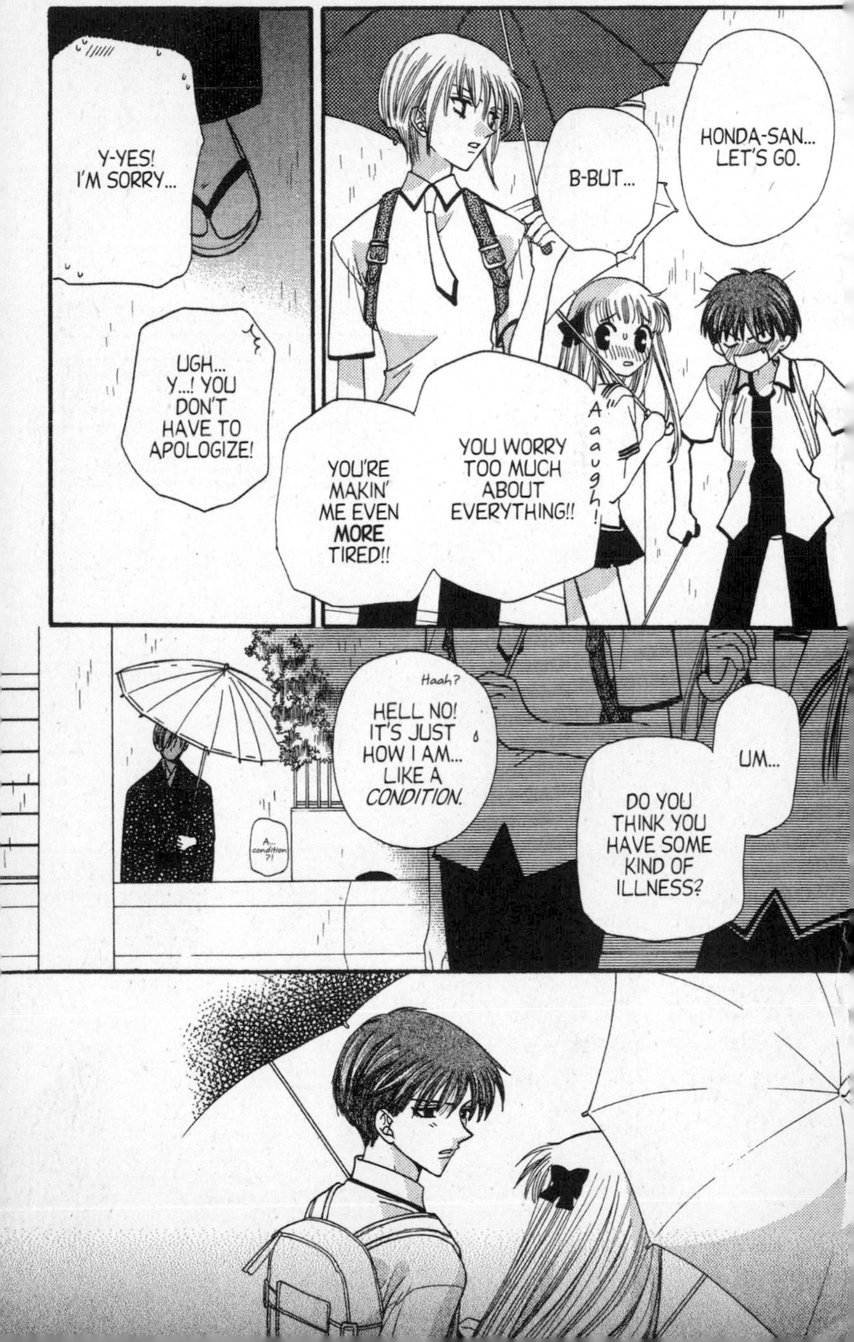
HONDA-SAN... LET'S GO.
B-BUT...
YOU WORRY TOO MUCH ABOUT EVERYTHING!!
YOU'RE MAKIN' ME EVEN MORE TIRED!!
Aaaugh!
Y-YES! I'M SORRY...
UGH... Y...! YOU DON'T HAVE TO APOLOGIZE!
UM...
DO YOU THINK YOU HAVE SOME KIND OF ILLNESS?
Haah?
HELL NO! IT'S JUST HOW I AM... LIKE A CONDITION.
A... condition?!

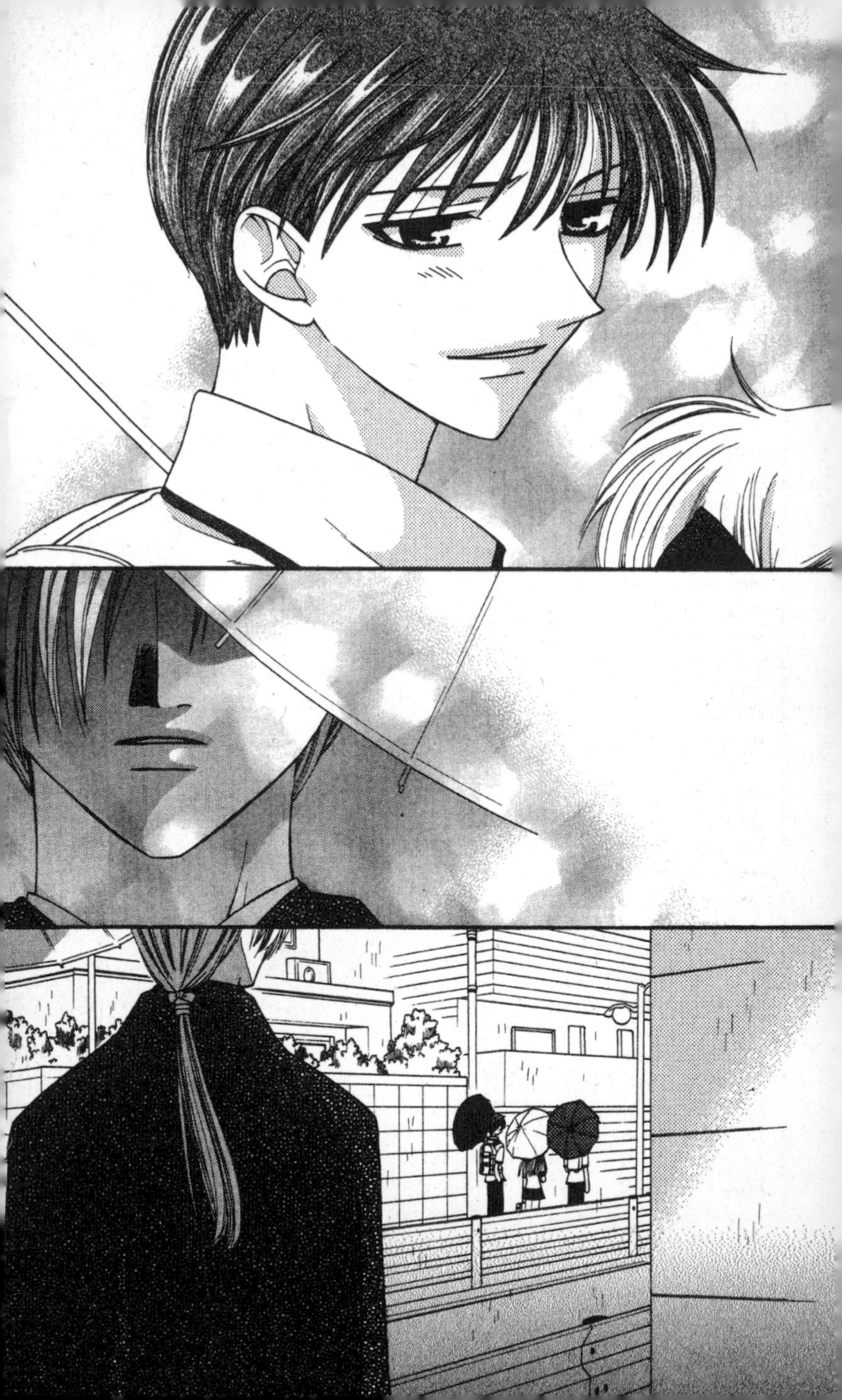

Fruits Basket 6 Part 1:

Hajimemashite and hello! I'm Takaya. Furuba has made it to the sixth volume. That means it's been almost two years since I started drawing it. Woooow... (Gazing into the distance.) So the volume 6 cover features Momiji. You know, **Momitchi!** He looks very young, but inside, he's the most mature of his generation of Sohmas. Right? "He had to be mature to deal with his youthful appearance and parental situation, right?" Well, yeah. It's kinda sad that way. But I also made him that way because it's cute! Recently, my hand hasn't been doing very well, so my handwriting is harder to read than usual, so gomen nasai. (I'm sorry!) Please enjoy volume 6.

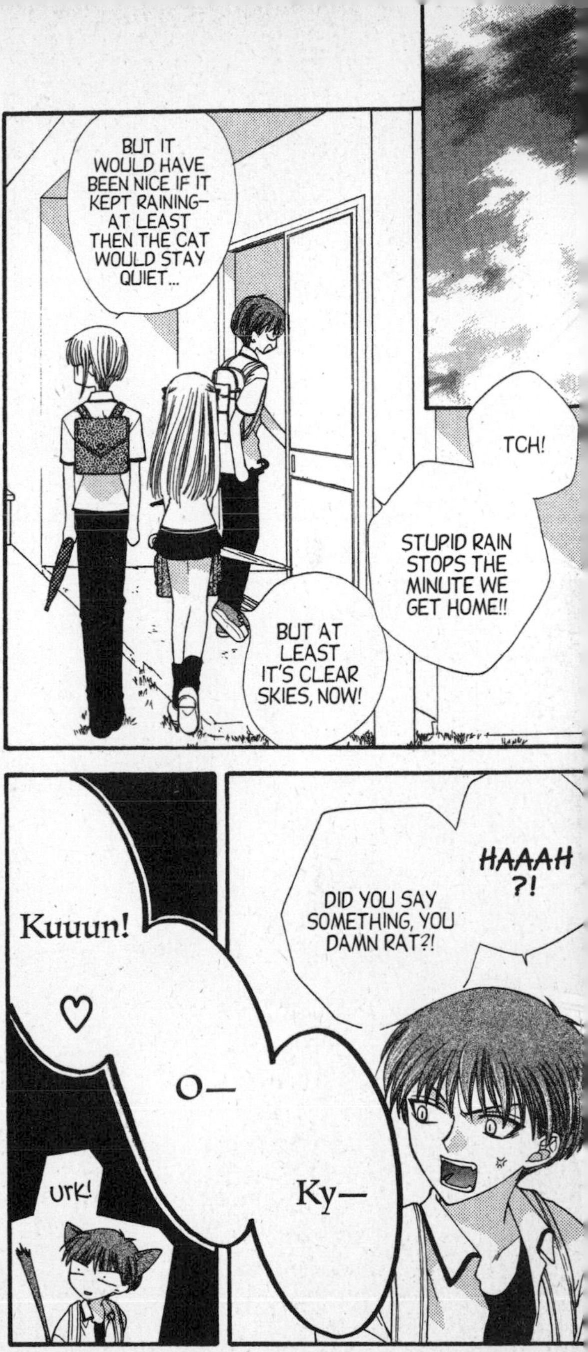
TCH!
STUPID RAIN STOPS THE MINUTE WE GET HOME!!
BUT AT LEAST IT'S CLEAR SKIES, NOW!
BUT IT WOULD HAVE BEEN NICE IF IT KEPT RAINING—AT LEAST THEN THE CAT WOULD STAY QUIET...
HAAAH ?!
DID YOU SAY SOMETHING, YOU DAMN RAT?!
Kuuun! ♡
O— Ky—
Urk!

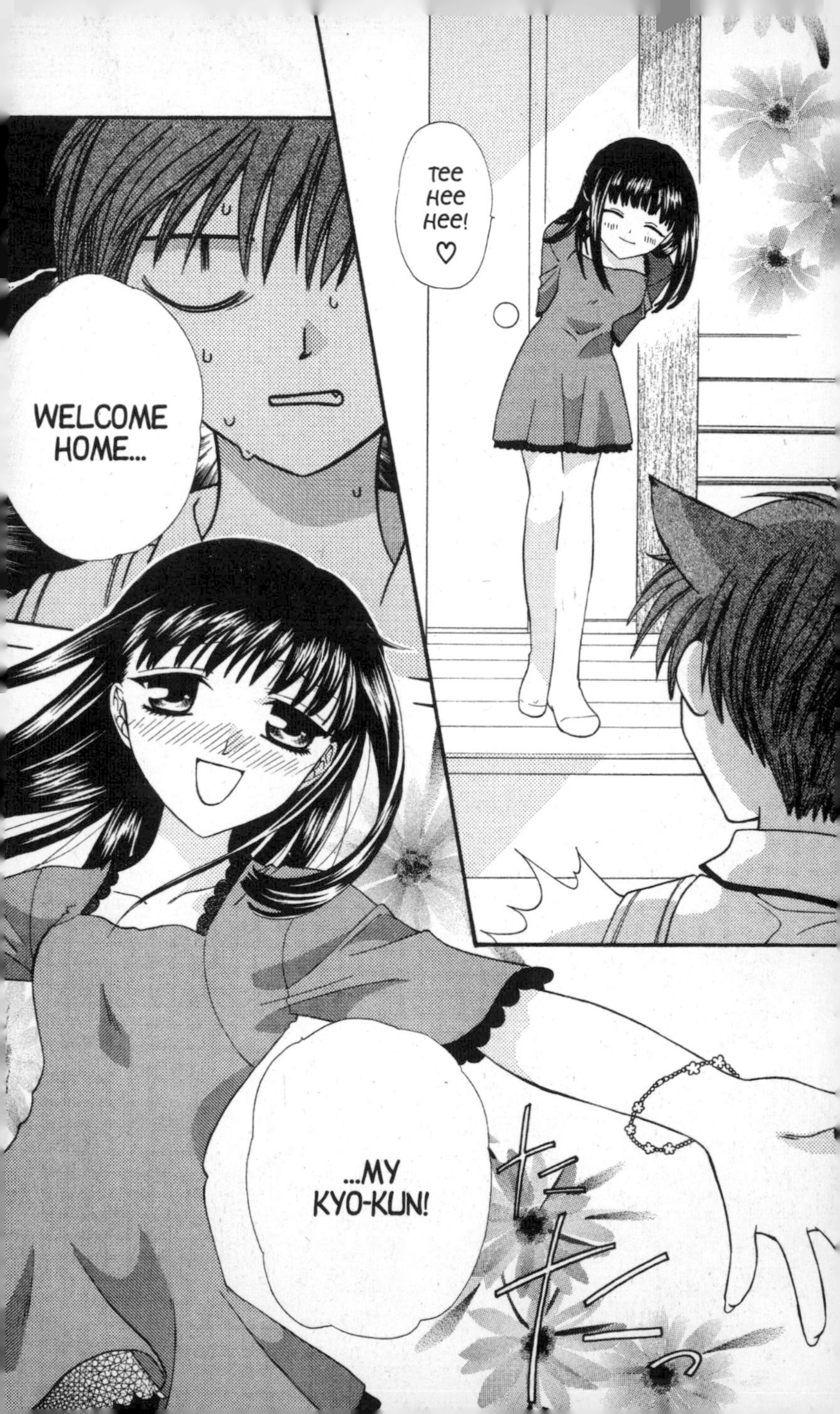
TEE HEE HEE! ♡
WELCOME HOME...
...MY KYO-KUN!

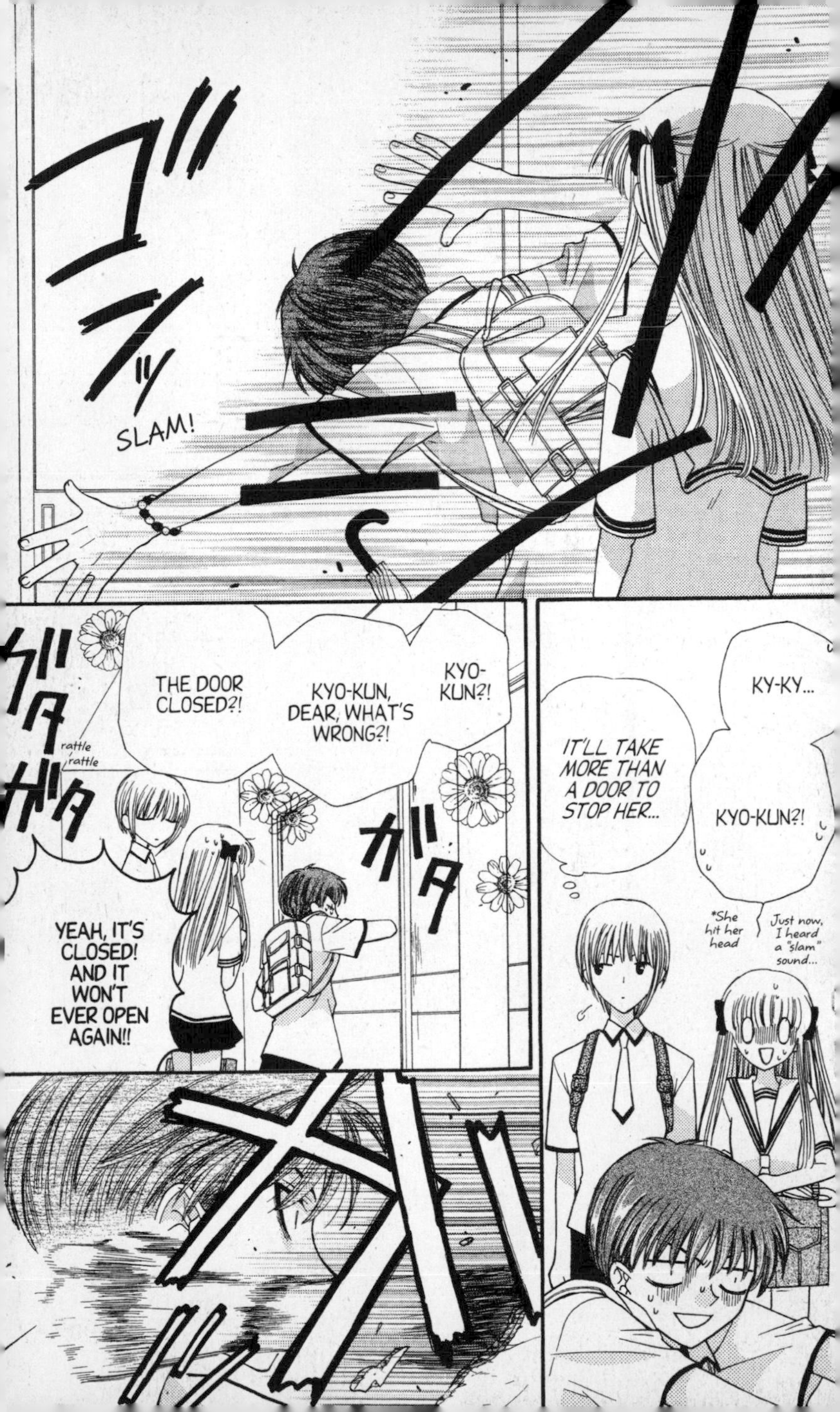
SLAM!
KY-KY...
KYO-KUN?!
IT'LL TAKE MORE THAN A DOOR TO STOP HER...
Just now, I heard a "slam" sound...
*She hit her head
KYO-KUN?!
KYO-KUN, DEAR, WHAT'S WRONG?!
THE DOOR CLOSED?!
ガタ
ガタガタ
rattle rattle
YEAH, IT'S CLOSED! AND IT WON'T EVER OPEN AGAIN!!

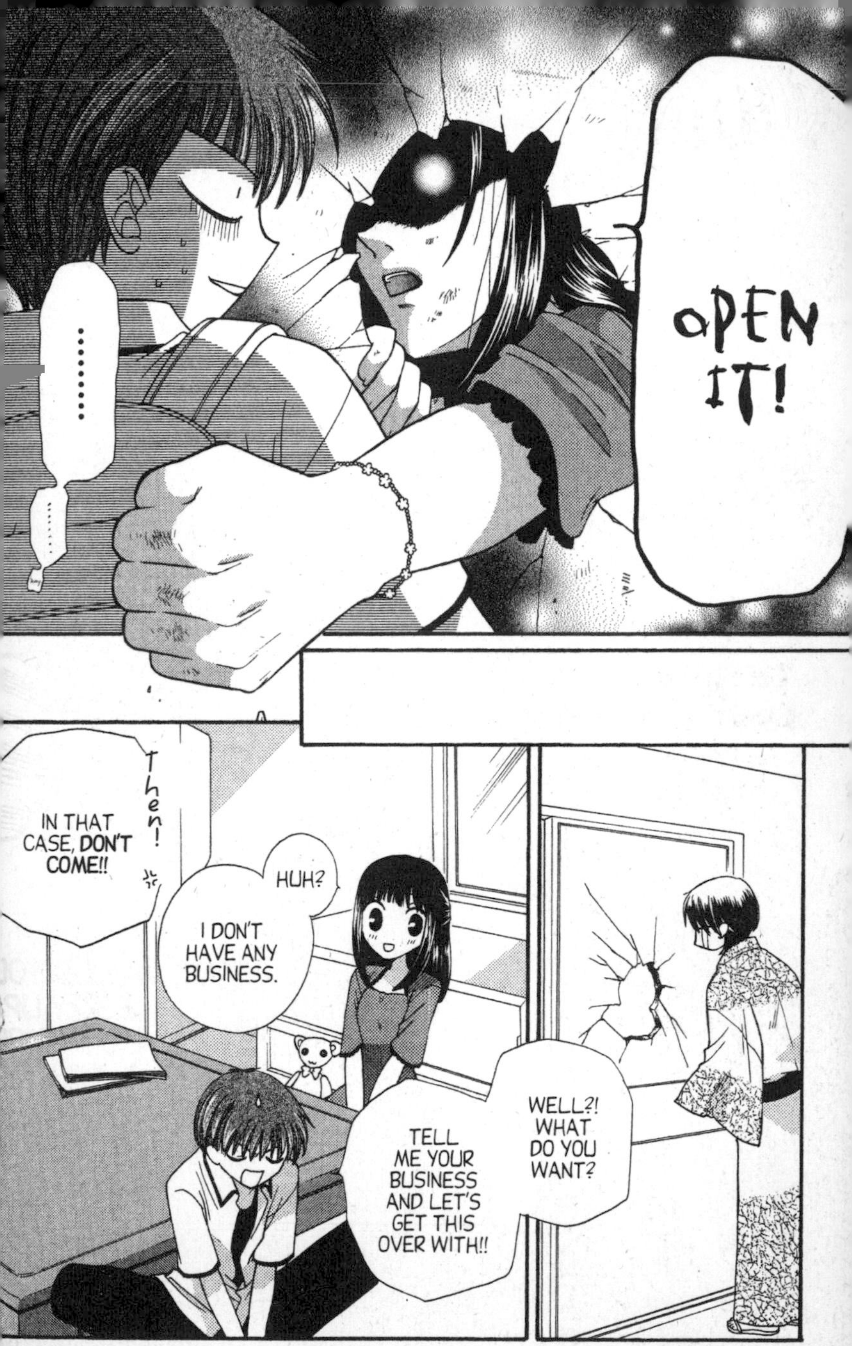

OPEN IT!
......
......
WELL?! WHAT DO YOU WANT?
TELL ME YOUR BUSINESS AND LET'S GET THIS OVER WITH!!
HUH?
I DON'T HAVE ANY BUSINESS.
Then!
IN THAT CASE, DON'T COME!!

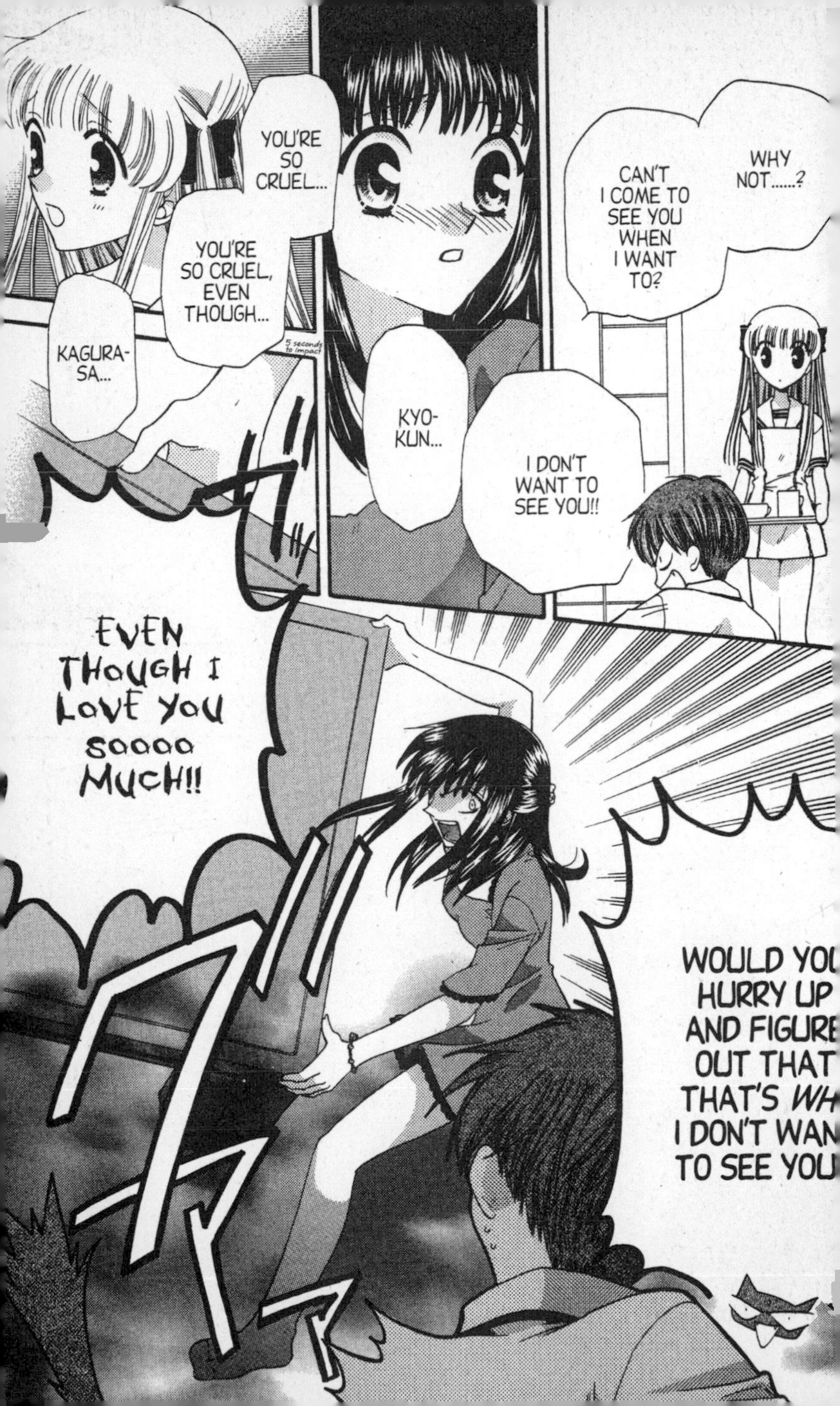
WHY NOT......?
CAN'T I COME TO SEE YOU WHEN I WANT TO?
I DON'T WANT TO SEE YOU!!
KYO-KUN...
YOU'RE SO CRUEL...
YOU'RE SO CRUEL, EVEN THOUGH...
5 seconds to impact
KAGURA-SA...
EVEN THOUGH I LOVE YOU SAAAA MUCH!!
WOULD YOU HURRY UP AND FIGURE OUT THAT THAT'S *WH* I DON'T WAN TO SEE YOU

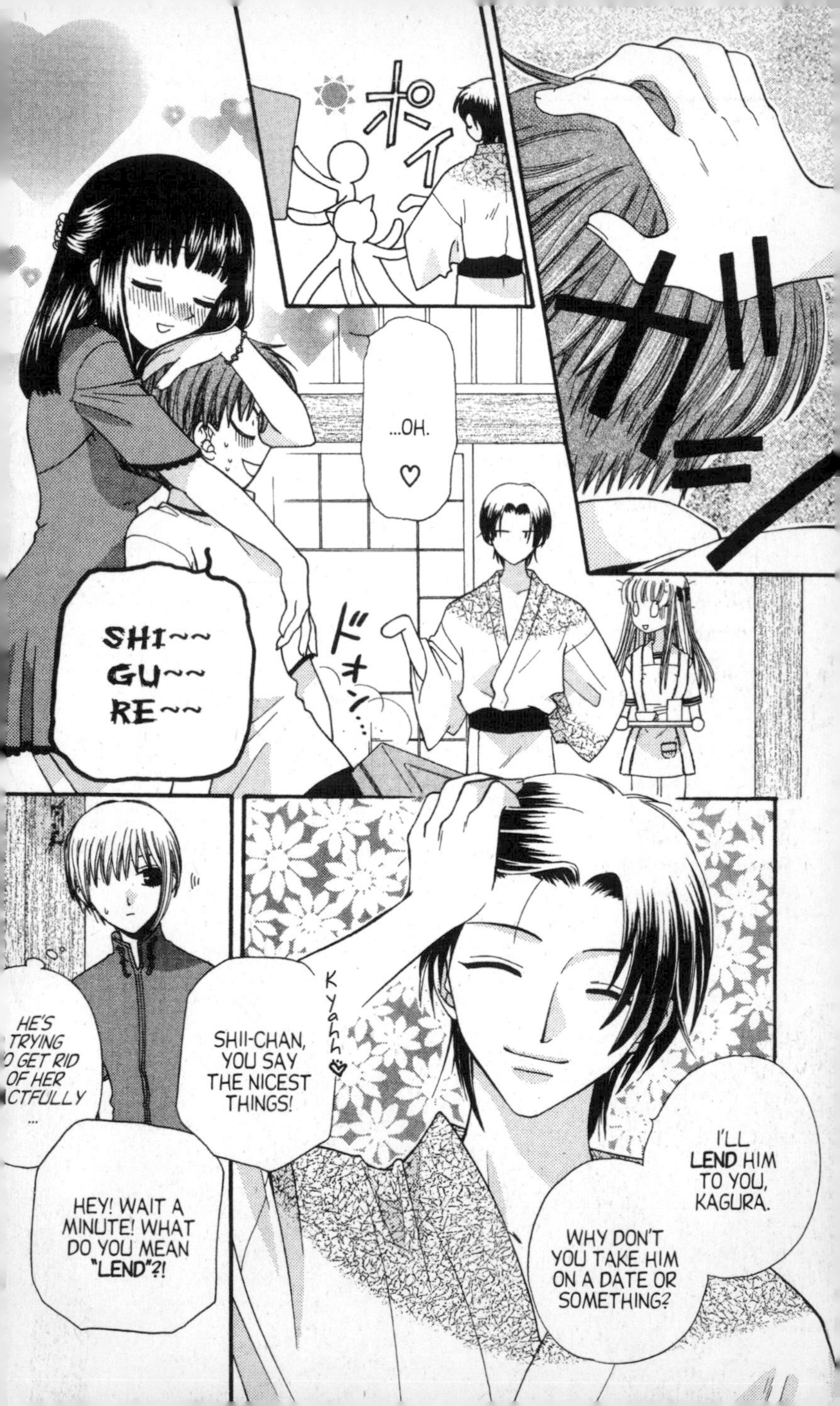

ポイ
...OH. ♡
ドオン...
SHI~~ GU~~ RE~~
I'LL **LEND** HIM TO YOU, KAGURA.
WHY DON'T YOU TAKE HIM ON A DATE OR SOMETHING?
Kyahh ♡
SHII-CHAN, YOU SAY THE NICEST THINGS!
HEY! WAIT A MINUTE! WHAT DO YOU MEAN "**LEND**"?!
HE'S TRYING O GET RID OF HER CTFULLY ...

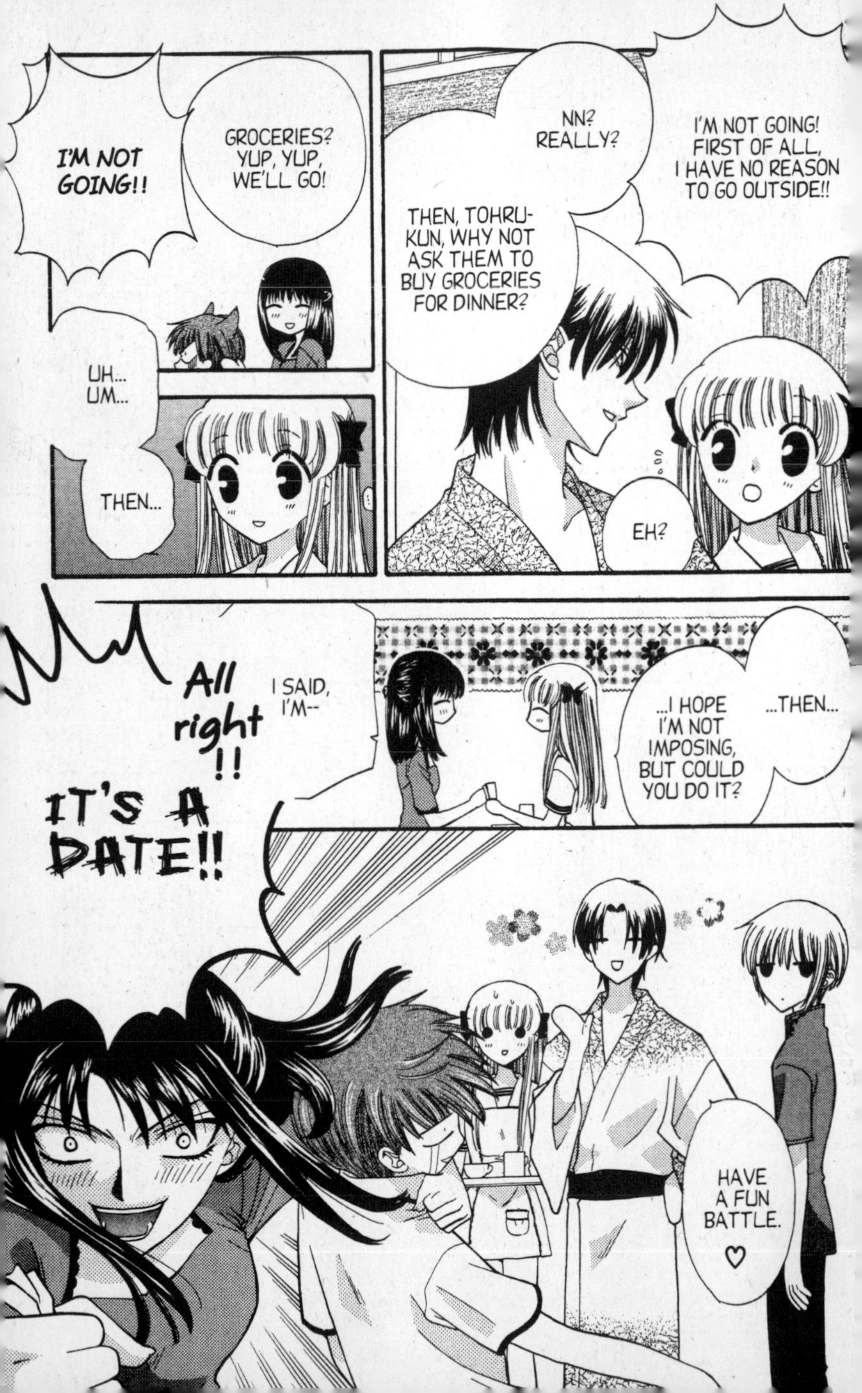
I'M NOT GOING! FIRST OF ALL, I HAVE NO REASON TO GO OUTSIDE!!
NN? REALLY?
THEN, TOHRU-KUN, WHY NOT ASK THEM TO BUY GROCERIES FOR DINNER?
EH?
GROCERIES? YUP, YUP, WE'LL GO!
I'M NOT GOING!!
UH... UM...
THEN...
...THEN...
...I HOPE I'M NOT IMPOSING, BUT COULD YOU DO IT?
I SAID, I'M--
All right!!
IT'S A DATE!!
HAVE A FUN BATTLE. ♡

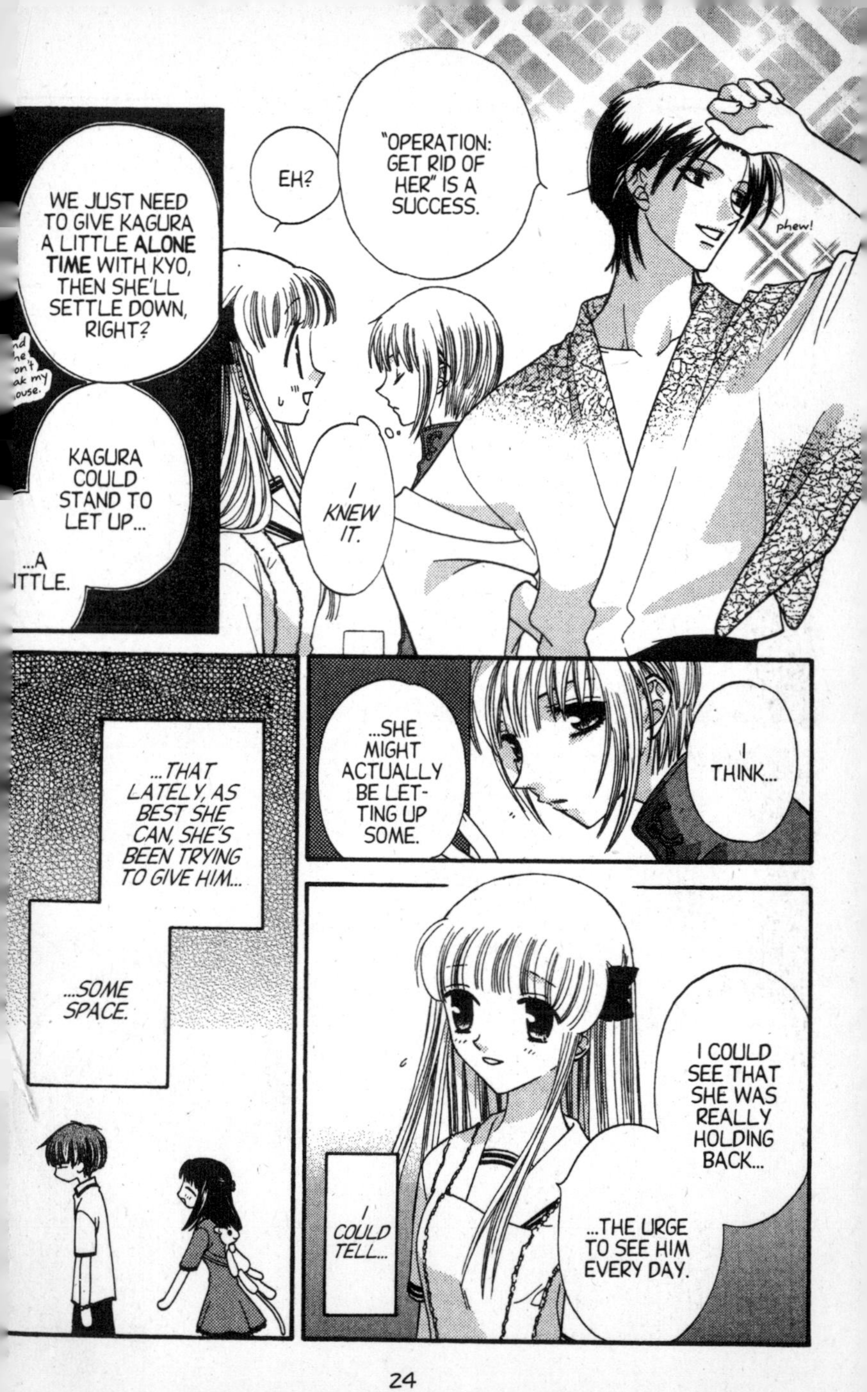
phew!
"OPERATION: GET RID OF HER" IS A SUCCESS.
EH?
WE JUST NEED TO GIVE KAGURA A LITTLE **ALONE TIME** WITH KYO, THEN SHE'LL SETTLE DOWN, RIGHT?
I KNEW IT.
KAGURA COULD STAND TO LET UP...
...A LITTLE.
I THINK...
...SHE MIGHT ACTUALLY BE LETTING UP SOME.
I COULD SEE THAT SHE WAS REALLY HOLDING BACK...
...THE URGE TO SEE HIM EVERY DAY.
I COULD TELL...
...THAT LATELY, AS BEST SHE CAN, SHE'S BEEN TRYING TO GIVE HIM...
...SOME SPACE.

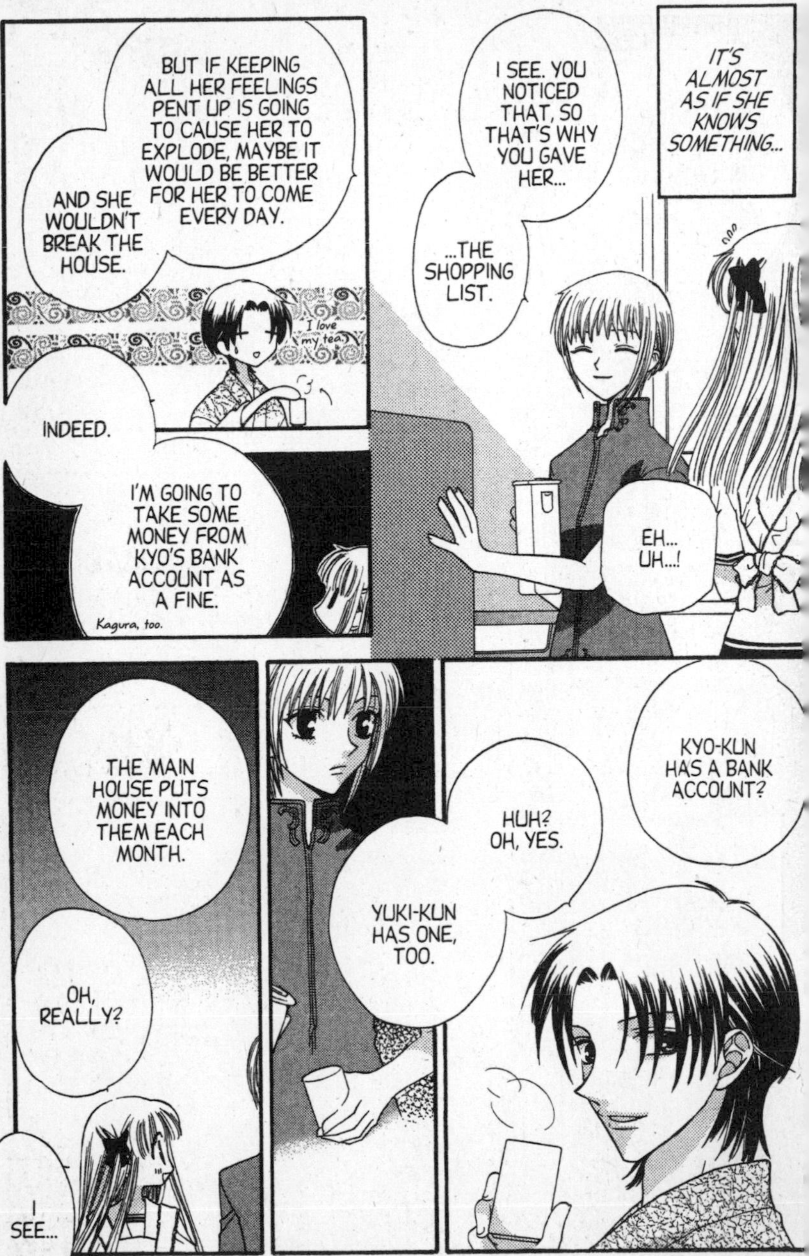
IT'S ALMOST AS IF SHE KNOWS SOMETHING...
I SEE. YOU NOTICED THAT, SO THAT'S WHY YOU GAVE HER...
...THE SHOPPING LIST.
EH... UH...!
BUT IF KEEPING ALL HER FEELINGS PENT UP IS GOING TO CAUSE HER TO EXPLODE, MAYBE IT WOULD BE BETTER FOR HER TO COME EVERY DAY.
AND SHE WOULDN'T BREAK THE HOUSE.
I love my tea.
INDEED.
I'M GOING TO TAKE SOME MONEY FROM KYO'S BANK ACCOUNT AS A FINE.
Kagura, too.
KYO-KUN HAS A BANK ACCOUNT?
HUH? OH, YES.
YUKI-KUN HAS ONE, TOO.
THE MAIN HOUSE PUTS MONEY INTO THEM EACH MONTH.
OH, REALLY?
I SEE...

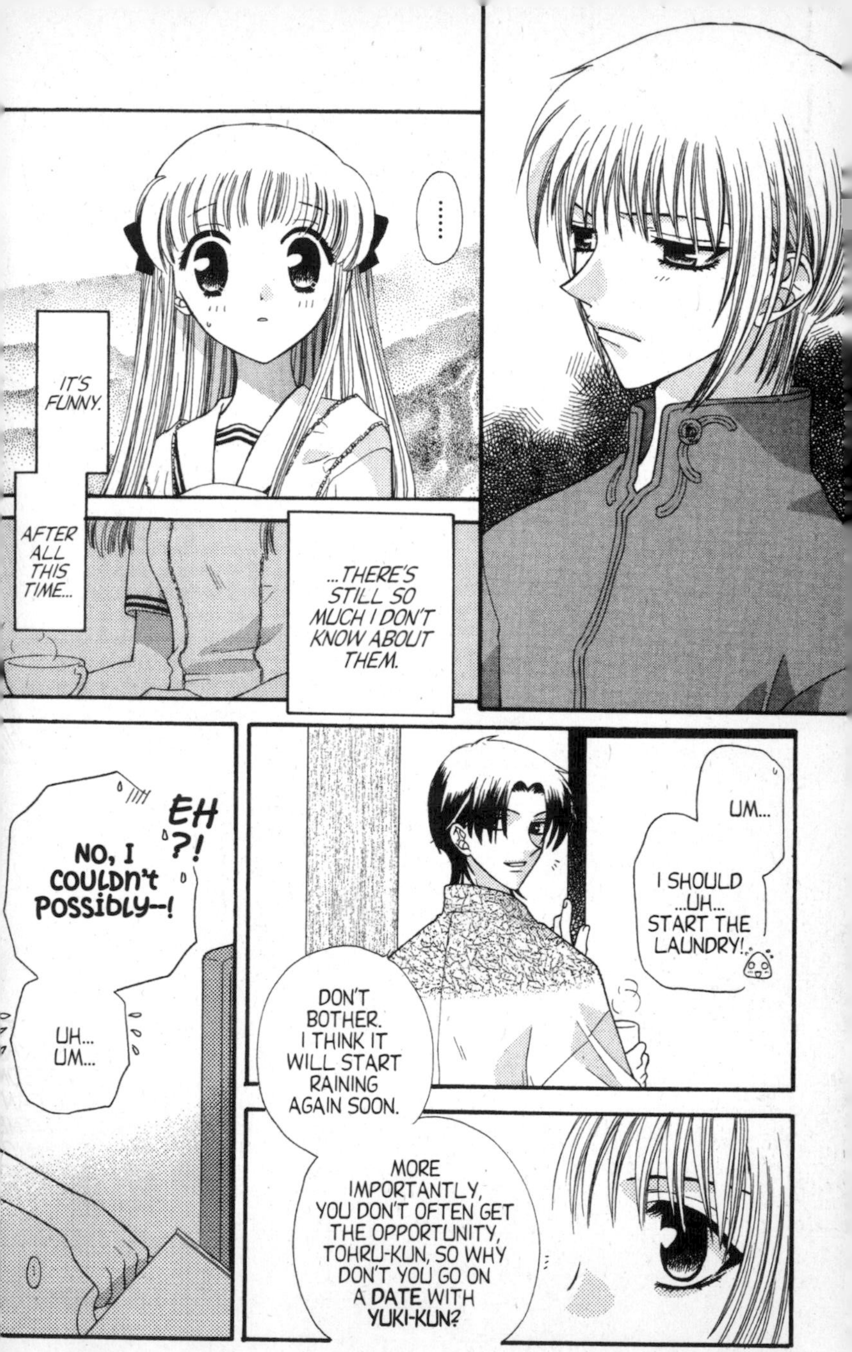
......
IT'S FUNNY.
AFTER ALL THIS TIME...
...THERE'S STILL SO MUCH I DON'T KNOW ABOUT THEM.
UM...
I SHOULD ...UH... START THE LAUNDRY!
DON'T BOTHER. I THINK IT WILL START RAINING AGAIN SOON.
MORE IMPORTANTLY, YOU DON'T OFTEN GET THE OPPORTUNITY, TOHRU-KUN, SO WHY DON'T YOU GO ON A **DATE** WITH **YUKI-KUN**?
EH?!
NO, I COULDN'T POSSIBLY--!
UH... UM...

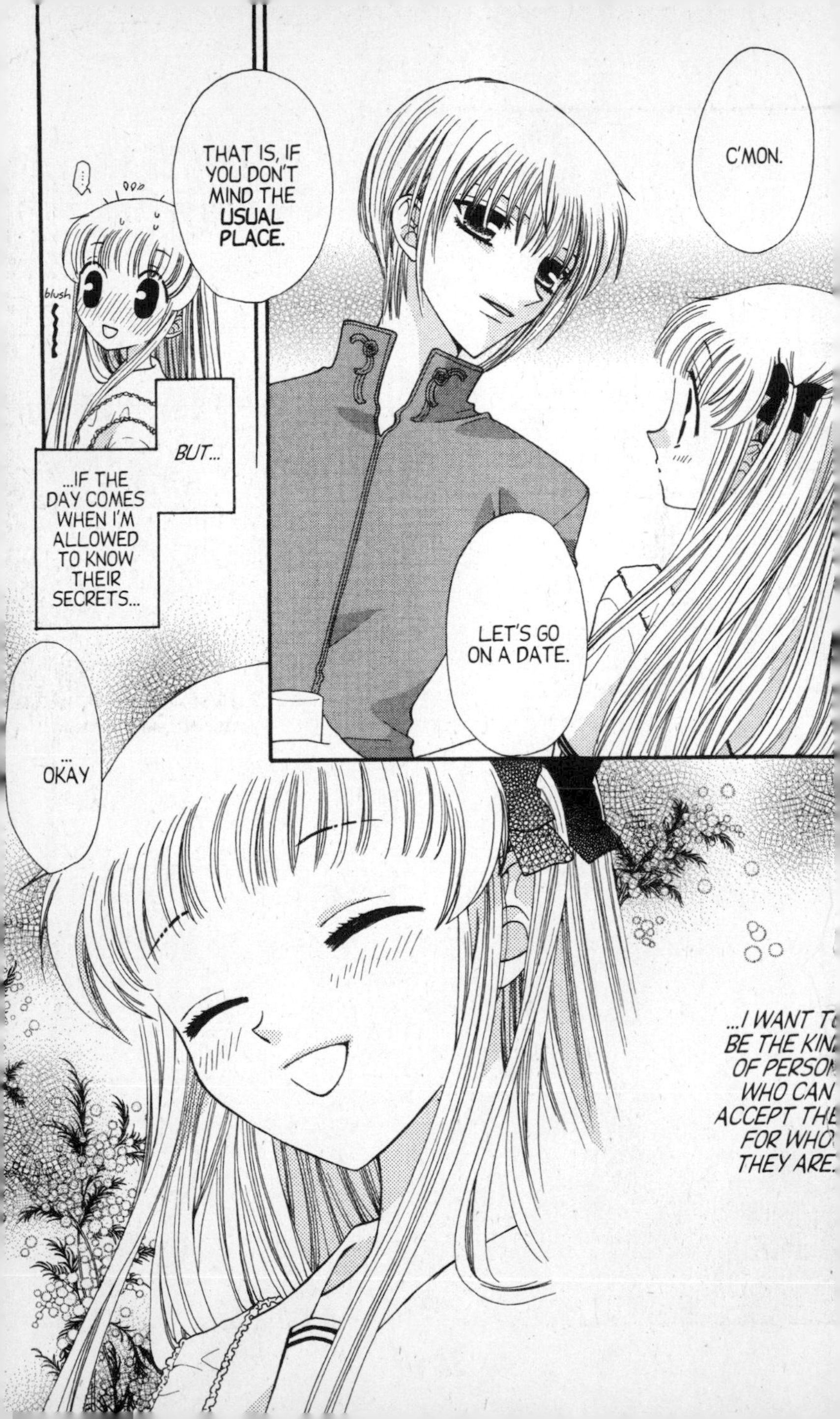
C'MON.
LET'S GO ON A DATE.
THAT IS, IF YOU DON'T MIND THE USUAL PLACE.
...
blush
BUT...
...IF THE DAY COMES WHEN I'M ALLOWED TO KNOW THEIR SECRETS...
...I WANT T BE THE KIN OF PERSO WHO CAN ACCEPT THE FOR WHO THEY ARE.
... OKAY

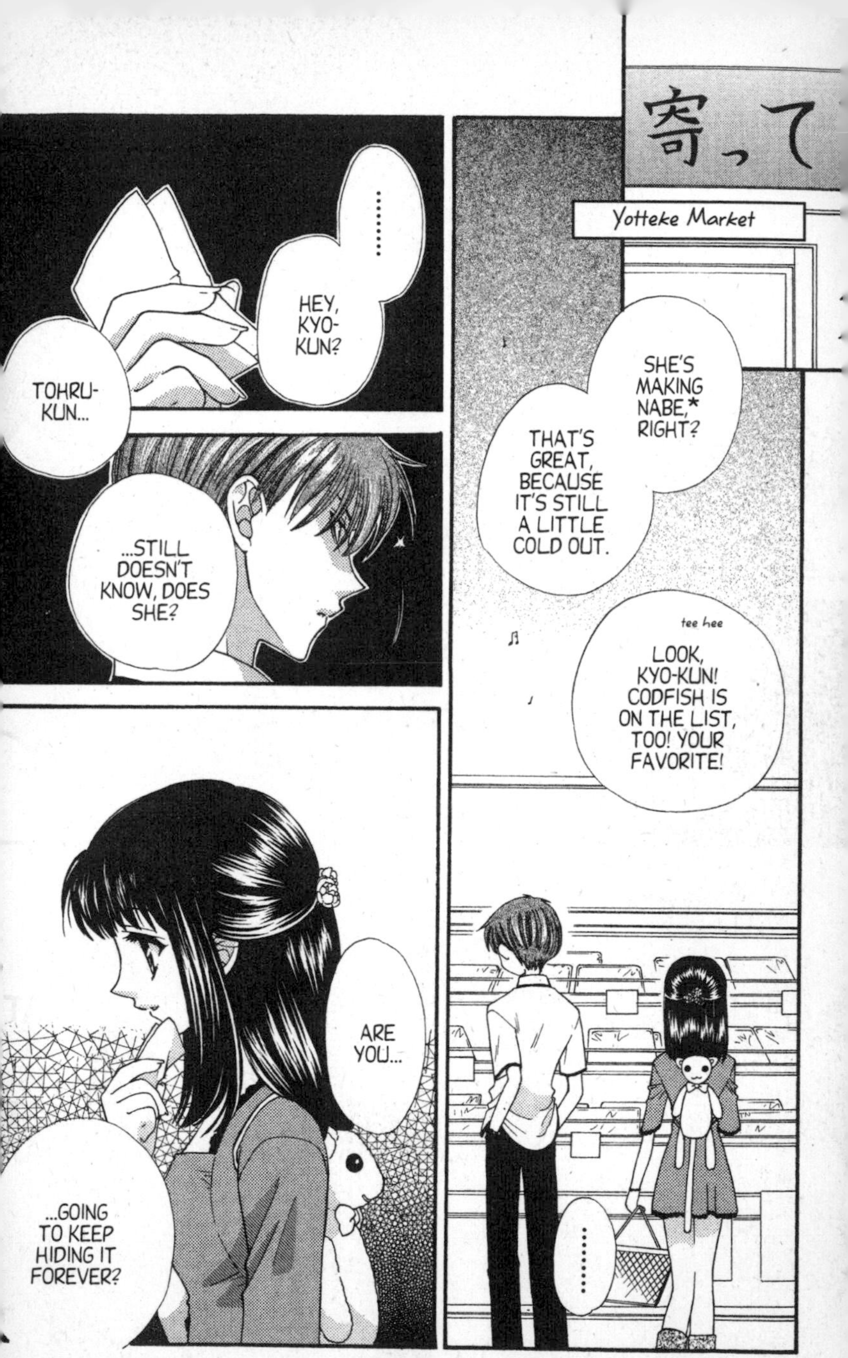
寄って
Yotteke Market
SHE'S MAKING NABE,* RIGHT?
THAT'S GREAT, BECAUSE IT'S STILL A LITTLE COLD OUT.
tee hee
LOOK, KYO-KUN! CODFISH IS ON THE LIST, TOO! YOUR FAVORITE!
....
....
HEY, KYO-KUN?
TOHRU-KUN...
...STILL DOESN'T KNOW, DOES SHE?
ARE YOU...
...GOING TO KEEP HIDING IT FOREVER?

*nabe: hot pot; stew

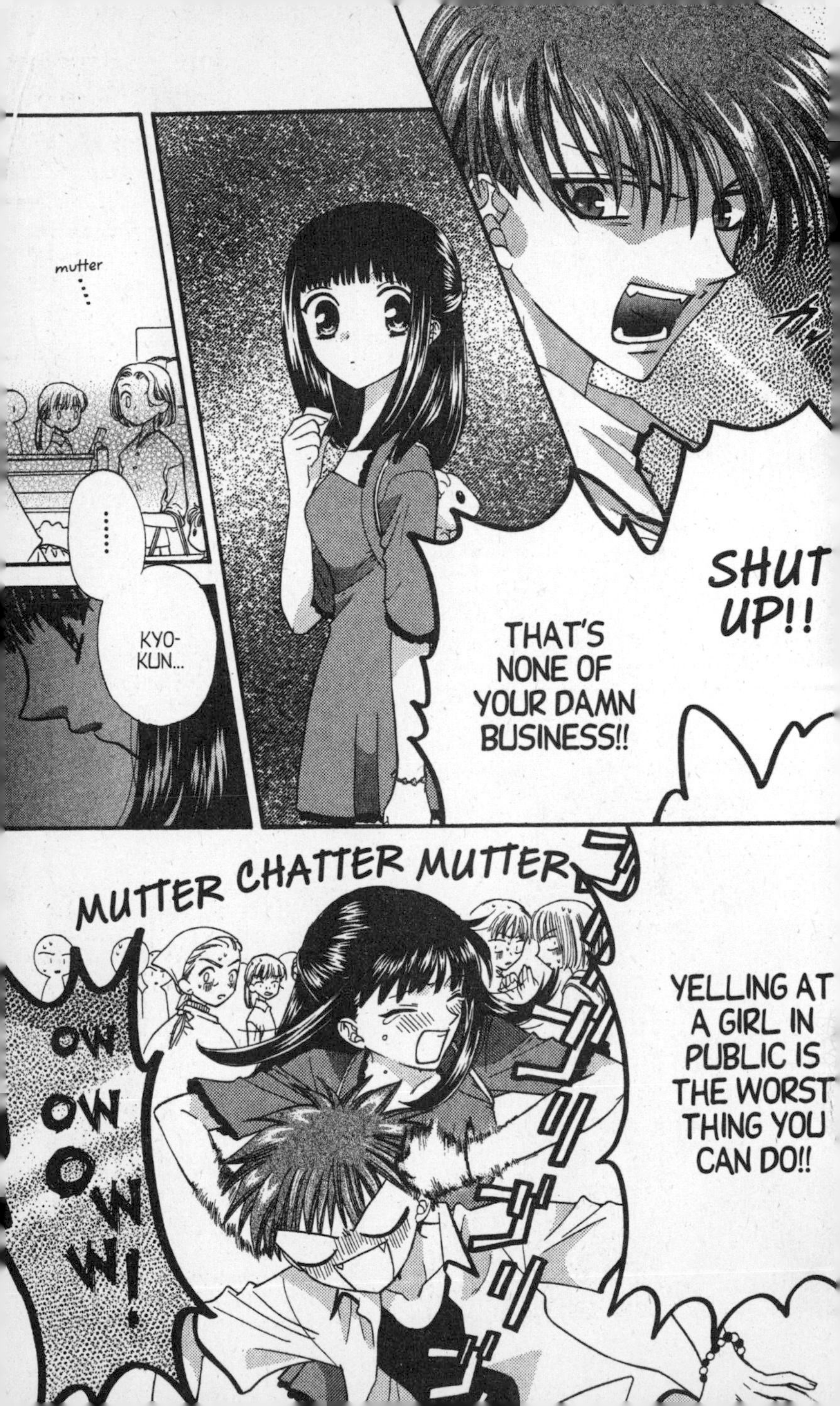
SHUT UP!!
THAT'S NONE OF YOUR DAMN BUSINESS!!
mutter
......
KYO-KUN...
MUTTER CHATTER MUTTER
YELLING AT A GIRL IN PUBLIC IS THE WORST THING YOU CAN DO!!
OW OW OWW!

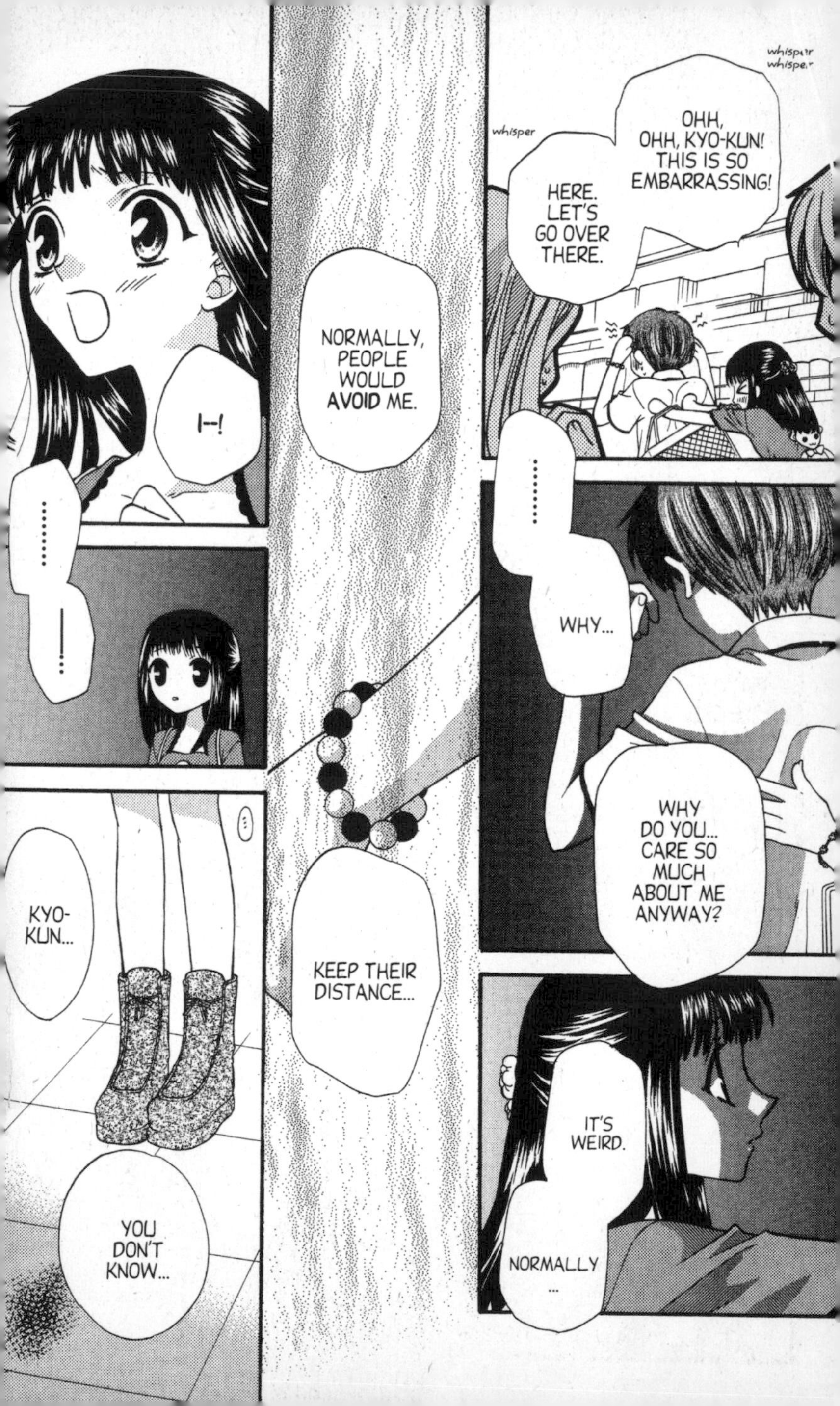

whisper whisper
OHH, OHH, KYO-KUN! THIS IS SO EMBARRASSING!
HERE. LET'S GO OVER THERE.
whisper
....
WHY...
WHY DO YOU... CARE SO MUCH ABOUT ME ANYWAY?
IT'S WEIRD.
NORMALLY ...
NORMALLY, PEOPLE WOULD AVOID ME.
KEEP THEIR DISTANCE...
I--!
........!
KYO-KUN...
YOU DON'T KNOW...

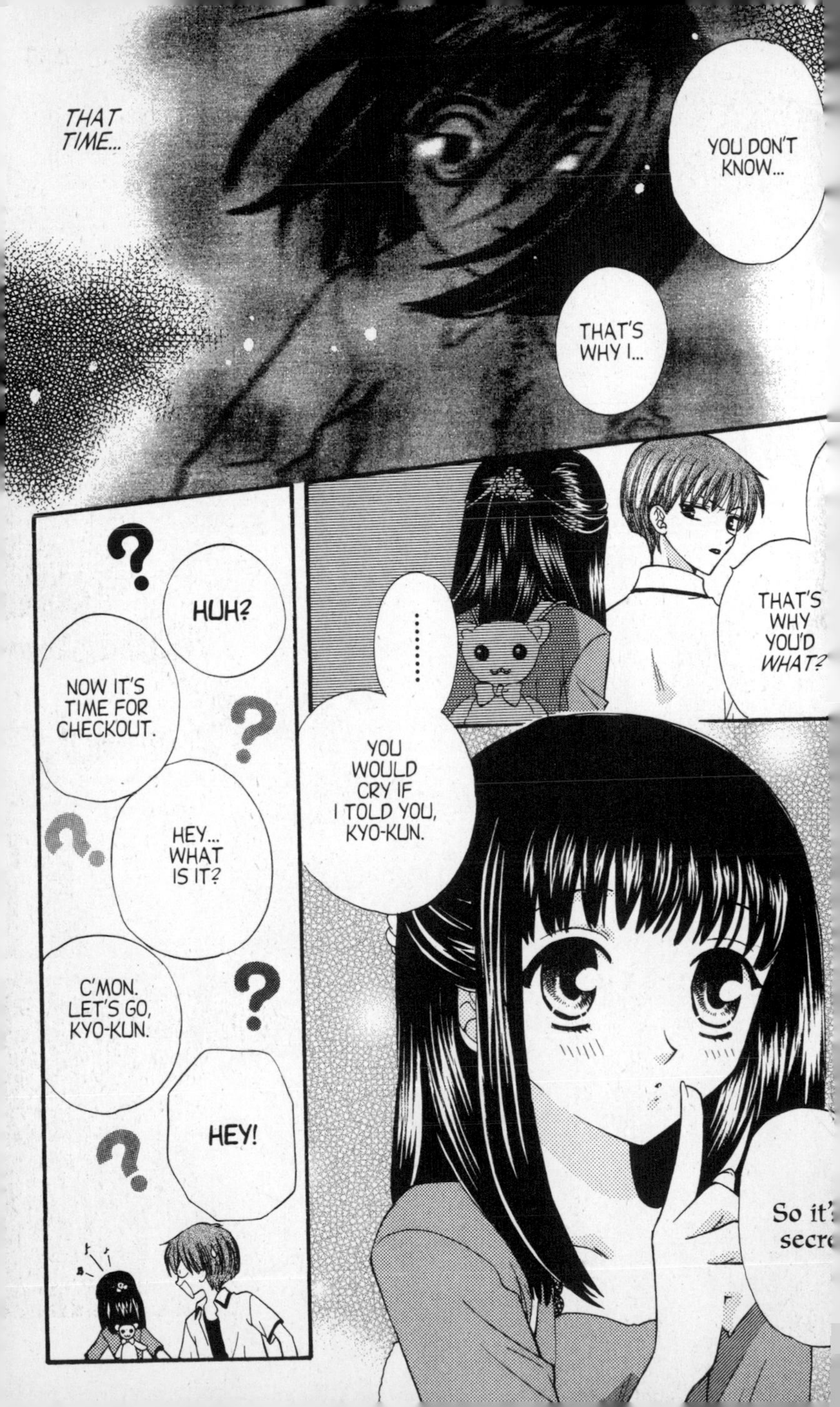
YOU DON'T KNOW...
THAT'S WHY I...
THAT TIME...
THAT'S WHY YOU'D WHAT?
......
YOU WOULD CRY IF I TOLD YOU, KYO-KUN.
So it' secre
HUH?
NOW IT'S TIME FOR CHECKOUT.
HEY... WHAT IS IT?
C'MON. LET'S GO, KYO-KUN.
HEY!

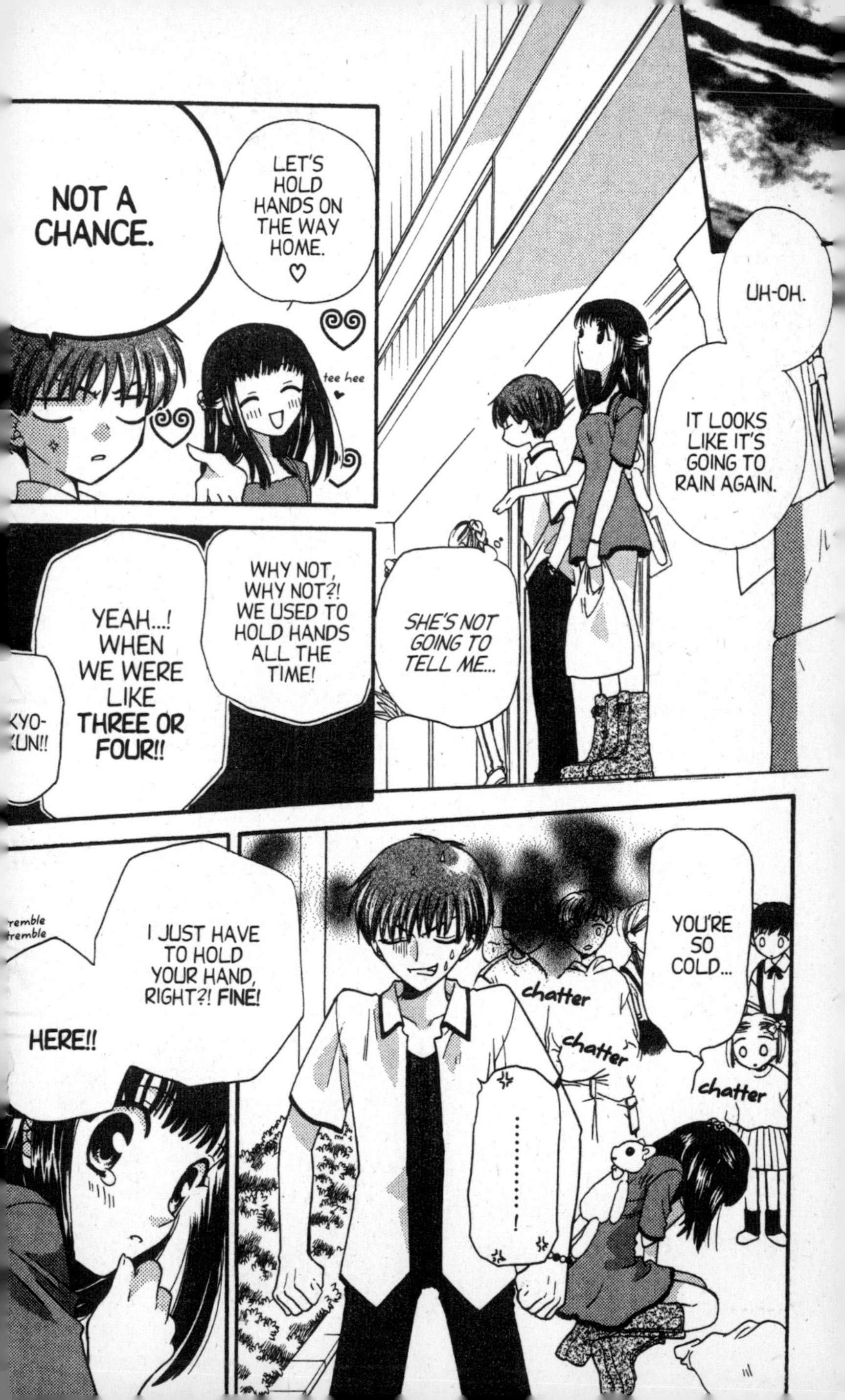
UH-OH.
IT LOOKS LIKE IT'S GOING TO RAIN AGAIN.
SHE'S NOT GOING TO TELL ME...
LET'S HOLD HANDS ON THE WAY HOME. ♡
NOT A CHANCE.
tee hee
WHY NOT, WHY NOT?! WE USED TO HOLD HANDS ALL THE TIME!
YEAH...! WHEN WE WERE LIKE THREE OR FOUR!!
KYO-KUN!!
YOU'RE SO COLD...
chatter
chatter
chatter
......!
tremble tremble
I JUST HAVE TO HOLD YOUR HAND, RIGHT?! FINE!
HERE!!

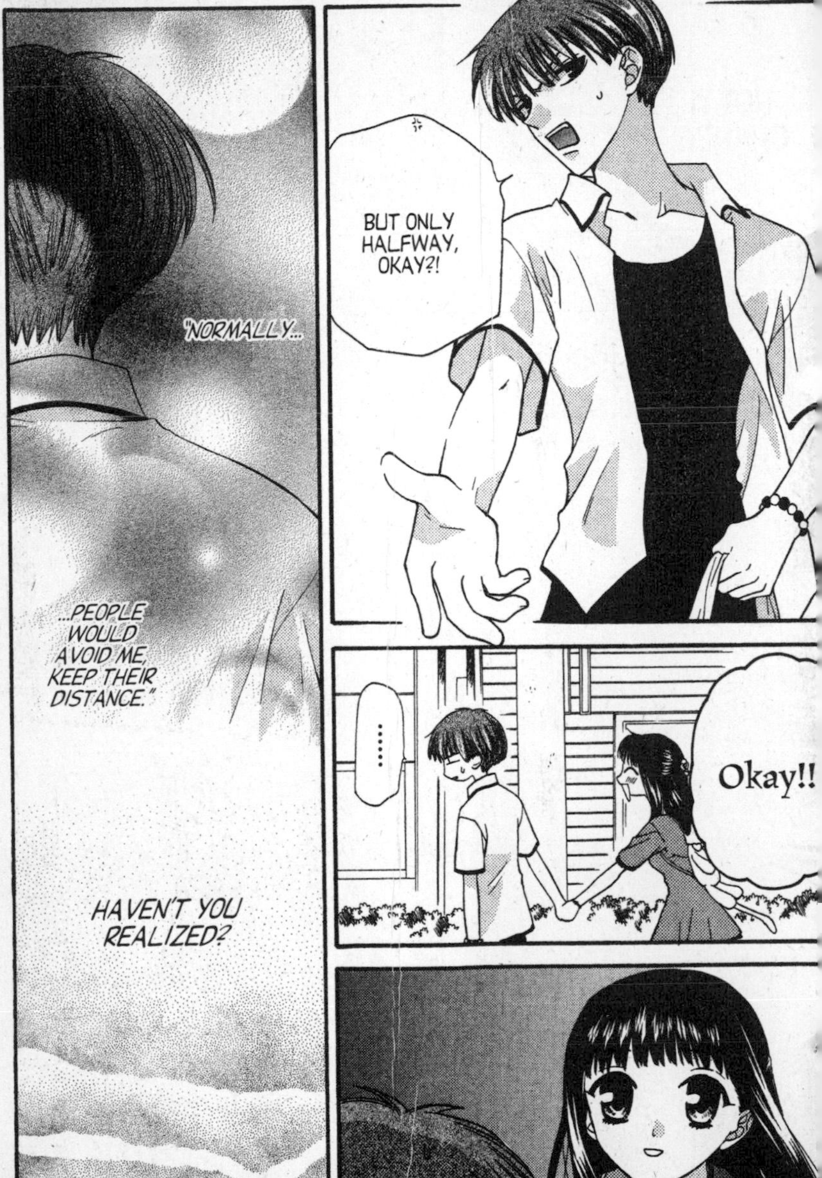
BUT ONLY HALFWAY, OKAY?!
Okay!!
......
"NORMALLY...
...PEOPLE WOULD AVOID ME, KEEP THEIR DISTANCE."
HAVEN'T YOU REALIZED?

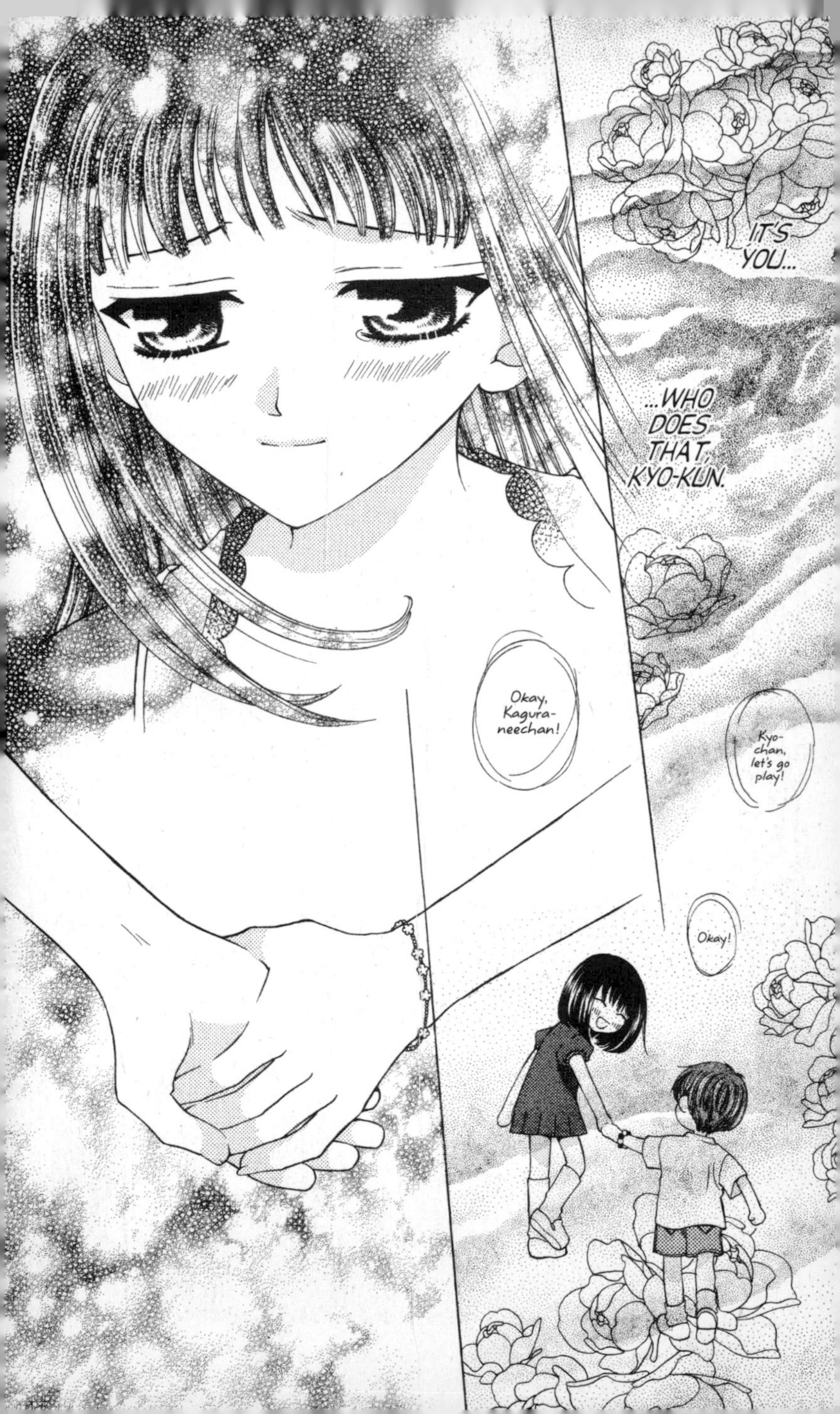
IT'S YOU...
...WHO DOES THAT, KYO-KUN.
Kyo-chan, let's go play!
Okay, Kagura-neechan!
Okay!

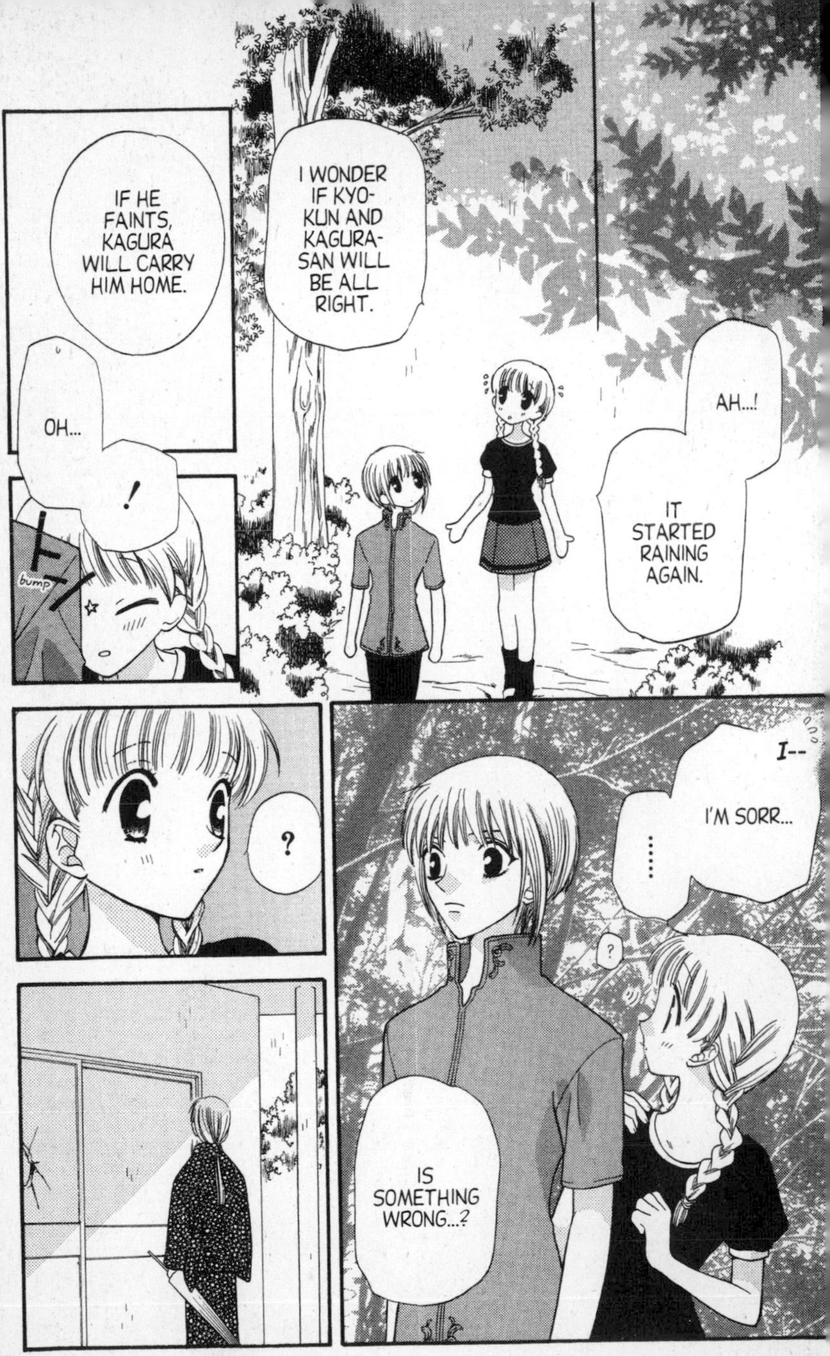
I WONDER IF KYO-KUN AND KAGURA-SAN WILL BE ALL RIGHT.
AH...!
IT STARTED RAINING AGAIN.
IF HE FAINTS, KAGURA WILL CARRY HIM HOME.
OH...
bump
!
I--
I'M SORR...
......
?
IS SOMETHING WRONG...?
?

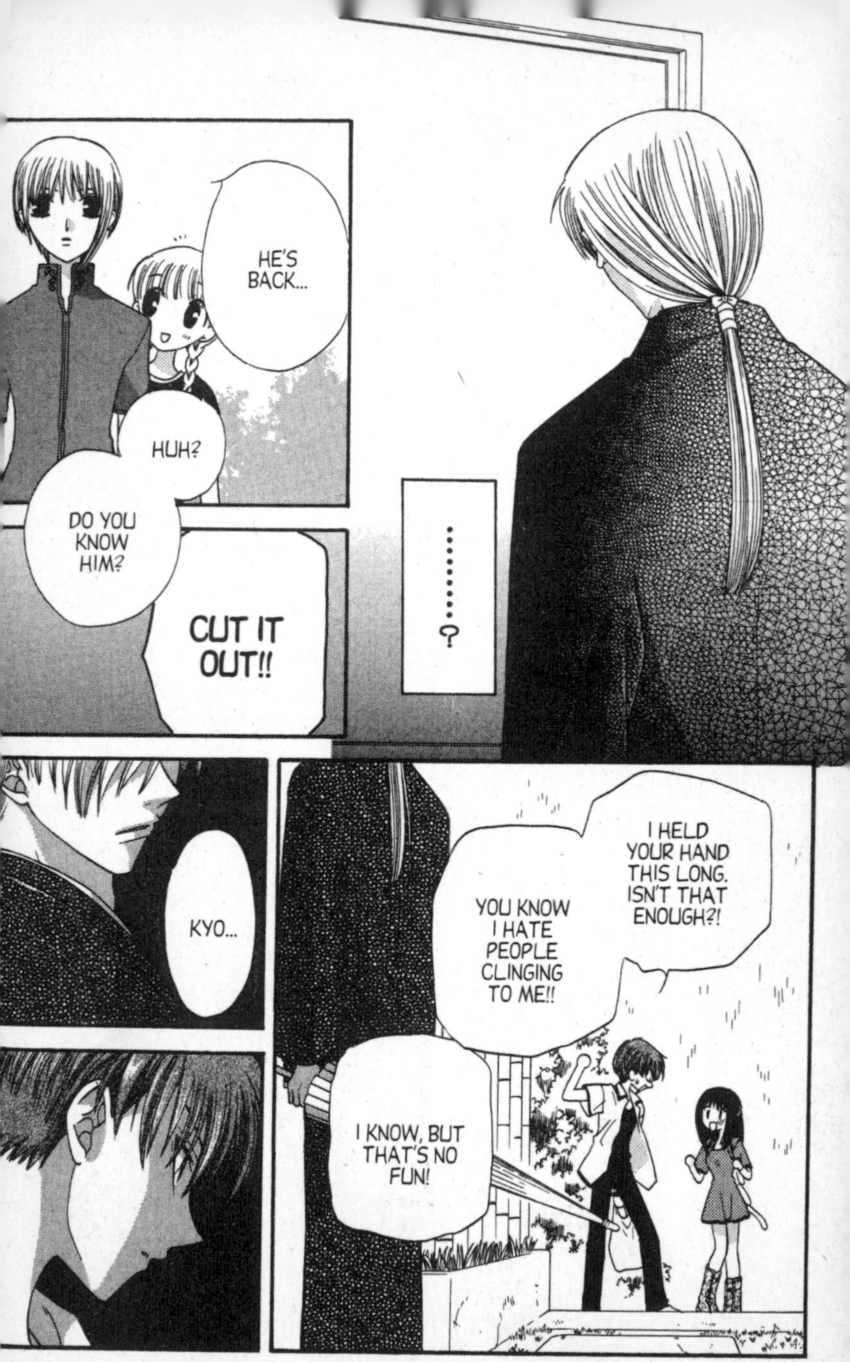
......?
HE'S BACK...
HUH?
DO YOU KNOW HIM?
CUT IT OUT!!
I HELD YOUR HAND THIS LONG. ISN'T THAT ENOUGH?!
YOU KNOW I HATE PEOPLE CLINGING TO ME!!
I KNOW, BUT THAT'S NO FUN!
KYO...

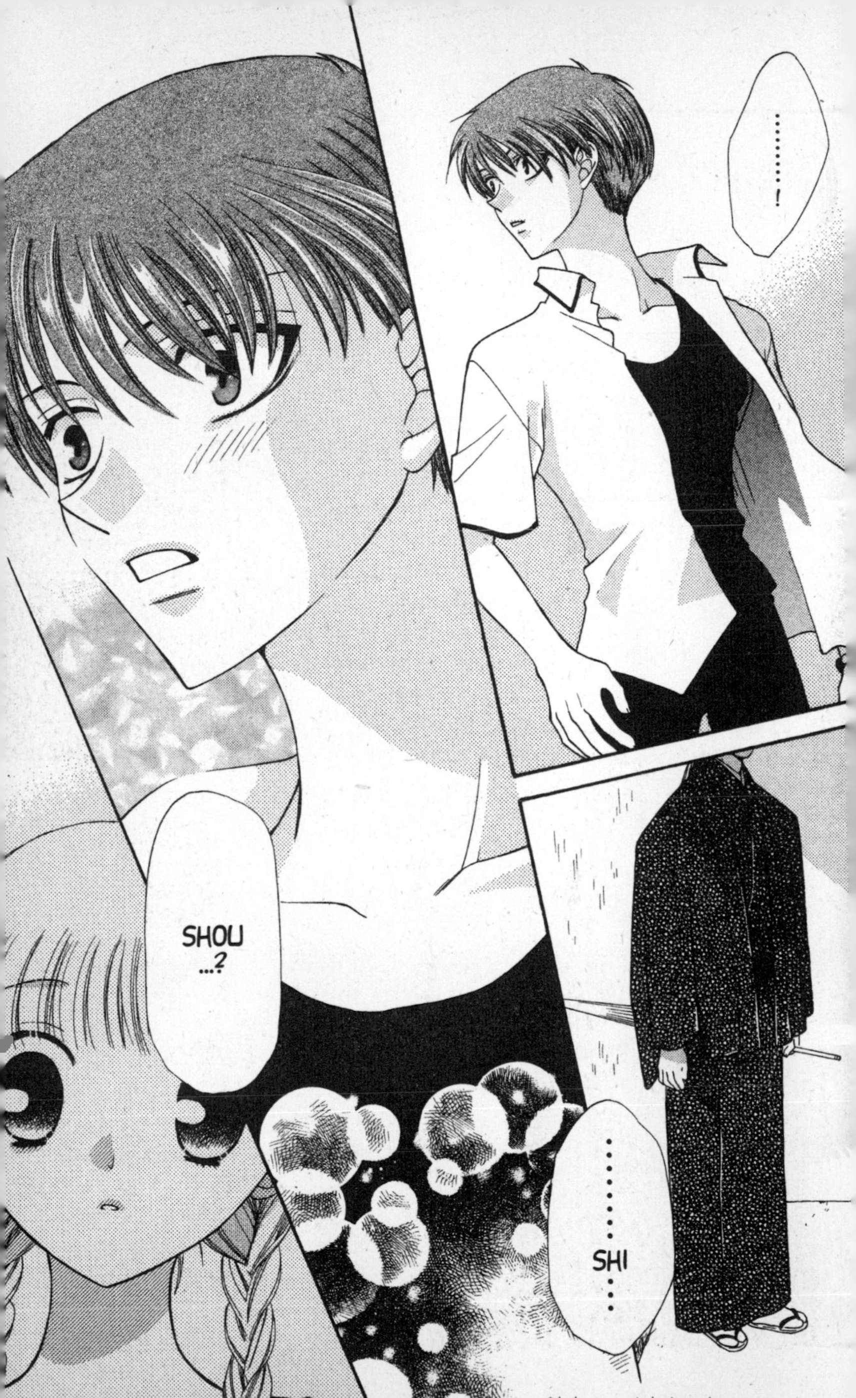
......!
......SHI......
SHOU ...?

*shishou: a martial arts master

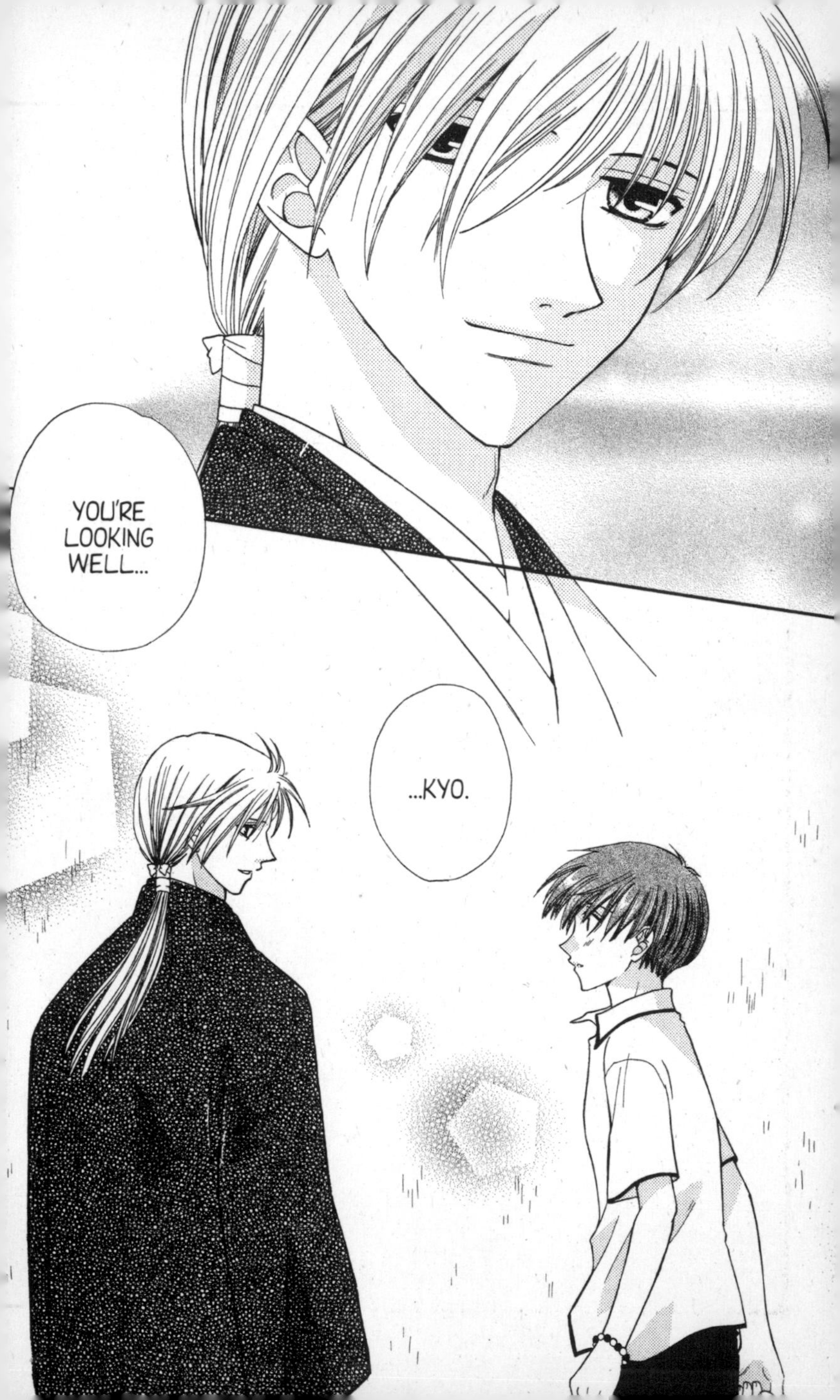
YOU'RE LOOKING WELL...
...KYO.

People say to use everything...

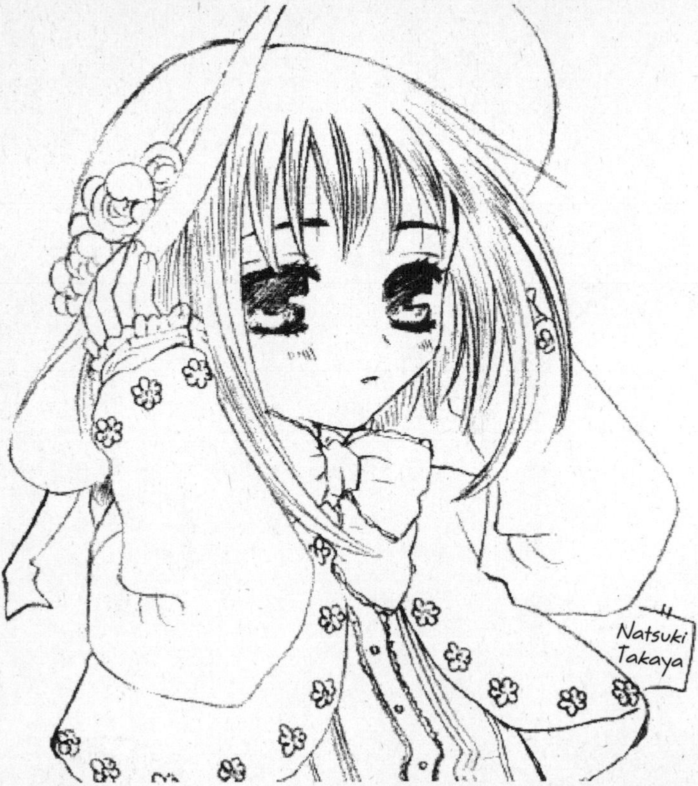
Natsuki Takaya

Like pictures that you can only see online and stuff. Like Momiji, I put a lot of my own preferences into Kisa. It's really fun to draw her. I'm a real girly-girl at heart, so I would have liked to try wearing flowy dresses or maid outfits at least once, but it looks like that dream will go unfulfilled (laugh). Too bad.

Chapter 32

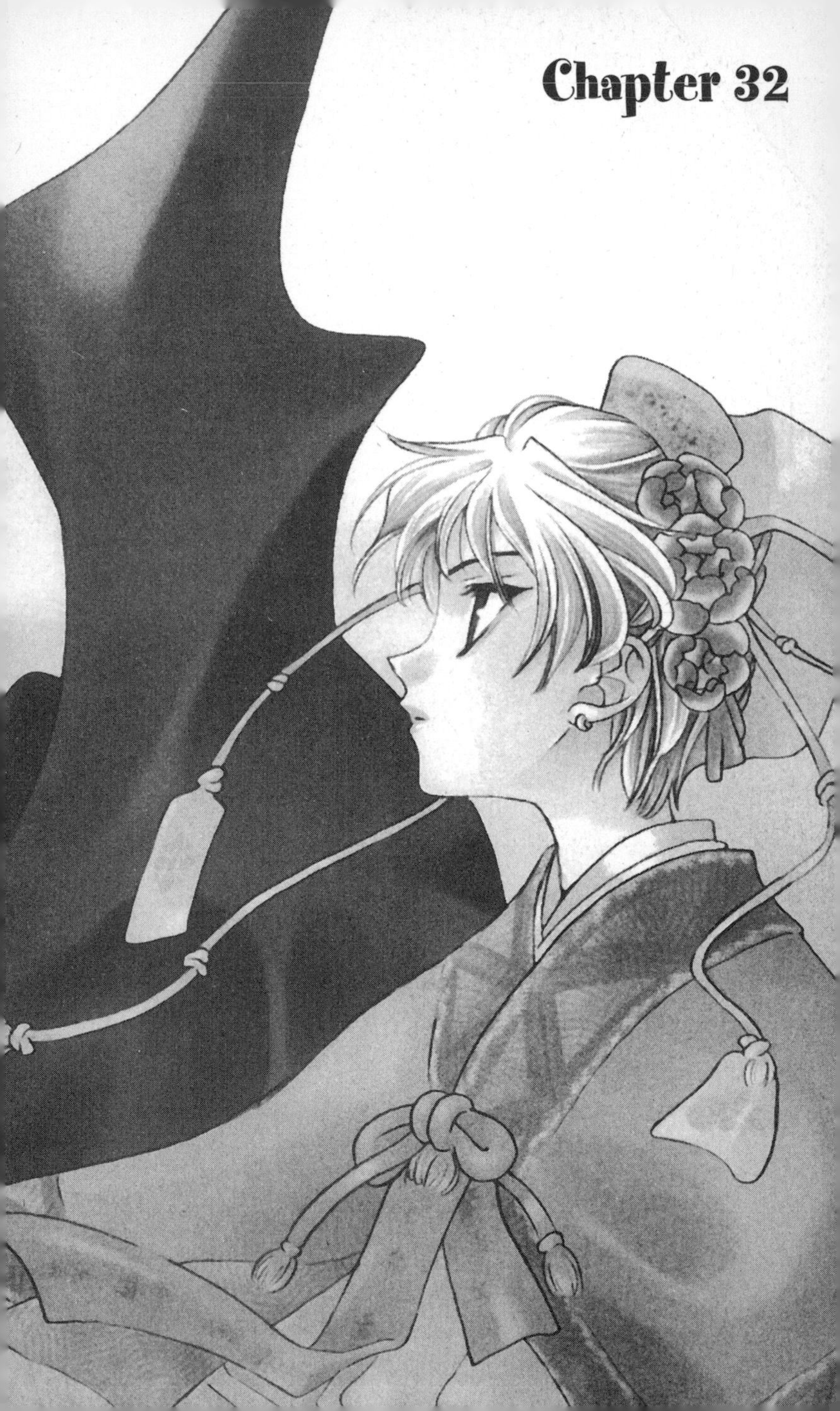

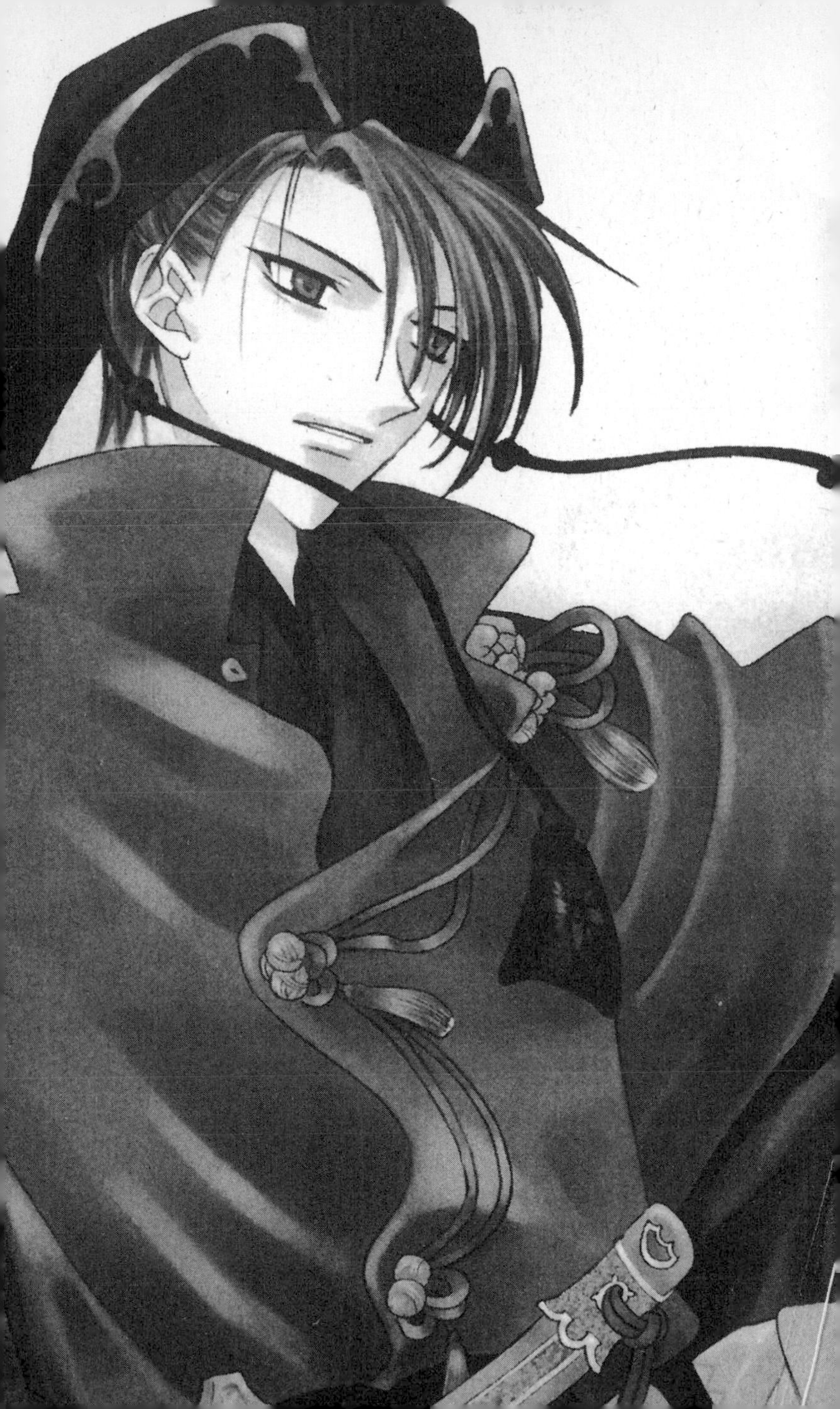

…ople say to use...

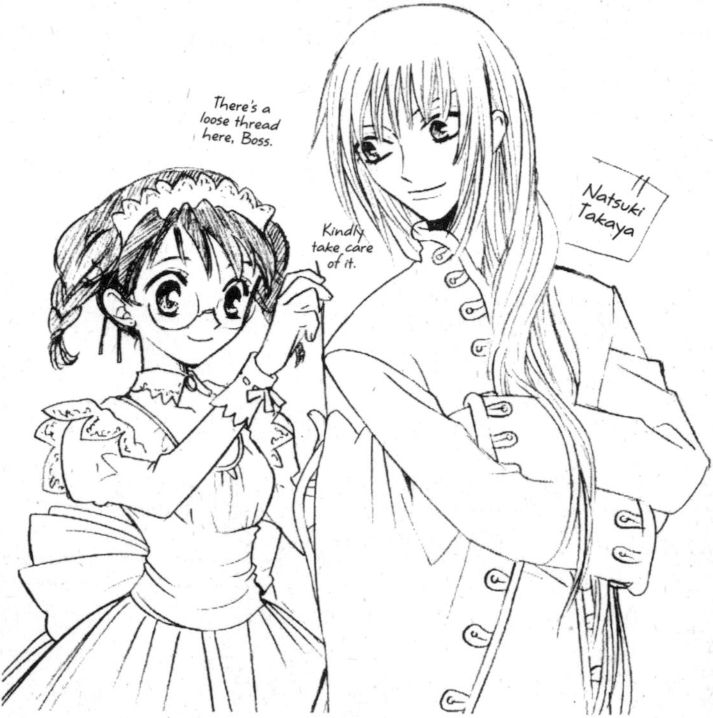

There's a loose thread here, Boss.
Kindly take care of it.
Natsuki Takaya

It's a rough sketch, so Mine's maid outfit is too plain. I'm sorry. Next time I'll draw it more seriously. (Huh?) The outfit Aaya is wearing was mostly designed by Aaya and made by Mine.

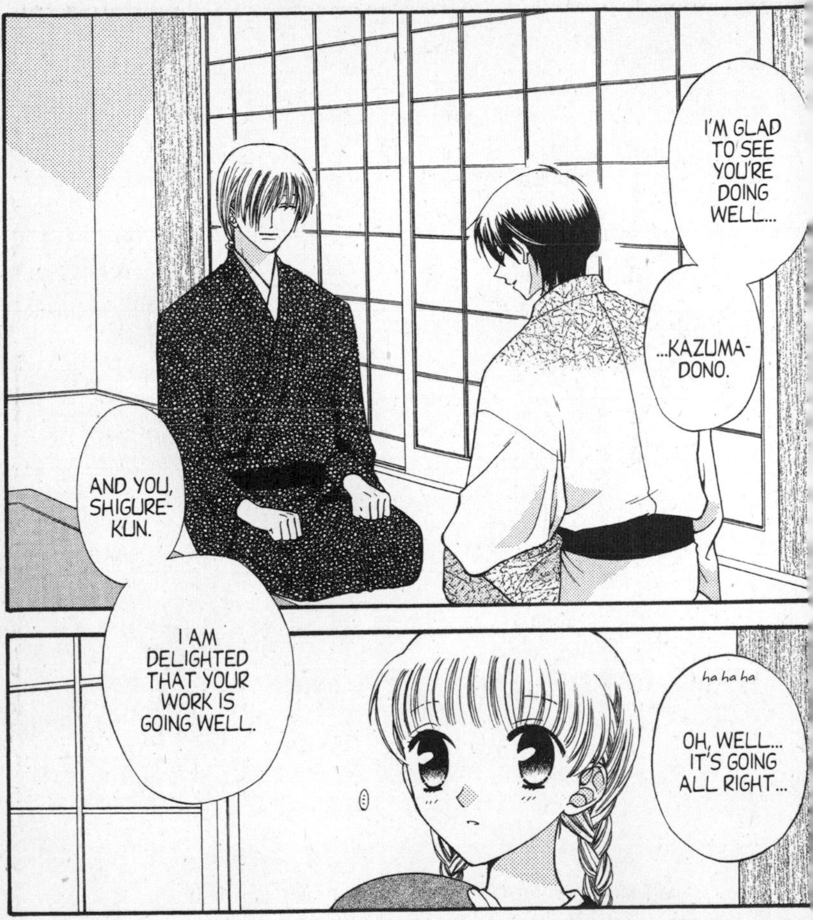
I'M GLAD TO SEE YOU'RE DOING WELL...
...KAZUMA-DONO.
AND YOU, SHIGURE-KUN.
I AM DELIGHTED THAT YOUR WORK IS GOING WELL.
ha ha ha
OH, WELL... IT'S GOING ALL RIGHT...

ULTRA SPECIAL BLAH BLAH BLAH. 2

There are those who think "I don't need them to love everything about me"... And there are others who think that, "I want them to love everything." Both are valid points of view. I really can't say one way is better than the other. Both exist. Kyo is the former.

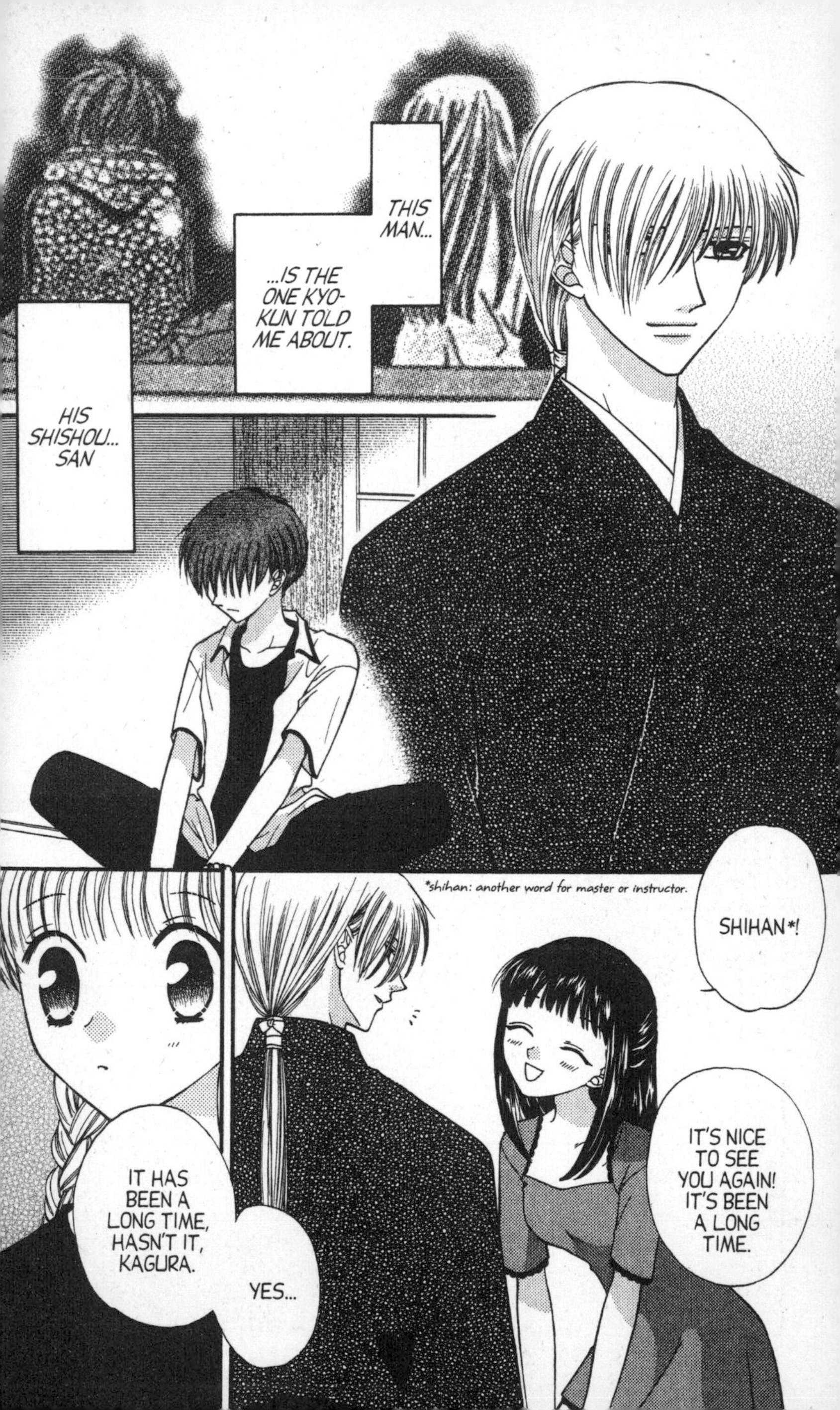
THIS MAN...
...IS THE ONE KYO-KUN TOLD ME ABOUT.
HIS SHISHOU... SAN
SHIHAN*!
IT'S NICE TO SEE YOU AGAIN! IT'S BEEN A LONG TIME.
IT HAS BEEN A LONG TIME, HASN'T IT, KAGURA.
YES...
*shihan: another word for master or instructor.

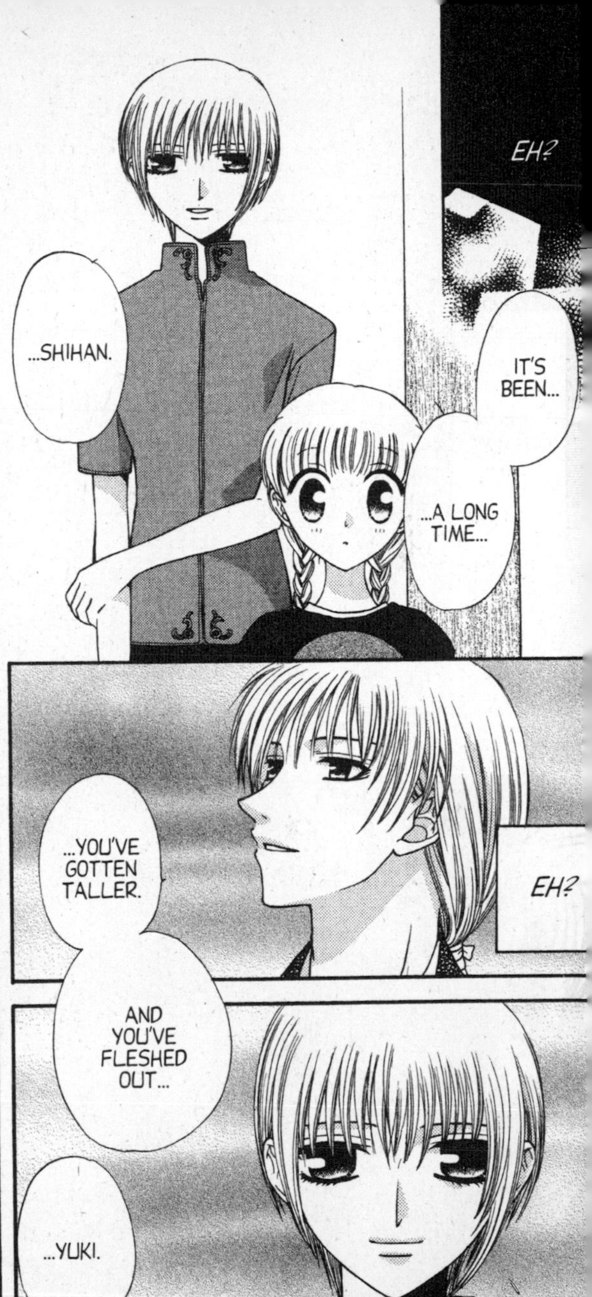
EH?
IT'S BEEN...
...A LONG TIME...
...SHIHAN.
EH?
...YOU'VE GOTTEN TALLER.
AND YOU'VE FLESHED OUT...
...YUKI.

Fruits Basket 6 Part 2:

A lot of people have told me, "It's okay to talk about games!" I'm glad. And so, without delay... (laugh) I finally finished *PERSONA 2: INNOCENT SIN.* (I had stopped in the middle.) I stopped right before the last boss, like with the first game. I wonder if it's inevitable...? For me, it is. I really liked Ginko. She was so cute when she said, "Aiya~" and stuff. Sadly, my Playstation is on its last legs, so during the ending song, it started skipping (laugh). Talk about Aiya~. Letting the credits go without sound... I'm playing *ETERNAL PUNISHMENT* on my PS2. (laugh)

(*INNOCENT SIN* and *ETERNAL PUNISHMENT* are both sequels to the sleeper hit RPG *PERSONA*. Only *ETERNAL PUNISHMENT* was released in the U.S. -ed.)

*ohisashiburi: The reason everyone is saying "It's been a long time," is because in Japan, there is a ritual phrase, "ohisashiburi," which is used when greeting someone you haven't seen in a while. It's similar to the way Japanese folk always say "Okaeri" (welcome home) when someone comes home, or "itadakimasu" (thanks for the food) before eating.

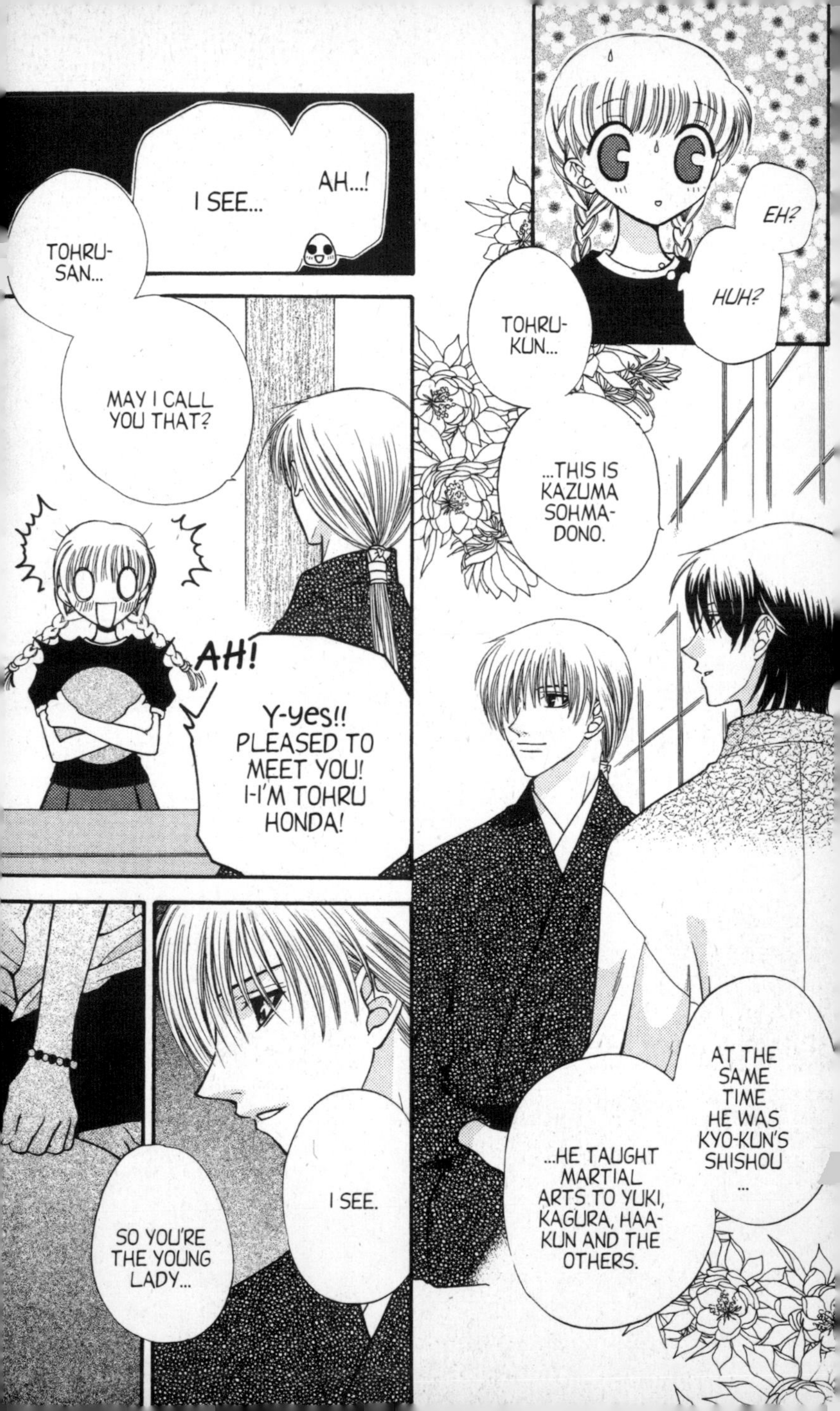
EH?
HUH?
TOHRU-KUN...
...THIS IS KAZUMA SOHMA-DONO.
AT THE SAME TIME HE WAS KYO-KUN'S SHISHOU ...
...HE TAUGHT MARTIAL ARTS TO YUKI, KAGURA, HAA-KUN AND THE OTHERS.
AH...!
I SEE...
TOHRU-SAN...
MAY I CALL YOU THAT?
AH!
Y-yes!! PLEASED TO MEET YOU! I-I'M TOHRU HONDA!
I SEE.
SO YOU'RE THE YOUNG LADY...

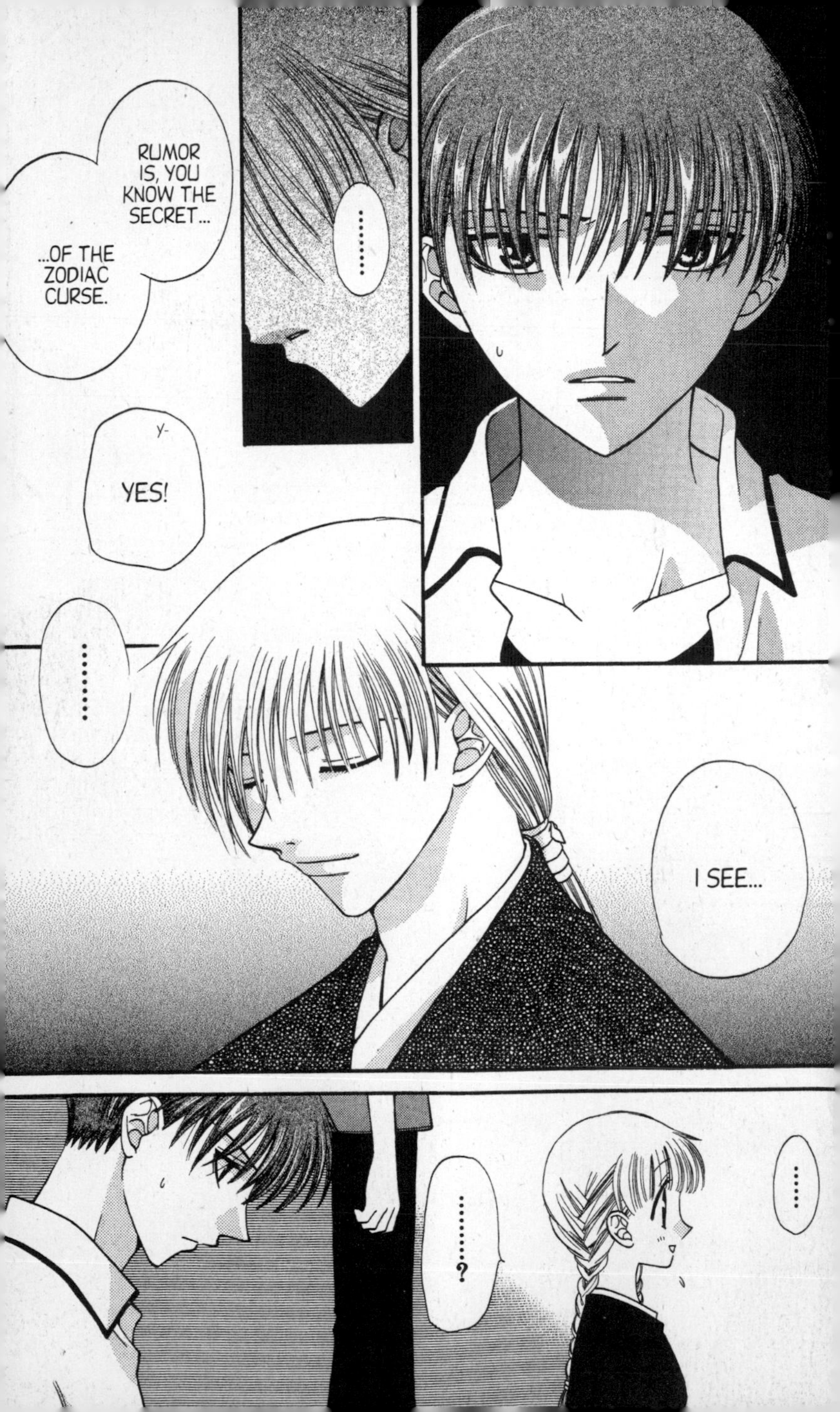
......
RUMOR IS, YOU KNOW THE SECRET...
...OF THE ZODIAC CURSE.
Y- YES!
I SEE...
......
......
......?

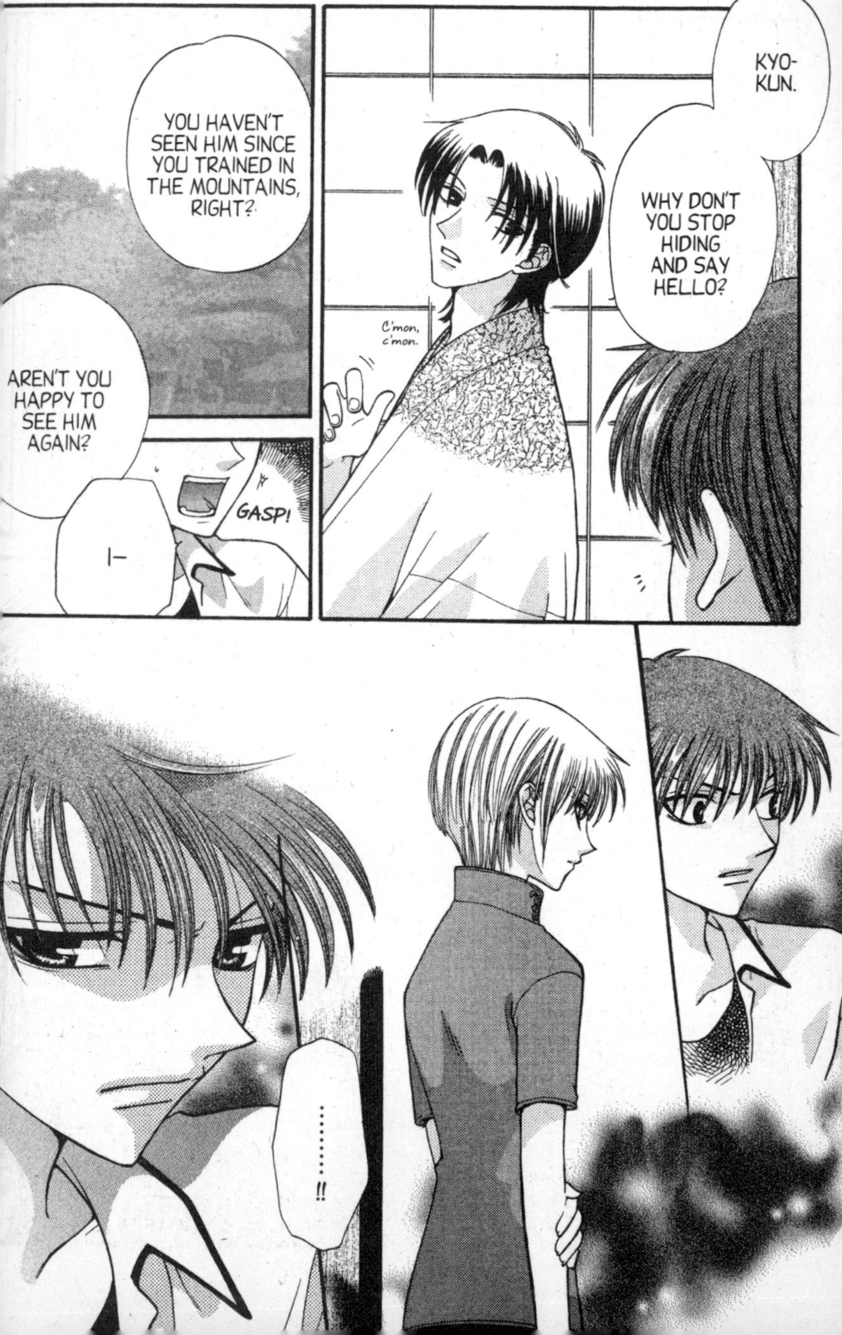
KYO-KUN.
WHY DON'T YOU STOP HIDING AND SAY HELLO?
C'mon, c'mon.
YOU HAVEN'T SEEN HIM SINCE YOU TRAINED IN THE MOUNTAINS, RIGHT?
AREN'T YOU HAPPY TO SEE HIM AGAIN?
GASP!
I—
......!!

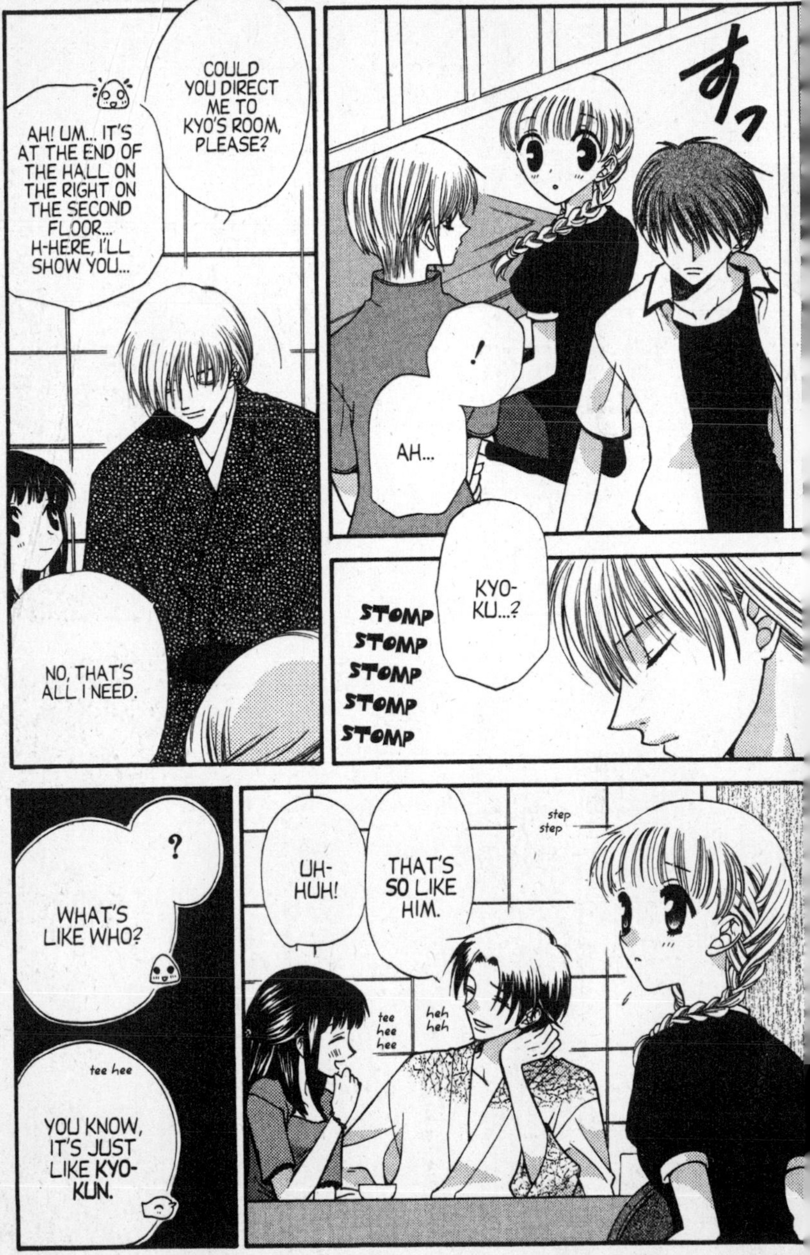
すっ
!
AH...
KYO-KU...?
STOMP STOMP STOMP STOMP STOMP
COULD YOU DIRECT ME TO KYO'S ROOM, PLEASE?
AH! UM... IT'S AT THE END OF THE HALL ON THE RIGHT ON THE SECOND FLOOR... H-HERE, I'LL SHOW YOU...
NO, THAT'S ALL I NEED.
step step
THAT'S SO LIKE HIM.
UH-HUH!
heh heh
tee hee hee
?
WHAT'S LIKE WHO?
tee hee
YOU KNOW, IT'S JUST LIKE KYO-KUN.

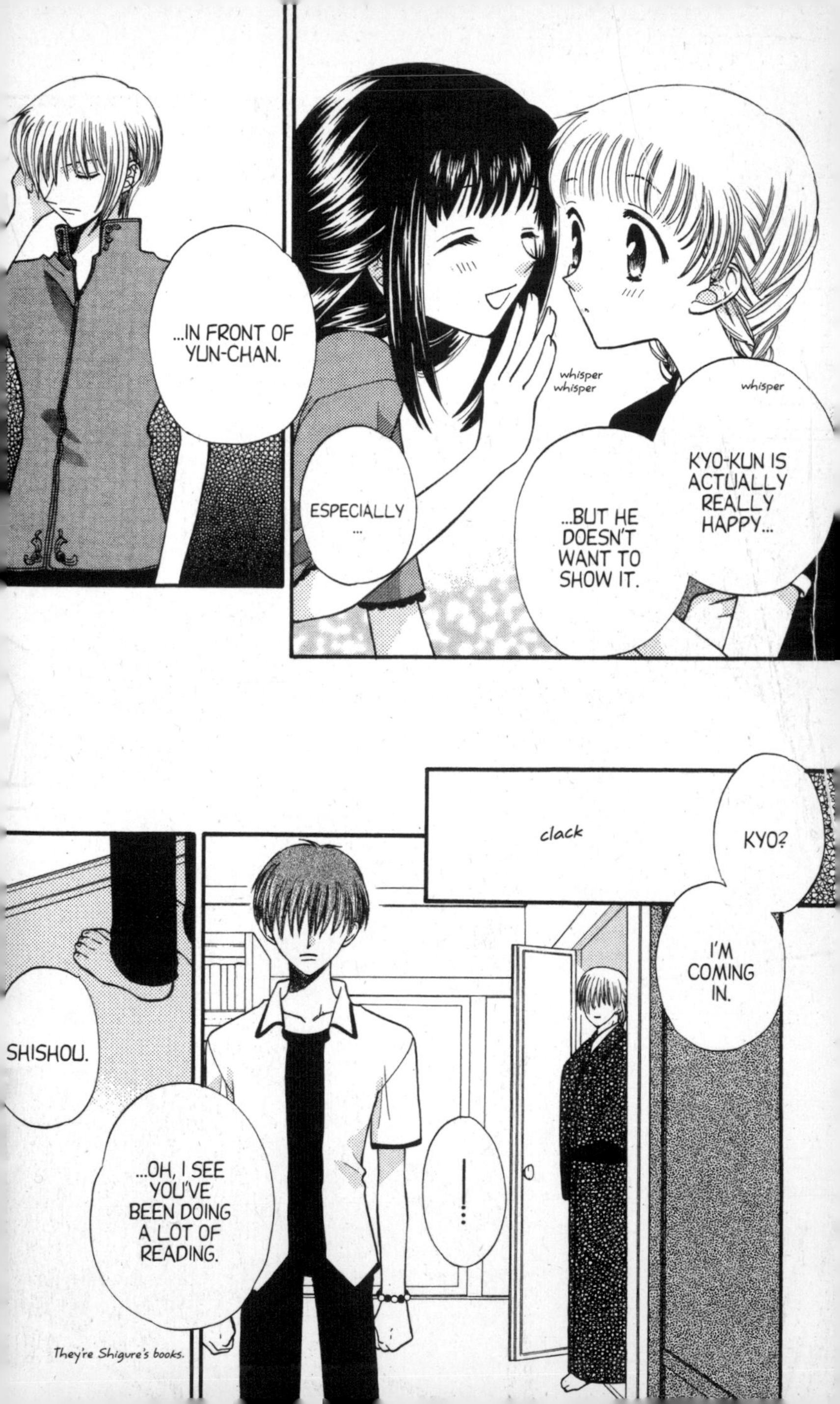
whisper
KYO-KUN IS ACTUALLY REALLY HAPPY...
whisper whisper
...BUT HE DOESN'T WANT TO SHOW IT.
ESPECIALLY ...
...IN FRONT OF YUN-CHAN.
KYO?
clack
I'M COMING IN.
SHISHOU.
!...
...OH, I SEE YOU'VE BEEN DOING A LOT OF READING.
They're Shigure's books.

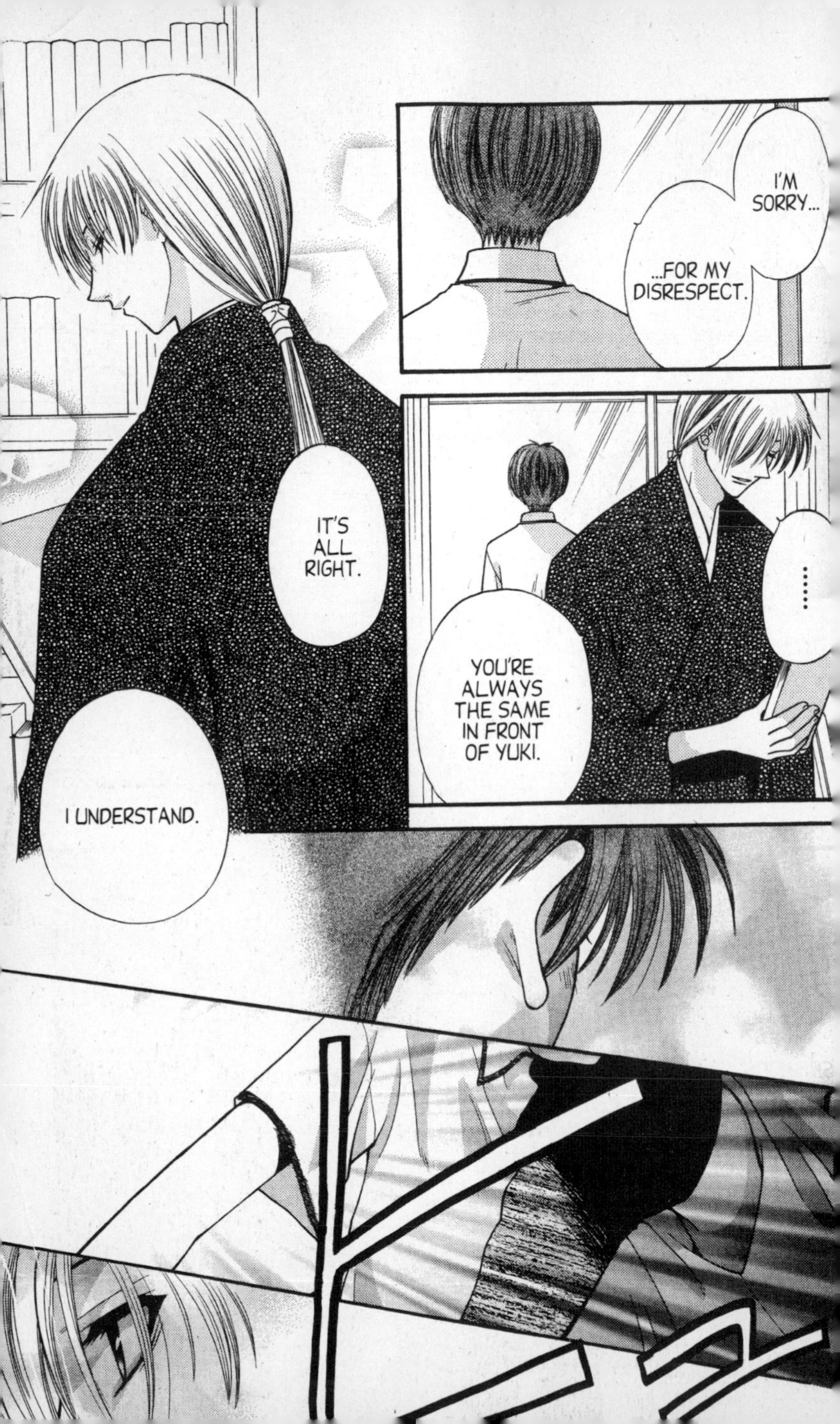
I'M SORRY...
...FOR MY DISRESPECT.
......
YOU'RE ALWAYS THE SAME IN FRONT OF YUKI.
IT'S ALL RIGHT.
I UNDERSTAND.

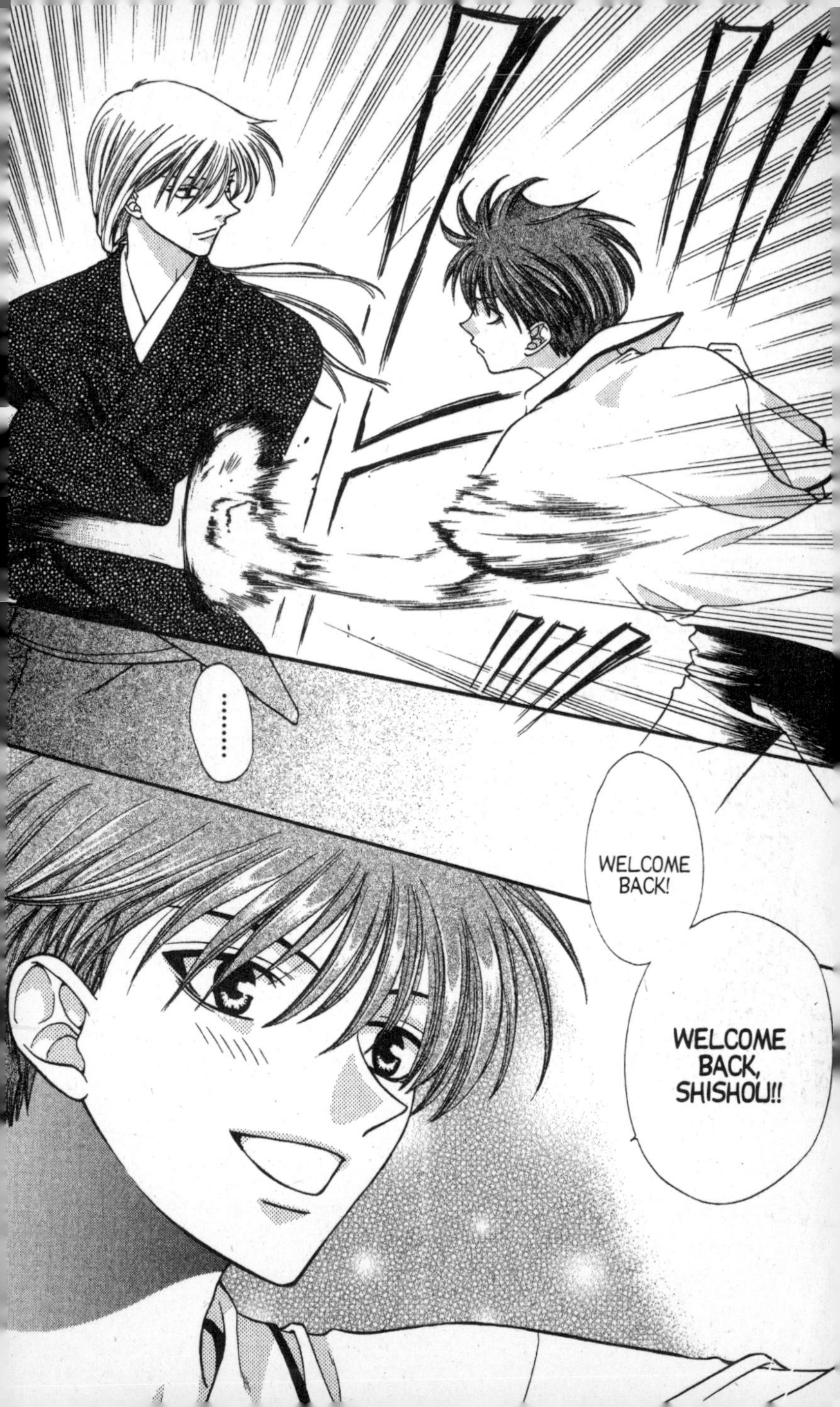
......
WELCOME BACK!
WELCOME BACK, SHISHOU!!

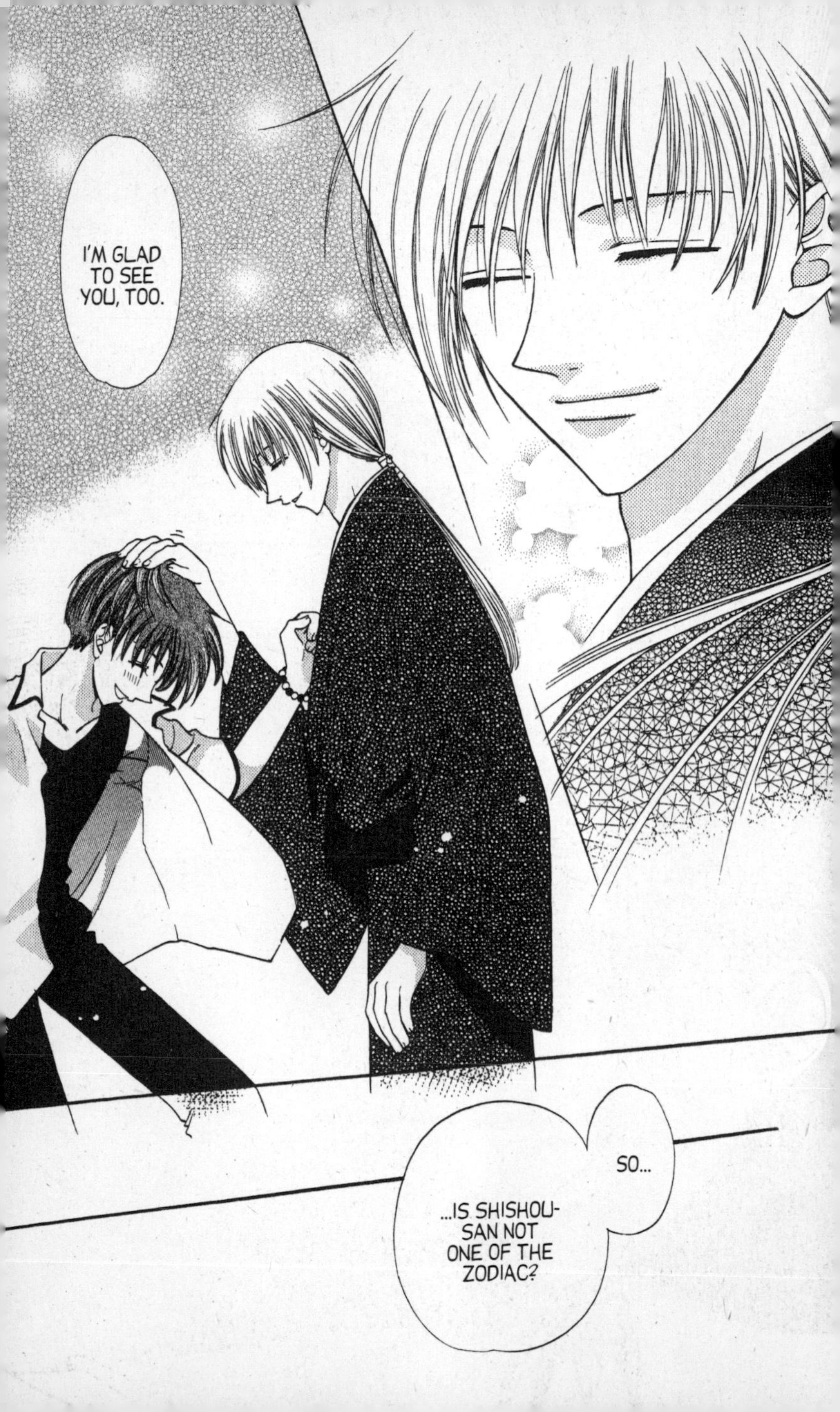
I'M GLAD TO SEE YOU, TOO.
SO...
...IS SHISHOU-SAN NOT ONE OF THE ZODIAC?

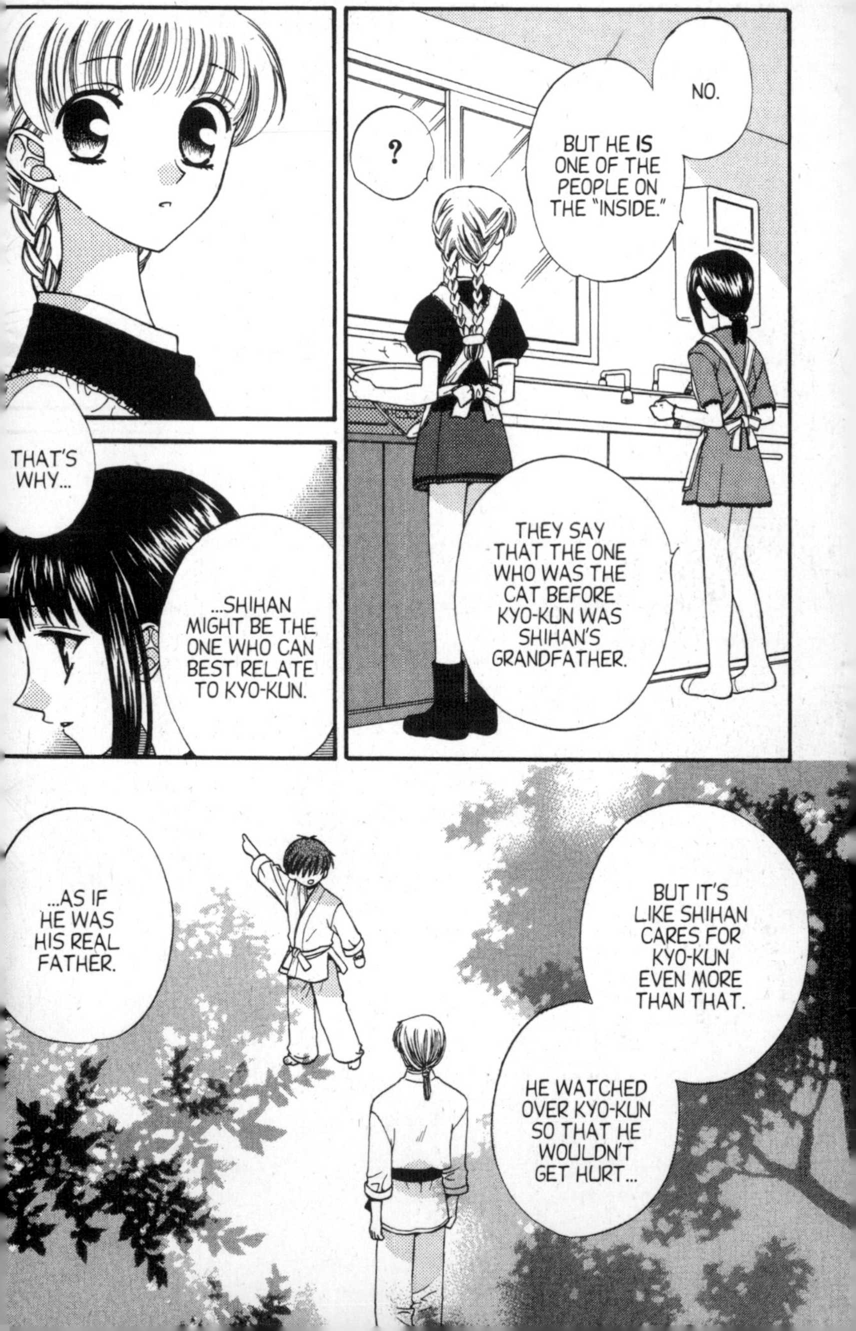
NO.
BUT HE **IS** ONE OF THE PEOPLE ON THE "INSIDE."
?
THEY SAY THAT THE ONE WHO WAS THE CAT BEFORE KYO-KUN WAS SHIHAN'S GRANDFATHER.
THAT'S WHY...
...SHIHAN MIGHT BE THE ONE WHO CAN BEST RELATE TO KYO-KUN.
BUT IT'S LIKE SHIHAN CARES FOR KYO-KUN EVEN MORE THAN THAT.
HE WATCHED OVER KYO-KUN SO THAT HE WOULDN'T GET HURT...
...AS IF HE WAS HIS REAL FATHER.

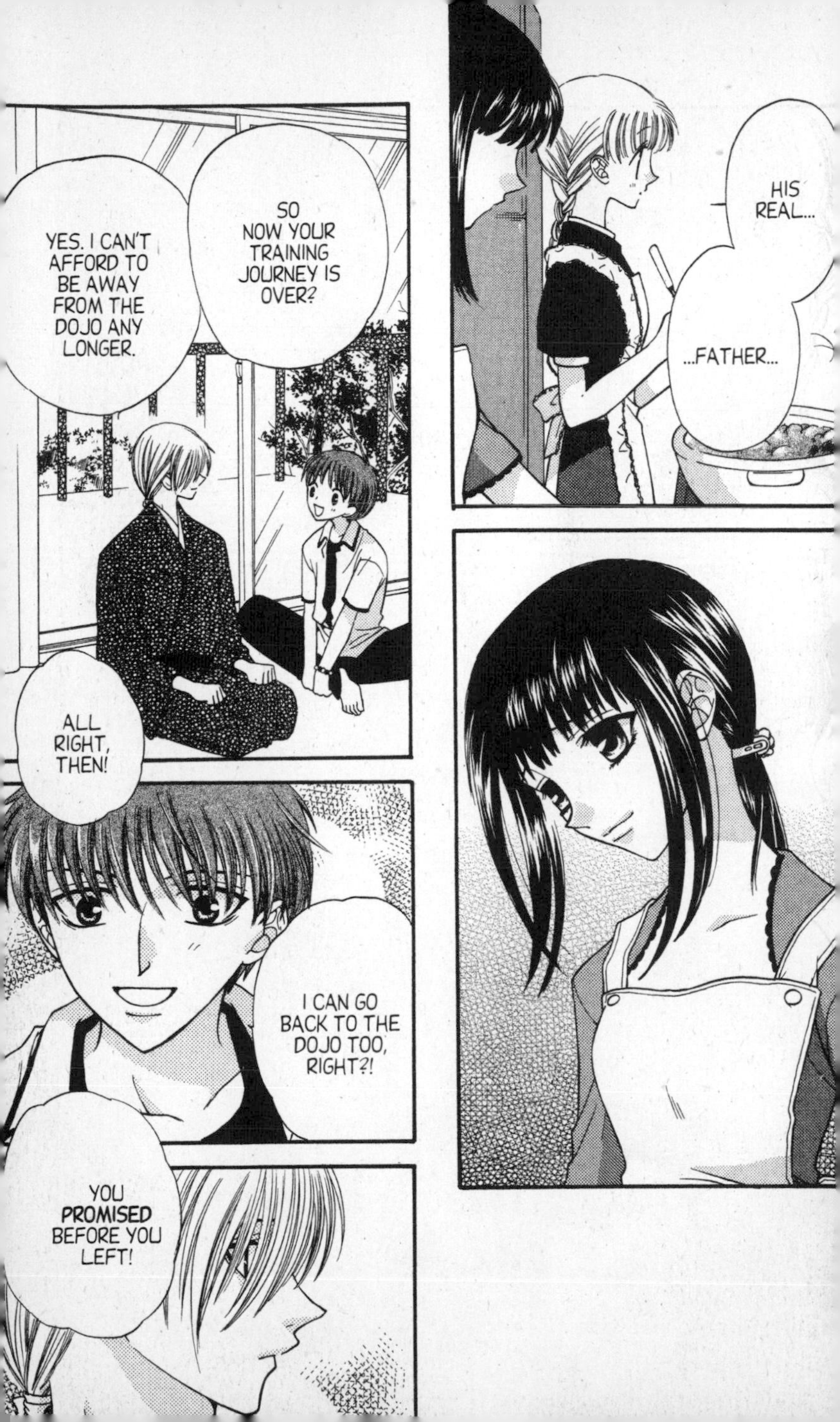
HIS REAL...
...FATHER...
SO NOW YOUR TRAINING JOURNEY IS OVER?
YES. I CAN'T AFFORD TO BE AWAY FROM THE DOJO ANY LONGER.
ALL RIGHT, THEN!
I CAN GO BACK TO THE DOJO TOO, RIGHT?!
YOU **PROMISED** BEFORE YOU LEFT!

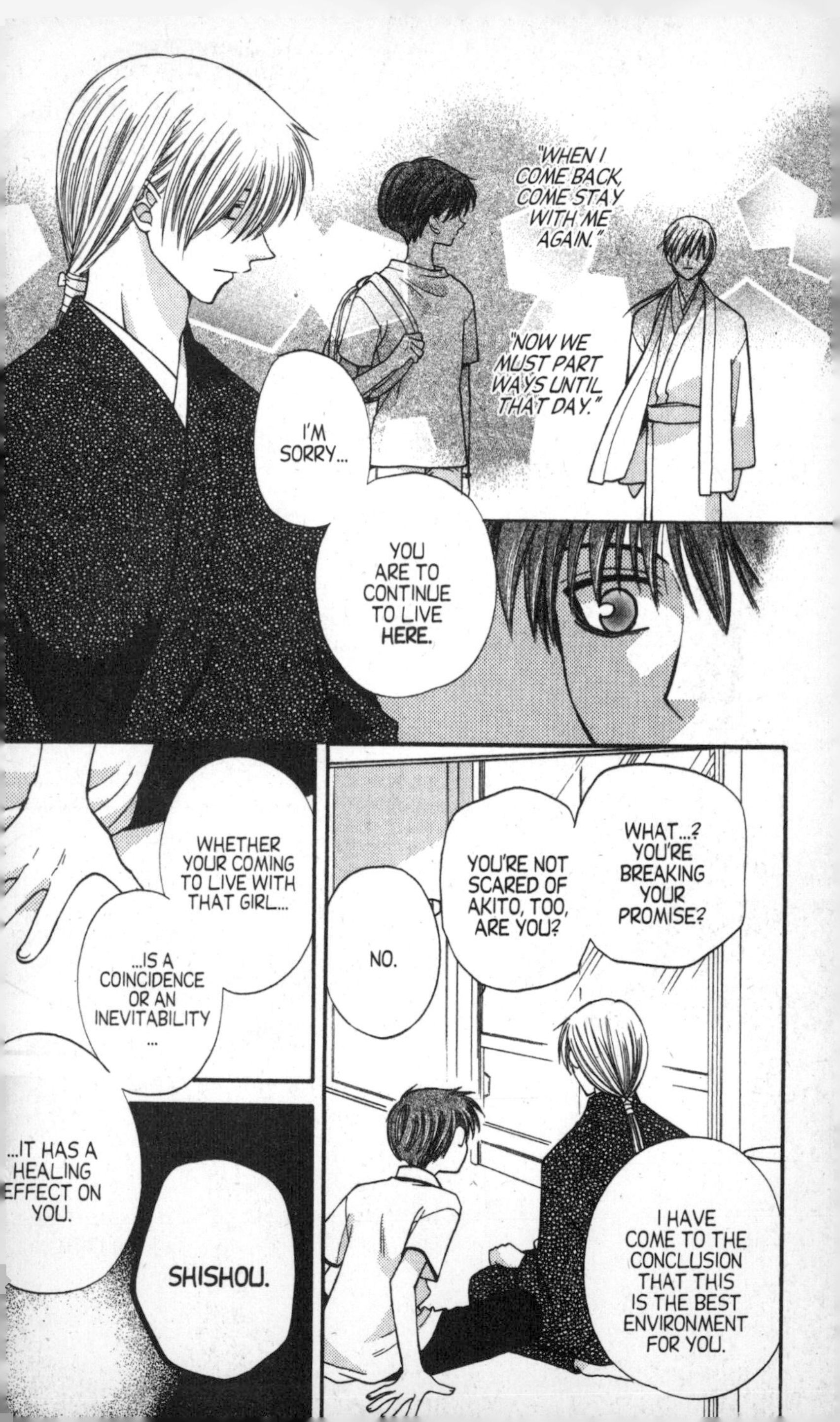
"WHEN I COME BACK, COME STAY WITH ME AGAIN."
"NOW WE MUST PART WAYS UNTIL THAT DAY."
I'M SORRY...
YOU ARE TO CONTINUE TO LIVE HERE.
WHAT...? YOU'RE BREAKING YOUR PROMISE?
YOU'RE NOT SCARED OF AKITO, TOO, ARE YOU?
NO.
I HAVE COME TO THE CONCLUSION THAT THIS IS THE BEST ENVIRONMENT FOR YOU.
WHETHER YOUR COMING TO LIVE WITH THAT GIRL...
...IS A COINCIDENCE OR AN INEVITABILITY...
...IT HAS A HEALING EFFECT ON YOU.
SHISHOU.

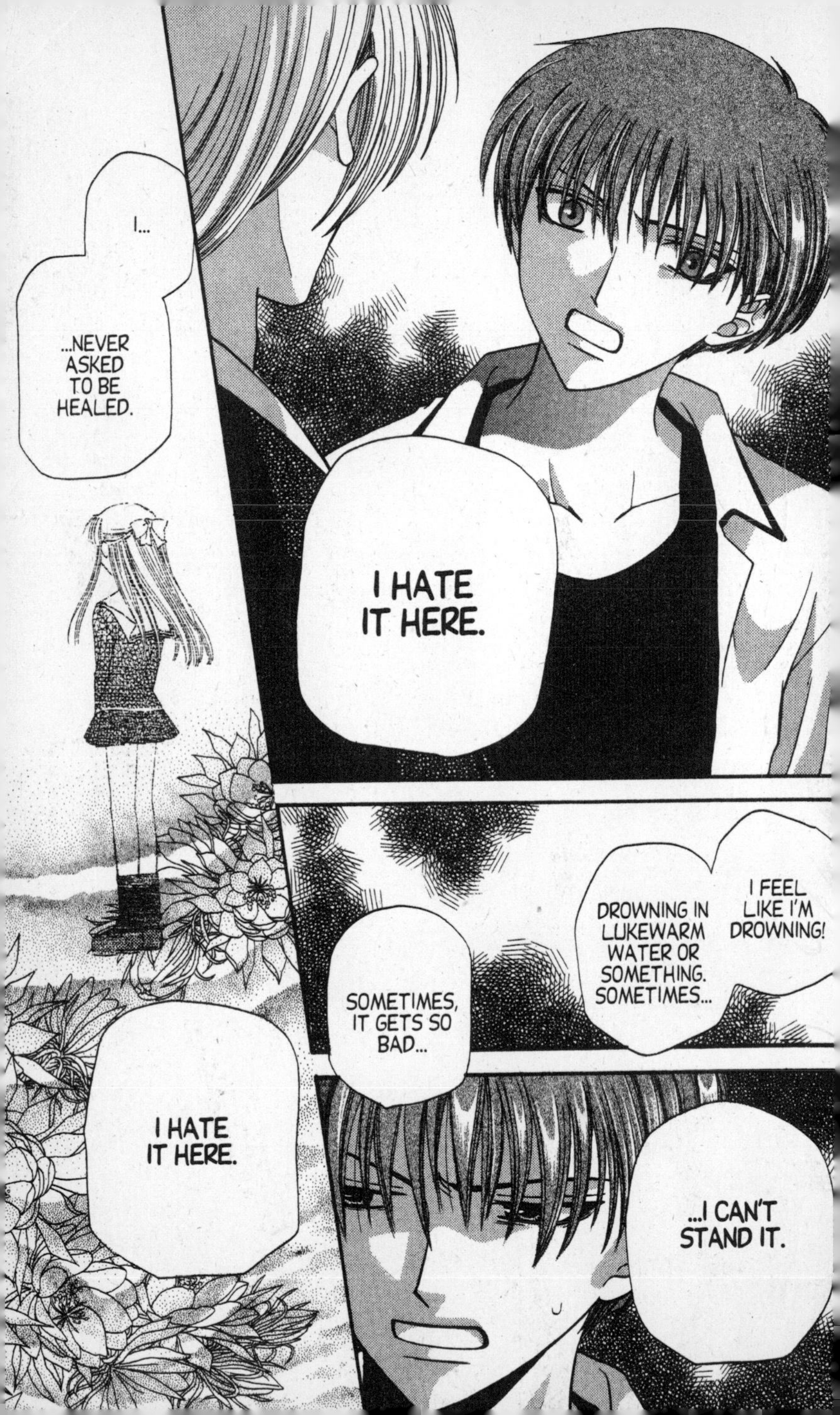
I HATE IT HERE.
I FEEL LIKE I'M DROWNING!
DROWNING IN LUKEWARM WATER OR SOMETHING. SOMETIMES...
SOMETIMES, IT GETS SO BAD...
...I CAN'T STAND IT.
I...
...NEVER ASKED TO BE HEALED.
I HATE IT HERE.

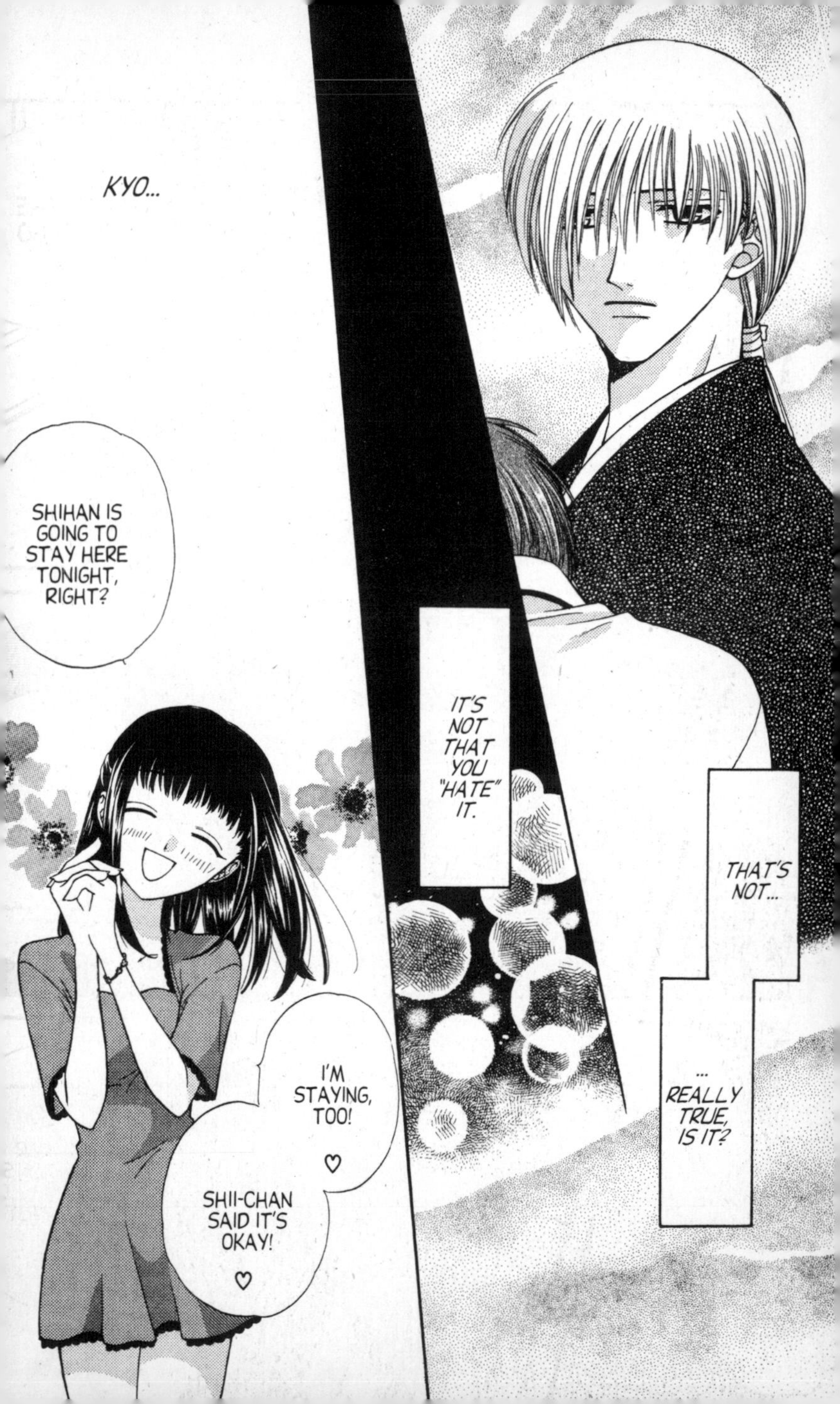

IT'S NOT THAT YOU "HATE" IT.
THAT'S NOT...
... REALLY TRUE, IS IT?
KYO...
SHIHAN IS GOING TO STAY HERE TONIGHT, RIGHT?
I'M STAYING, TOO! ♡
SHII-CHAN SAID IT'S OKAY! ♡

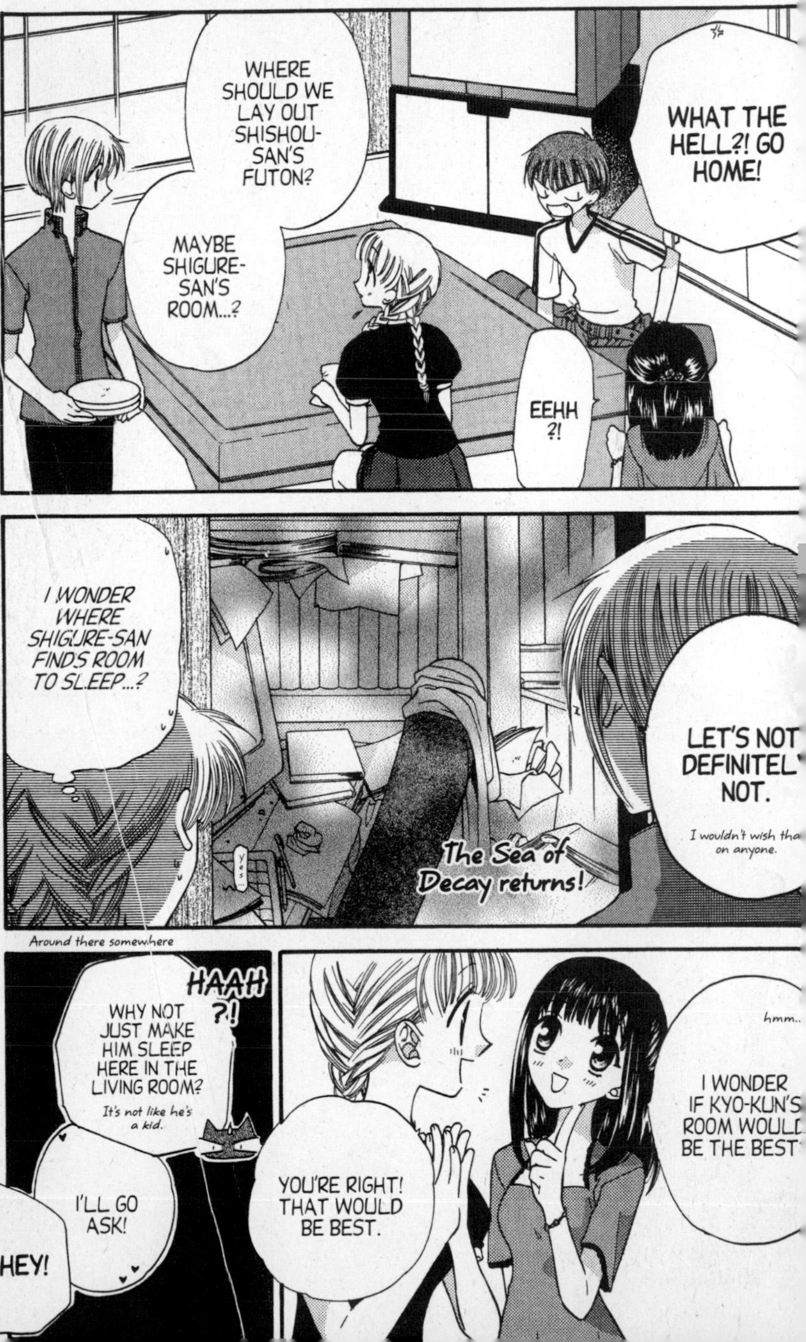
WHAT THE HELL?! GO HOME!
WHERE SHOULD WE LAY OUT SHISHOU-SAN'S FUTON?
MAYBE SHIGURE-SAN'S ROOM...?
EEHH ?!
LET'S NOT DEFINITEL NOT.
I wouldn't wish tha on anyone.
The Sea of Decay returns!
I WONDER WHERE SHIGURE-SAN FINDS ROOM TO SLEEP...?
yes...
Around there somewhere
hmm..
I WONDER IF KYO-KUN'S ROOM WOULD BE THE BEST
YOU'RE RIGHT! THAT WOULD BE BEST.
HAAH ?!
WHY NOT JUST MAKE HIM SLEEP HERE IN THE LIVING ROOM?
It's not like he's a kid.
I'LL GO ASK!
HEY!

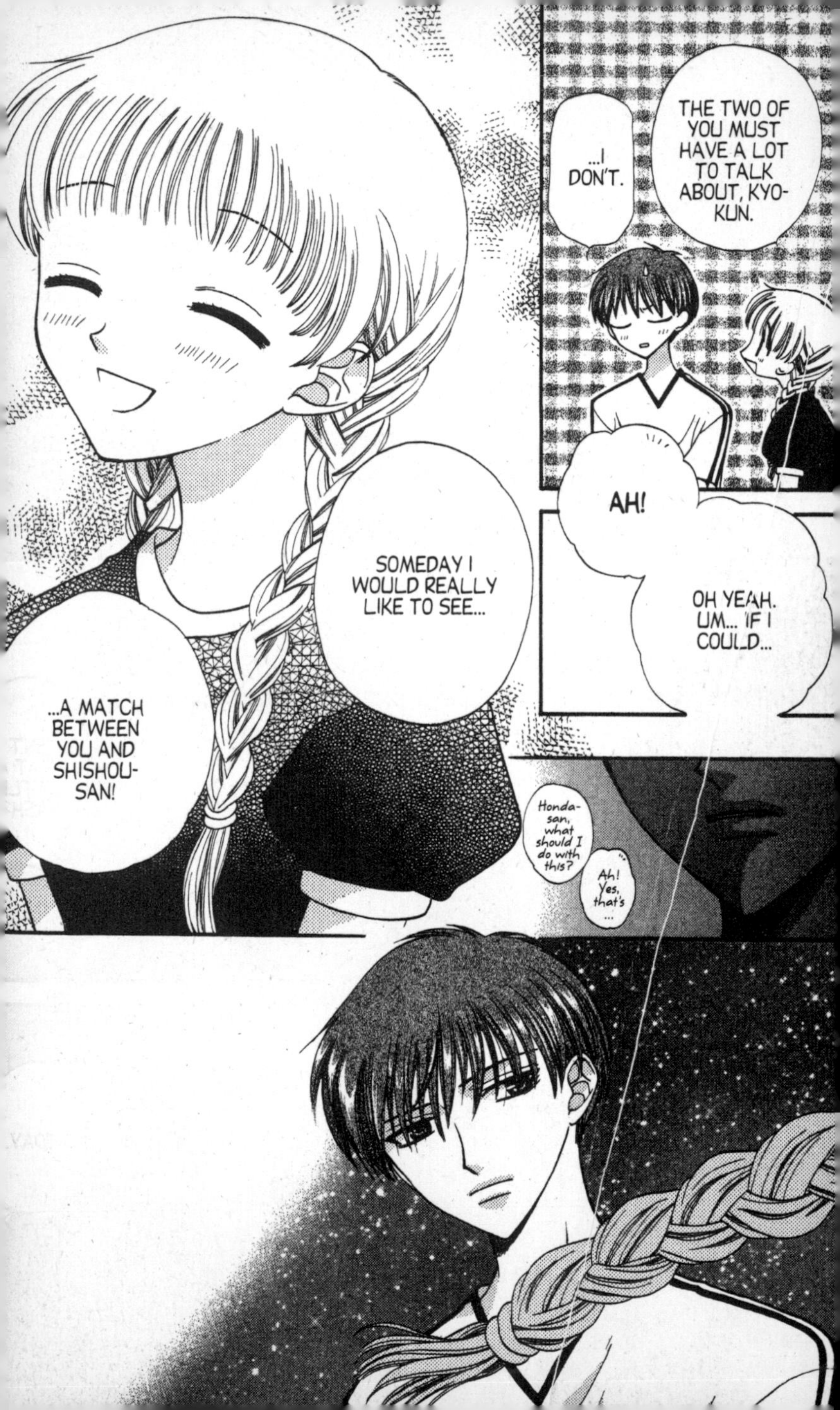
THE TWO OF YOU MUST HAVE A LOT TO TALK ABOUT, KYO-KUN.
...I DON'T.
AH!
OH YEAH. UM... IF I COULD...
Honda-san, what should I do with this?
Ah! Yes, that's ...
SOMEDAY I WOULD REALLY LIKE TO SEE...
...A MATCH BETWEEN YOU AND SHISHOU-SAN!

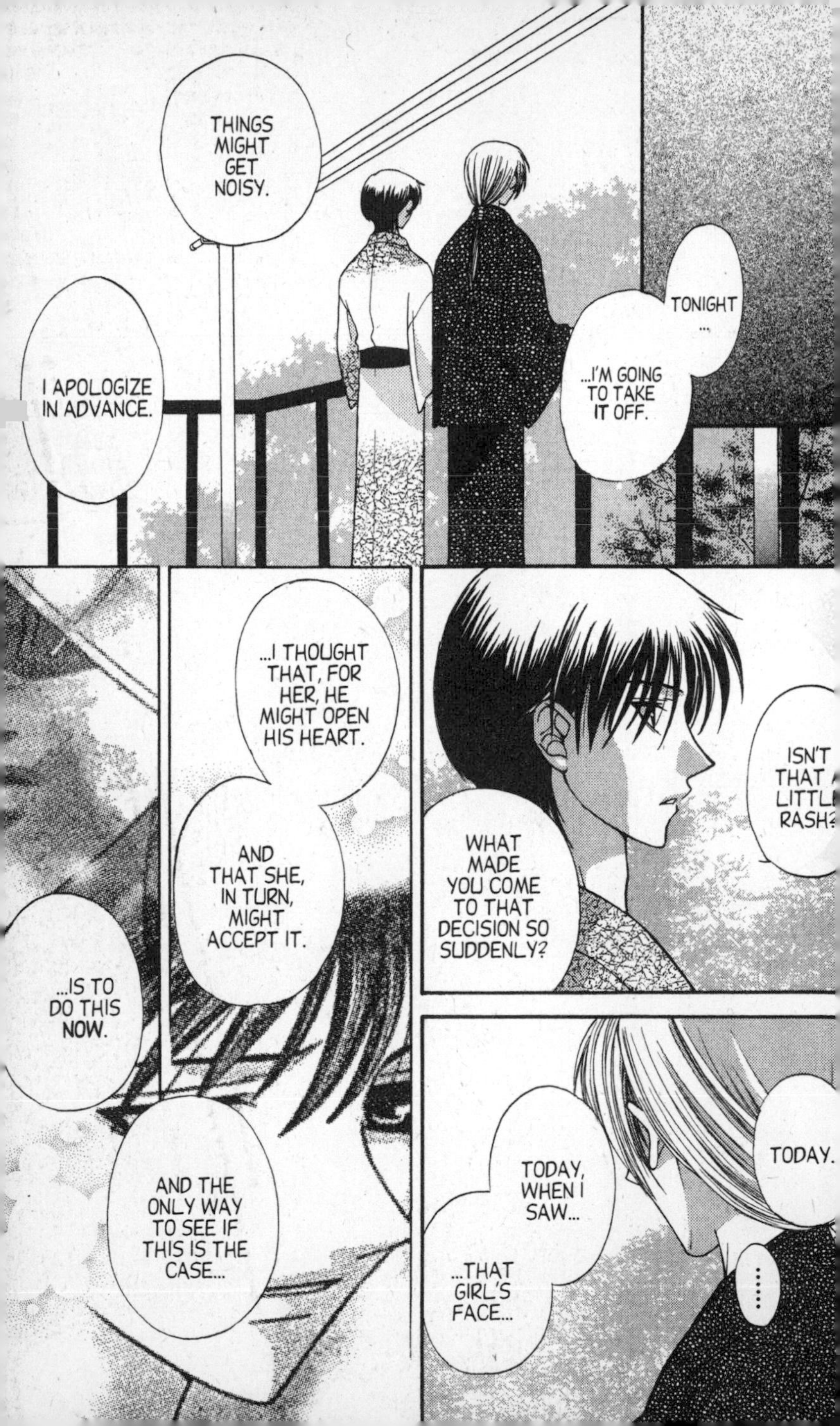
TONIGHT ...
...I'M GOING TO TAKE IT OFF.
THINGS MIGHT GET NOISY.
I APOLOGIZE IN ADVANCE.
ISN'T THAT LITTL RASH?
WHAT MADE YOU COME TO THAT DECISION SO SUDDENLY?
TODAY.
......
TODAY, WHEN I SAW...
...THAT GIRL'S FACE...
...I THOUGHT THAT, FOR HER, HE MIGHT OPEN HIS HEART.
AND THAT SHE, IN TURN, MIGHT ACCEPT IT.
AND THE ONLY WAY TO SEE IF THIS IS THE CASE...
...IS TO DO THIS NOW.

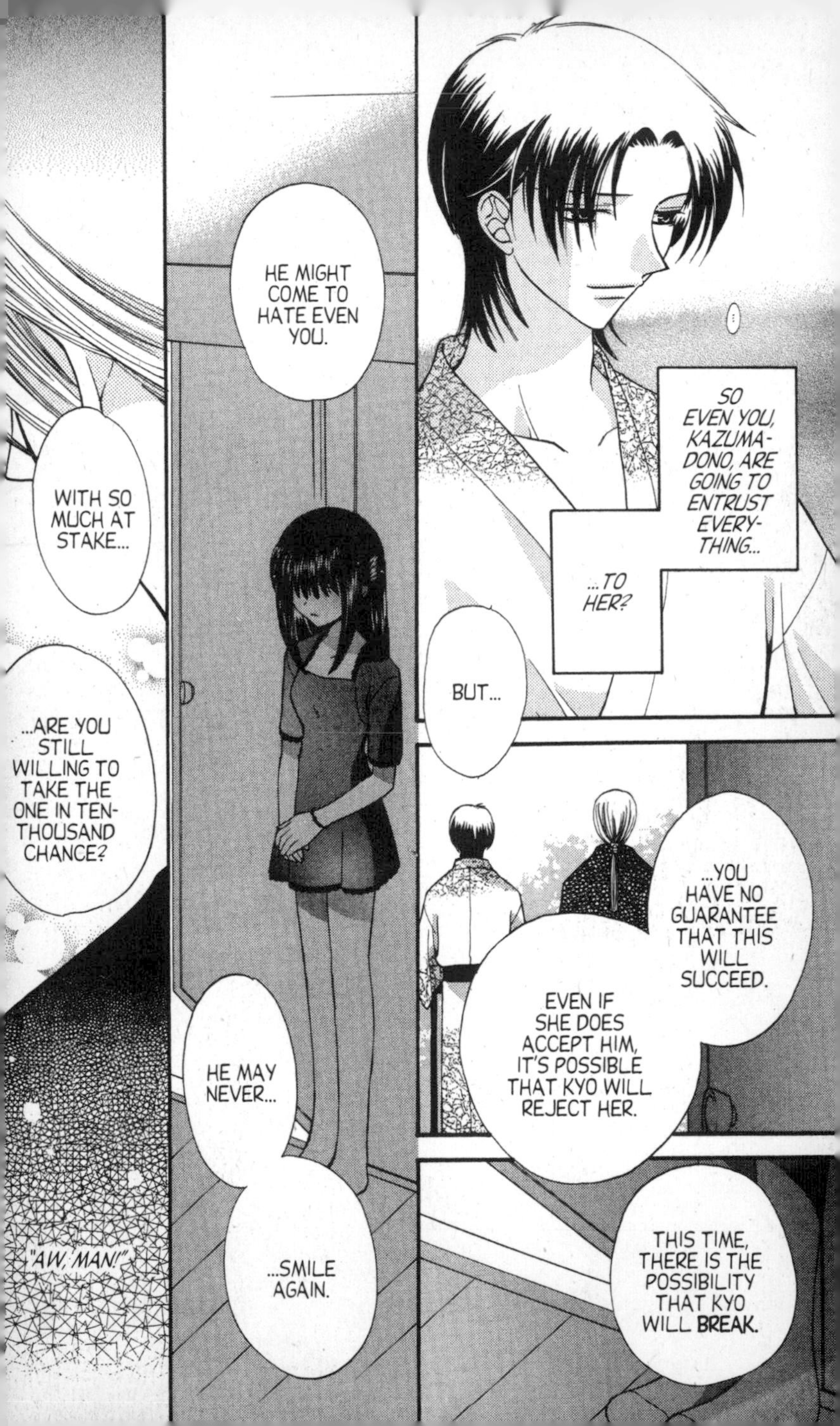

SO EVEN YOU, KAZUMA-DONO, ARE GOING TO ENTRUST EVERYTHING...
...TO HER?
BUT...
...YOU HAVE NO GUARANTEE THAT THIS WILL SUCCEED.
EVEN IF SHE DOES ACCEPT HIM, IT'S POSSIBLE THAT KYO WILL REJECT HER.
THIS TIME, THERE IS THE POSSIBILITY THAT KYO WILL **BREAK.**
HE MIGHT COME TO HATE EVEN YOU.
HE MAY NEVER...
...SMILE AGAIN.
WITH SO MUCH AT STAKE...
...ARE YOU STILL WILLING TO TAKE THE ONE IN TEN-THOUSAND CHANCE?
"AW, MAN!"

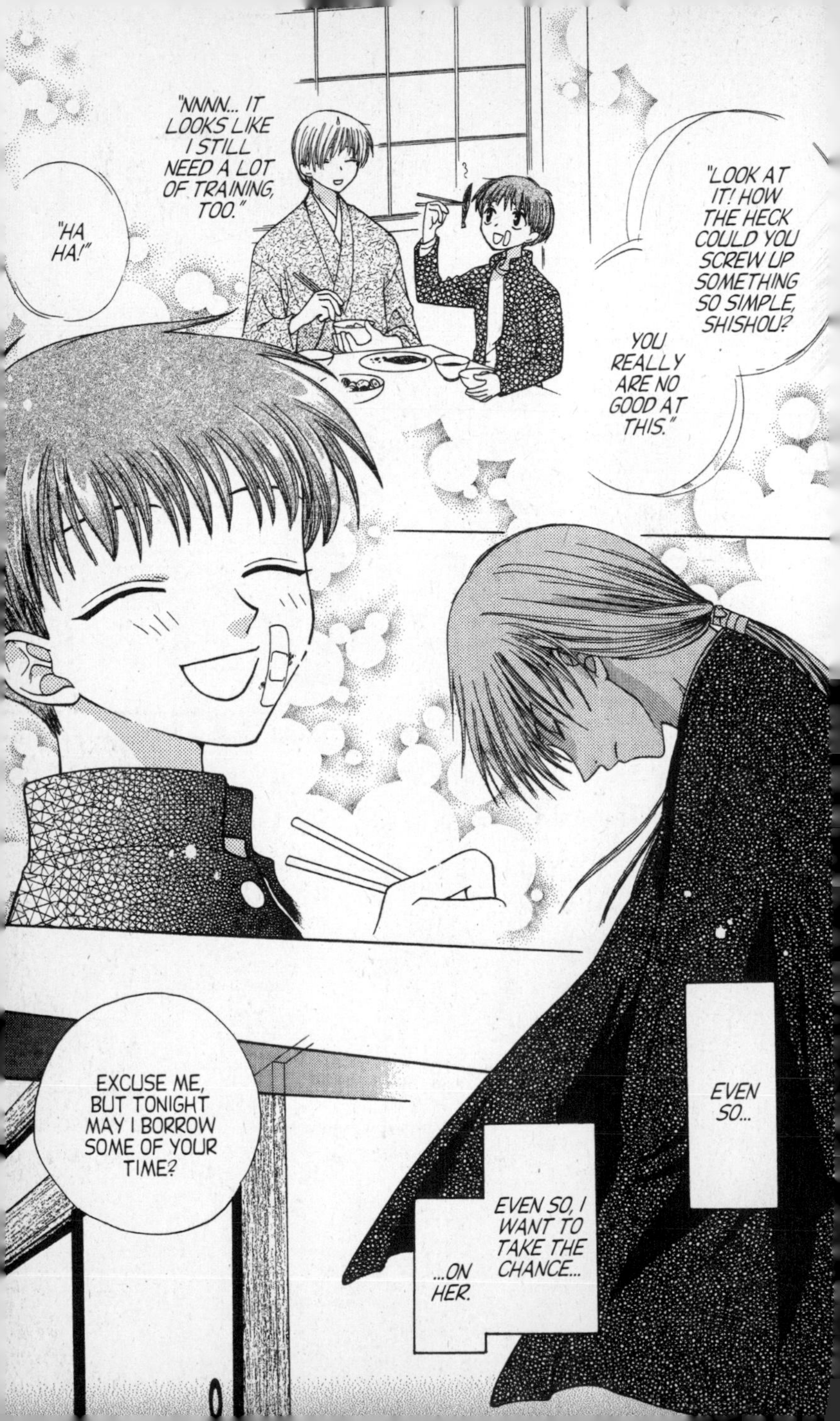
"LOOK AT IT! HOW THE HECK COULD YOU SCREW UP SOMETHING SO SIMPLE, SHISHOU?
YOU REALLY ARE NO GOOD AT THIS."
"NNNN... IT LOOKS LIKE I STILL NEED A LOT OF TRAINING, TOO."
"HA HA!"
EVEN SO...
EVEN SO, I WANT TO TAKE THE CHANCE...
...ON HER.
EXCUSE ME, BUT TONIGHT MAY I BORROW SOME OF YOUR TIME?

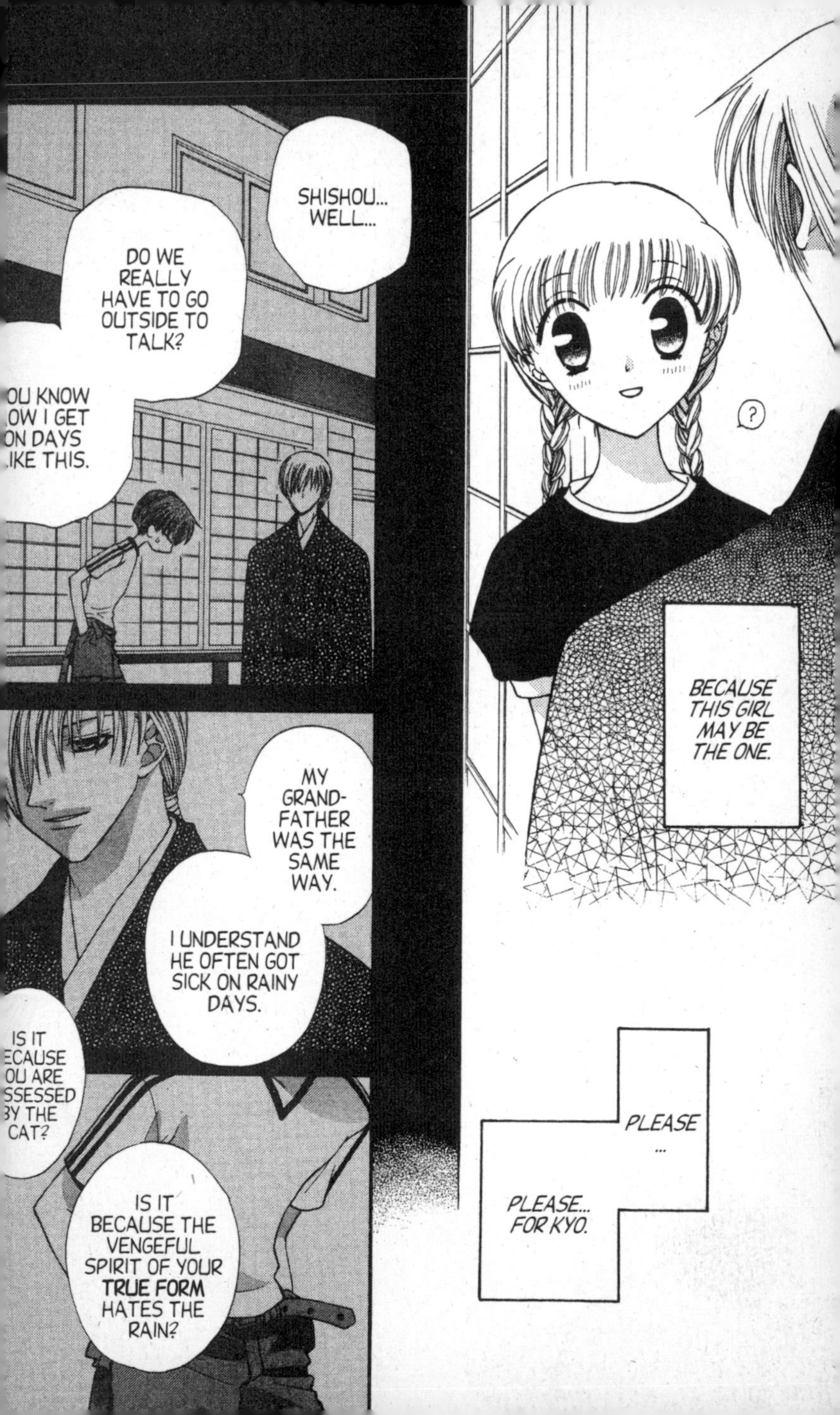
?
BECAUSE THIS GIRL MAY BE THE ONE.
PLEASE...
PLEASE... FOR KYO.
SHISHOU... WELL...
DO WE REALLY HAVE TO GO OUTSIDE TO TALK?
OU KNOW OW I GET ON DAYS IKE THIS.
MY GRAND-FATHER WAS THE SAME WAY.
I UNDERSTAND HE OFTEN GOT SICK ON RAINY DAYS.
IS IT ECAUSE OU ARE SSESSED BY THE CAT?
IS IT BECAUSE THE VENGEFUL SPIRIT OF YOUR **TRUE FORM** HATES THE RAIN?

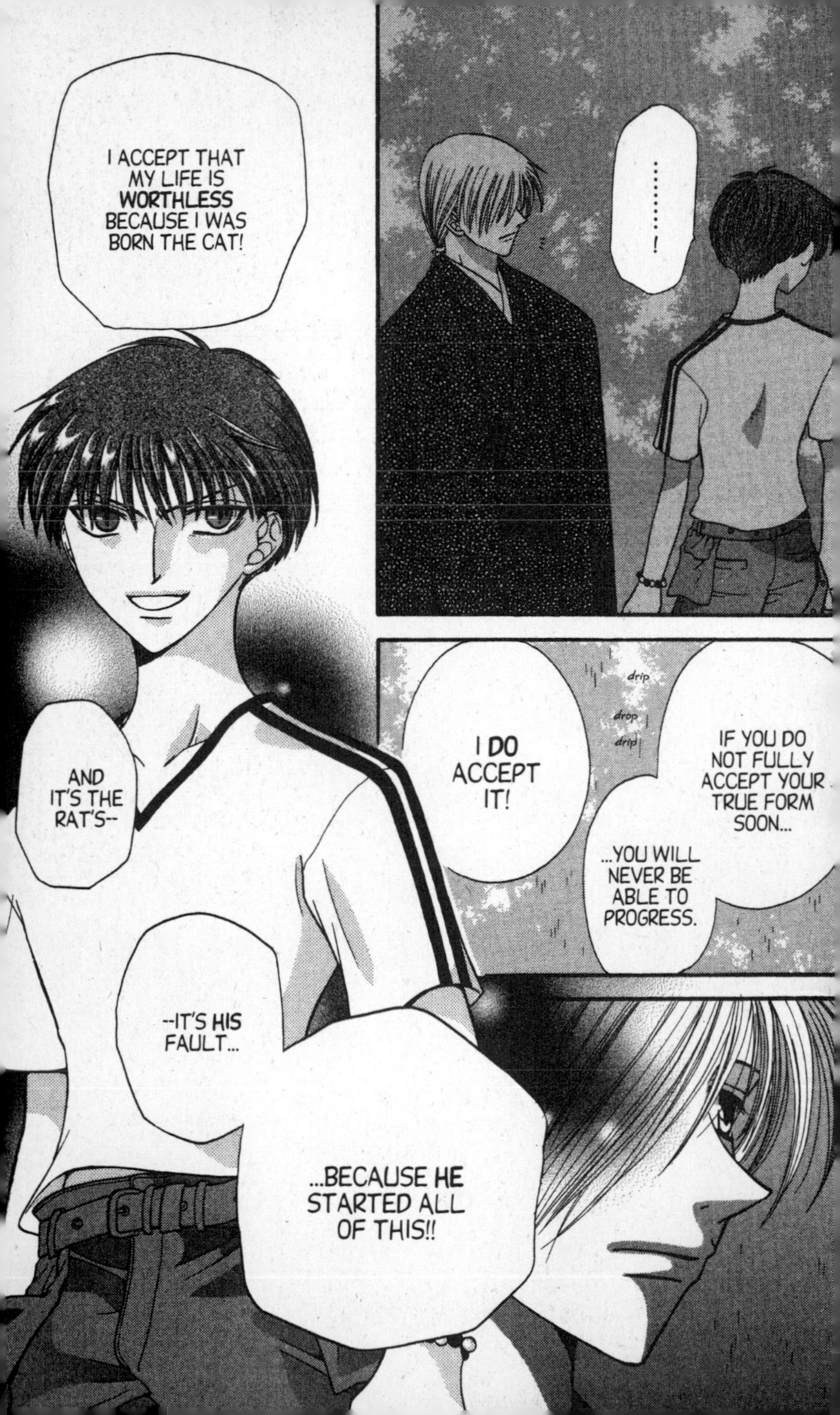
......!
IF YOU DO NOT FULLY ACCEPT YOUR TRUE FORM SOON...
...YOU WILL NEVER BE ABLE TO PROGRESS.
drip
drop
drip
I DO ACCEPT IT!
I ACCEPT THAT MY LIFE IS **WORTHLESS** BECAUSE I WAS BORN THE CAT!
AND IT'S THE RAT'S--
--IT'S HIS FAULT...
...BECAUSE HE STARTED ALL OF THIS!!

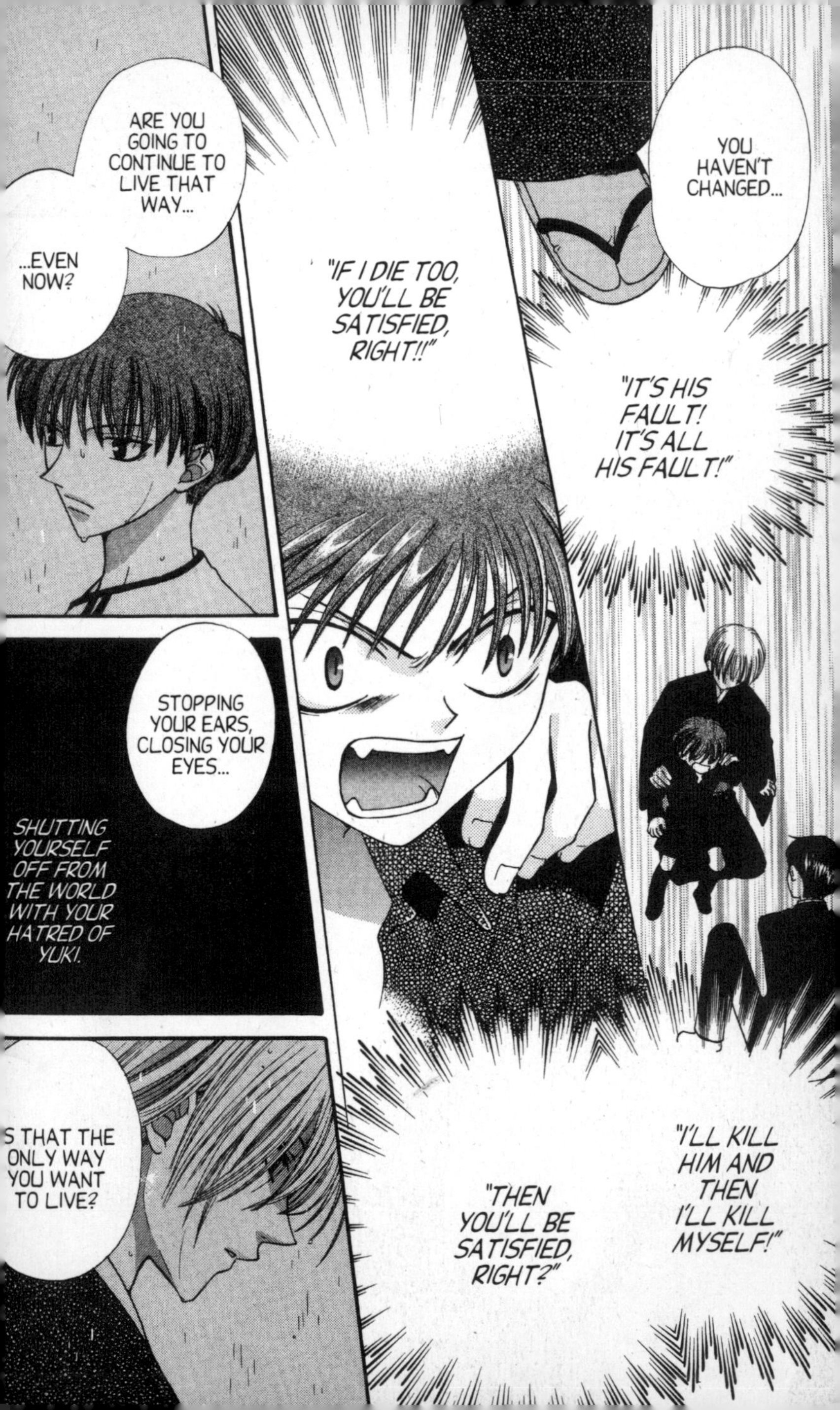
YOU HAVEN'T CHANGED...
"IT'S HIS FAULT! IT'S ALL HIS FAULT!"
"I'LL KILL HIM AND THEN I'LL KILL MYSELF!"
"THEN YOU'LL BE SATISFIED, RIGHT?"
"IF I DIE TOO, YOU'LL BE SATISFIED, RIGHT!!"
ARE YOU GOING TO CONTINUE TO LIVE THAT WAY...
...EVEN NOW?
STOPPING YOUR EARS, CLOSING YOUR EYES...
SHUTTING YOURSELF OFF FROM THE WORLD WITH YOUR HATRED OF YUKI.
S THAT THE ONLY WAY YOU WANT TO LIVE?

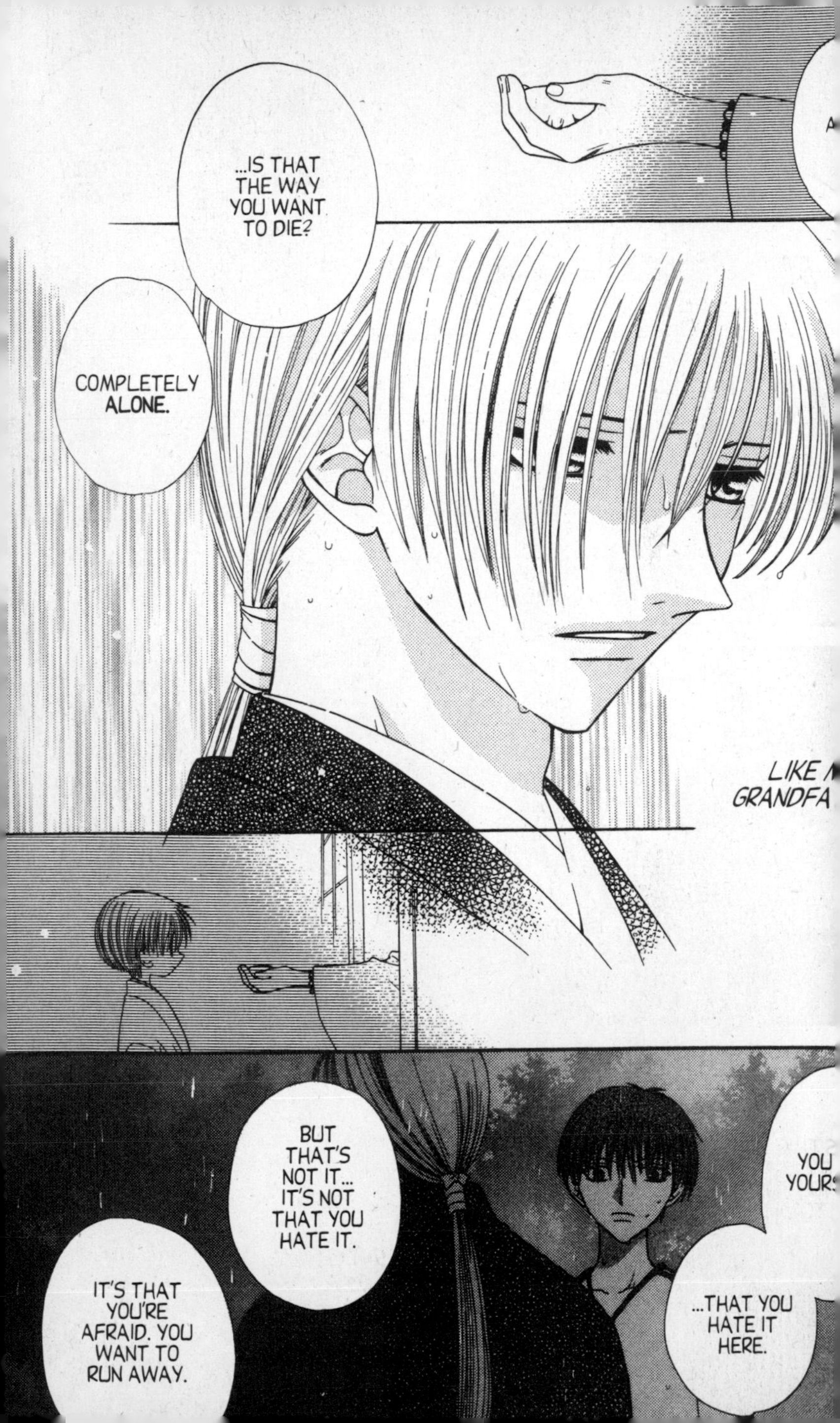
...IS THAT THE WAY YOU WANT TO DIE?
COMPLETELY ALONE.
...THAT YOU HATE IT HERE.
BUT THAT'S NOT IT... IT'S NOT THAT YOU HATE IT.
IT'S THAT YOU'RE AFRAID. YOU WANT TO RUN AWAY.

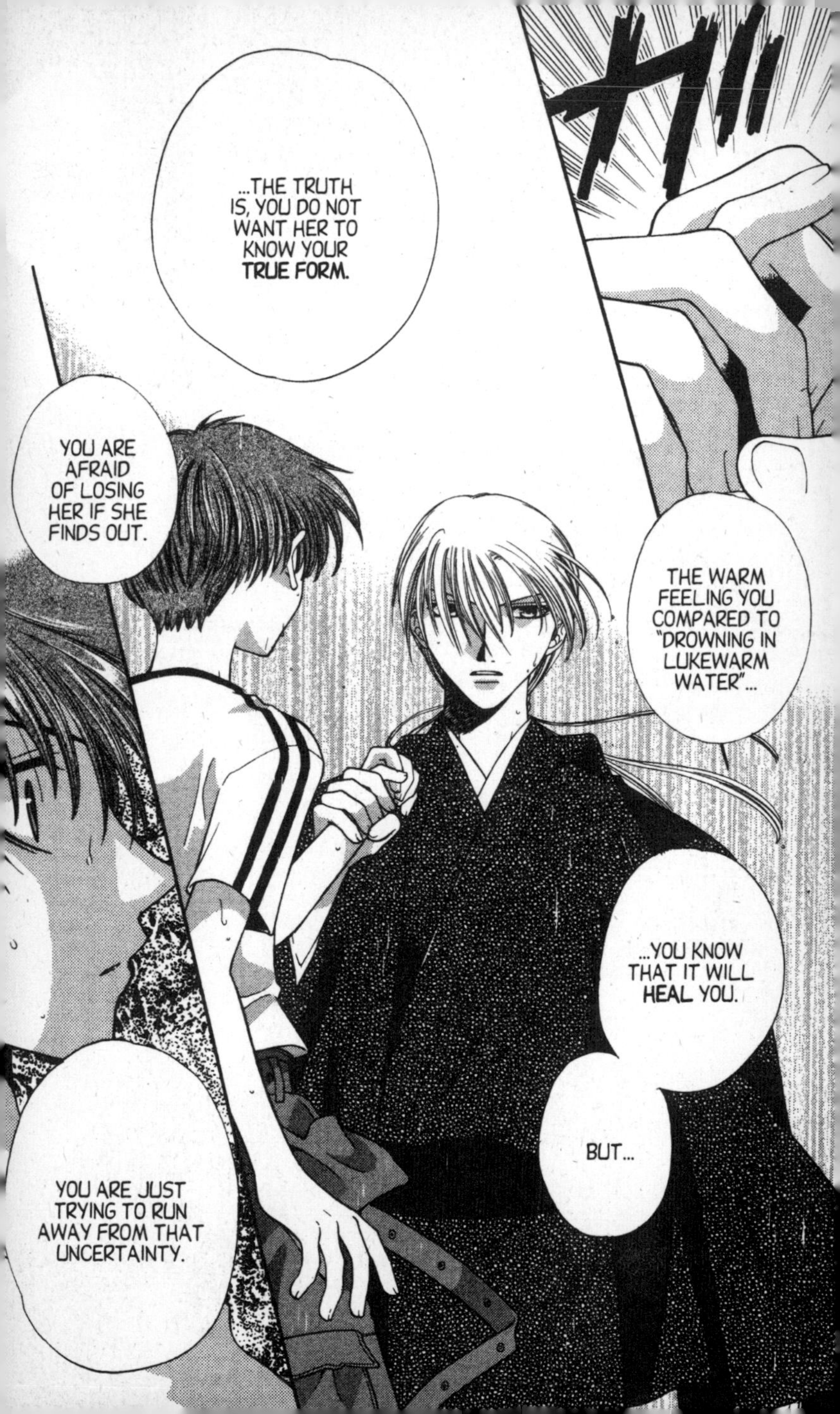
...THE TRUTH IS, YOU DO NOT WANT HER TO KNOW YOUR **TRUE FORM.**
THE WARM FEELING YOU COMPARED TO "DROWNING IN LUKEWARM WATER"...
...YOU KNOW THAT IT WILL **HEAL YOU.**
BUT...
YOU ARE AFRAID OF LOSING HER IF SHE FINDS OUT.
YOU ARE JUST TRYING TO RUN AWAY FROM THAT UNCERTAINTY.

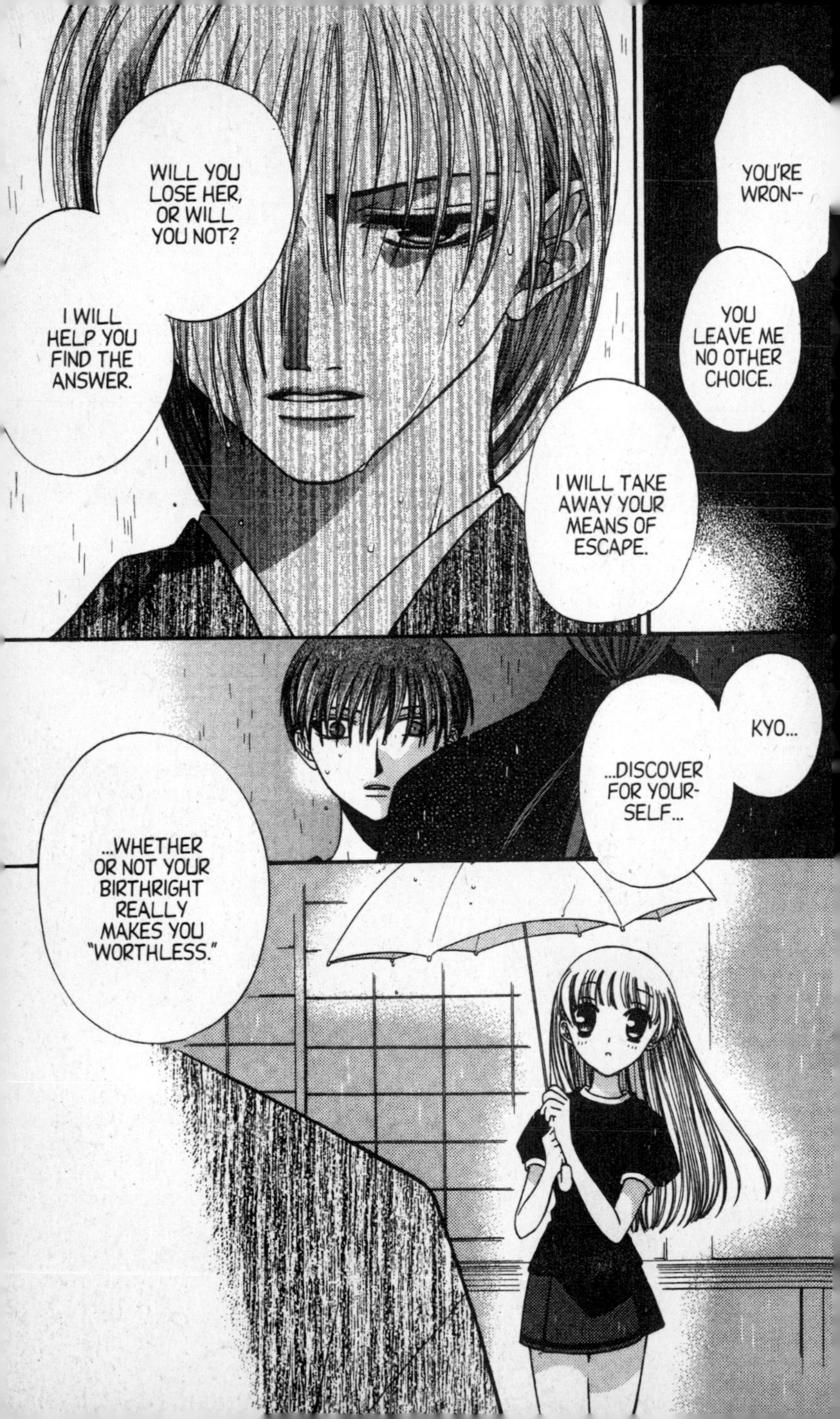
YOU'RE WRON--
YOU LEAVE ME NO OTHER CHOICE.
I WILL TAKE AWAY YOUR MEANS OF ESCAPE.
WILL YOU LOSE HER, OR WILL YOU NOT?
I WILL HELP YOU FIND THE ANSWER.
KYO...
...DISCOVER FOR YOUR-SELF...
...WHETHER OR NOT YOUR BIRTHRIGHT REALLY MAKES YOU "WORTHLESS."

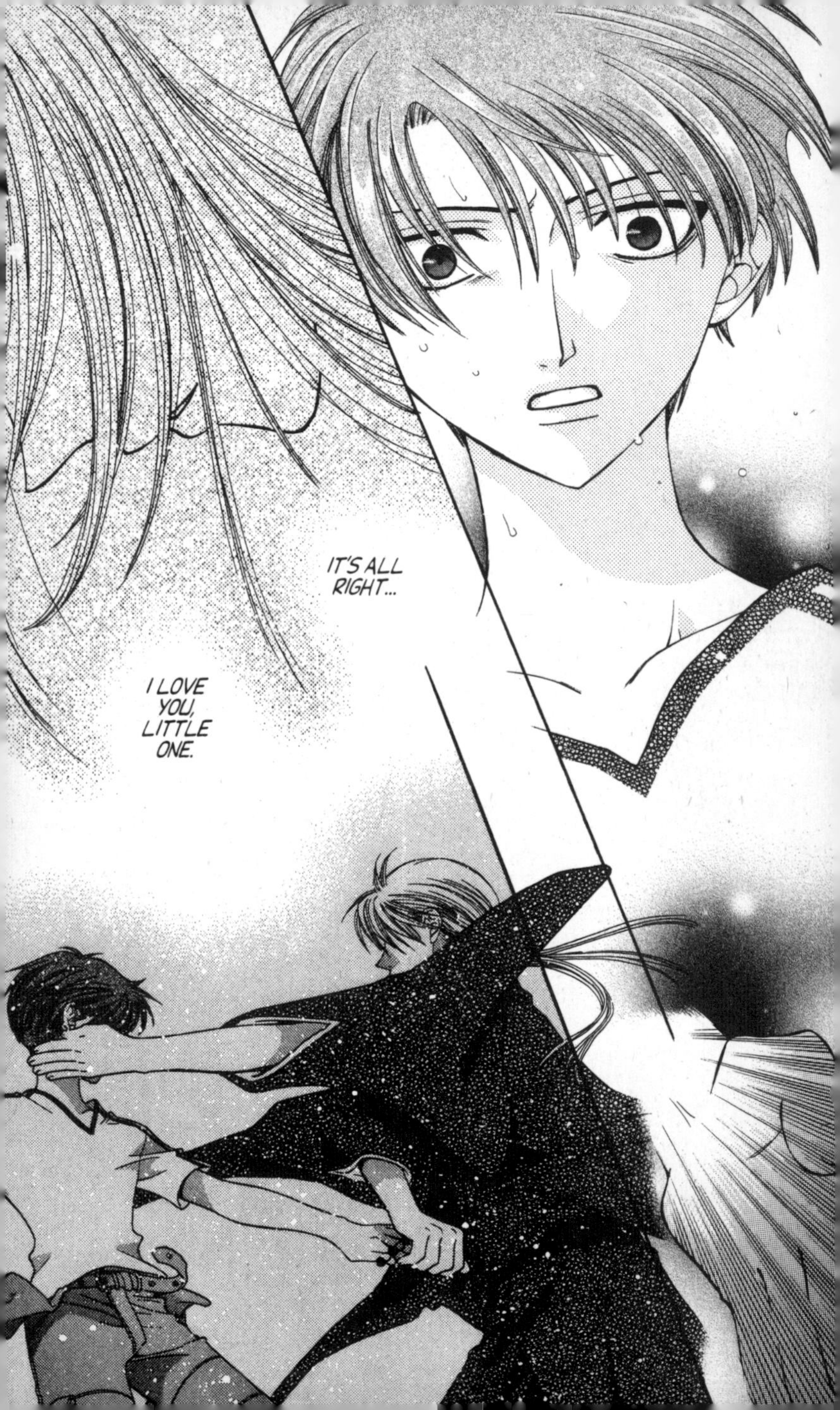
IT'S ALL RIGHT...
I LOVE YOU, LITTLE ONE.

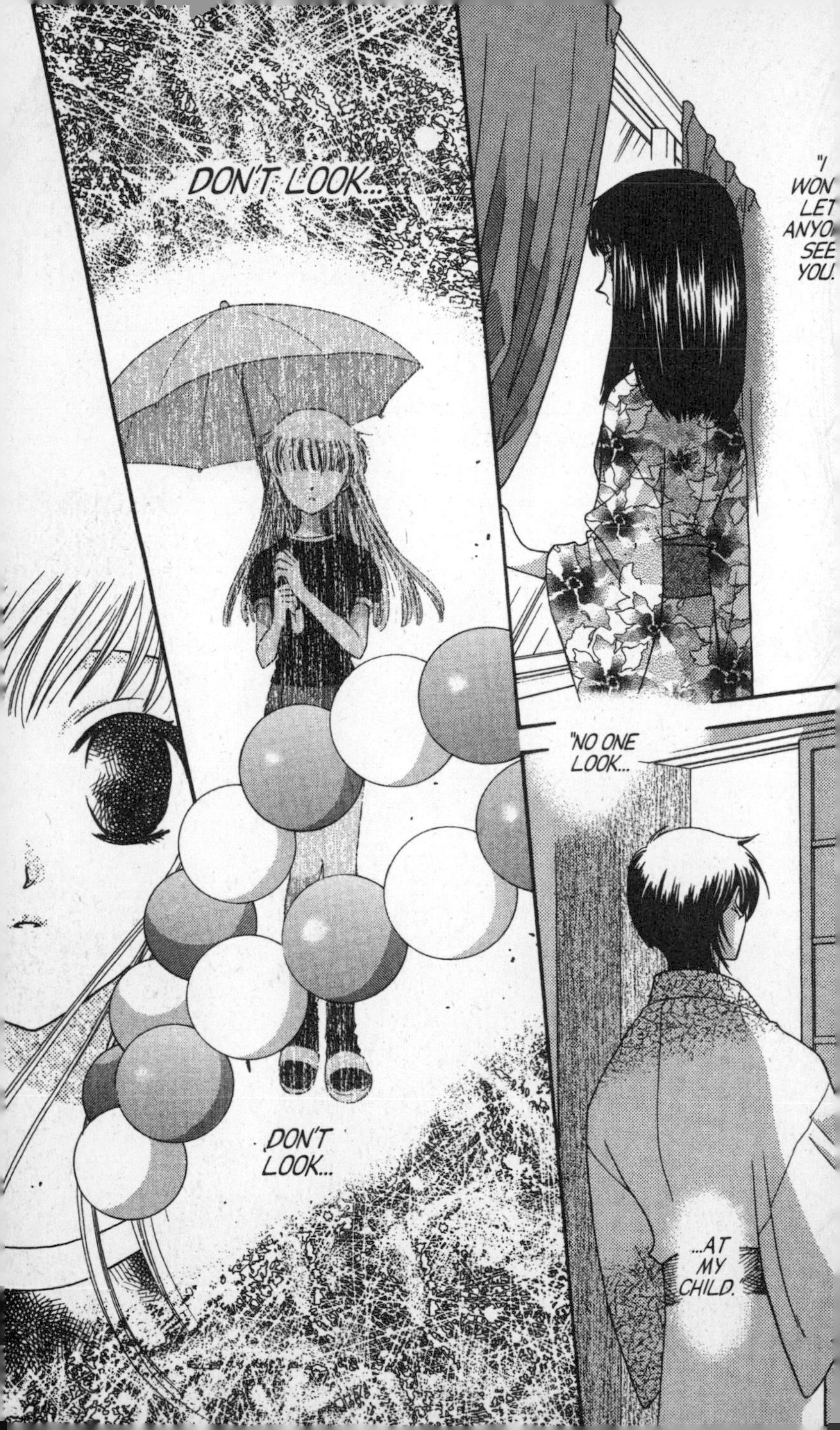
"I WON LET ANYO SEE YOU.
"NO ONE LOOK...
...AT MY CHILD."
DON'T LOOK...
DON'T LOOK...

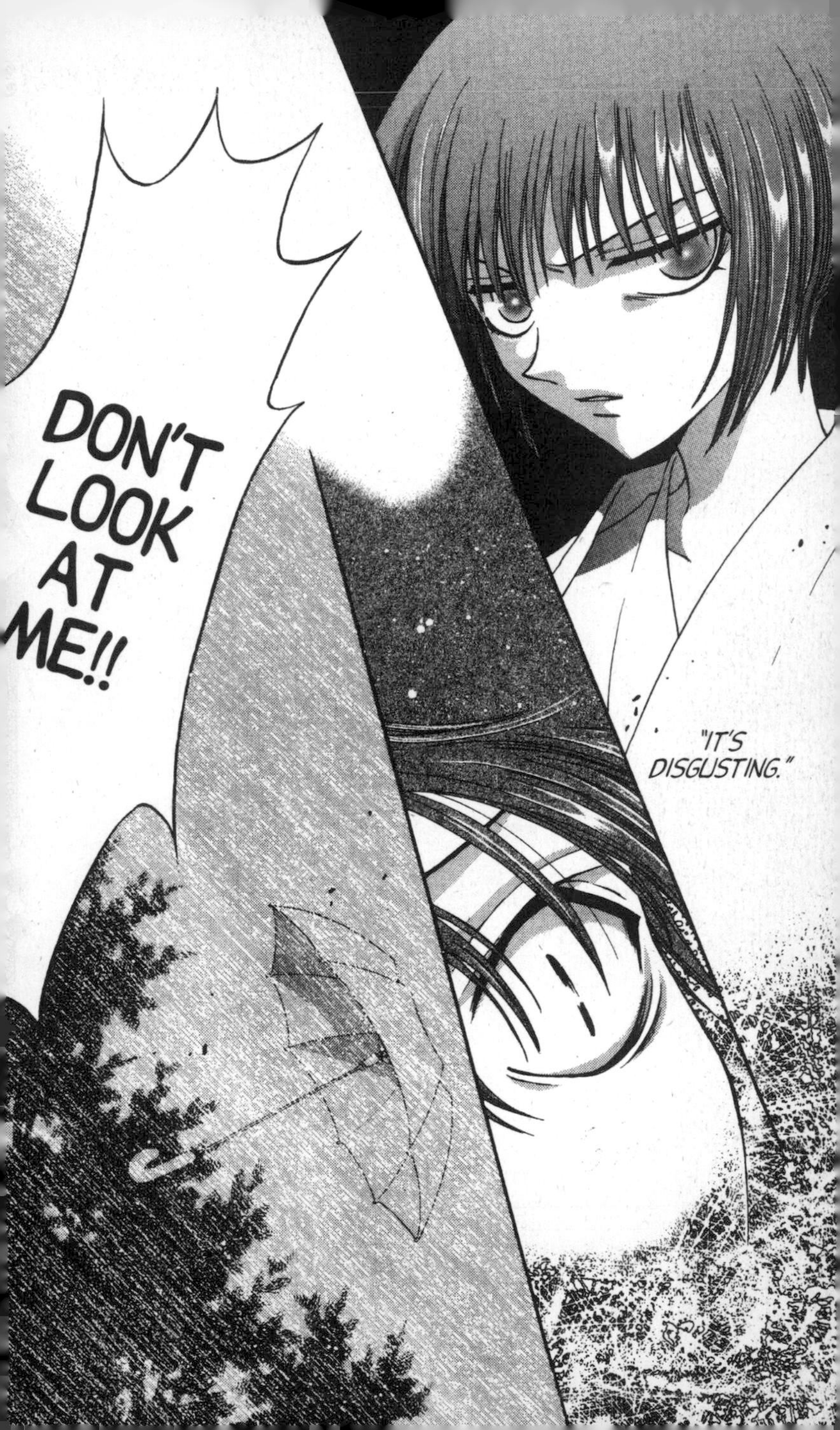
"IT'S DISGUSTING."
DON'T LOOK AT ME!!

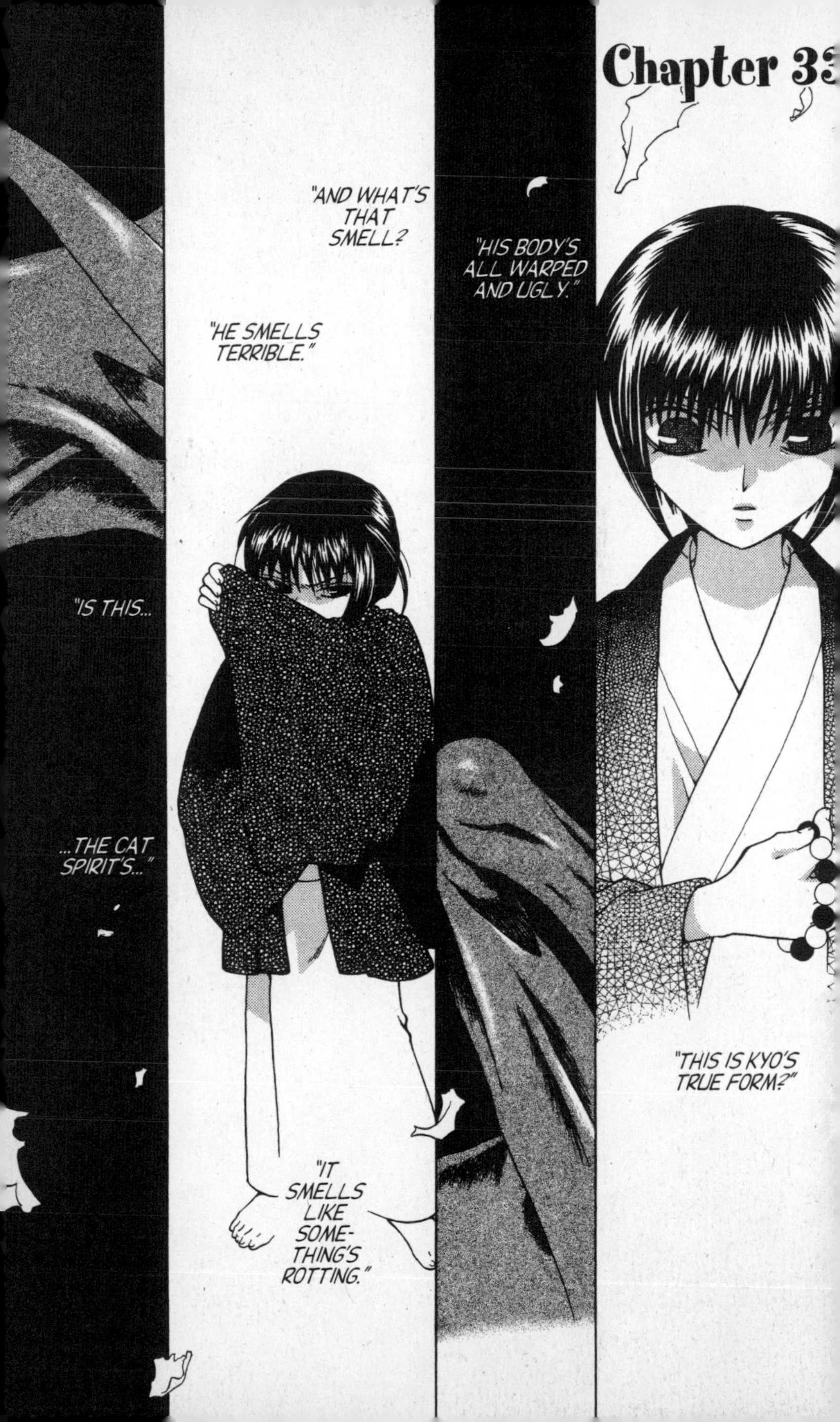
Chapter 33
"THIS IS KYO'S TRUE FORM?"
"HIS BODY'S ALL WARPED AND UGLY."
"AND WHAT'S THAT SMELL?
"HE SMELLS TERRIBLE."
"IT SMELLS LIKE SOME-THING'S ROTTING."
"IS THIS...
...THE CAT SPIRIT'S..."

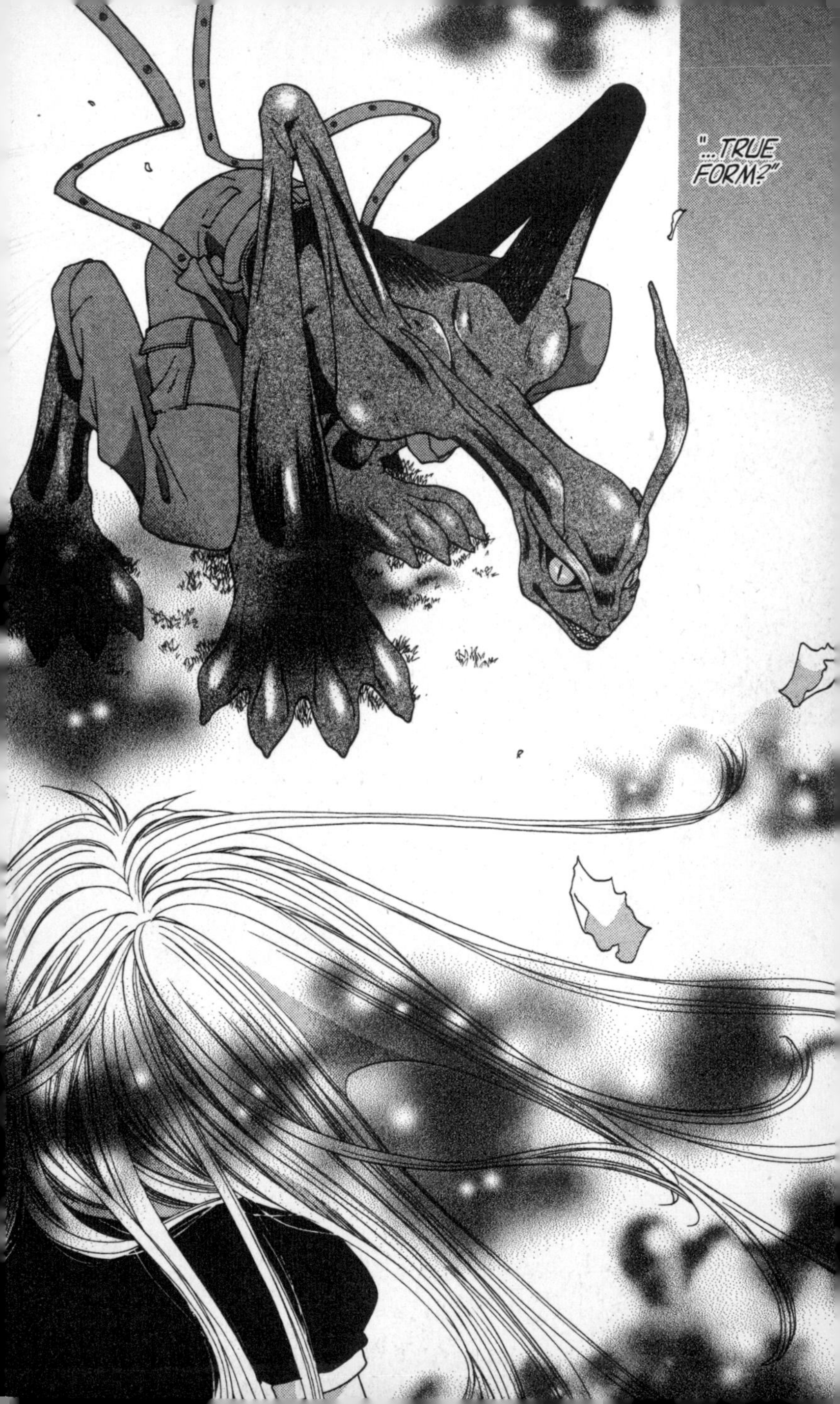
"...TRUE FORM?"

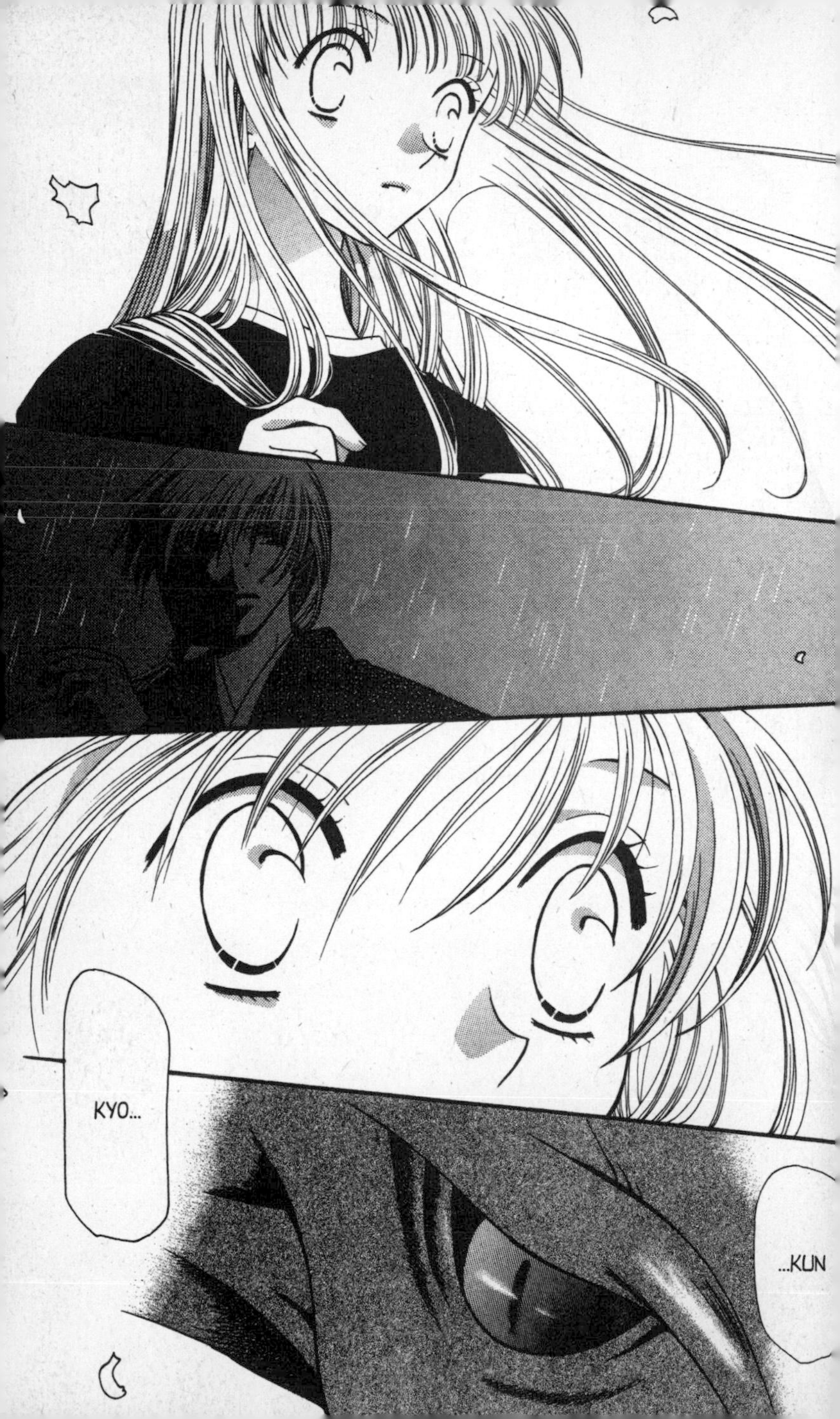
...KUN
KYO...

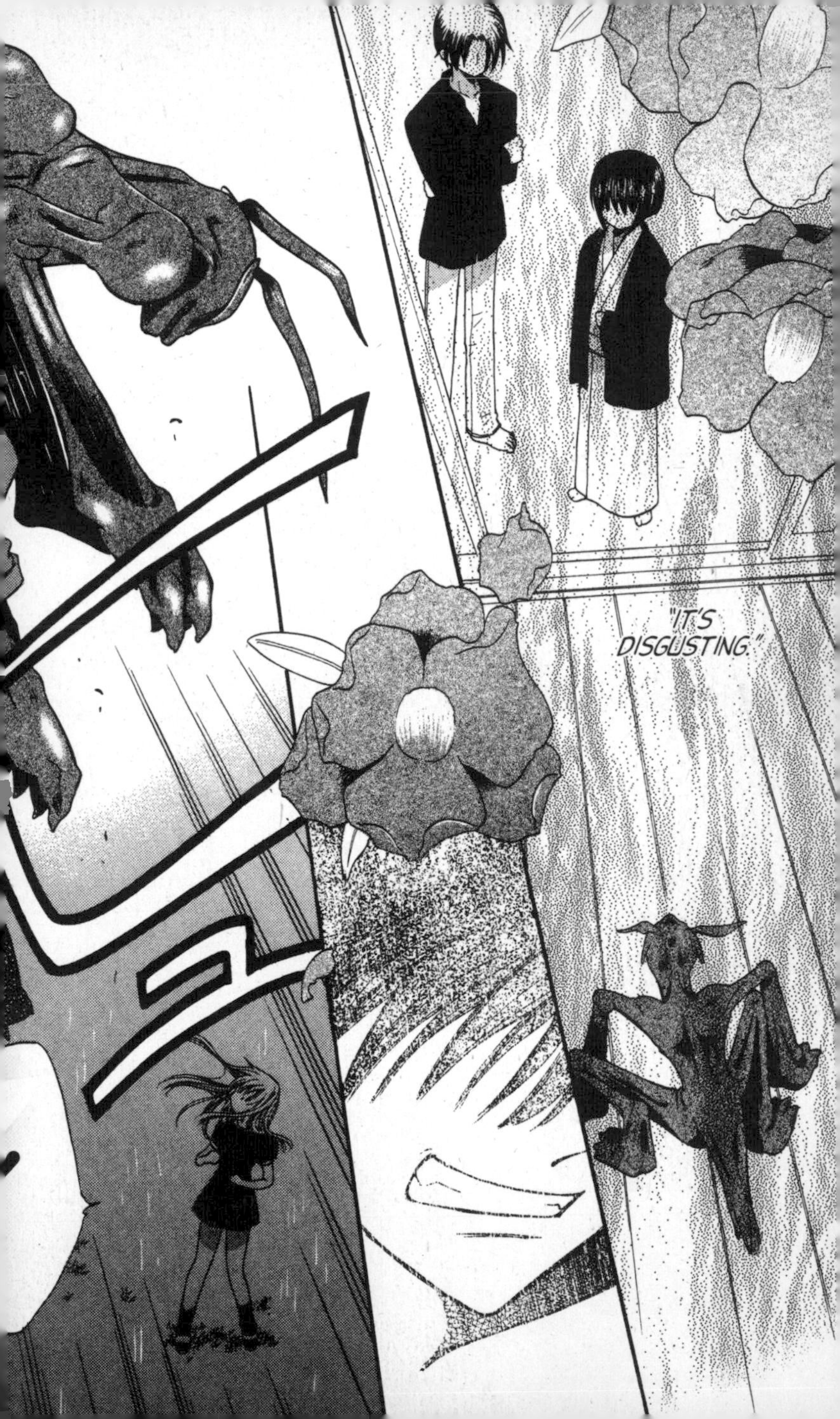
"IT'S DISGUSTING."

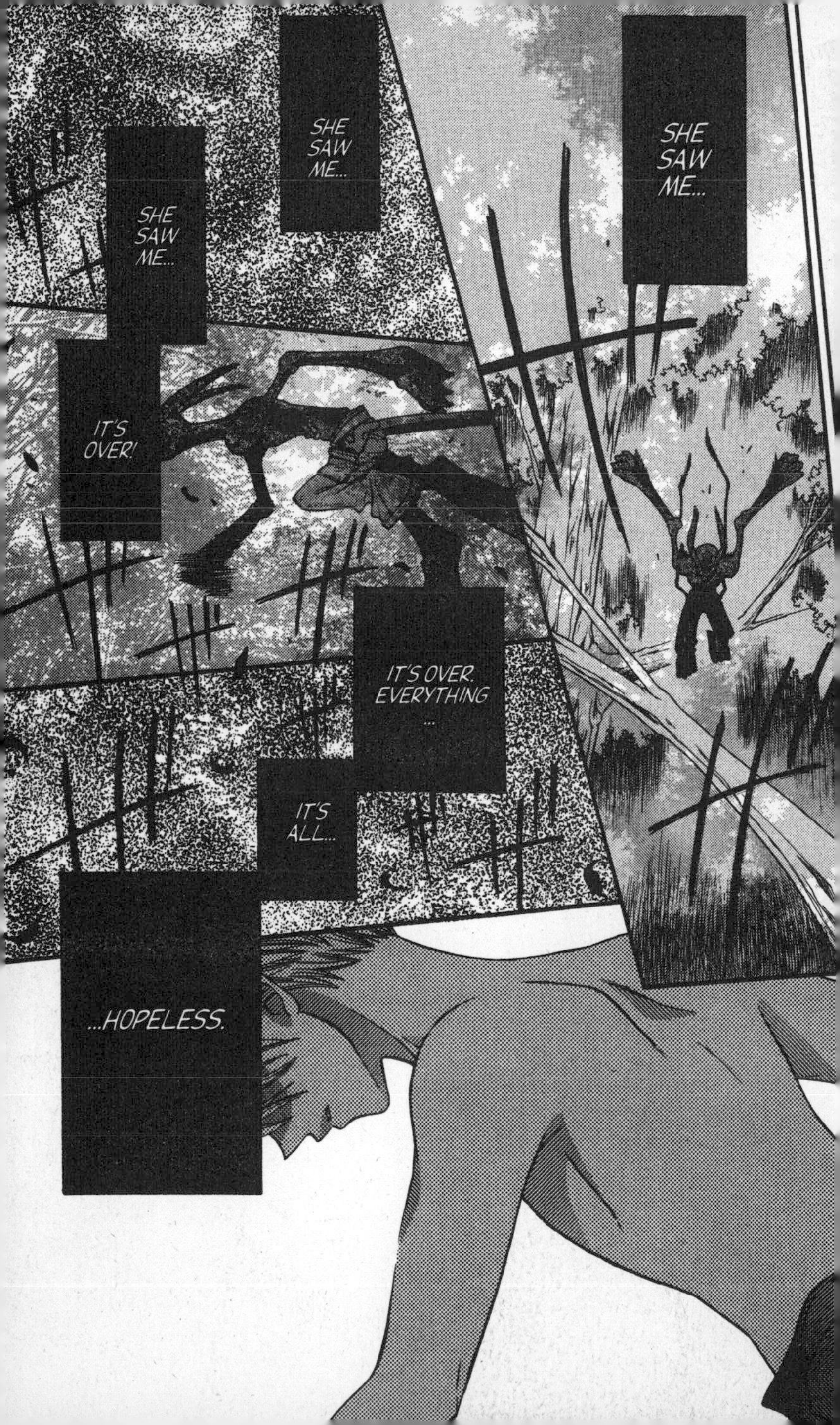
SHE SAW ME...
SHE SAW ME...
SHE SAW ME...
IT'S OVER!
IT'S OVER. EVERYTHING ...
IT'S ALL...
...HOPELESS.

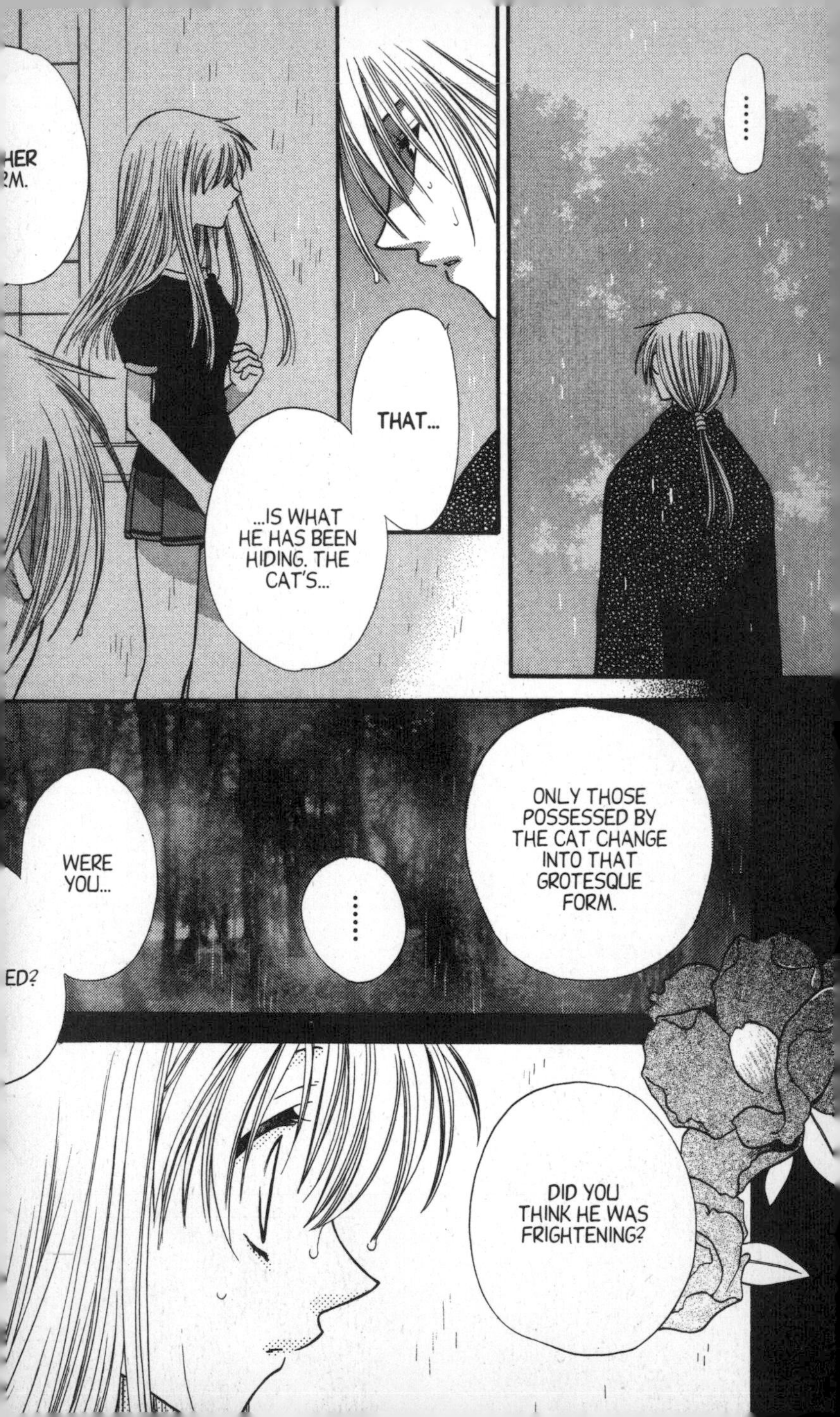
......
THAT...
...IS WHAT HE HAS BEEN HIDING. THE CAT'S...
HER RM.
ONLY THOSE POSSESSED BY THE CAT CHANGE INTO THAT GROTESQUE FORM.
......
WERE YOU... ED?
DID YOU THINK HE WAS FRIGHTENING?

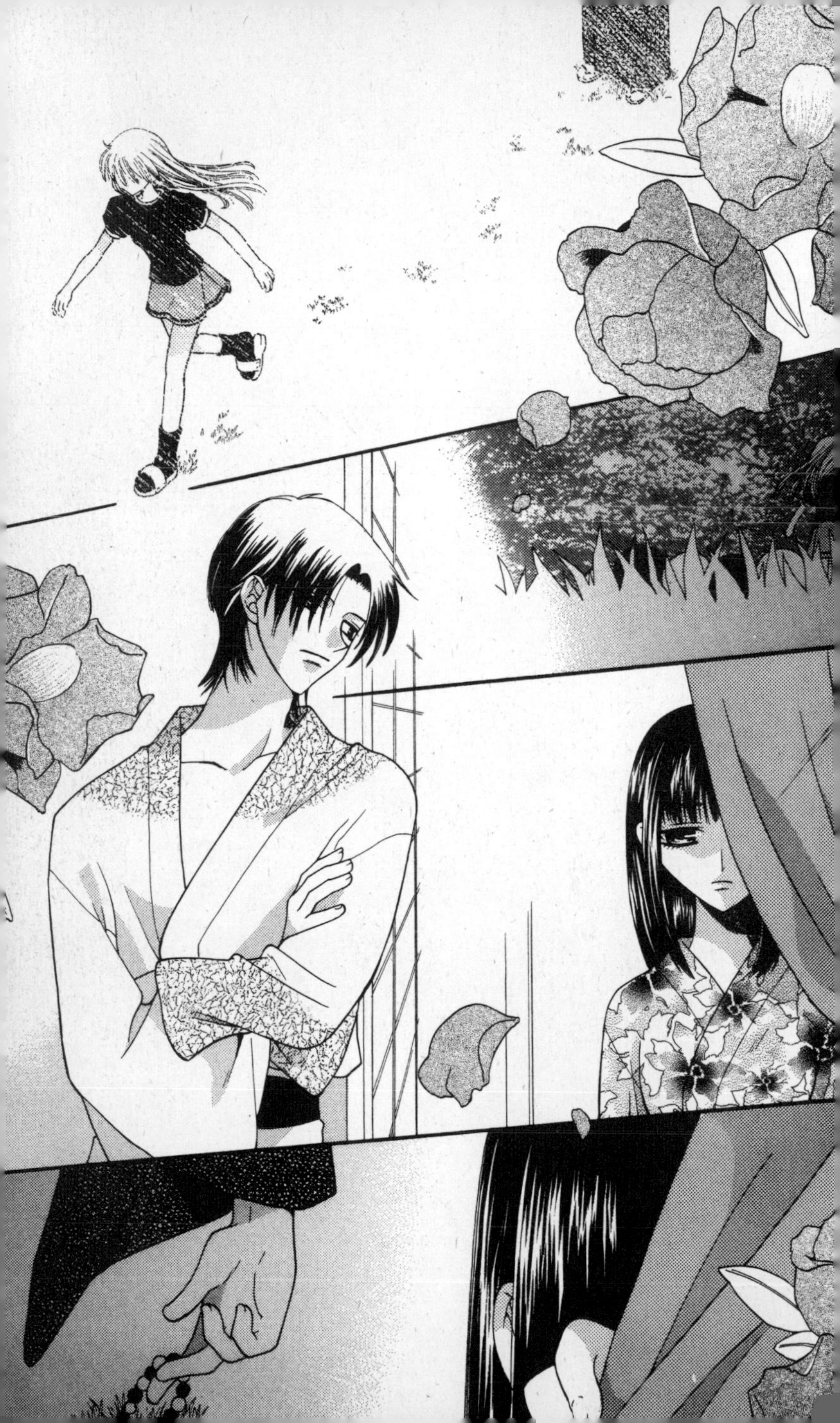

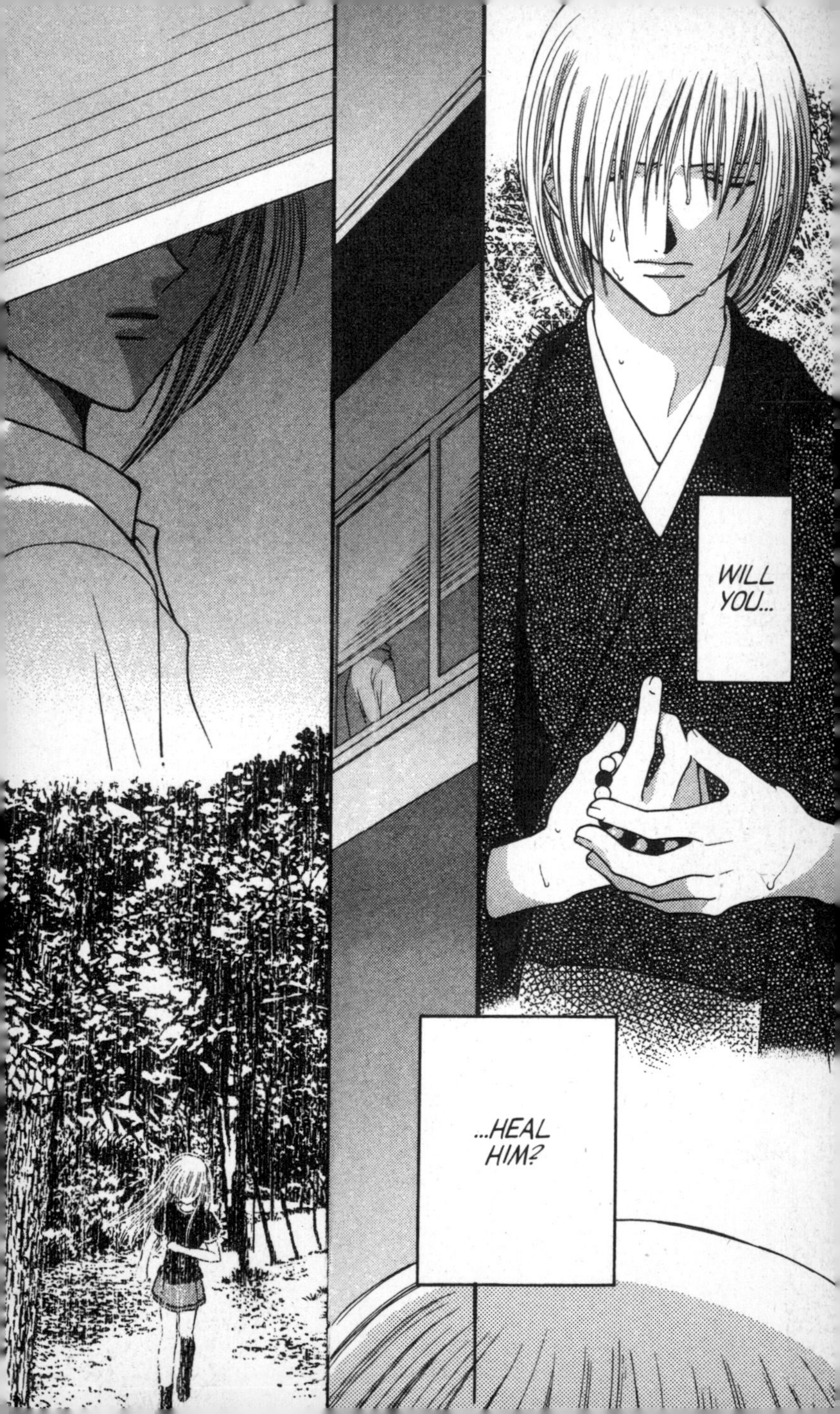
WILL YOU...
...HEAL HIM?

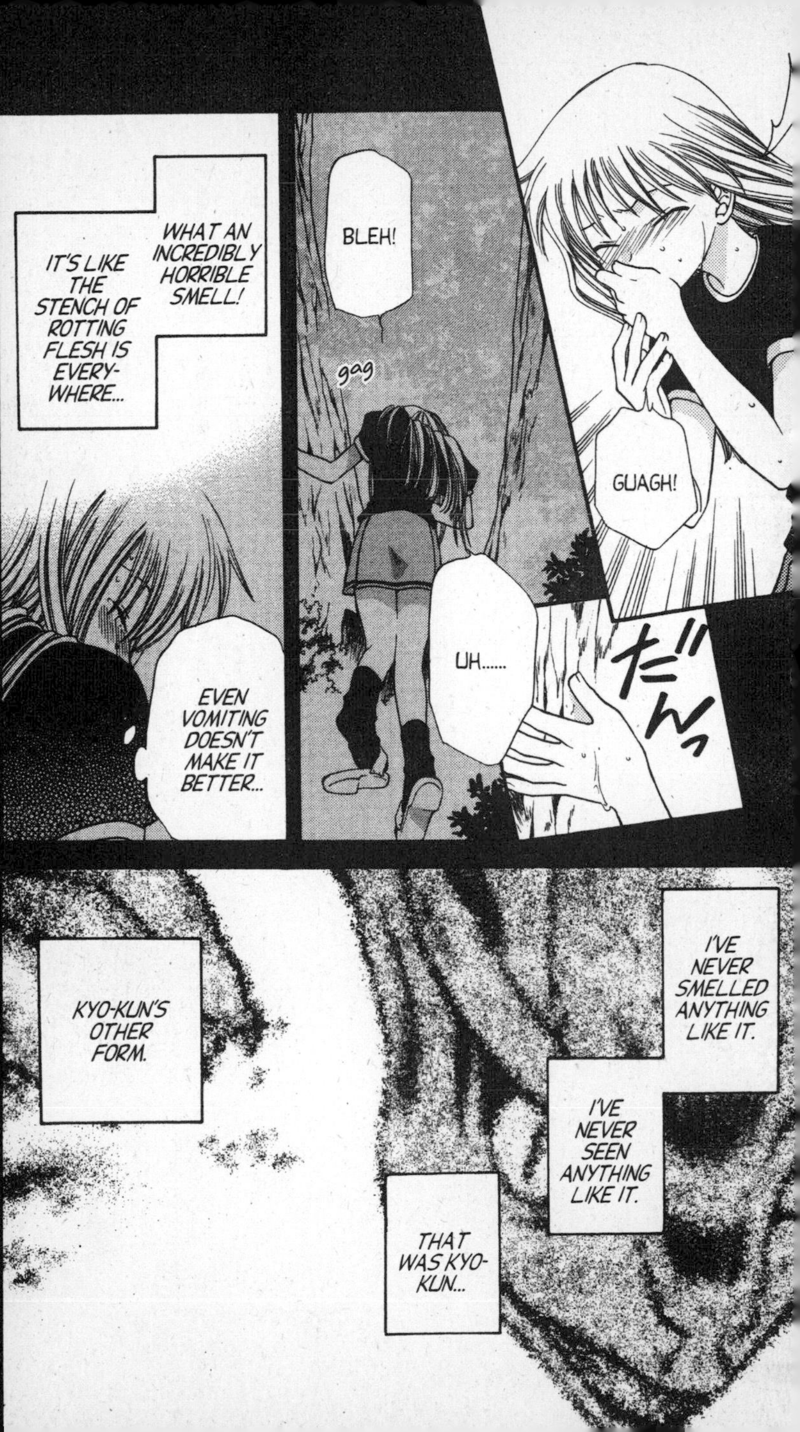
GUAGH!
だんっ
UH......
BLEH!
gag
WHAT AN INCREDIBLY HORRIBLE SMELL!
IT'S LIKE THE STENCH OF ROTTING FLESH IS EVERY-WHERE...
EVEN VOMITING DOESN'T MAKE IT BETTER...
I'VE NEVER SMELLED ANYTHING LIKE IT.
I'VE NEVER SEEN ANYTHING LIKE IT.
THAT WAS KYO-KUN...
KYO-KUN'S OTHER FORM.

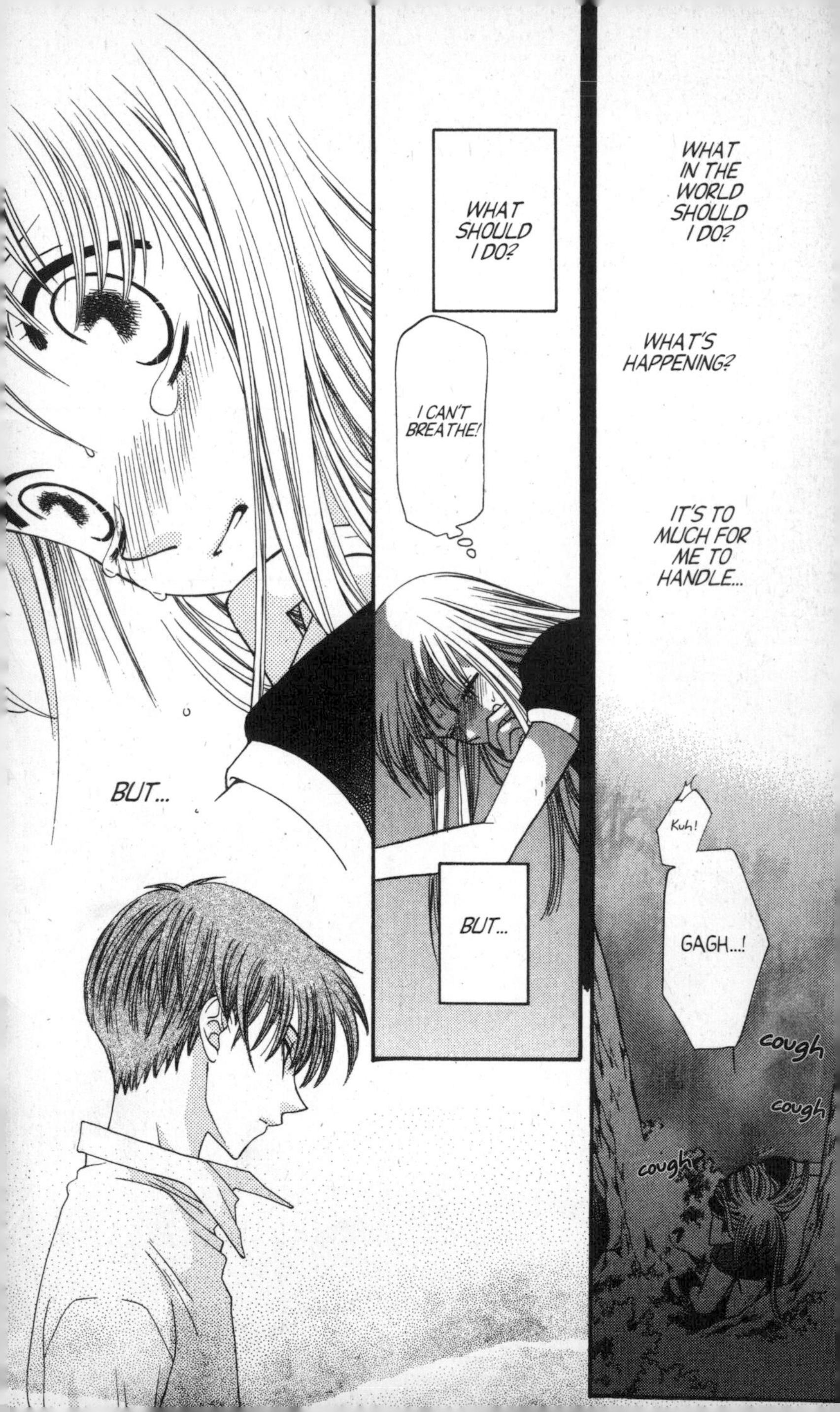
WHAT IN THE WORLD SHOULD I DO?
WHAT'S HAPPENING?
IT'S TO MUCH FOR ME TO HANDLE...
Kuh!
GAGH...!
cough
cough
cough
WHAT SHOULD I DO?
I CAN'T BREATHE!
BUT...
BUT...

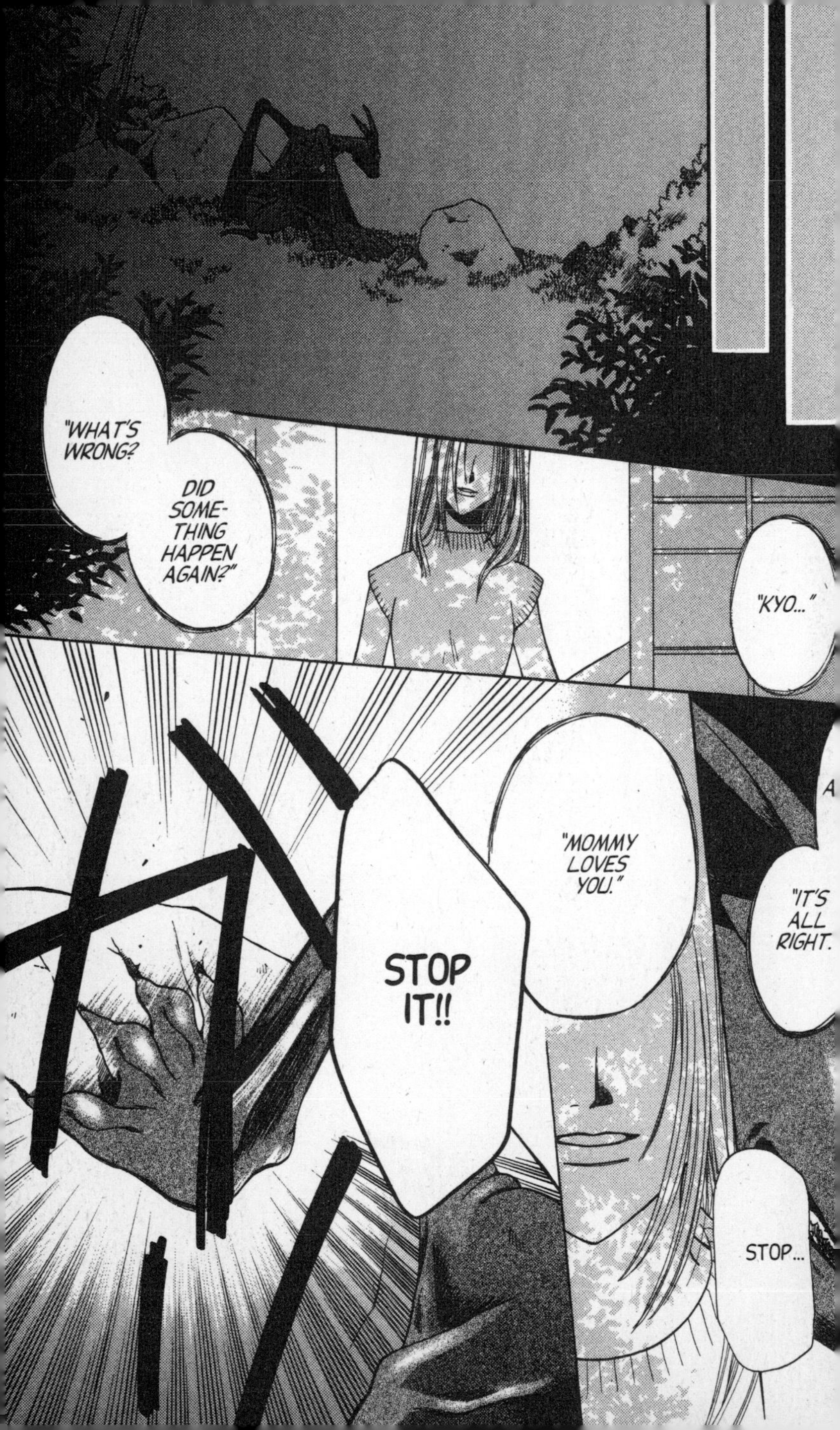
"KYO..."
"WHAT'S WRONG?
DID SOMETHING HAPPEN AGAIN?"
"IT'S ALL RIGHT.
"MOMMY LOVES YOU."
STOP...
STOP IT!!

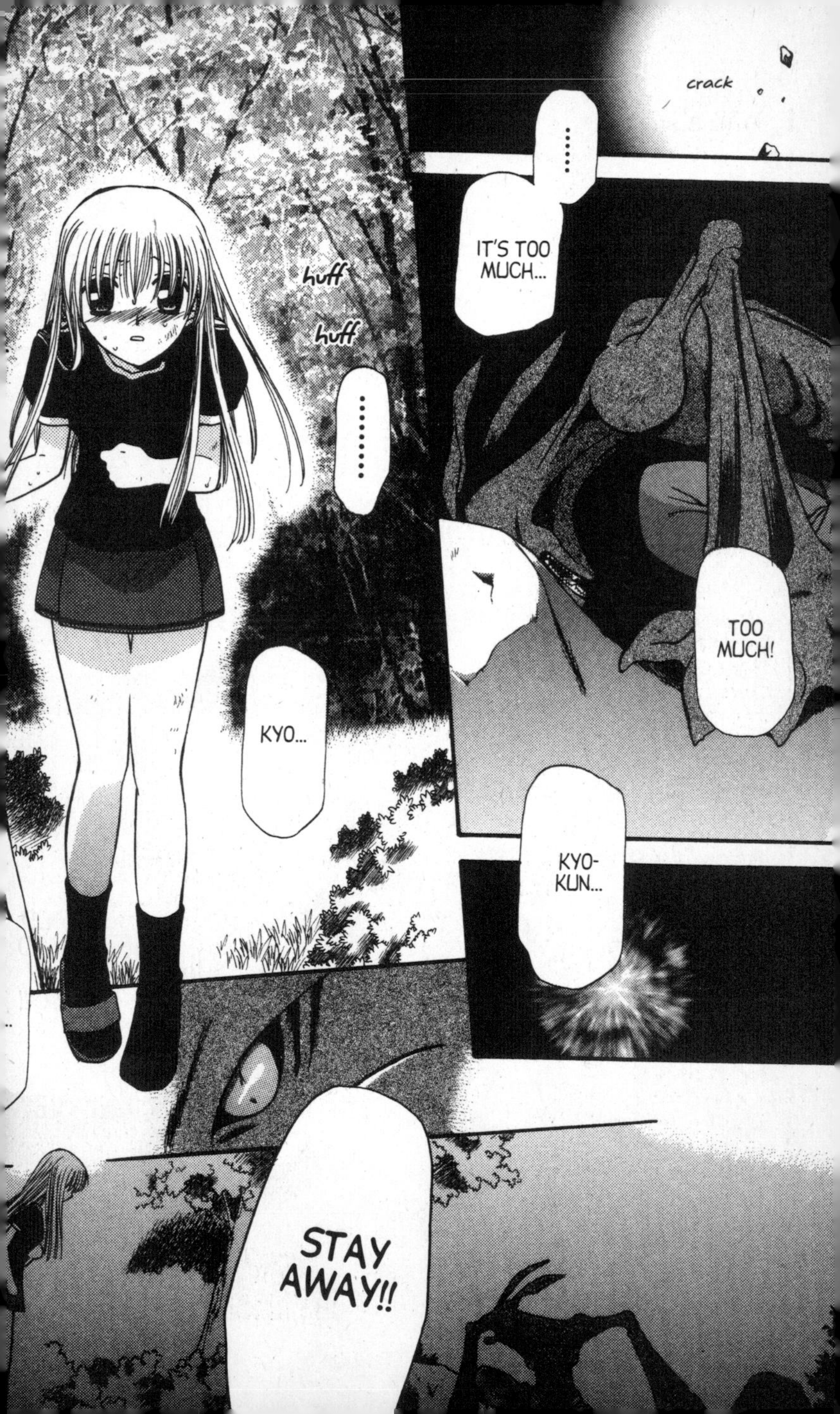
crack
......
IT'S TOO MUCH...
TOO MUCH!
KYO-KUN...
huff
huff
......
KYO...
STAY AWAY!!

Fruits Basket 6 Part 3:

I'm still in the middle of *SUMMON NIGHT*. But *HARUKANARU TOKI NO NAKA DE* was amazing. This might be the fastest I've ever completed a game. I think the captures I made might have even been helpful to someone. (Don't flatter yourself. They weren't.) And again, my Playstation's in bad shape, so there were sound issues. Such a tragedy... Still, I played as if entranced. I love Tomomasa-san and Inori-kun. (Those two don't match, Takaya.) I can't wait to play *ANGELIQUE TROIS*. There should be a lot more of them! I love Love-sim games! They fill my heart with joy. Even when a game isn't a love-sim, I like it when designers throw in a little romance. Yay!

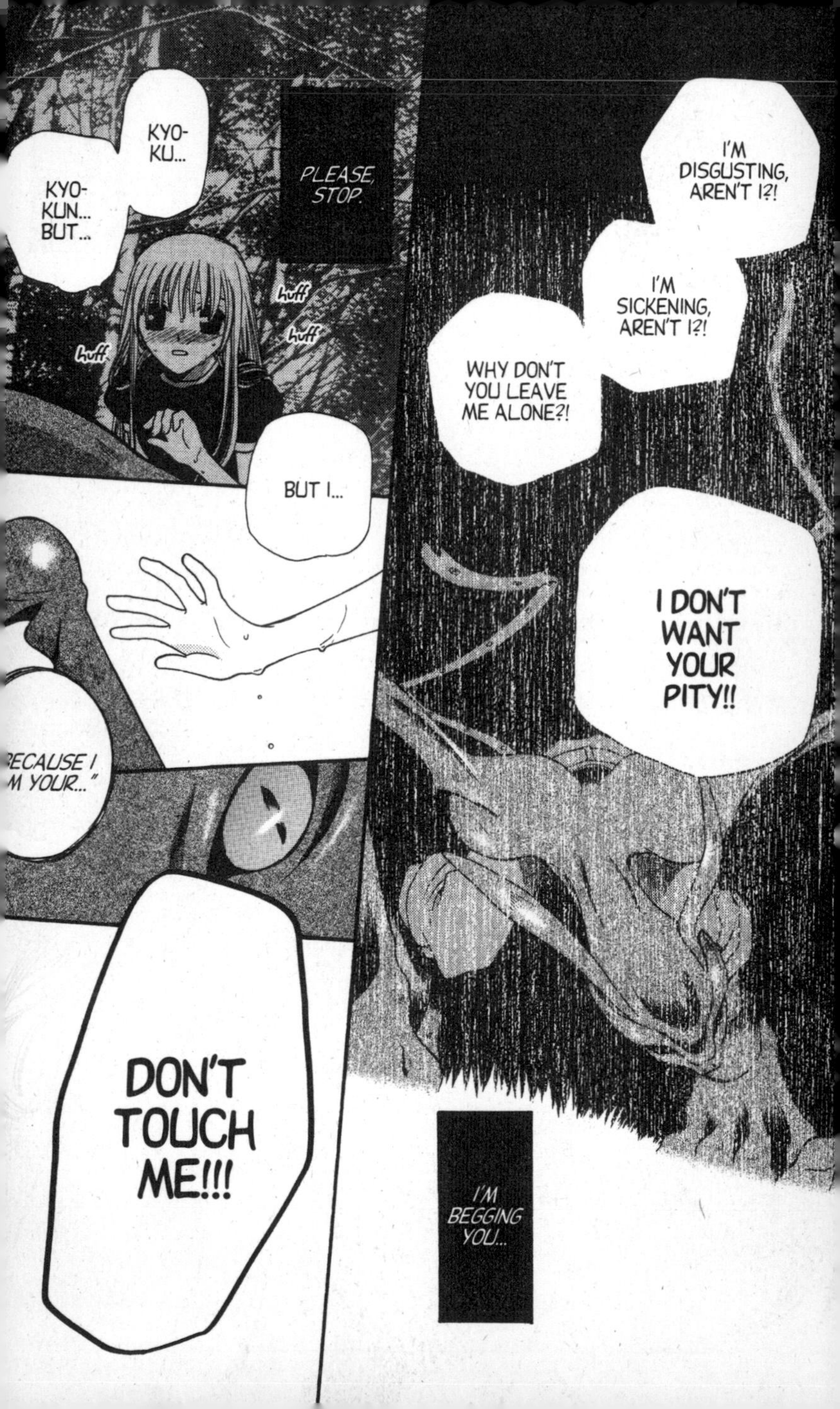
I'M DISGUSTING, AREN'T I?!
I'M SICKENING, AREN'T I?!
WHY DON'T YOU LEAVE ME ALONE?!
I DON'T WANT YOUR PITY!!
I'M BEGGING YOU...
PLEASE, STOP.
KYO-KU...
KYO-KUN... BUT...
huff
huff
huff
BUT I...
ECAUSE I M YOUR..."
DON'T TOUCH ME!!!

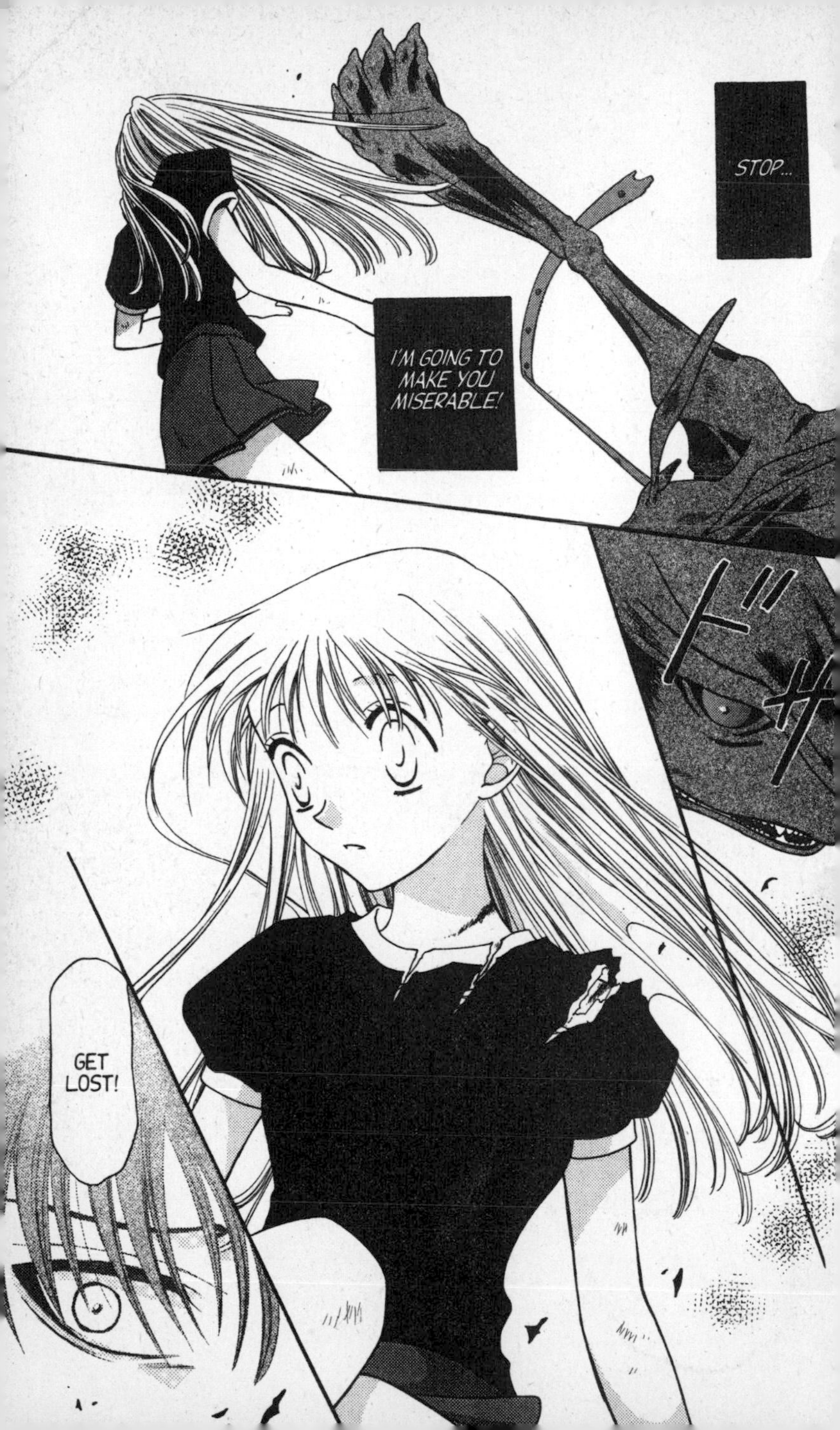
STOP...
I'M GOING TO MAKE YOU MISERABLE!
ドザ
GET LOST!

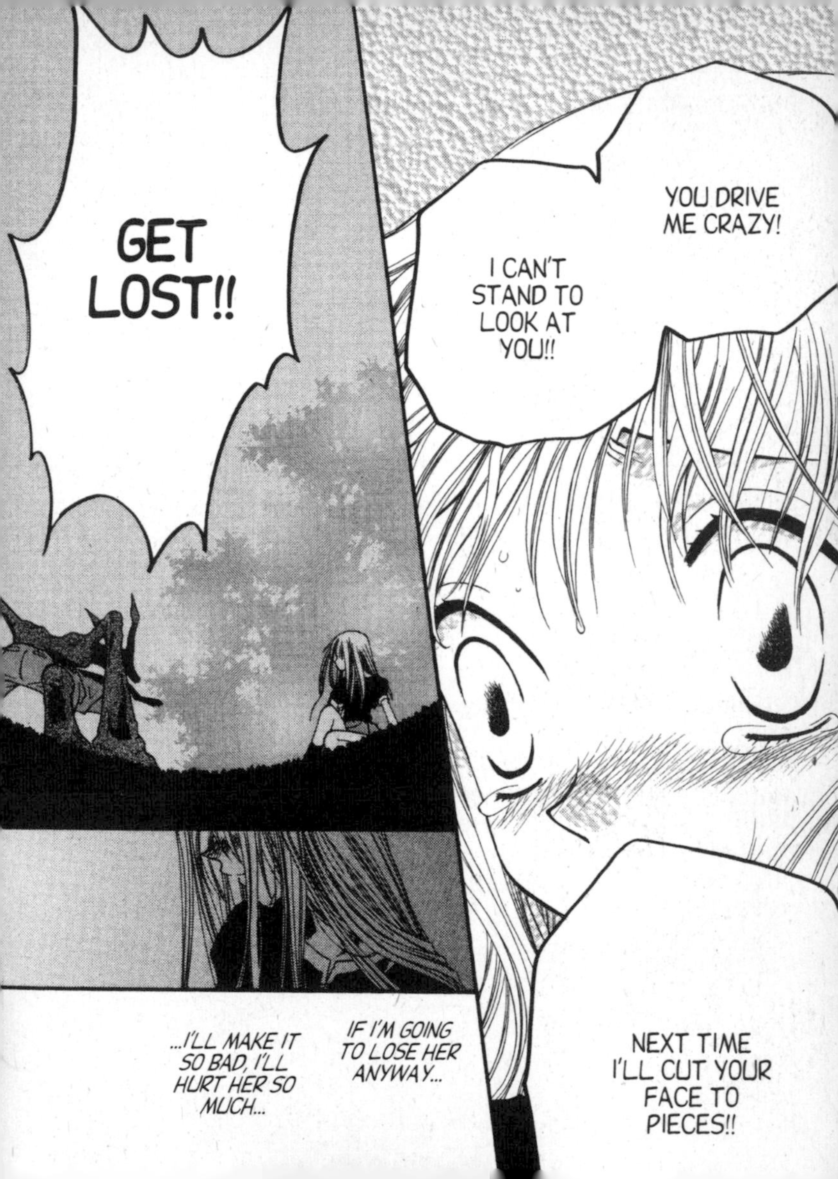
YOU DRIVE ME CRAZY!
I CAN'T STAND TO LOOK AT YOU!!
NEXT TIME I'LL CUT YOUR FACE TO PIECES!!
GET LOST!!
IF I'M GOING TO LOSE HER ANYWAY...
...I'LL MAKE IT SO BAD, I'LL HURT HER SO MUCH...

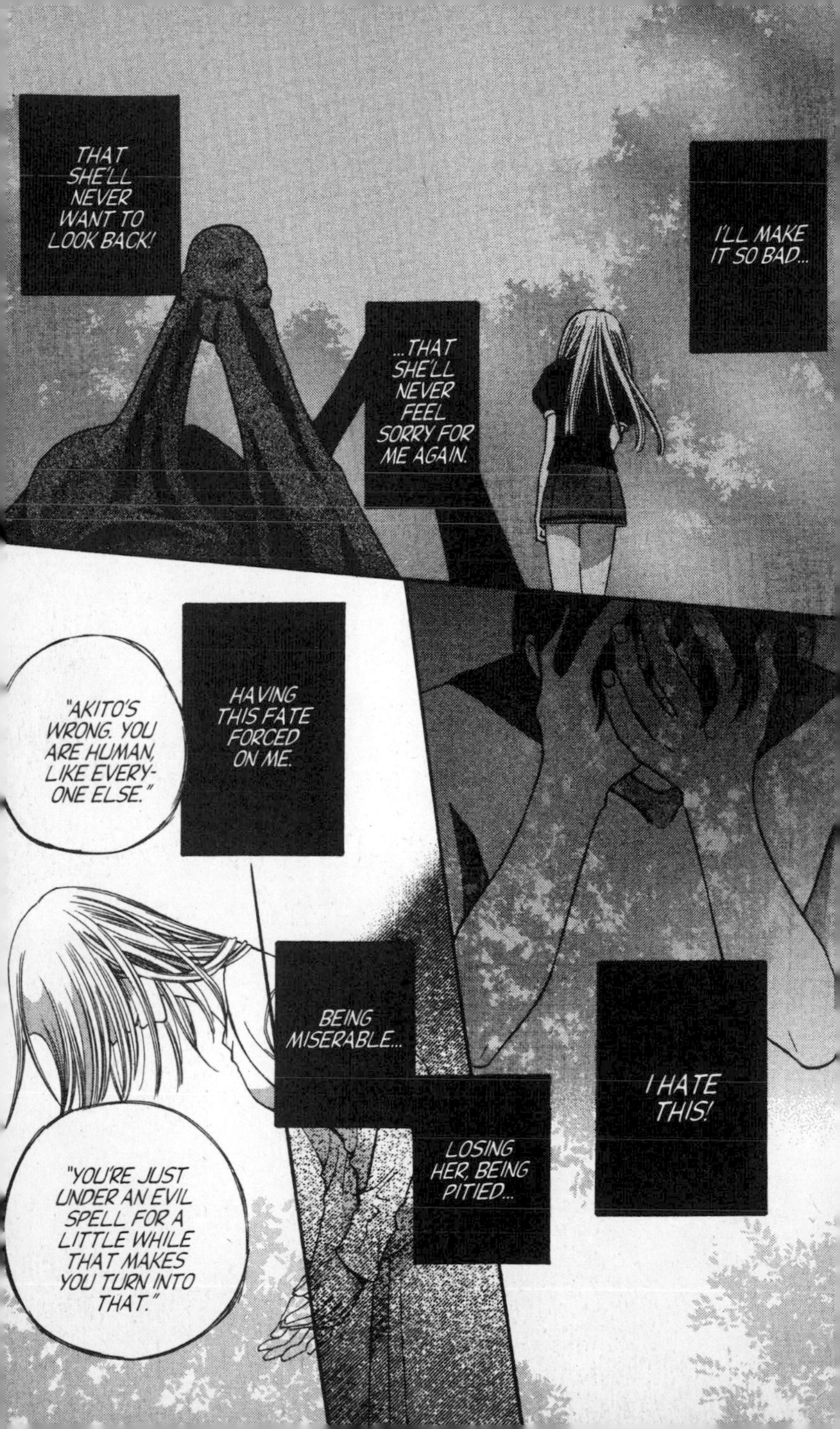
I'LL MAKE IT SO BAD...
...THAT SHE'LL NEVER FEEL SORRY FOR ME AGAIN.
THAT SHE'LL NEVER WANT TO LOOK BACK!
I HATE THIS!
LOSING HER, BEING PITIED...
BEING MISERABLE...
HAVING THIS FATE FORCED ON ME.
"AKITO'S WRONG. YOU ARE HUMAN, LIKE EVERY-ONE ELSE."
"YOU'RE JUST UNDER AN EVIL SPELL FOR A LITTLE WHILE THAT MAKES YOU TURN INTO THAT."

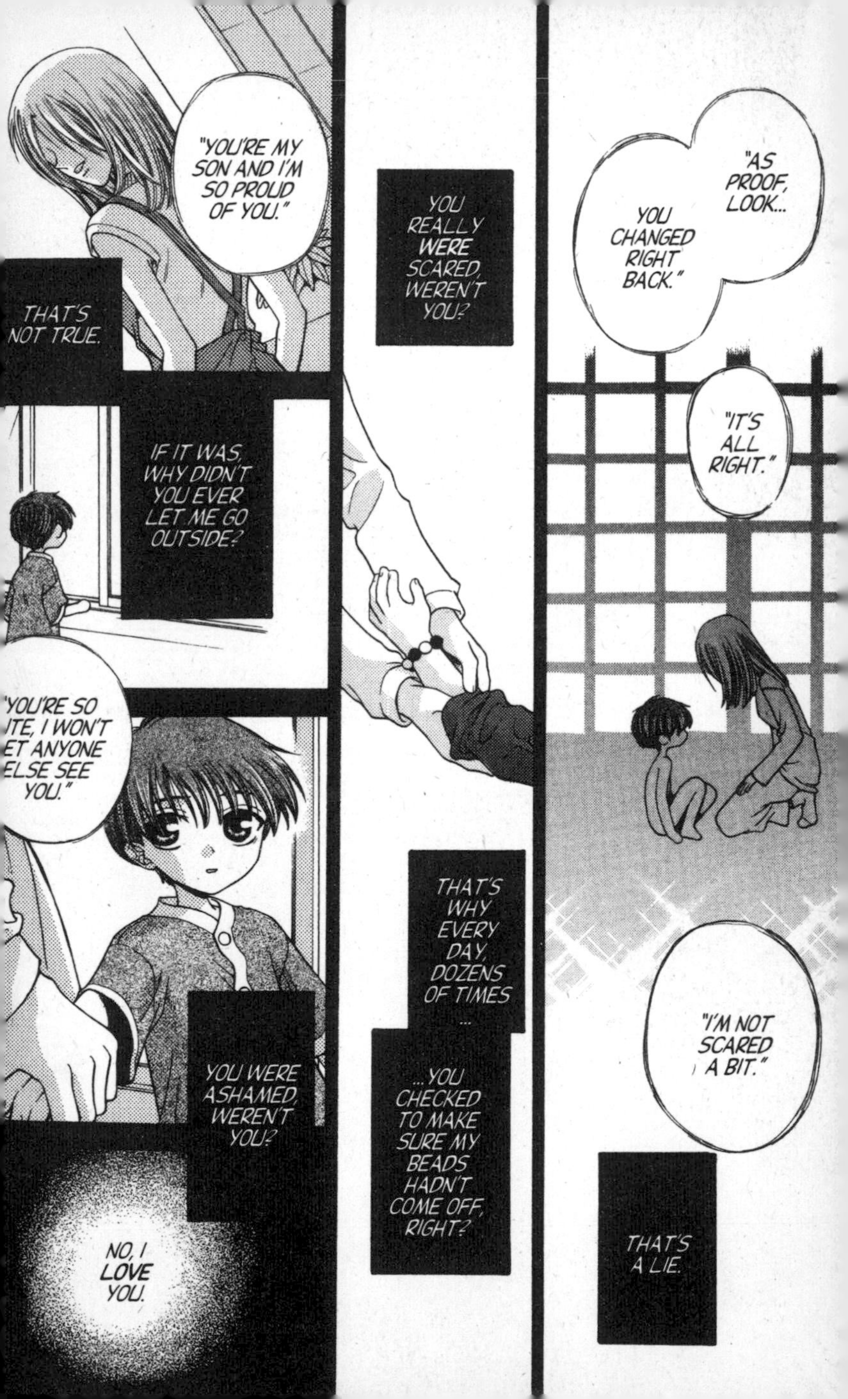
"AS PROOF, LOOK... YOU CHANGED RIGHT BACK."
"IT'S ALL RIGHT."
"I'M NOT SCARED A BIT."
THAT'S A LIE.
YOU REALLY WERE SCARED, WEREN'T YOU?
THAT'S WHY EVERY DAY, DOZENS OF TIMES ...
...YOU CHECKED TO MAKE SURE MY BEADS HADN'T COME OFF, RIGHT?
"YOU'RE MY SON AND I'M SO PROUD OF YOU."
THAT'S NOT TRUE.
IF IT WAS, WHY DIDN'T YOU EVER LET ME GO OUTSIDE?
"YOU'RE SO ITE, I WON'T ET ANYONE ELSE SEE YOU."
YOU WERE ASHAMED, WEREN'T YOU?
NO, I LOVE YOU.

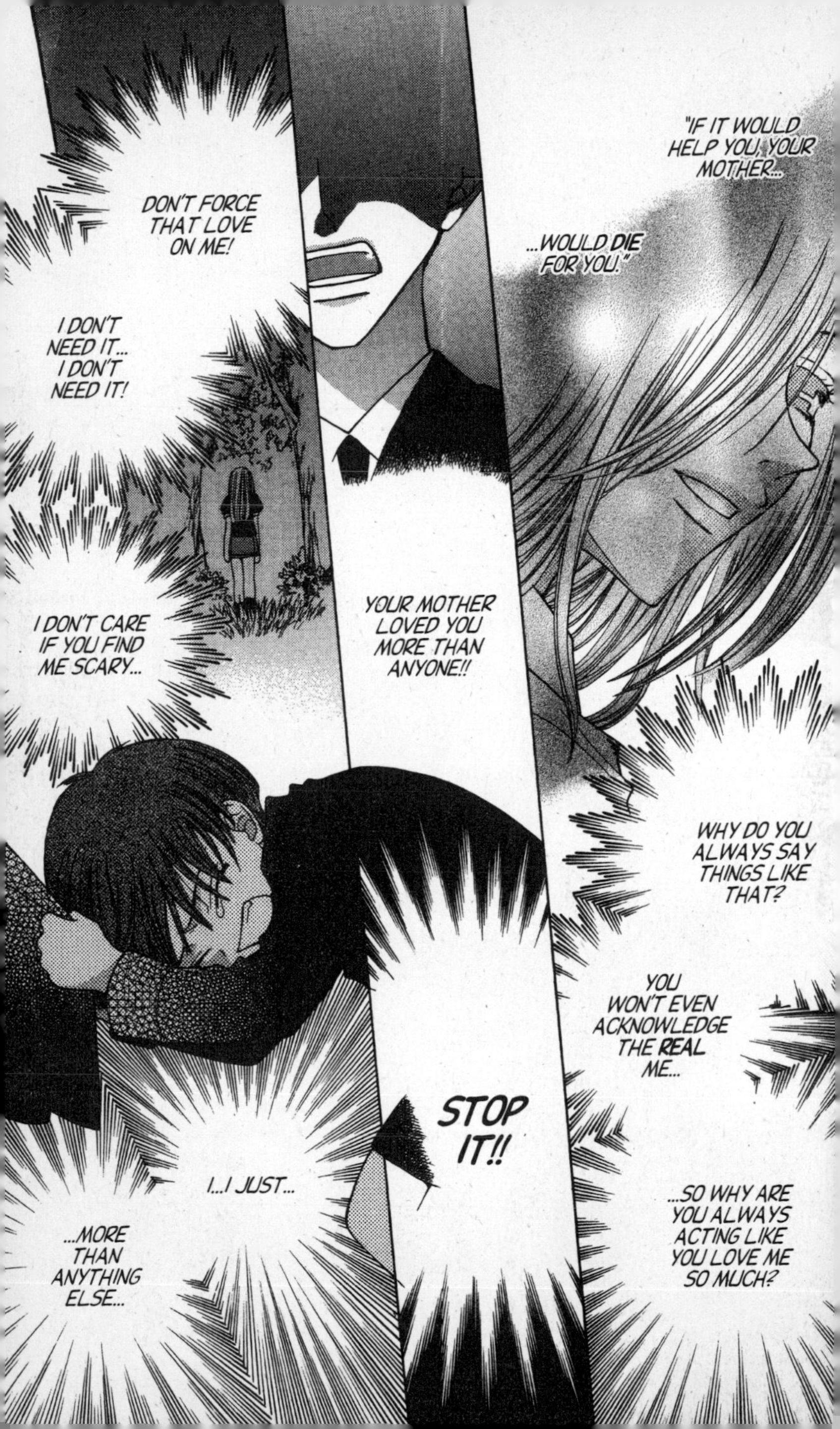
"IF IT WOULD HELP YOU, YOUR MOTHER...
...WOULD DIE FOR YOU."
WHY DO YOU ALWAYS SAY THINGS LIKE THAT?
YOU WON'T EVEN ACKNOWLEDGE THE REAL ME...
...SO WHY ARE YOU ALWAYS ACTING LIKE YOU LOVE ME SO MUCH?
YOUR MOTHER LOVED YOU MORE THAN ANYONE!!
STOP IT!!
DON'T FORCE THAT LOVE ON ME!
I DON'T NEED IT... I DON'T NEED IT!
I DON'T CARE IF YOU FIND ME SCARY...
I...I JUST...
...MORE THAN ANYTHING ELSE...

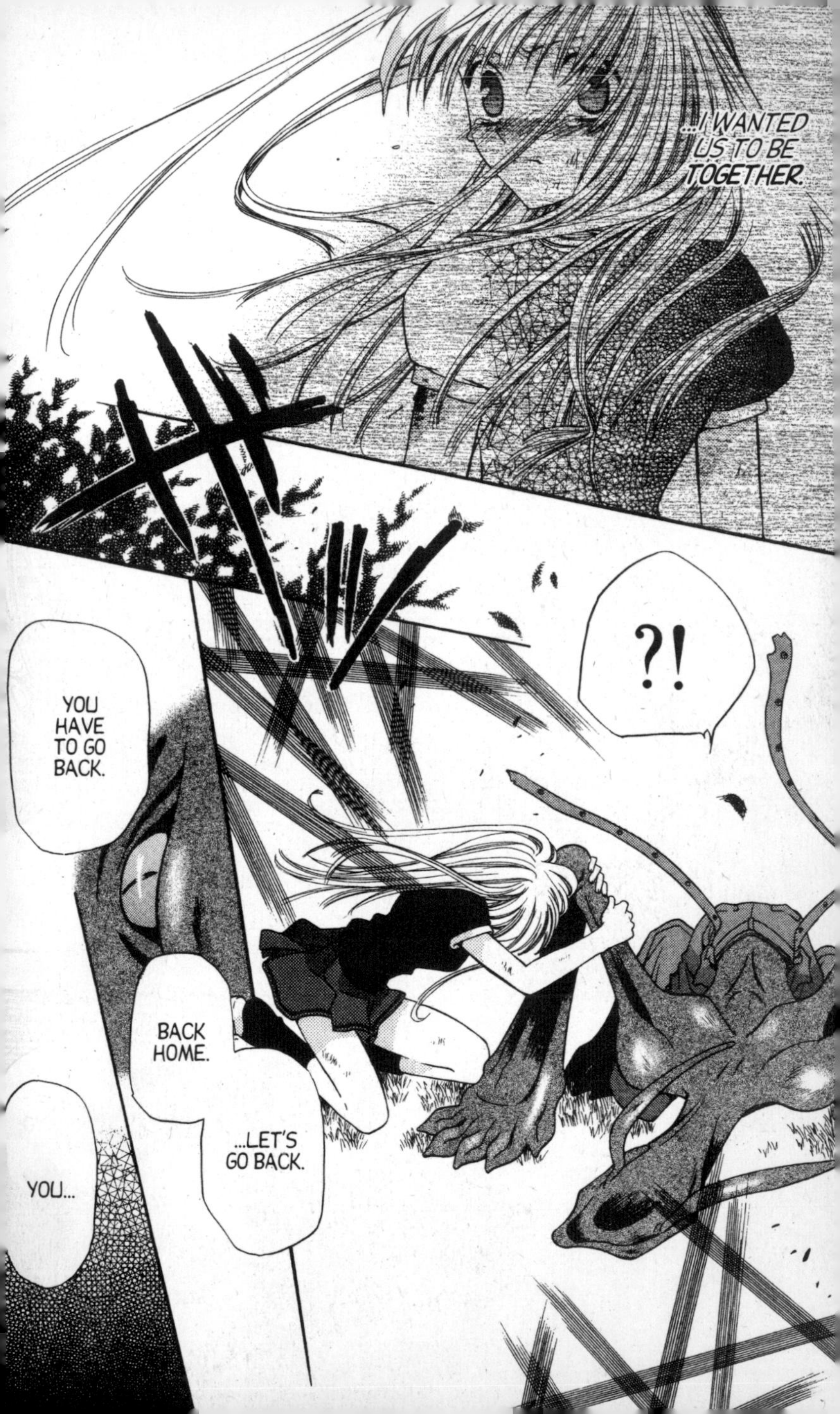
...I WANTED US TO BE TOGETHER.
?!
YOU HAVE TO GO BACK.
BACK HOME.
...LET'S GO BACK.
YOU...

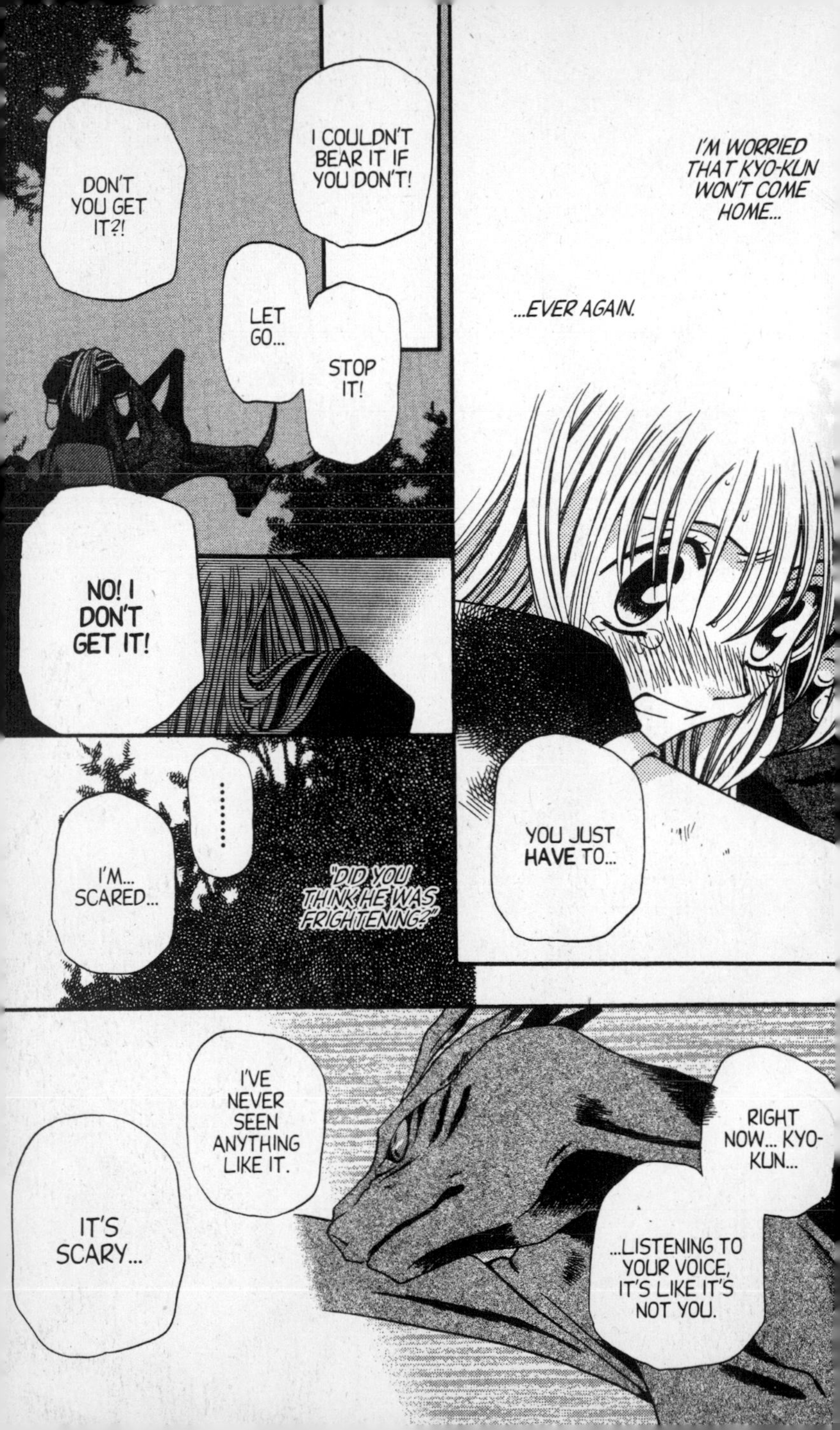
I'M WORRIED THAT KYO-KUN WON'T COME HOME...
...EVER AGAIN.
YOU JUST HAVE TO...
I COULDN'T BEAR IT IF YOU DON'T!
DON'T YOU GET IT?!
STOP IT!
LET GO...
NO! I DON'T GET IT!
......
"DID YOU THINK HE WAS FRIGHTENING?"
I'M... SCARED...
RIGHT NOW... KYO-KUN...
...LISTENING TO YOUR VOICE, IT'S LIKE IT'S NOT YOU.
I'VE NEVER SEEN ANYTHING LIKE IT.
IT'S SCARY...

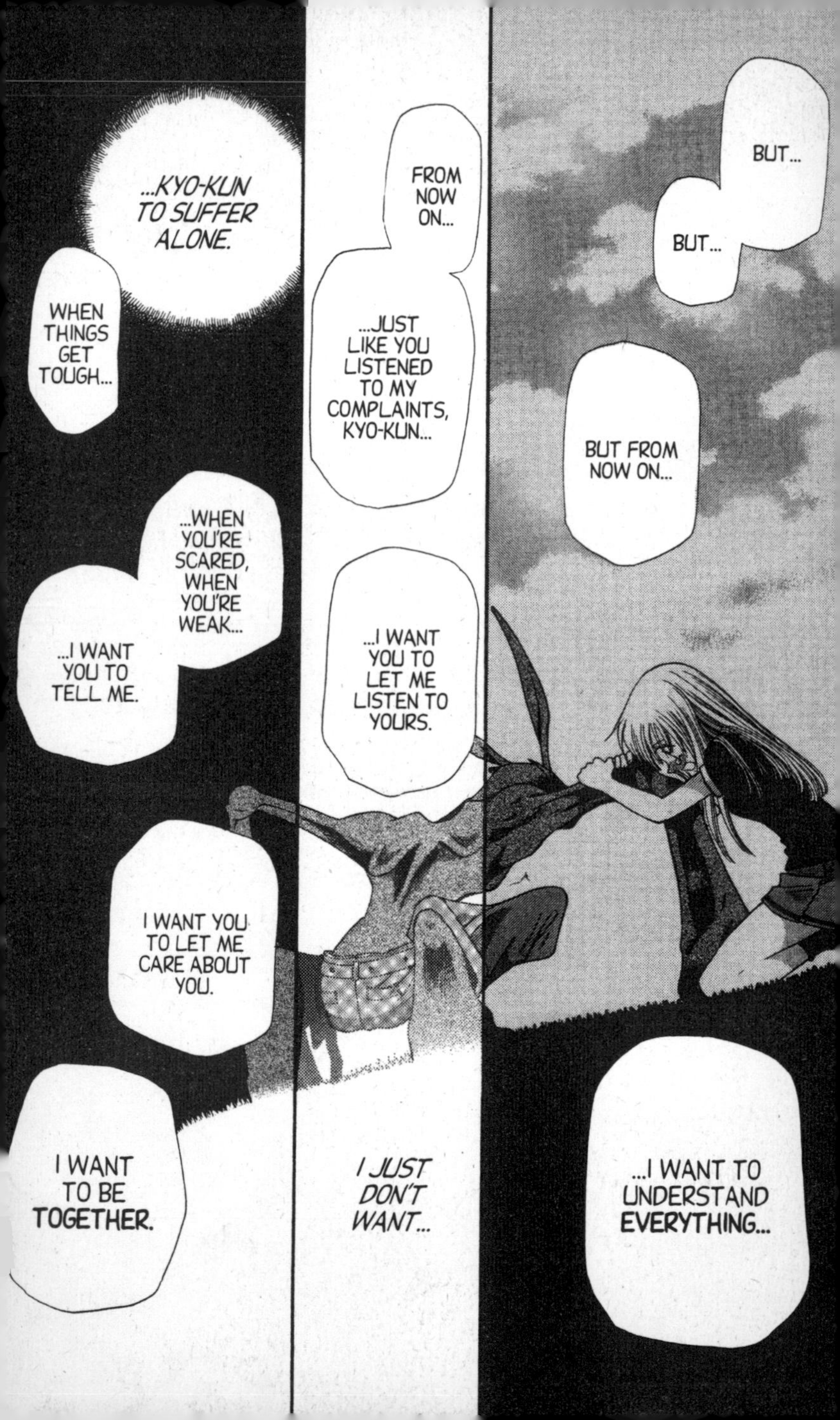

BUT...
BUT...
BUT FROM NOW ON...
...I WANT TO UNDERSTAND EVERYTHING...
FROM NOW ON...
...JUST LIKE YOU LISTENED TO MY COMPLAINTS, KYO-KUN...
...I WANT YOU TO LET ME LISTEN TO YOURS.
I JUST DON'T WANT...
...KYO-KUN TO SUFFER ALONE.
WHEN THINGS GET TOUGH...
...WHEN YOU'RE SCARED, WHEN YOU'RE WEAK...
...I WANT YOU TO TELL ME.
I WANT YOU TO LET ME CARE ABOUT YOU.
I WANT TO BE TOGETHER.

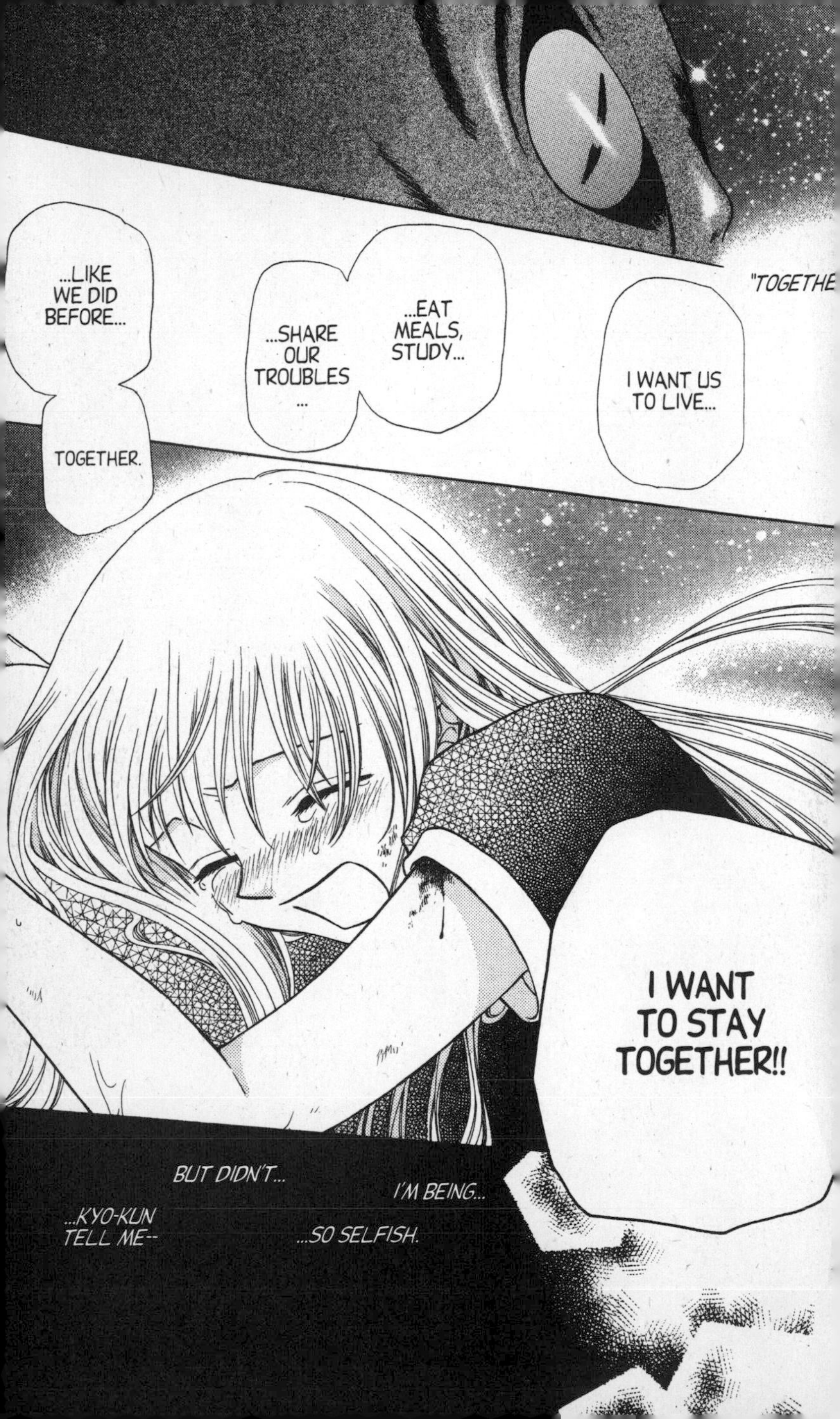

"TOGETHE
I WANT US TO LIVE...
...EAT MEALS, STUDY...
...SHARE OUR TROUBLES ...
...LIKE WE DID BEFORE...
TOGETHER.
I WANT TO STAY TOGETHER!!
I'M BEING...
...SO SELFISH.
BUT DIDN'T...
...KYO-KUN TELL ME--

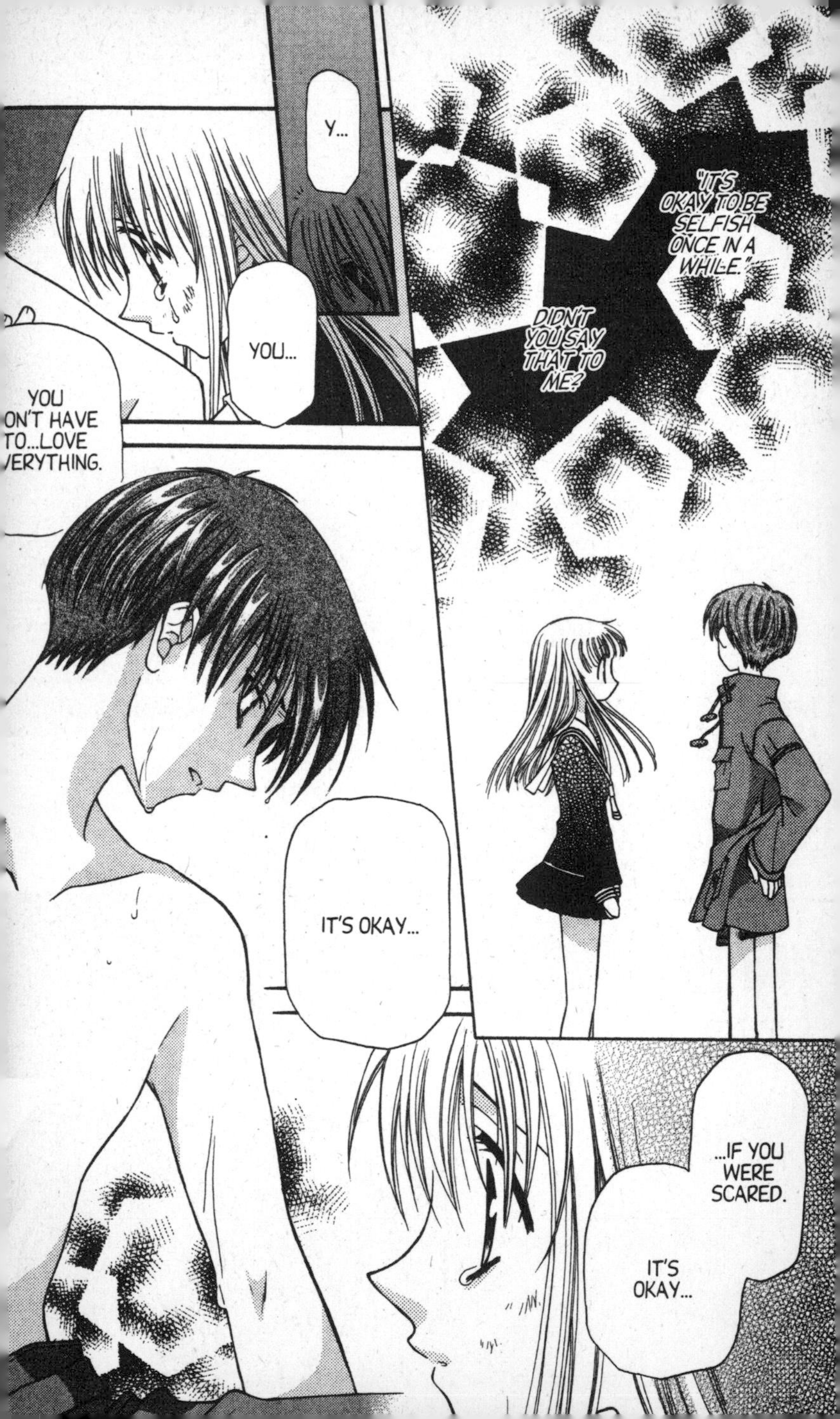
"IT'S OKAY TO BE SELFISH ONCE IN A WHILE."
DIDN'T YOU SAY THAT TO ME?
Y...
YOU...
YOU ON'T HAVE TO...LOVE VERYTHING.
IT'S OKAY...
...IF YOU WERE SCARED.
IT'S OKAY...

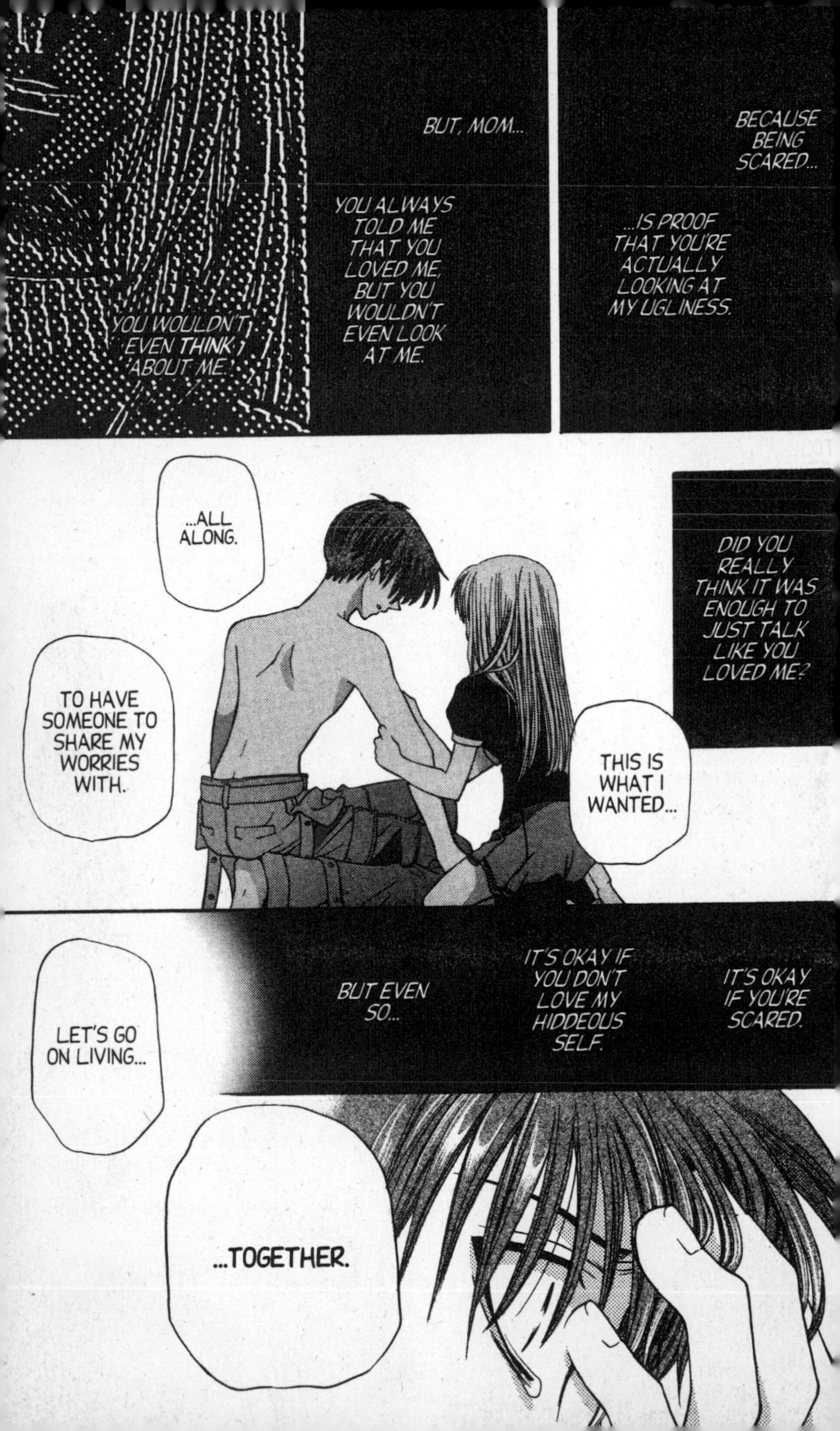
BECAUSE BEING SCARED...
...IS PROOF THAT YOU'RE ACTUALLY LOOKING AT MY UGLINESS.
BUT, MOM...
YOU ALWAYS TOLD ME THAT YOU LOVED ME, BUT YOU WOULDN'T EVEN LOOK AT ME.
YOU WOULDN'T EVEN THINK ABOUT ME.
DID YOU REALLY THINK IT WAS ENOUGH TO JUST TALK LIKE YOU LOVED ME?
THIS IS WHAT I WANTED...
TO HAVE SOMEONE TO SHARE MY WORRIES WITH.
...ALL ALONG.
IT'S OKAY IF YOU'RE SCARED.
IT'S OKAY IF YOU DON'T LOVE MY HIDDEOUS SELF.
BUT EVEN SO...
LET'S GO ON LIVING...
...TOGETHER.

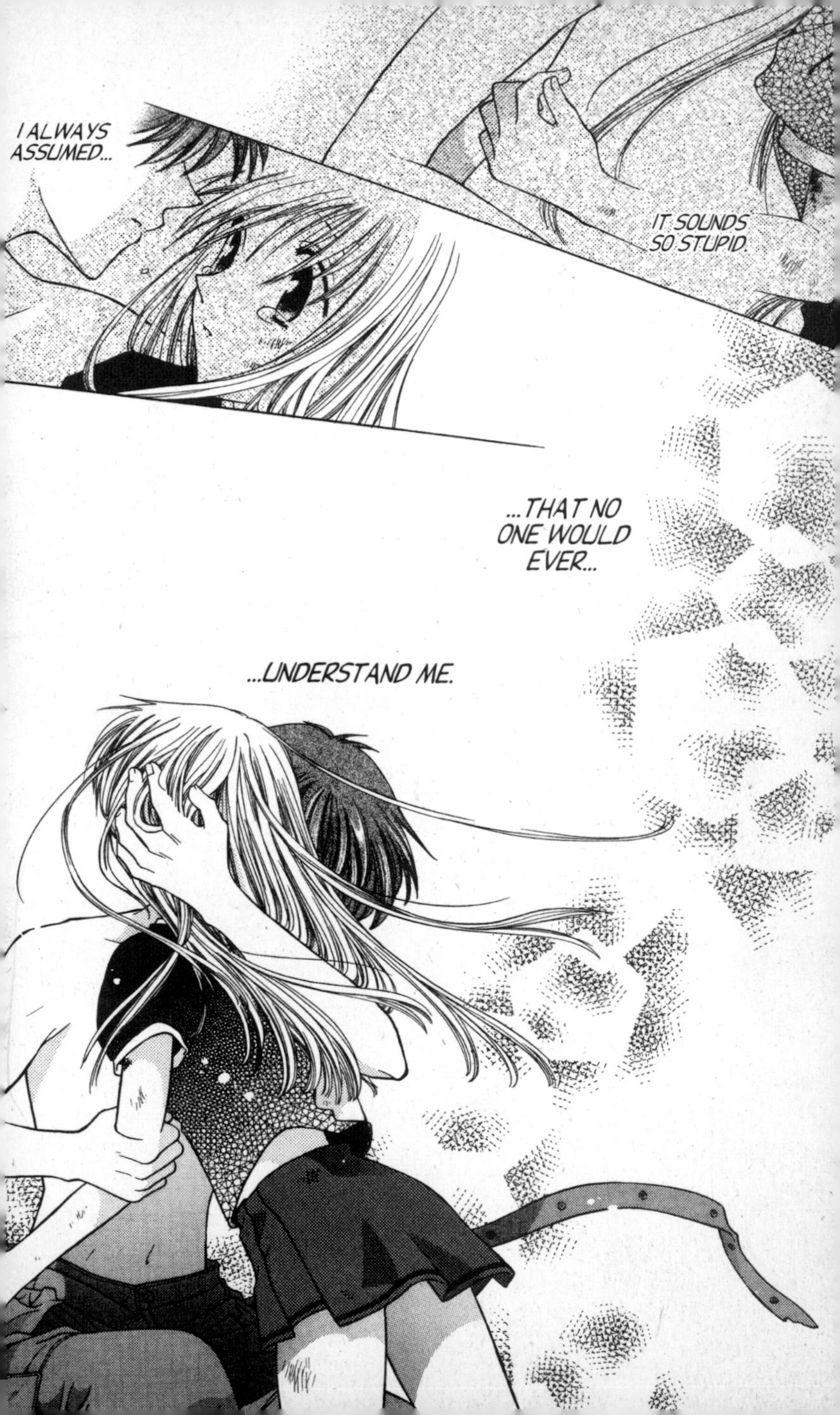
IT SOUNDS SO STUPID.
I ALWAYS ASSUMED...
...THAT NO ONE WOULD EVER...
...UNDERSTAND ME.

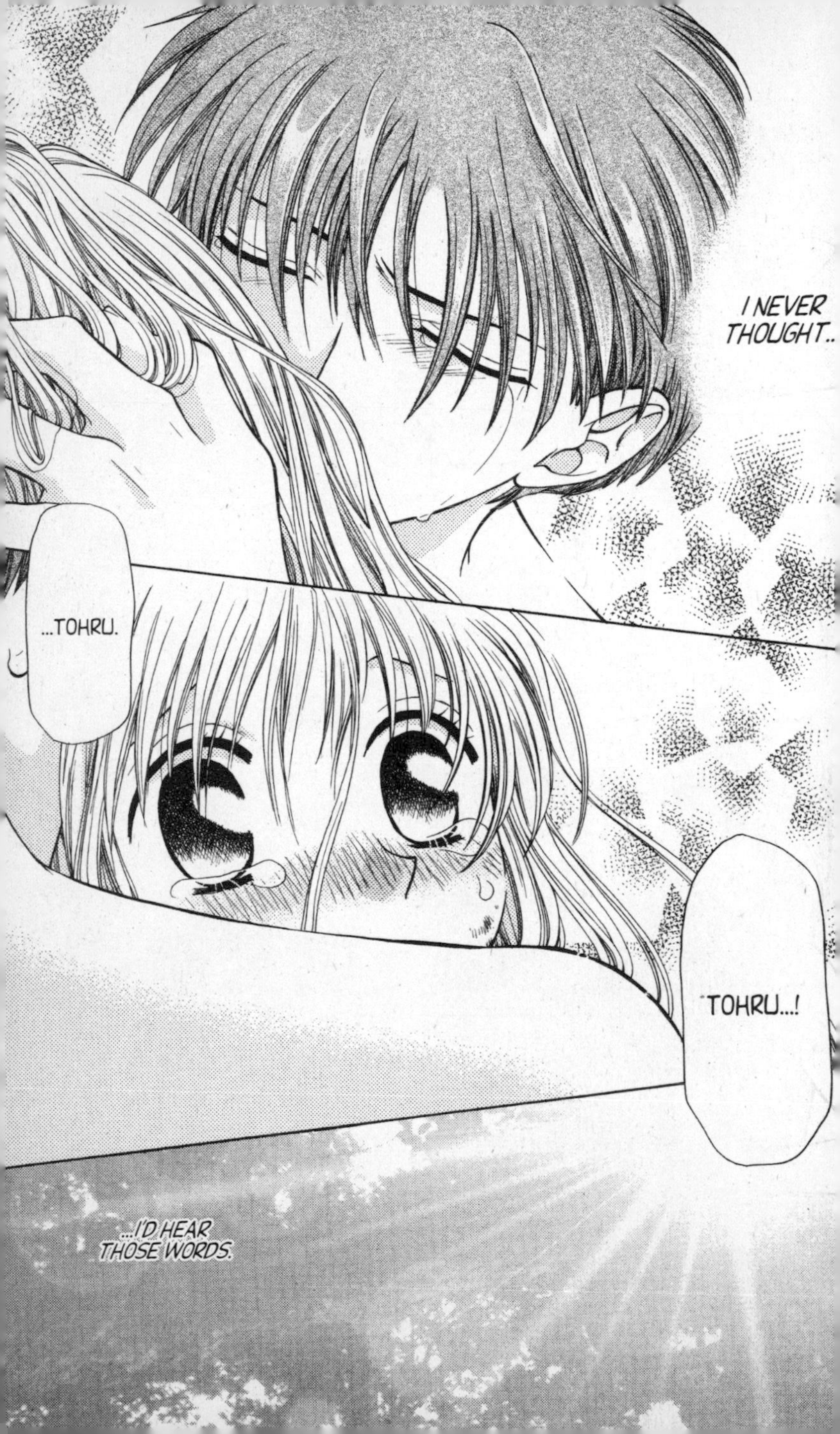
I NEVER THOUGHT..
...TOHRU.
TOHRU...!
...I'D HEAR THOSE WORDS.

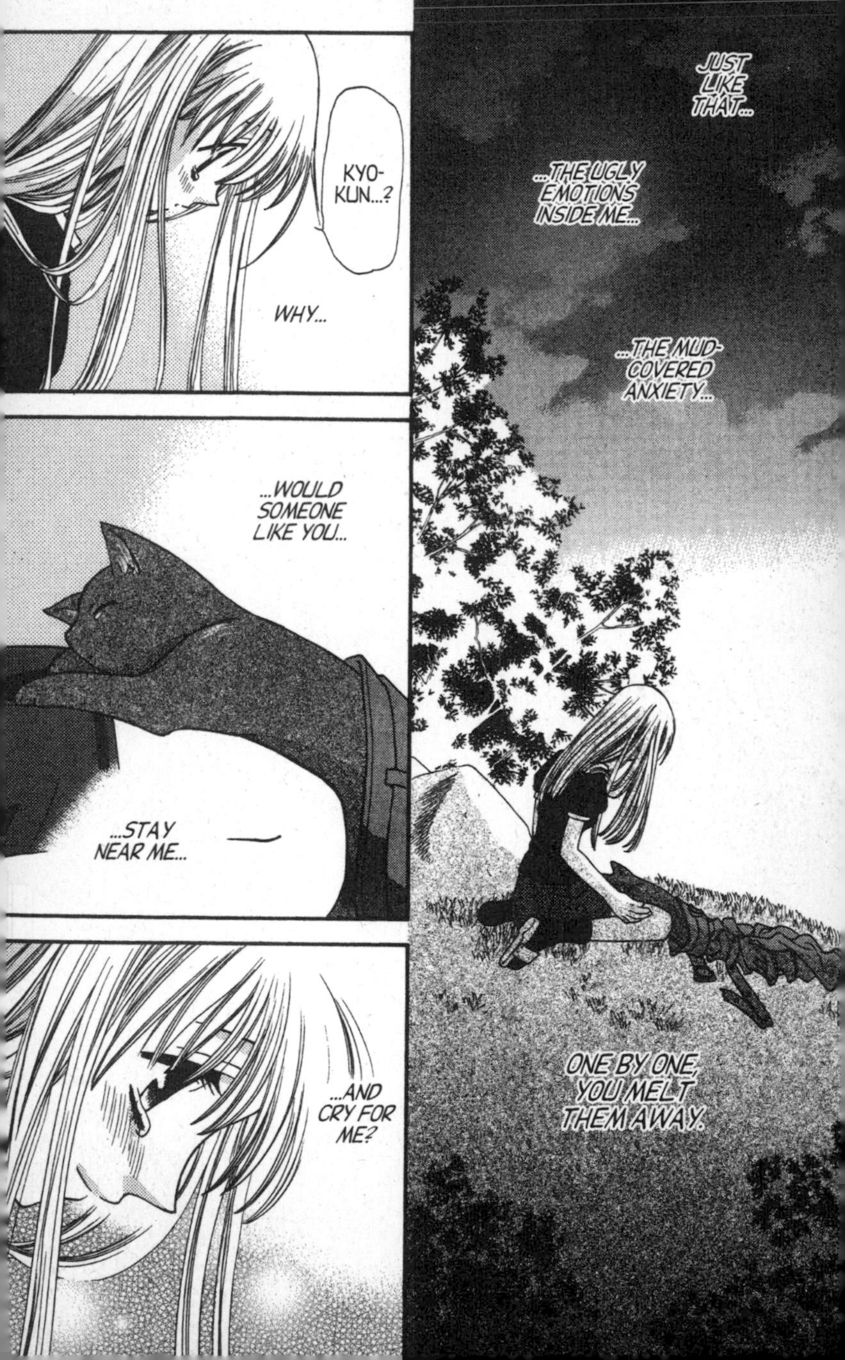
JUST LIKE THAT...
...THE UGLY EMOTIONS INSIDE ME...
...THE MUD-COVERED ANXIETY...
ONE BY ONE, YOU MELT THEM AWAY.
KYO-KUN...?
WHY...
...WOULD SOMEONE LIKE YOU...
...STAY NEAR ME...
...AND CRY FOR ME?

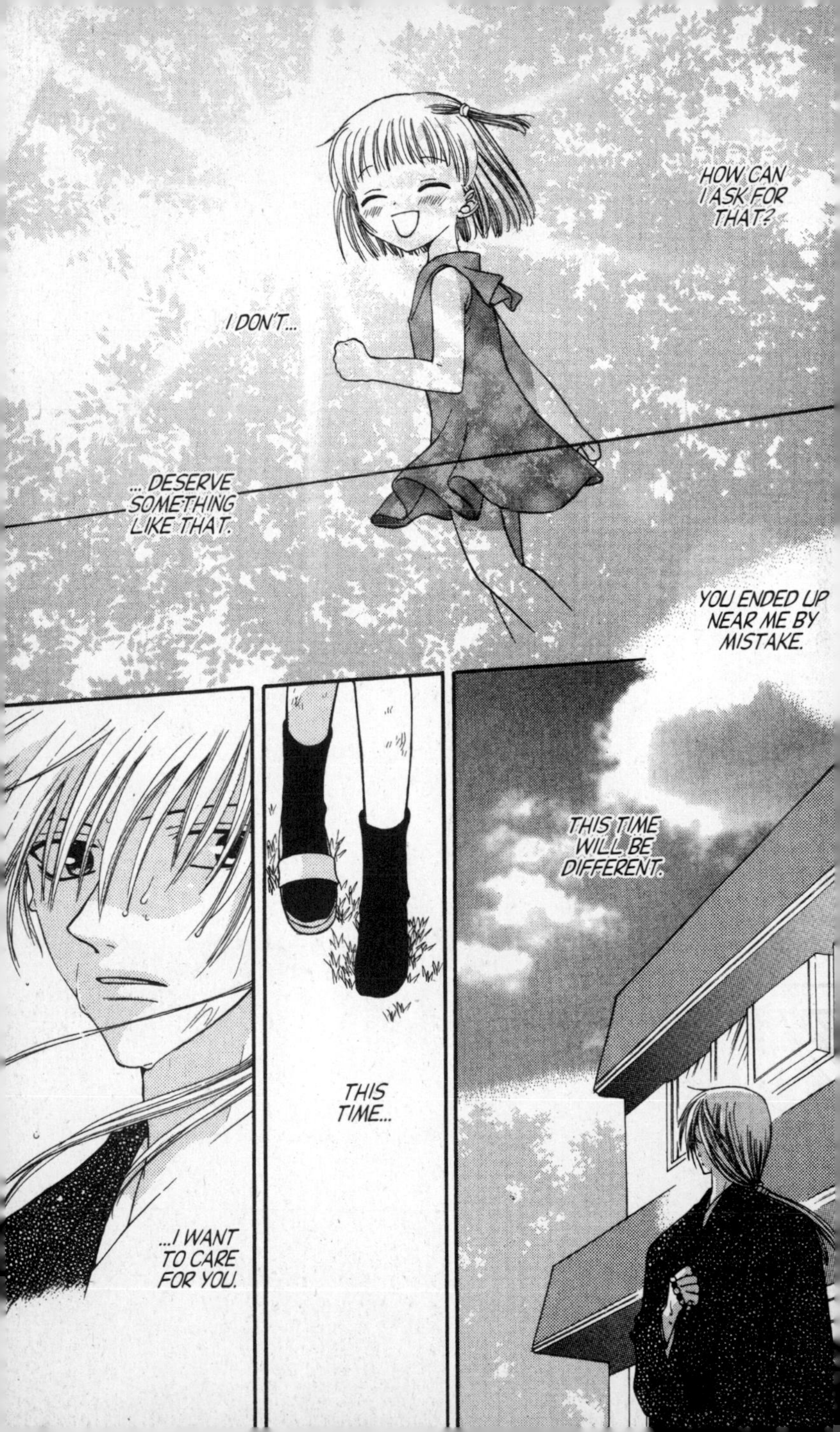
HOW CAN I ASK FOR THAT?
I DON'T...
... DESERVE SOMETHING LIKE THAT.
YOU ENDED UP NEAR ME BY MISTAKE.
THIS TIME WILL BE DIFFERENT.
THIS TIME...
...I WANT TO CARE FOR YOU.

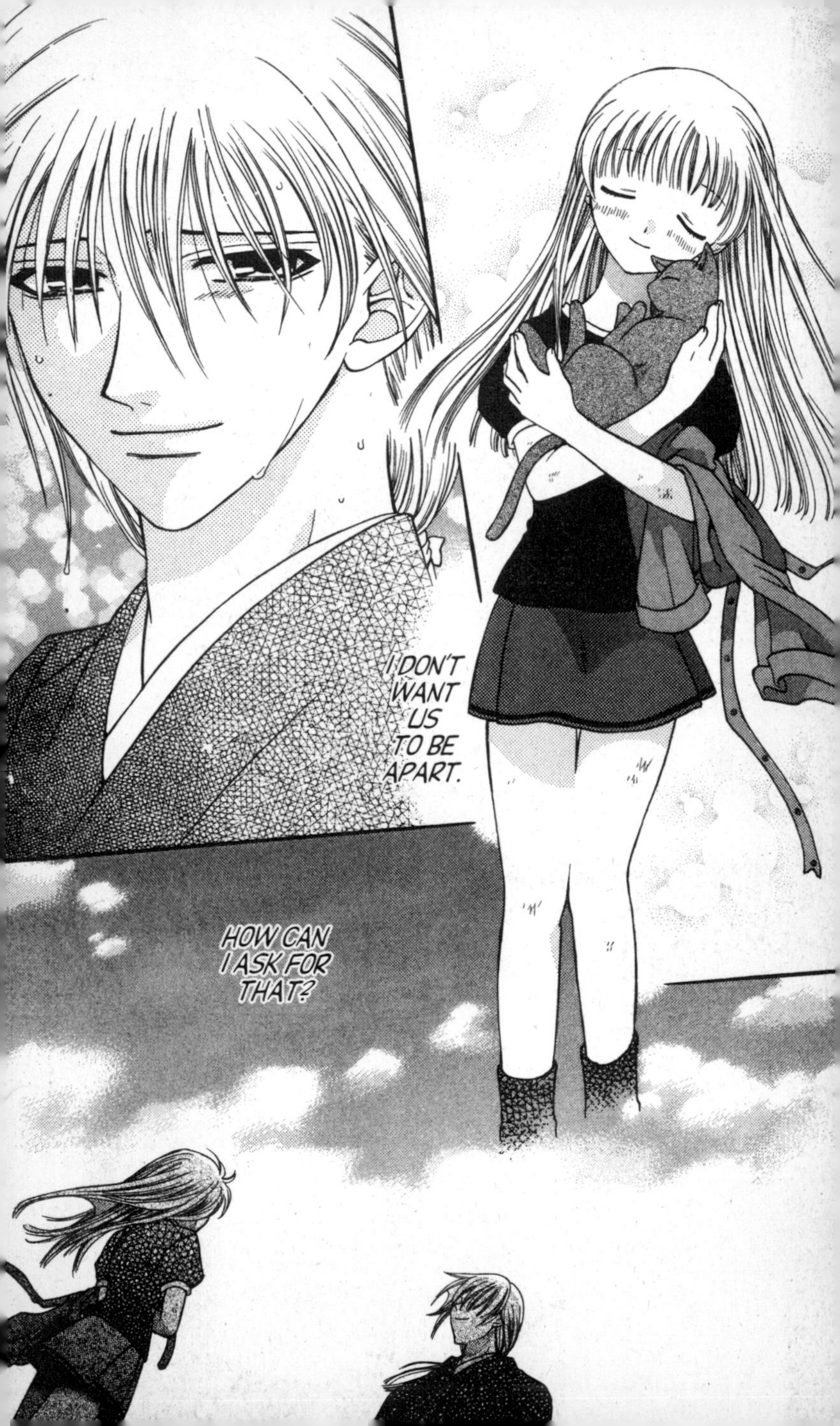
I DON'T WANT US TO BE APART.
HOW CAN I ASK FOR THAT?

Chapter 34

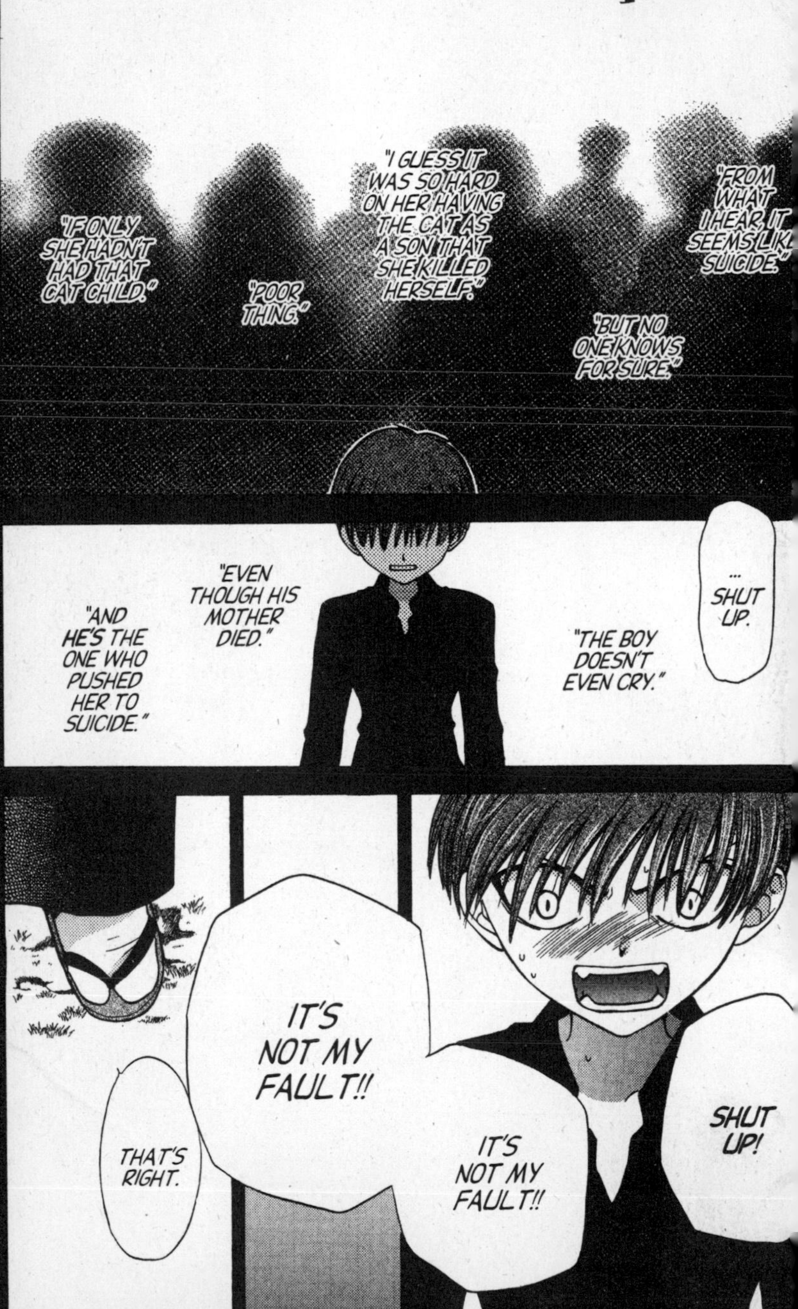
"FROM WHAT I HEAR, IT SEEMS LIK SUICIDE."
"BUT NO ONE KNOWS FOR SURE."
"I GUESS IT WAS SO HARD ON HER HAVING THE CAT AS A SON THAT SHE KILLED HERSELF."
"POOR THING."
"IF ONLY SHE HADN'T HAD THAT CAT CHILD."
... SHUT UP.
"THE BOY DOESN'T EVEN CRY."
"EVEN THOUGH HIS MOTHER DIED."
"AND HE'S THE ONE WHO PUSHED HER TO SUICIDE."
SHUT UP!
IT'S NOT MY FAULT!!
IT'S NOT MY FAULT!!
THAT'S RIGHT.

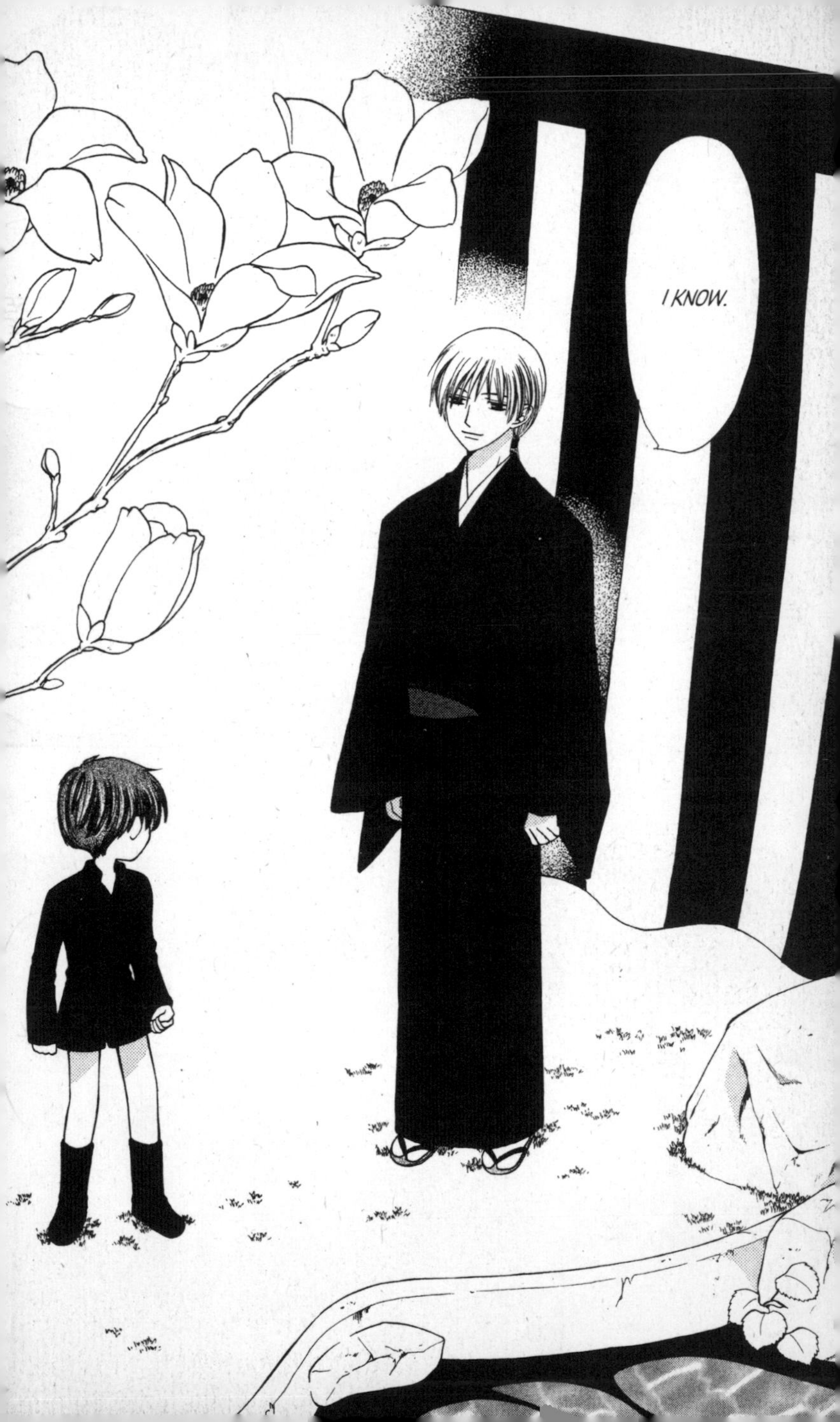
I KNOW.

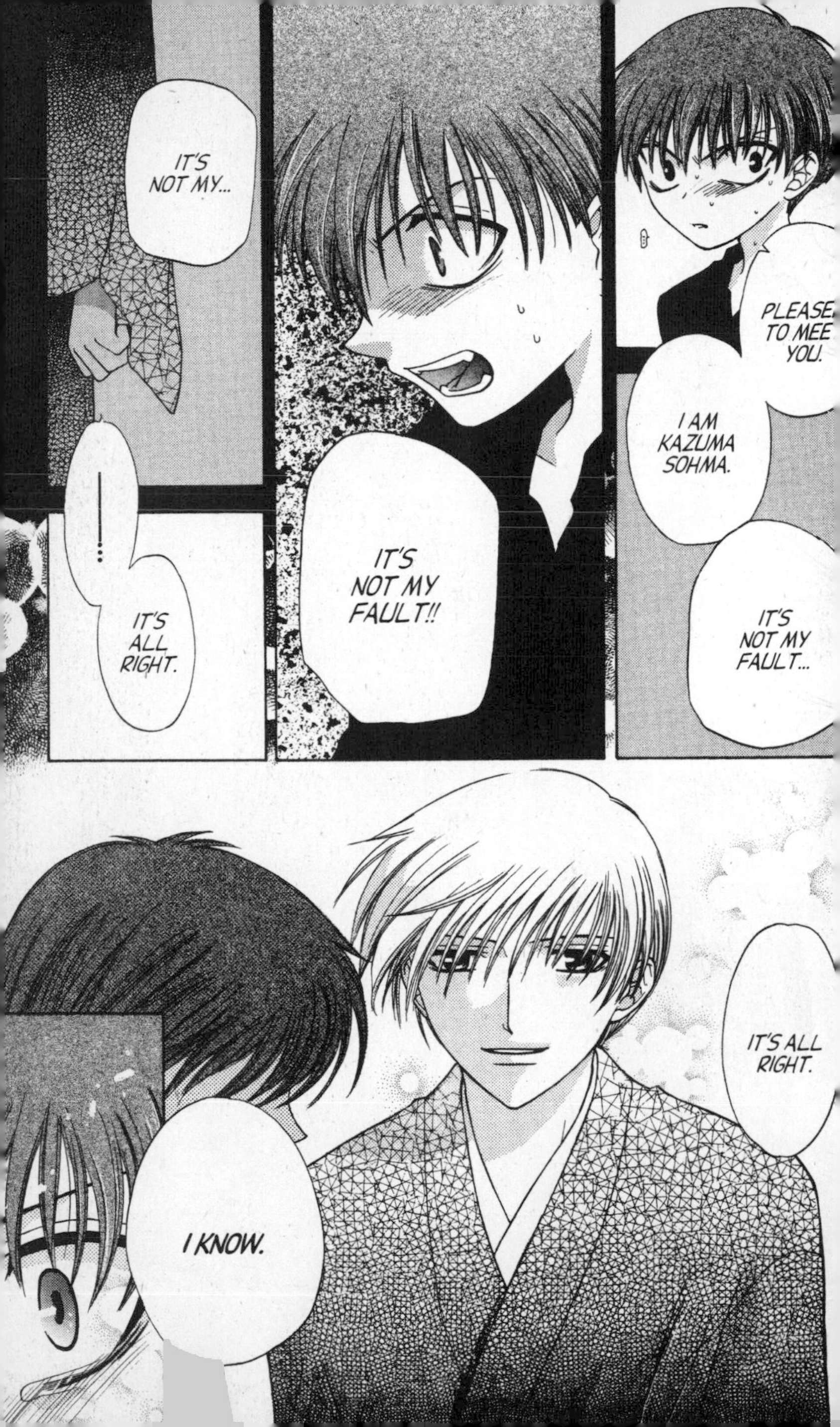
PLEASE TO MEE YOU.
I AM KAZUMA SOHMA.
IT'S NOT MY FAULT...
IT'S NOT MY FAULT!!
IT'S NOT MY...
......!
IT'S ALL RIGHT.
IT'S ALL RIGHT.
I KNOW.

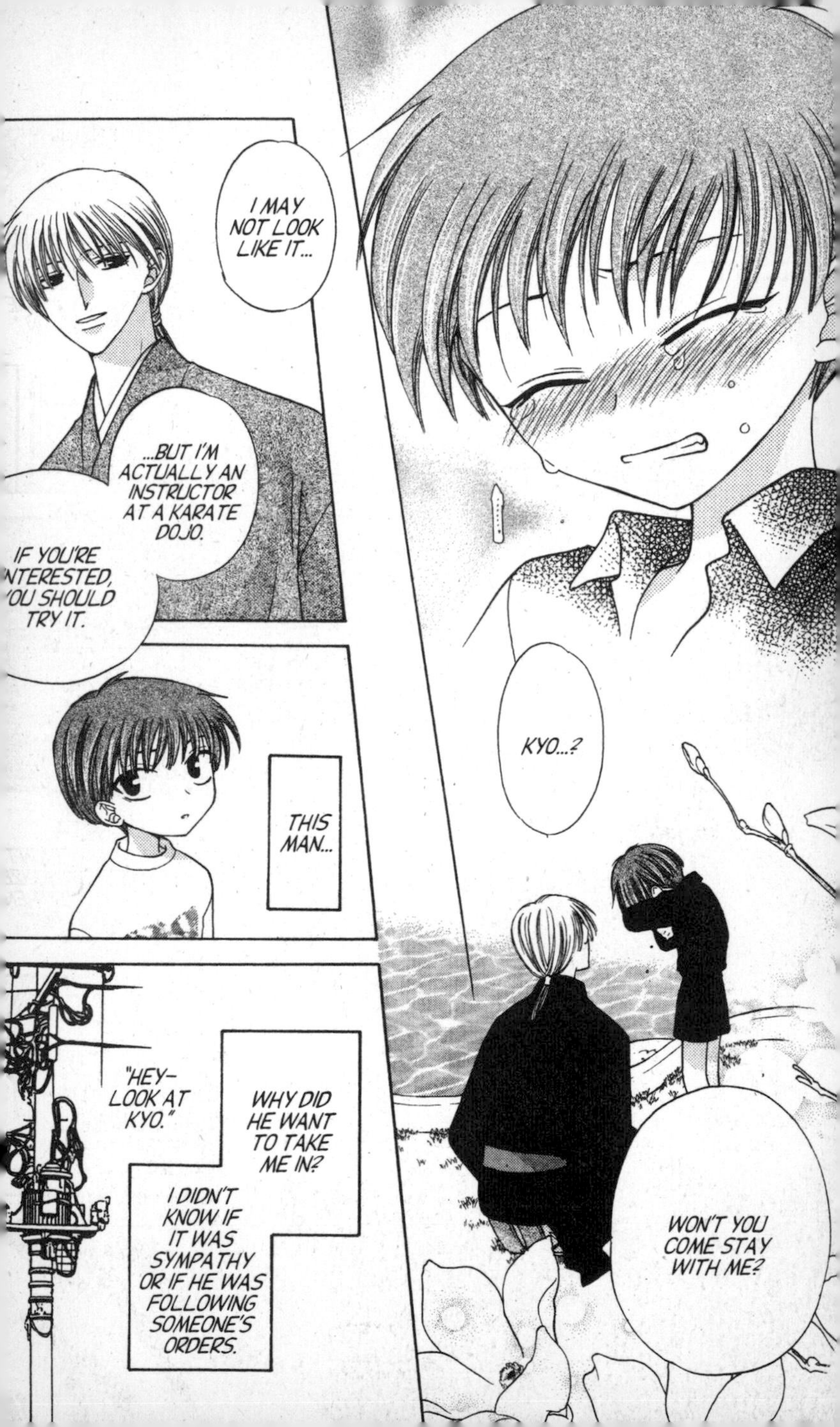
KYO...?
WON'T YOU COME STAY WITH ME?
I MAY NOT LOOK LIKE IT...
...BUT I'M ACTUALLY AN INSTRUCTOR AT A KARATE DOJO.
IF YOU'RE NTERESTED, OU SHOULD TRY IT.
THIS MAN...
WHY DID HE WANT TO TAKE ME IN?
I DIDN'T KNOW IF IT WAS SYMPATHY OR IF HE WAS FOLLOWING SOMEONE'S ORDERS.
"HEY– LOOK AT KYO."

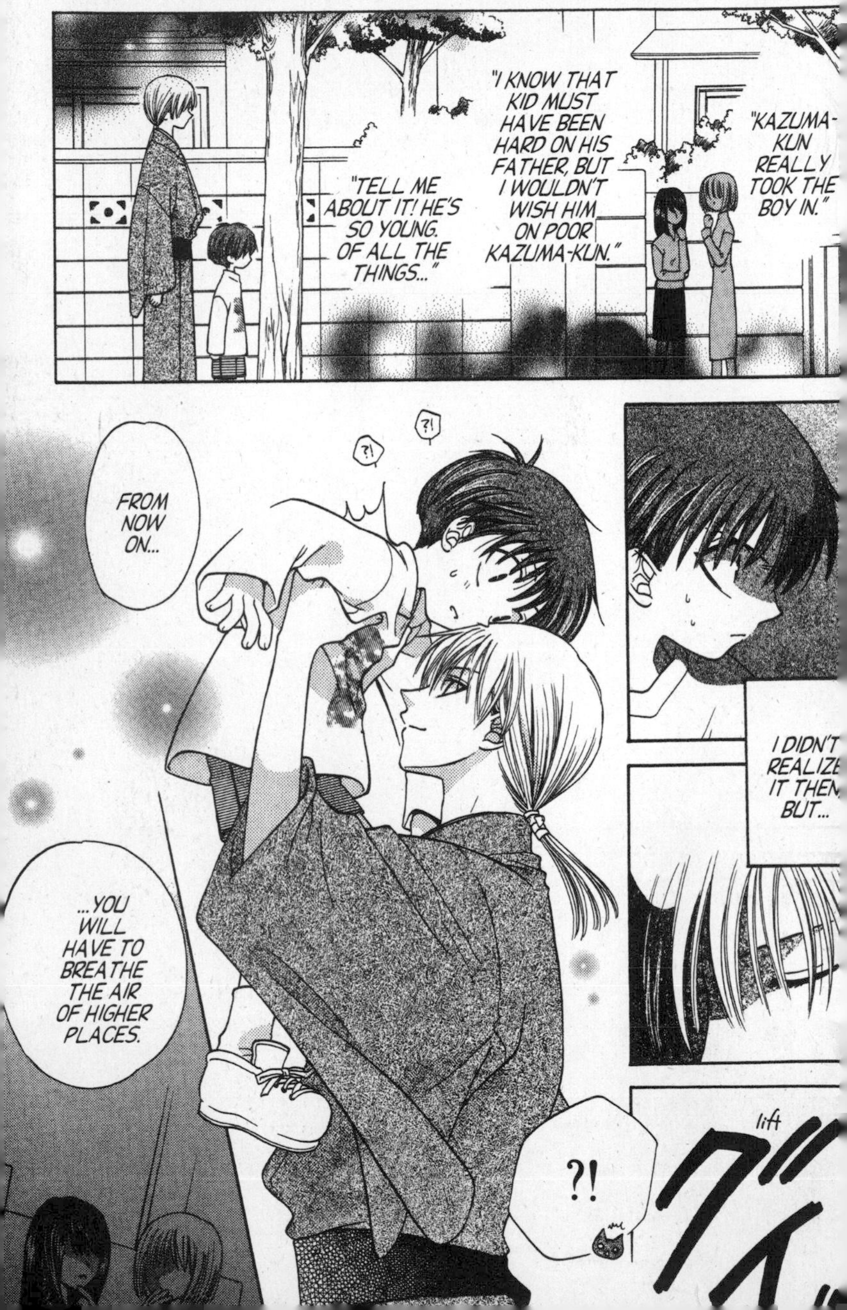
"KAZUMA-KUN REALLY TOOK THE BOY IN."
"I KNOW THAT KID MUST HAVE BEEN HARD ON HIS FATHER, BUT I WOULDN'T WISH HIM ON POOR KAZUMA-KUN."
"TELL ME ABOUT IT! HE'S SO YOUNG. OF ALL THE THINGS..."
I DIDN'T REALIZE IT THEN, BUT...
lift
?!
?!
?!
FROM NOW ON...
...YOU WILL HAVE TO BREATHE THE AIR OF HIGHER PLACES.

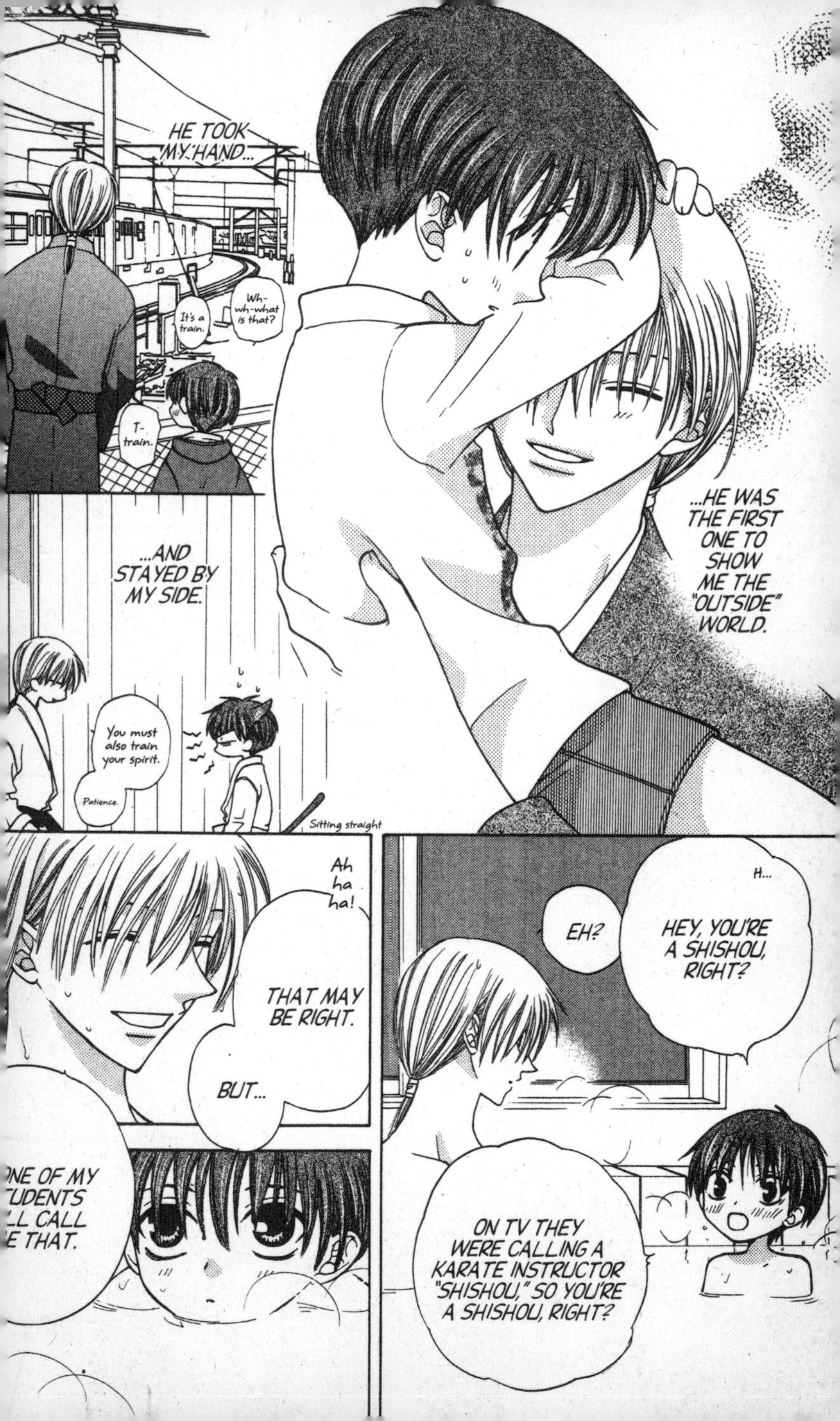
...HE WAS THE FIRST ONE TO SHOW ME THE "OUTSIDE" WORLD.
HE TOOK MY HAND...
Wh-wh-what is that?
It's a train.
T-train.
...AND STAYED BY MY SIDE.
You must also train your spirit.
Patience.
Sitting straight
H...
HEY, YOU'RE A SHISHOU, RIGHT?
EH?
ON TV THEY WERE CALLING A KARATE INSTRUCTOR "SHISHOU," SO YOU'RE A SHISHOU, RIGHT?
Ah ha ha!
THAT MAY BE RIGHT.
BUT...
ONE OF MY TUDENTS LL CALL E THAT.

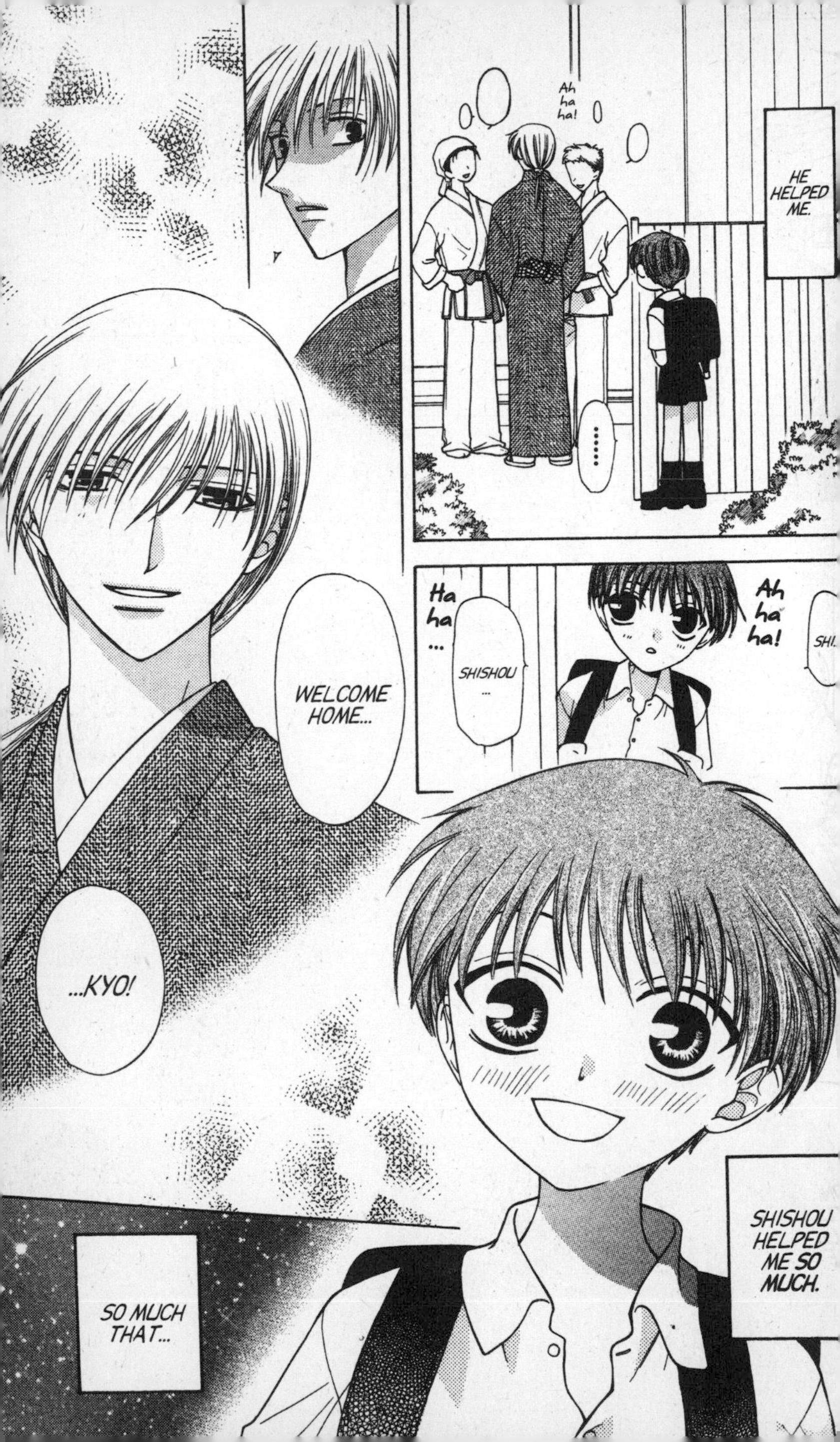
HE HELPED ME.
Ah ha ha!
......
Ah ha ha!
SHI...
Ha ha ...
SHISHOU ...
WELCOME HOME...
...KYO!
SHISHOU HELPED ME SO MUCH.
SO MUCH THAT...

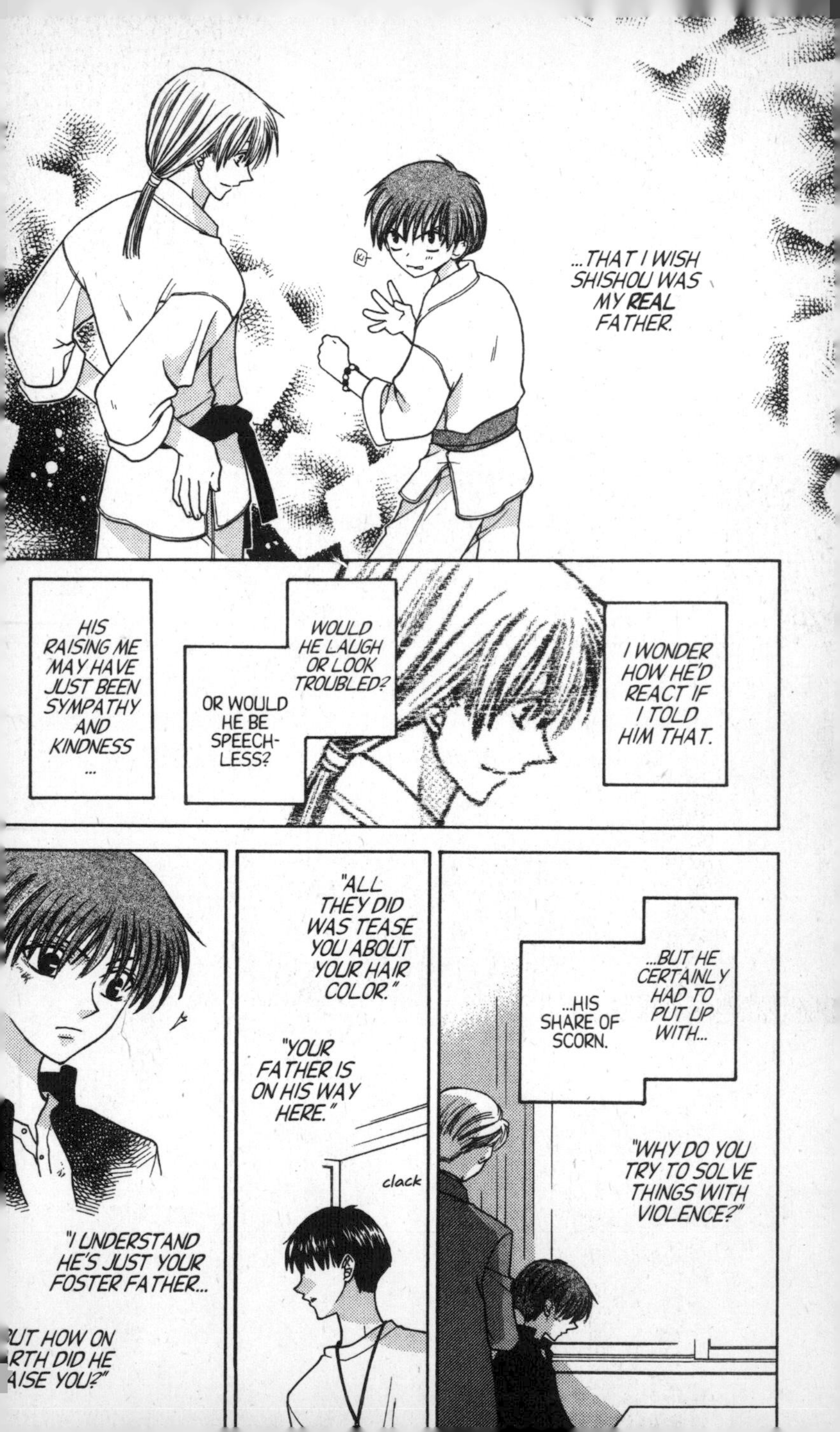
Ki
...THAT I WISH SHISHOU WAS MY REAL FATHER.
I WONDER HOW HE'D REACT IF I TOLD HIM THAT.
WOULD HE LAUGH OR LOOK TROUBLED?
OR WOULD HE BE SPEECH-LESS?
HIS RAISING ME MAY HAVE JUST BEEN SYMPATHY AND KINDNESS ...
...BUT HE CERTAINLY HAD TO PUT UP WITH...
...HIS SHARE OF SCORN.
"WHY DO YOU TRY TO SOLVE THINGS WITH VIOLENCE?"
"ALL THEY DID WAS TEASE YOU ABOUT YOUR HAIR COLOR."
"YOUR FATHER IS ON HIS WAY HERE."
clack
"I UNDERSTAND HE'S JUST YOUR FOSTER FATHER...
UT HOW ON RTH DID HE AISE YOU?"

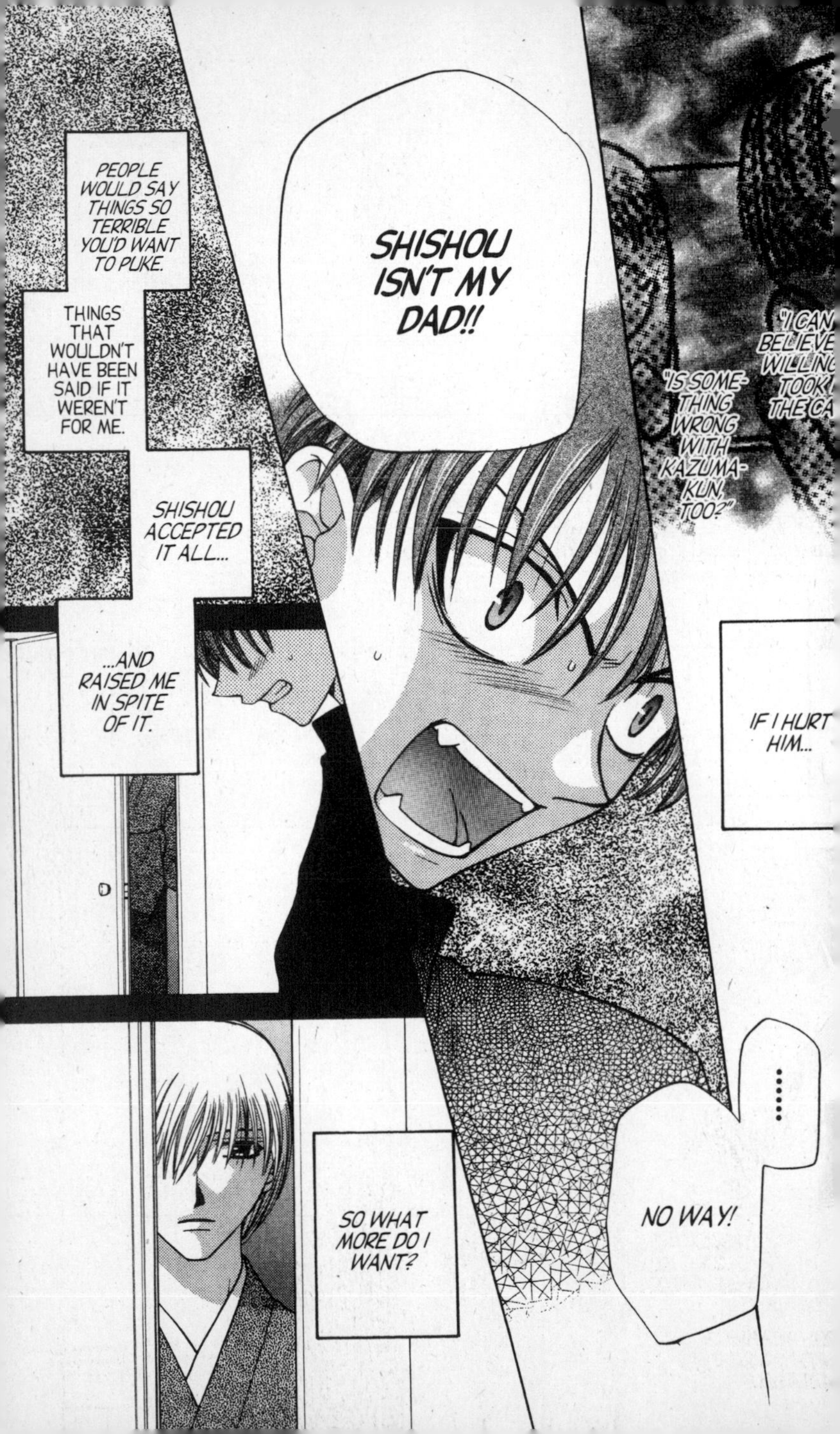
"I CAN BELIEVE WILLING TOOK THE CA
"IS SOME-THING WRONG WITH KAZUMA-KUN, TOO?"
SHISHOU ISN'T MY DAD!!
PEOPLE WOULD SAY THINGS SO TERRIBLE YOU'D WANT TO PUKE.
THINGS THAT WOULDN'T HAVE BEEN SAID IF IT WEREN'T FOR ME.
SHISHOU ACCEPTED IT ALL...
...AND RAISED ME IN SPITE OF IT.
IF I HURT HIM...
......
NO WAY!
SO WHAT MORE DO I WANT?

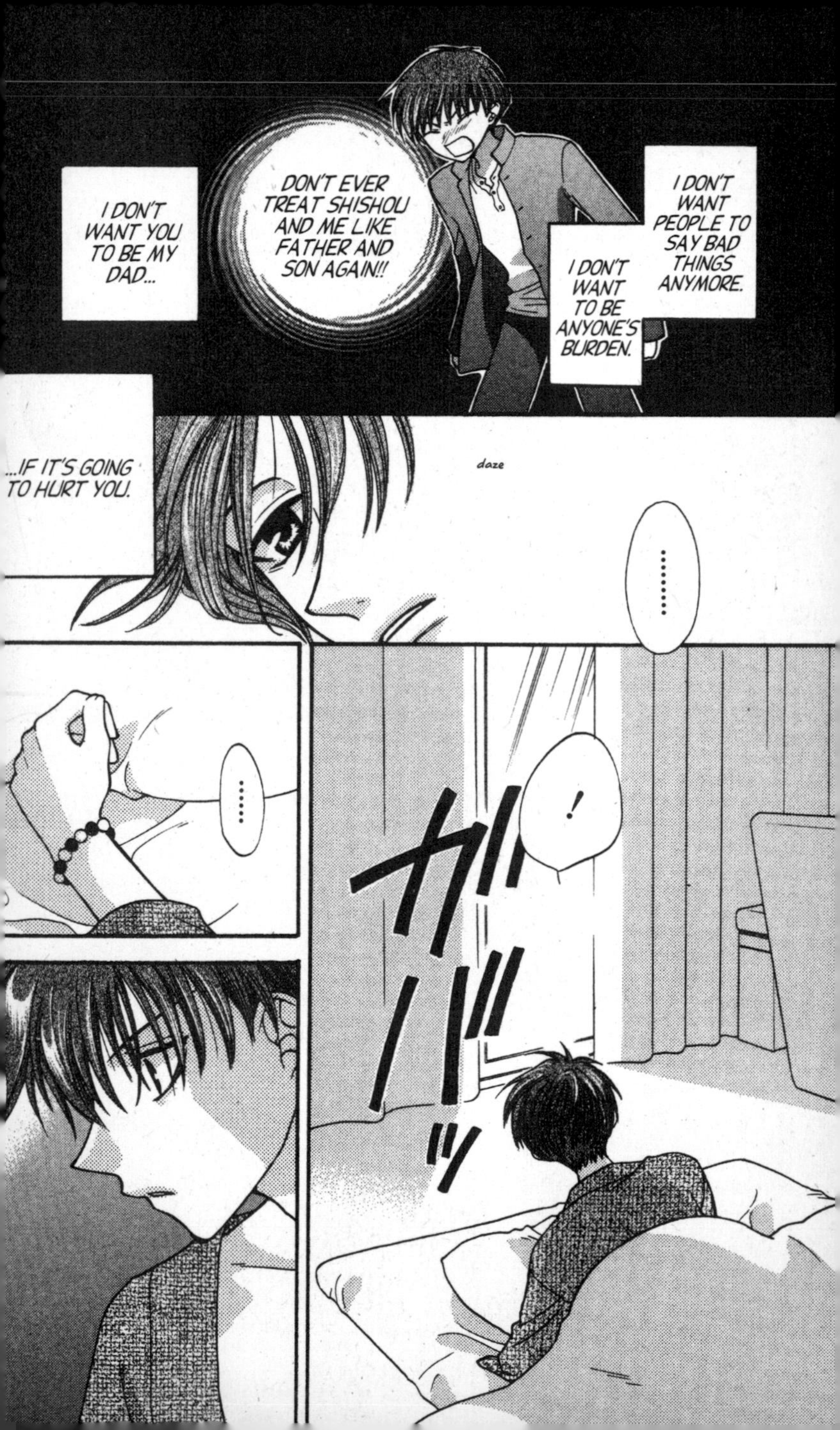
I DON'T WANT PEOPLE TO SAY BAD THINGS ANYMORE.
I DON'T WANT TO BE ANYONE'S BURDEN.
DON'T EVER TREAT SHISHOU AND ME LIKE FATHER AND SON AGAIN!!
I DON'T WANT YOU TO BE MY DAD...
...IF IT'S GOING TO HURT YOU.
daze
....
!
ガバッ
......

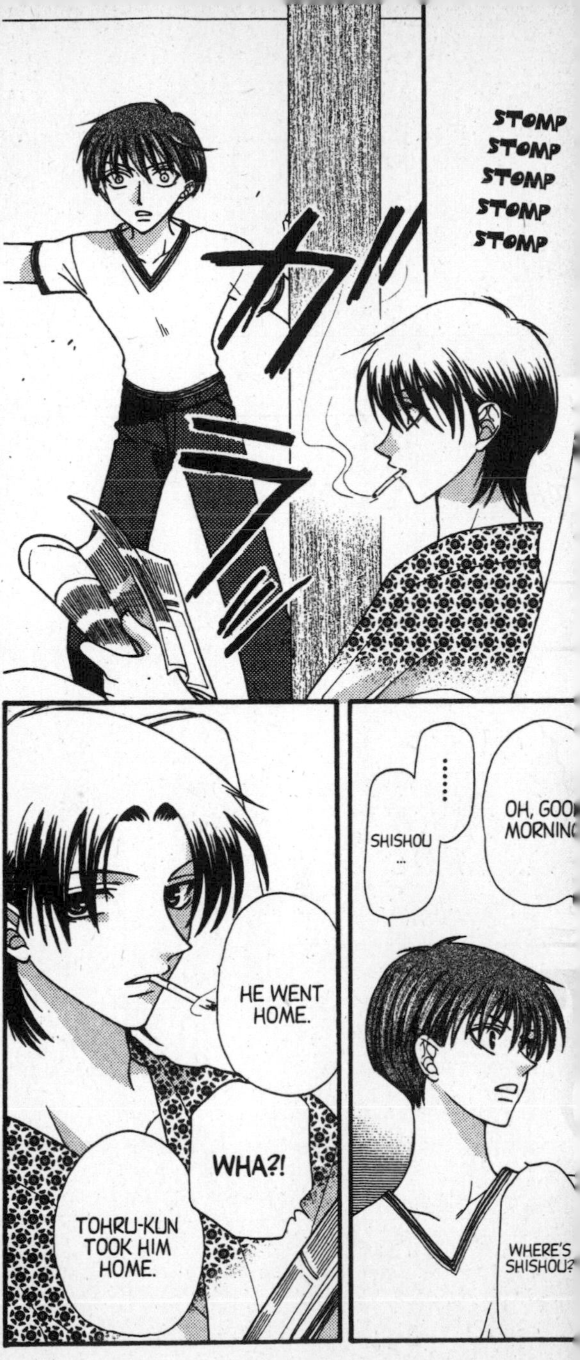
STOMP
STOMP
STOMP
STOMP
STOMP
OH, GOO
MORNIN
......
SHISHOU ...
WHERE'S SHISHOU?
HE WENT HOME.
WHA?!
TOHRU-KUN TOOK HIM HOME.

Fruits Basket 6 Part 4:

As I'm writing this, FF9 still hasn't come out. Just a little longer. Finally, the most dangerous game... The game that I will put everything aside for, even eating... No, if I get too hungry, I will eat. (So you will eat!) There are things in the world whose power to draw you in is strong. Things that fill you with anticipation are the strongest of all. Like Square-san's games. Y'know? You think, "I'm sleepy... I'm sleepy, but... I have to know what happens next!" Goodness gracious. And *GRANDIA 2* is coming out! I'm so happy I could scream. And a Dreamcast version of *SAKURA TAISEN* is on its way, so I scream even more. Aahh, there aren't enough hours in the day! (laugh)

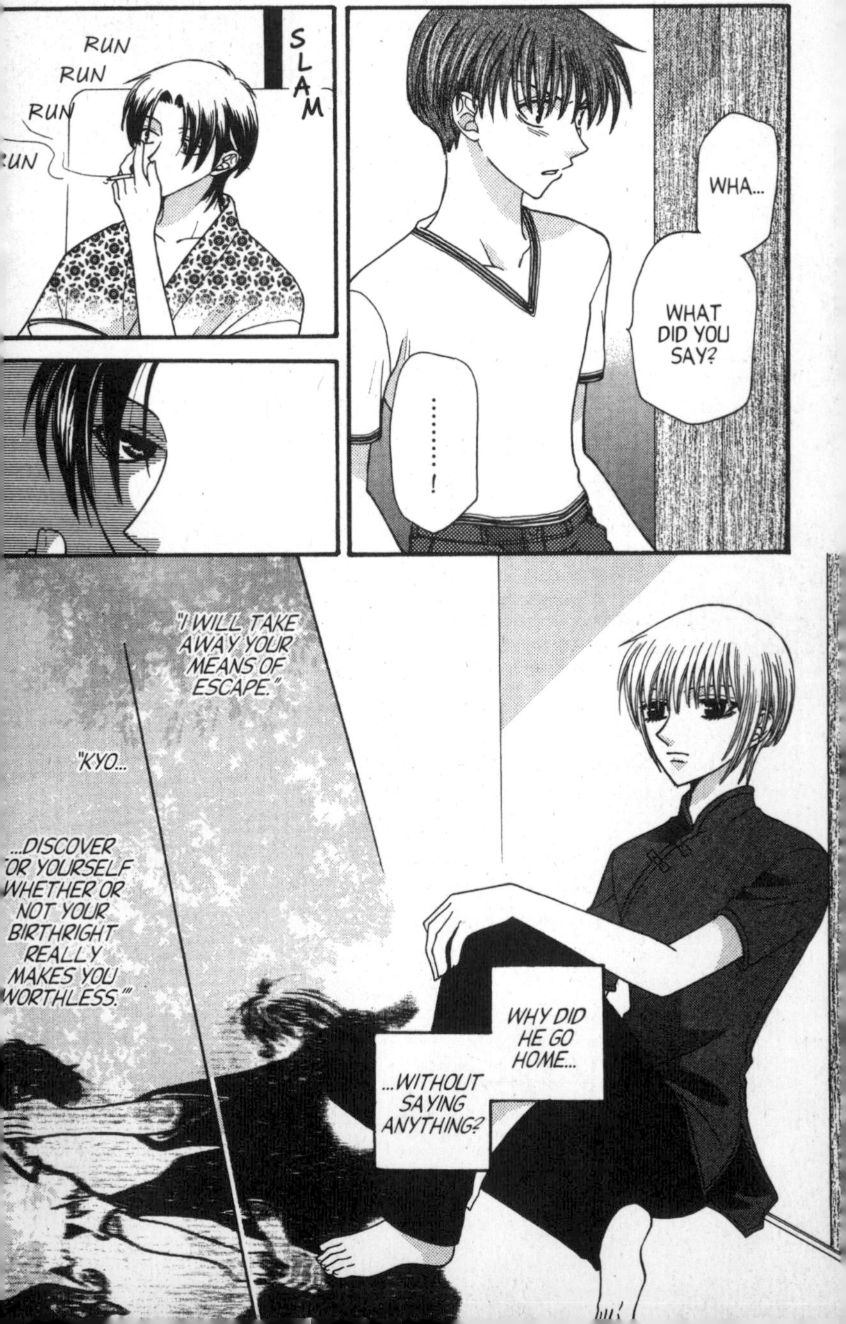
WHA...
WHAT DID YOU SAY?
......!
RUN
RUN
RUN
UN
SLAM
"I WILL TAKE AWAY YOUR MEANS OF ESCAPE."
"KYO...
...DISCOVER FOR YOURSELF WHETHER OR NOT YOUR BIRTHRIGHT REALLY MAKES YOU WORTHLESS.'"
WHY DID HE GO HOME...
...WITHOUT SAYING ANYTHING?

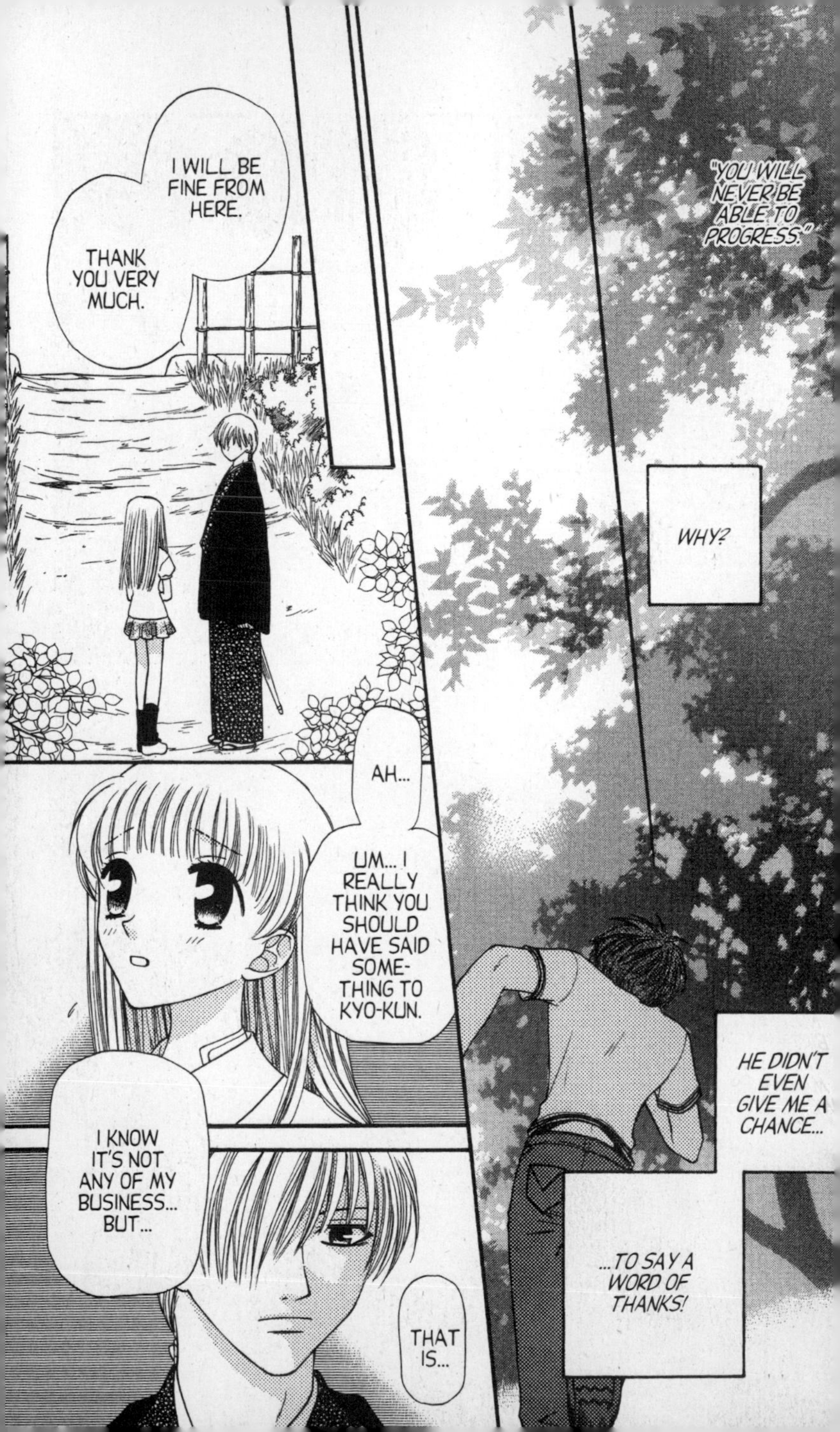
"YOU WILL NEVER BE ABLE TO PROGRESS."
WHY?
HE DIDN'T EVEN GIVE ME A CHANCE...
...TO SAY A WORD OF THANKS!
I WILL BE FINE FROM HERE.
THANK YOU VERY MUCH.
AH...
UM... I REALLY THINK YOU SHOULD HAVE SAID SOME-THING TO KYO-KUN.
I KNOW IT'S NOT ANY OF MY BUSINESS... BUT...
THAT IS...

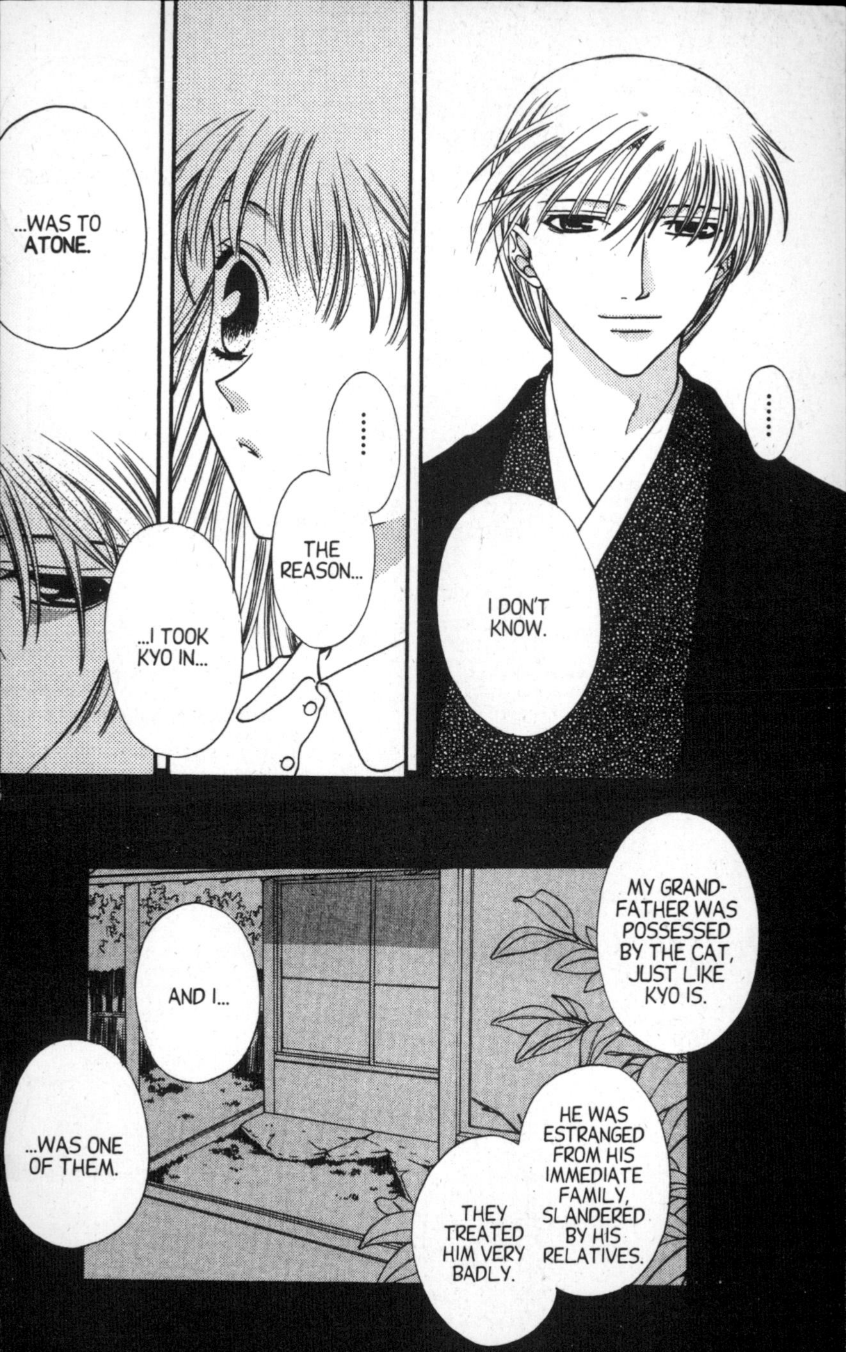
......
I DON'T KNOW.
......
THE REASON...
...I TOOK KYO IN...
...WAS TO ATONE.
MY GRAND-FATHER WAS POSSESSED BY THE CAT, JUST LIKE KYO IS.
HE WAS ESTRANGED FROM HIS IMMEDIATE FAMILY, SLANDERED BY HIS RELATIVES.
THEY TREATED HIM VERY BADLY.
AND I...
...WAS ONE OF THEM.

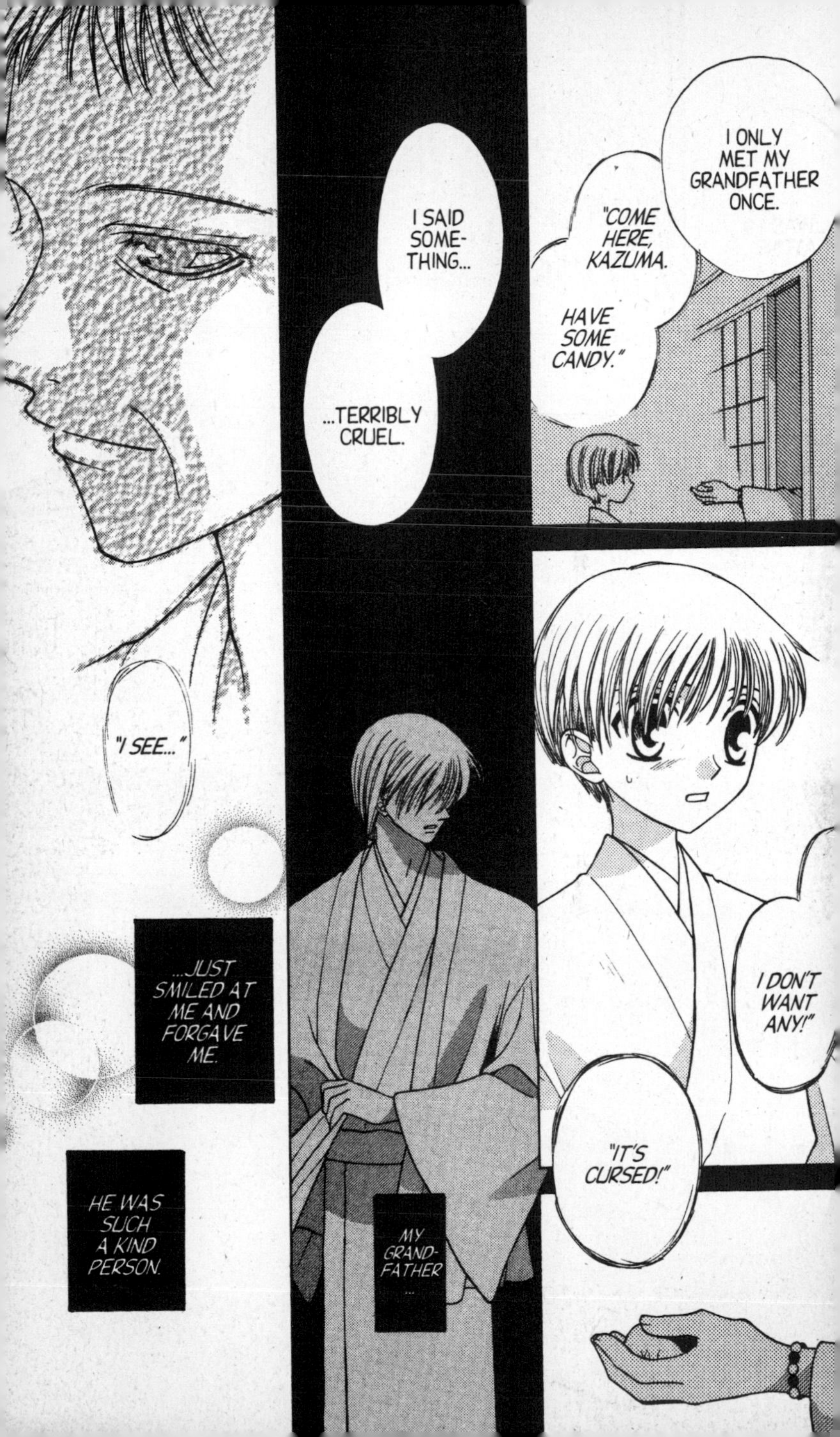
I ONLY MET MY GRANDFATHER ONCE.
"COME HERE, KAZUMA.
HAVE SOME CANDY."
I DON'T WANT ANY!"
"IT'S CURSED!"
I SAID SOME-THING...
...TERRIBLY CRUEL.
MY GRAND-FATHER ...
"I SEE..."
...JUST SMILED AT ME AND FORGAVE ME.
HE WAS SUCH A KIND PERSON.

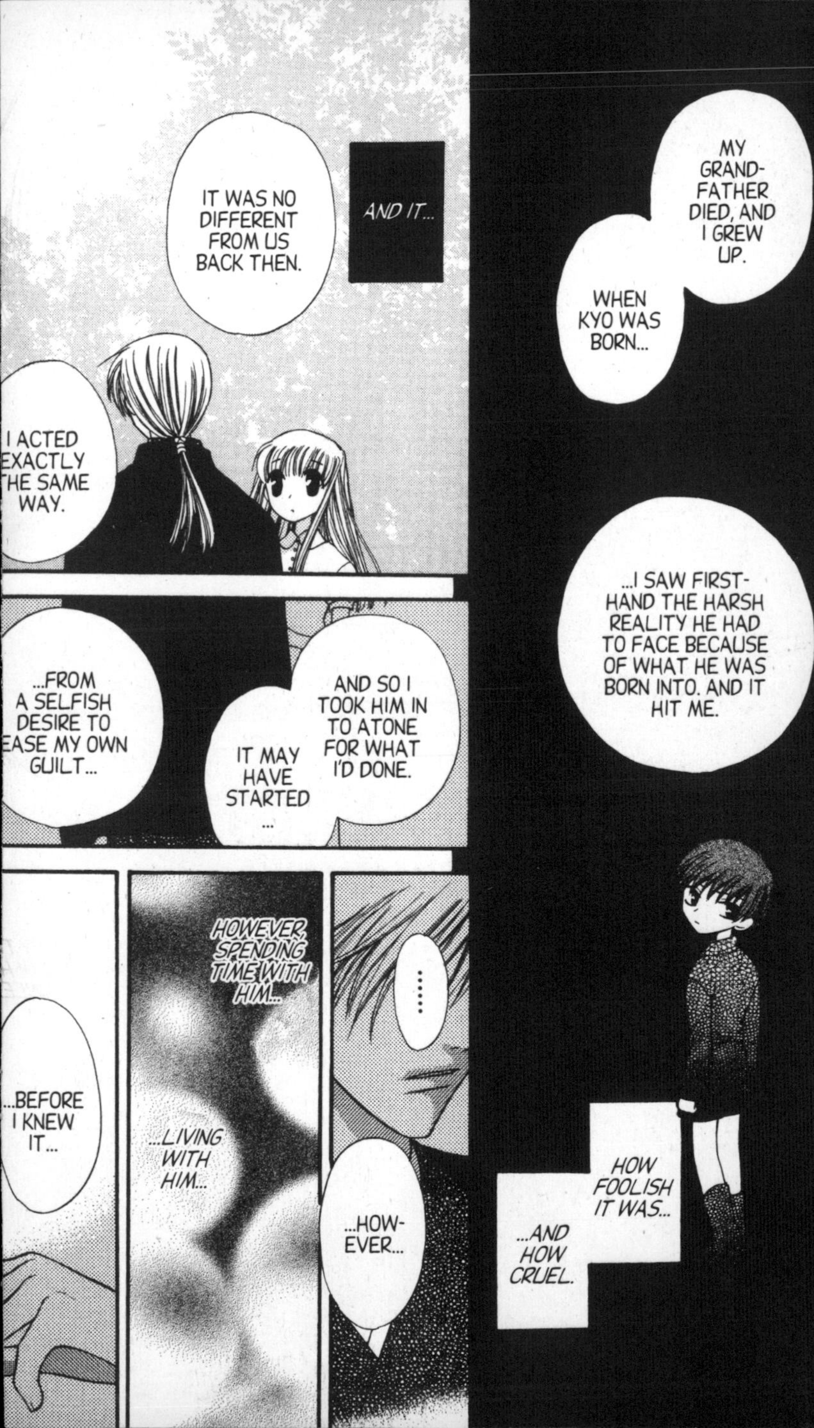

MY GRANDFATHER DIED, AND I GREW UP.
WHEN KYO WAS BORN...
...I SAW FIRST-HAND THE HARSH REALITY HE HAD TO FACE BECAUSE OF WHAT HE WAS BORN INTO. AND IT HIT ME.
HOW FOOLISH IT WAS...
...AND HOW CRUEL.
AND IT...
IT WAS NO DIFFERENT FROM US BACK THEN.
I ACTED EXACTLY THE SAME WAY.
AND SO I TOOK HIM IN TO ATONE FOR WHAT I'D DONE.
IT MAY HAVE STARTED...
...FROM A SELFISH DESIRE TO EASE MY OWN GUILT...
......
...HOW-EVER...
HOWEVER, SPENDING TIME WITH HIM...
...LIVING WITH HIM...
...BEFORE I KNEW IT...

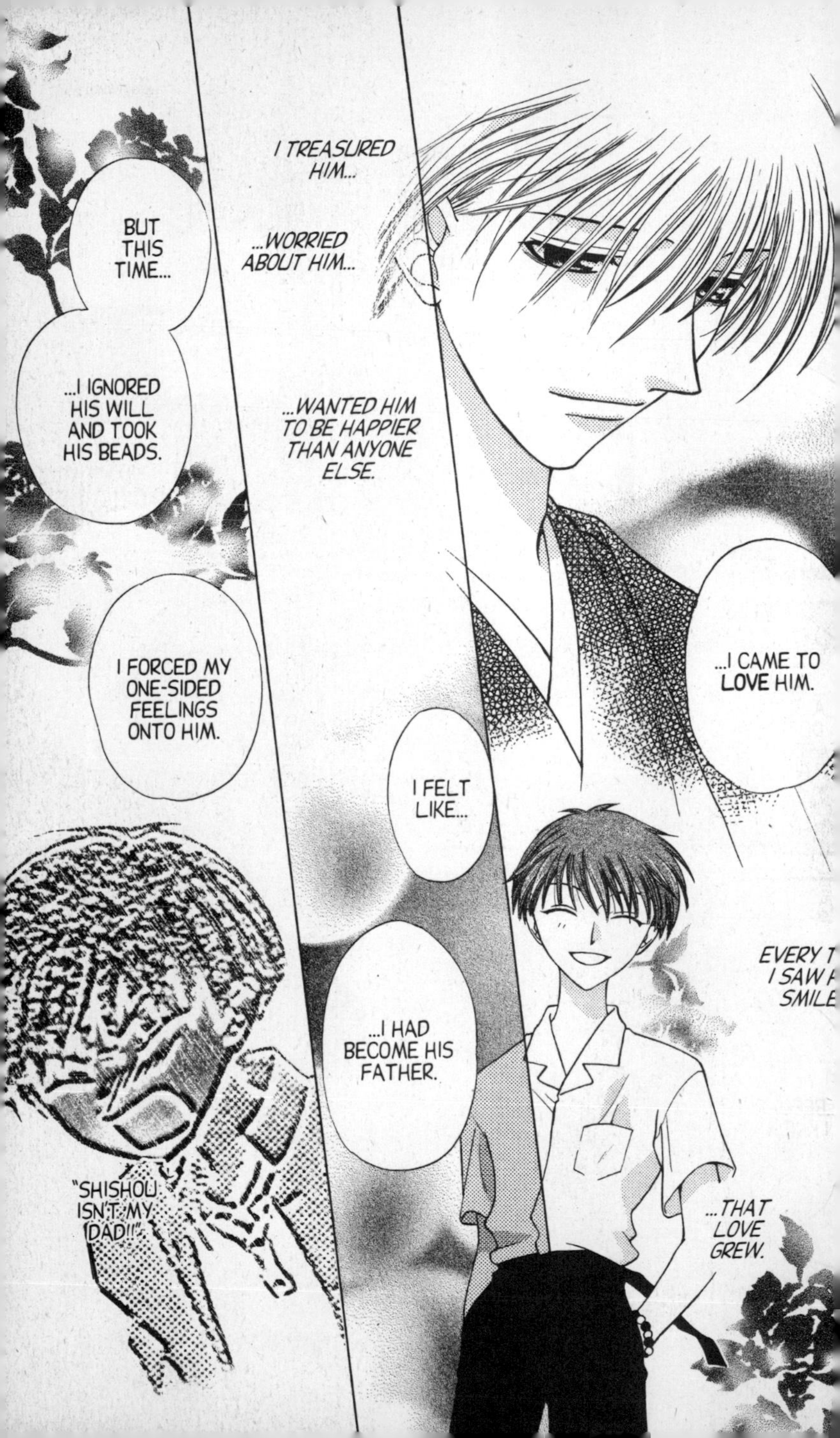
...I CAME TO LOVE HIM.
EVERY T
I SAW
SMILE
...THAT LOVE GREW.
I TREASURED HIM...
...WORRIED ABOUT HIM...
...WANTED HIM TO BE HAPPIER THAN ANYONE ELSE.
I FELT LIKE...
...I HAD BECOME HIS FATHER.
BUT THIS TIME...
...I IGNORED HIS WILL AND TOOK HIS BEADS.
I FORCED MY ONE-SIDED FEELINGS ONTO HIM.
"SHISHOU ISN'T MY DAD!!"

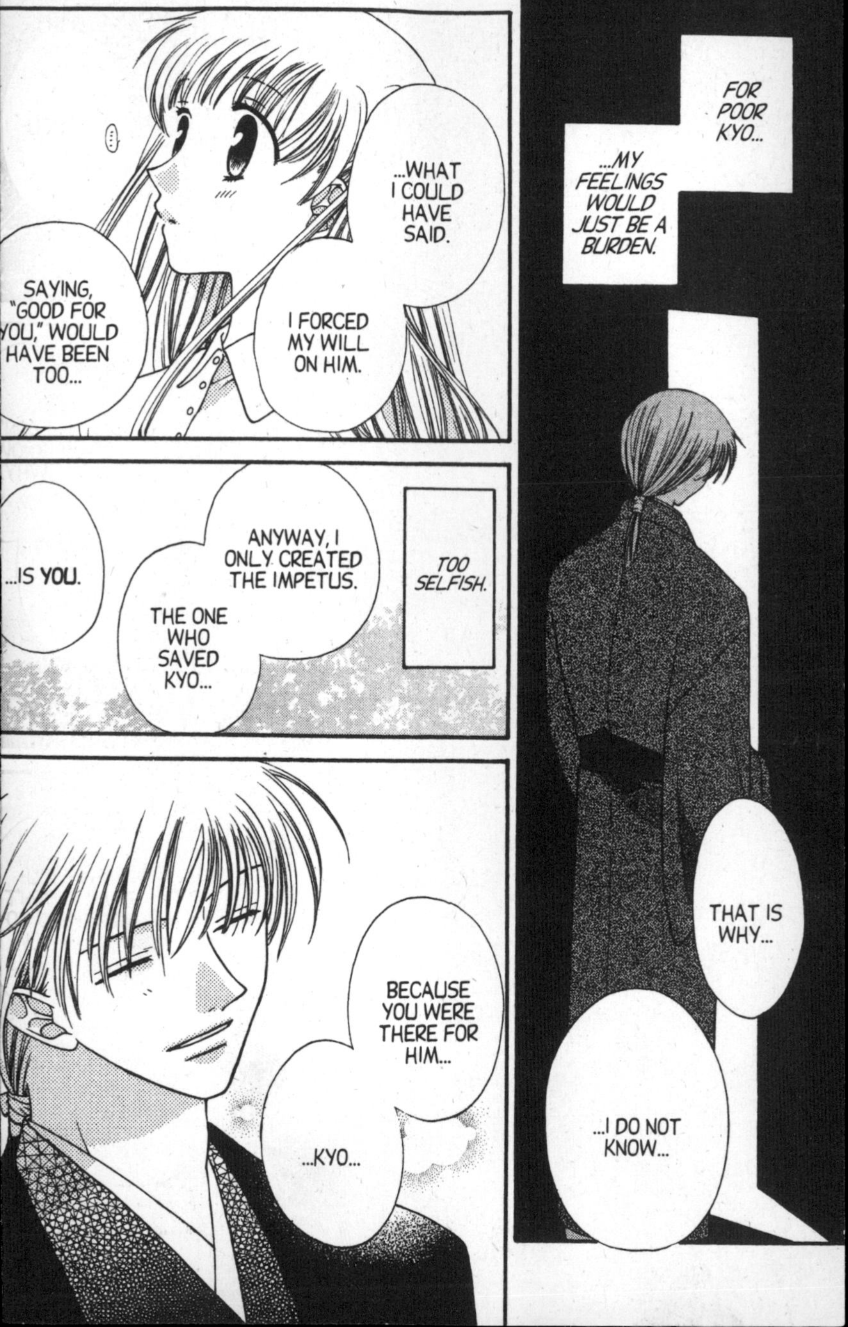
FOR POOR KYO...
...MY FEELINGS WOULD JUST BE A BURDEN.
THAT IS WHY...
...I DO NOT KNOW...
...WHAT I COULD HAVE SAID.
I FORCED MY WILL ON HIM.
SAYING, "GOOD FOR YOU," WOULD HAVE BEEN TOO...
TOO SELFISH.
ANYWAY, I ONLY CREATED THE IMPETUS.
THE ONE WHO SAVED KYO...
...IS **YOU**.
BECAUSE YOU WERE THERE FOR HIM...
...KYO...

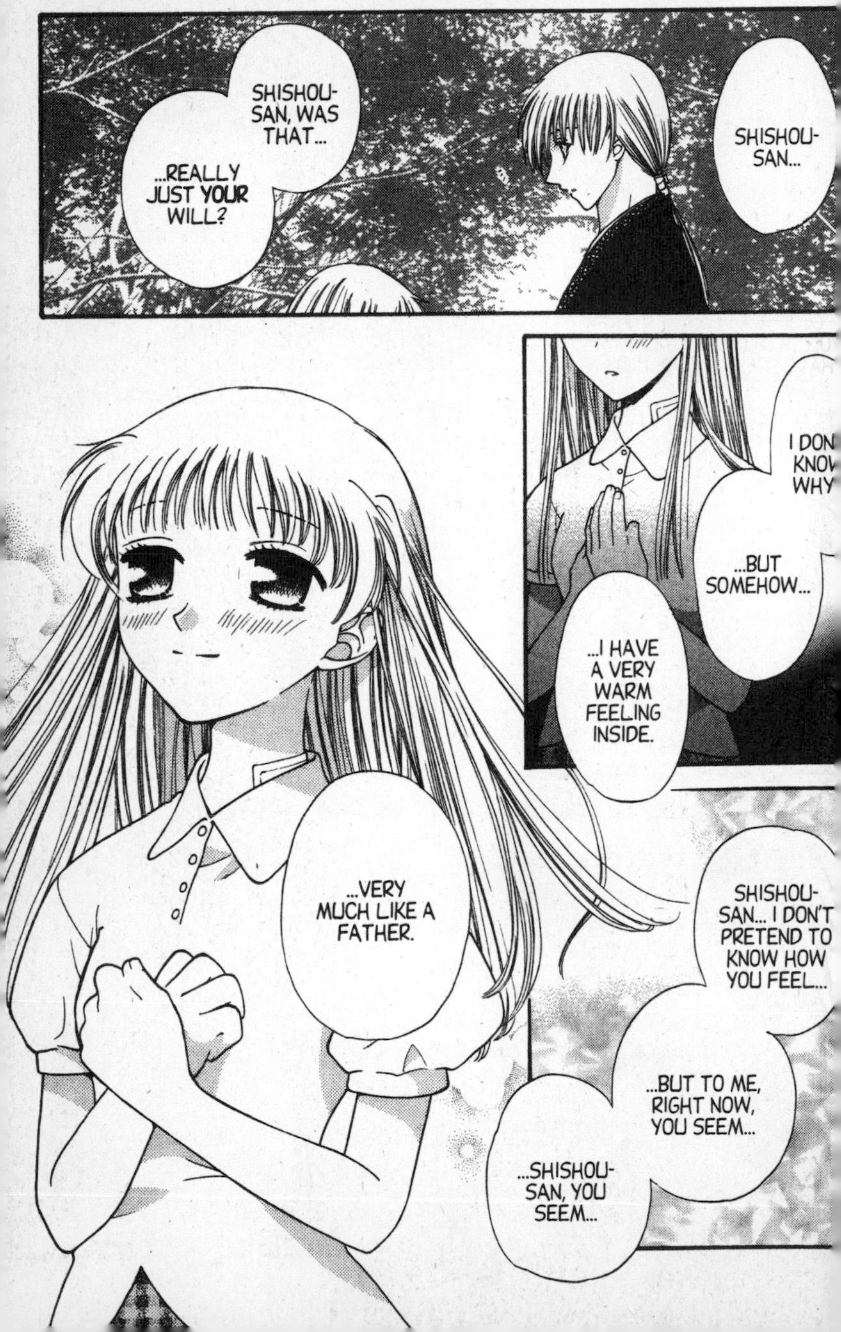
SHISHOU-SAN...
SHISHOU-SAN, WAS THAT...
...REALLY JUST **YOUR** WILL?
I DON KNOW WHY
...BUT SOMEHOW...
...I HAVE A VERY WARM FEELING INSIDE.
SHISHOU-SAN... I DON'T PRETEND TO KNOW HOW YOU FEEL...
...BUT TO ME, RIGHT NOW, YOU SEEM...
...SHISHOU-SAN, YOU SEEM...
...VERY MUCH LIKE A FATHER.

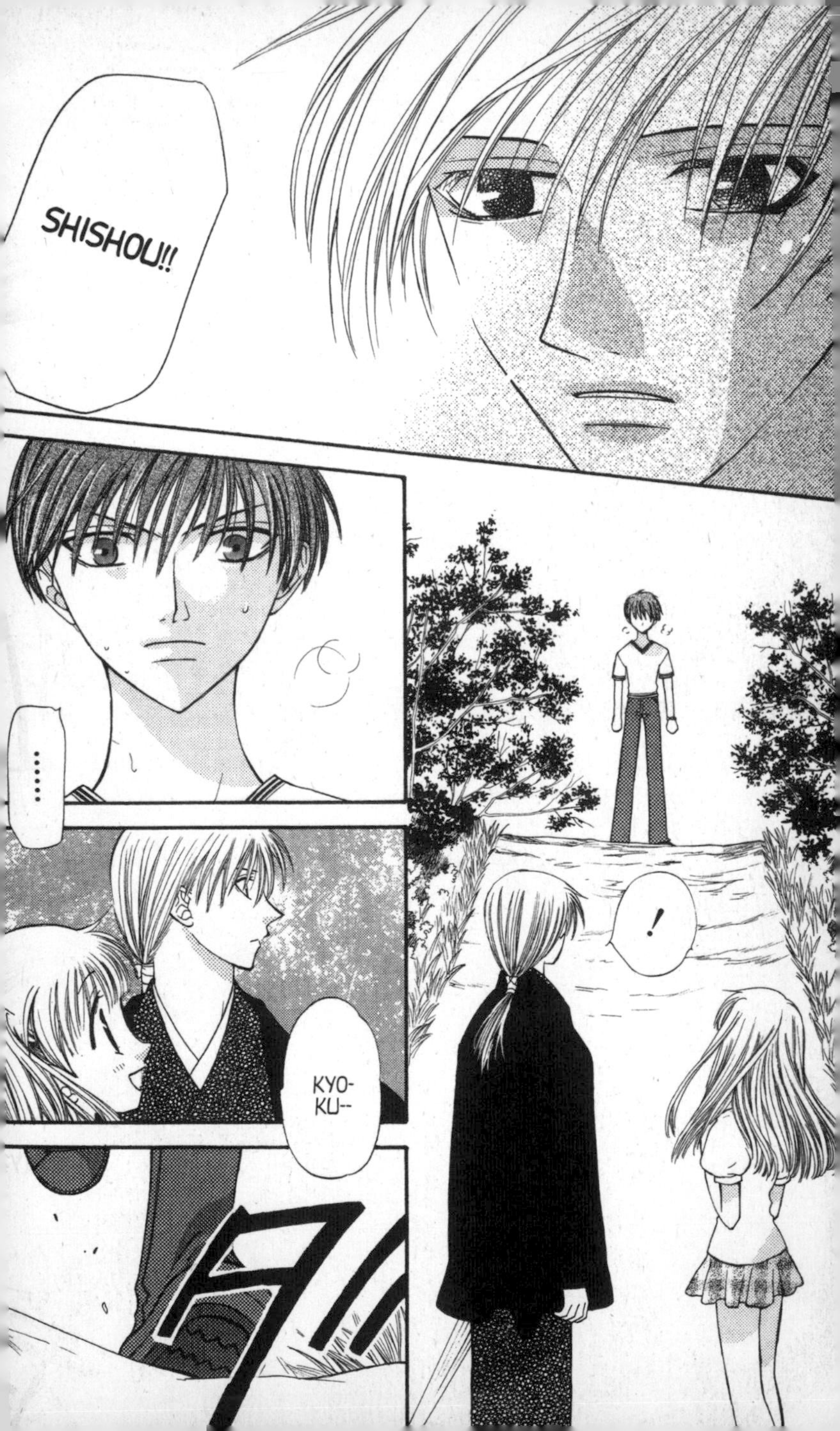
SHISHOU!!
!
......
KYO-KU--

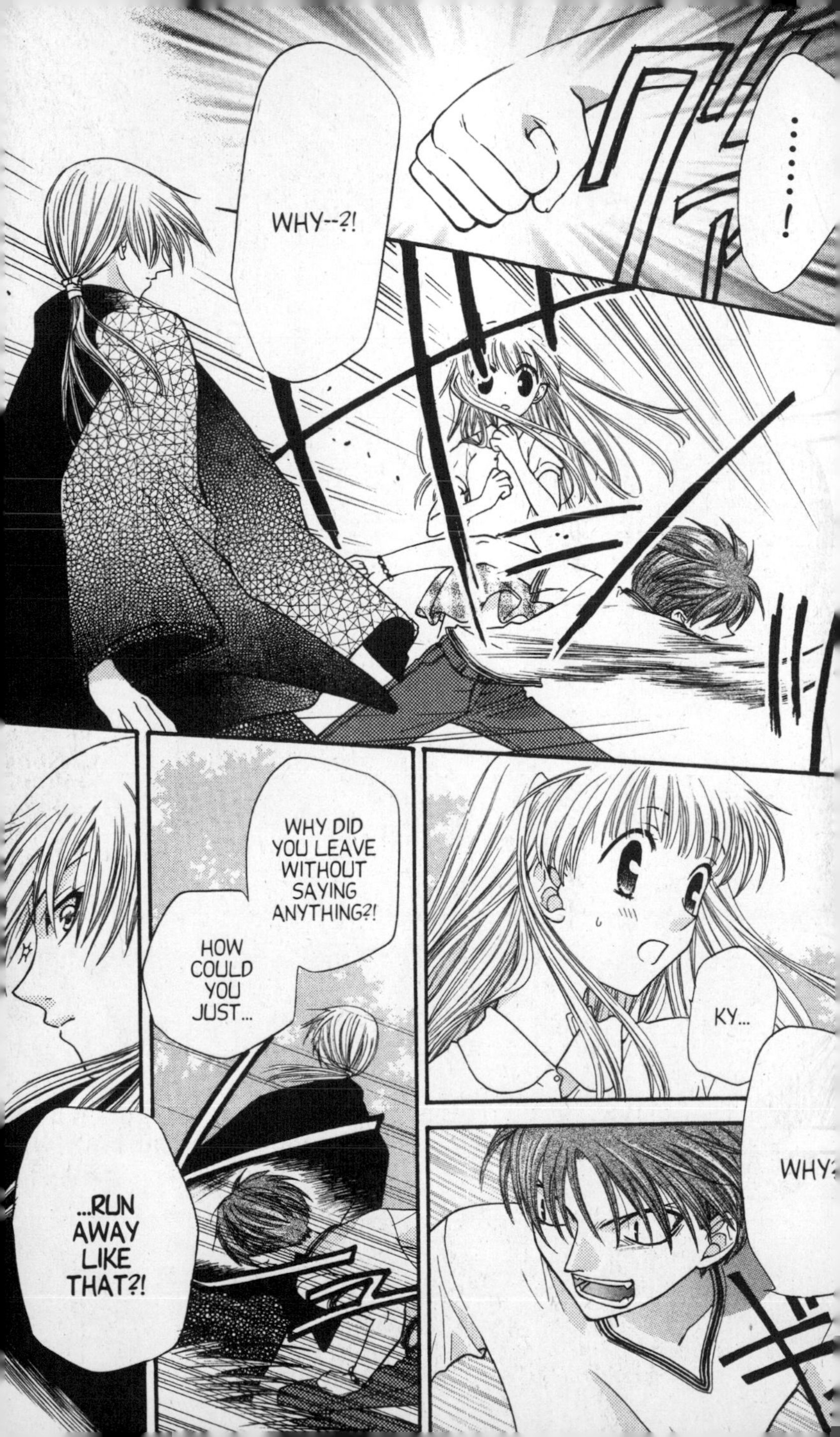

......!
WHY--?!
KY...
WHY?
WHY DID YOU LEAVE WITHOUT SAYING ANYTHING?!
HOW COULD YOU JUST...
...RUN AWAY LIKE THAT?!

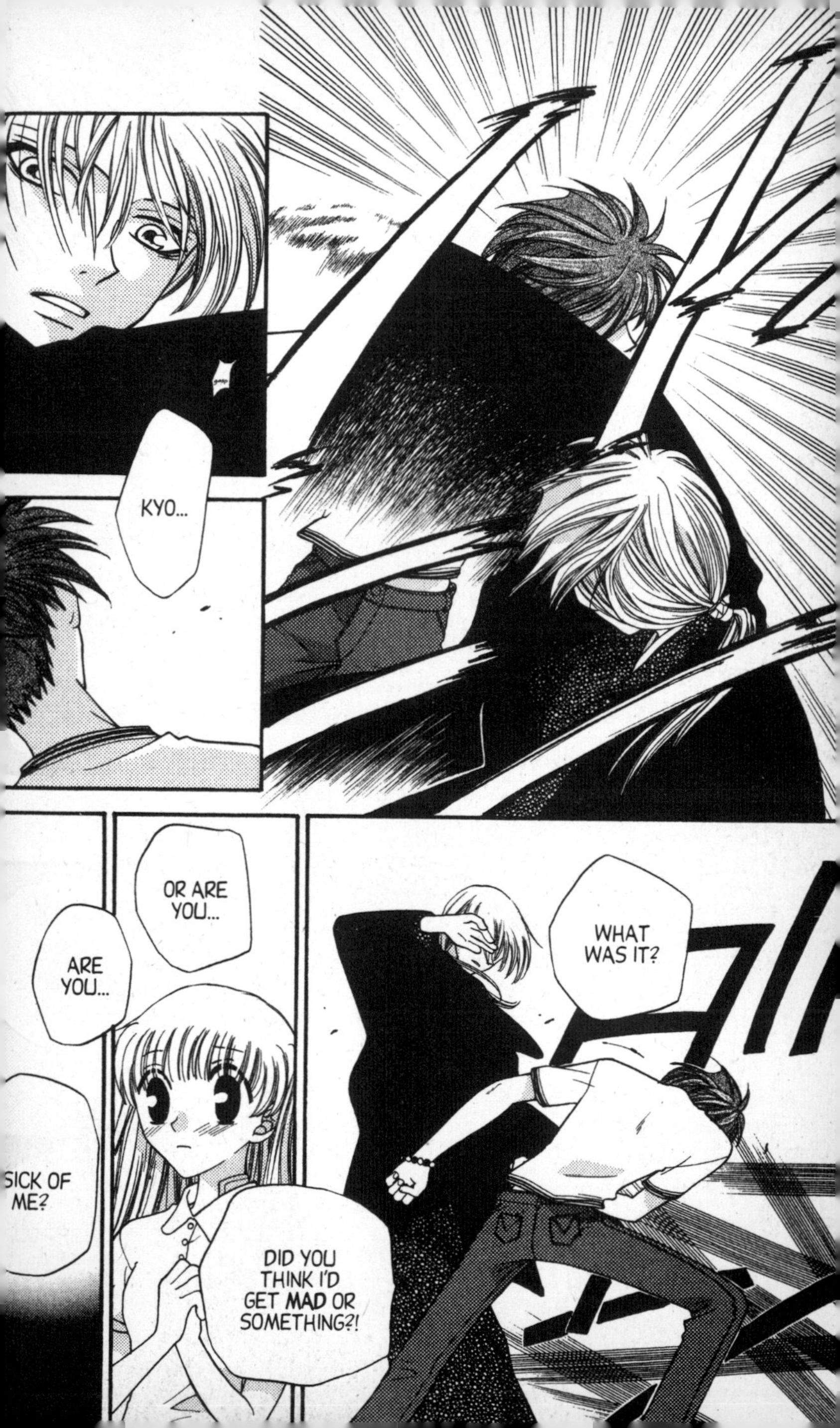
KYO...
WHAT WAS IT?
DID YOU THINK I'D GET MAD OR SOMETHING?!
OR ARE YOU...
ARE YOU...
SICK OF ME?

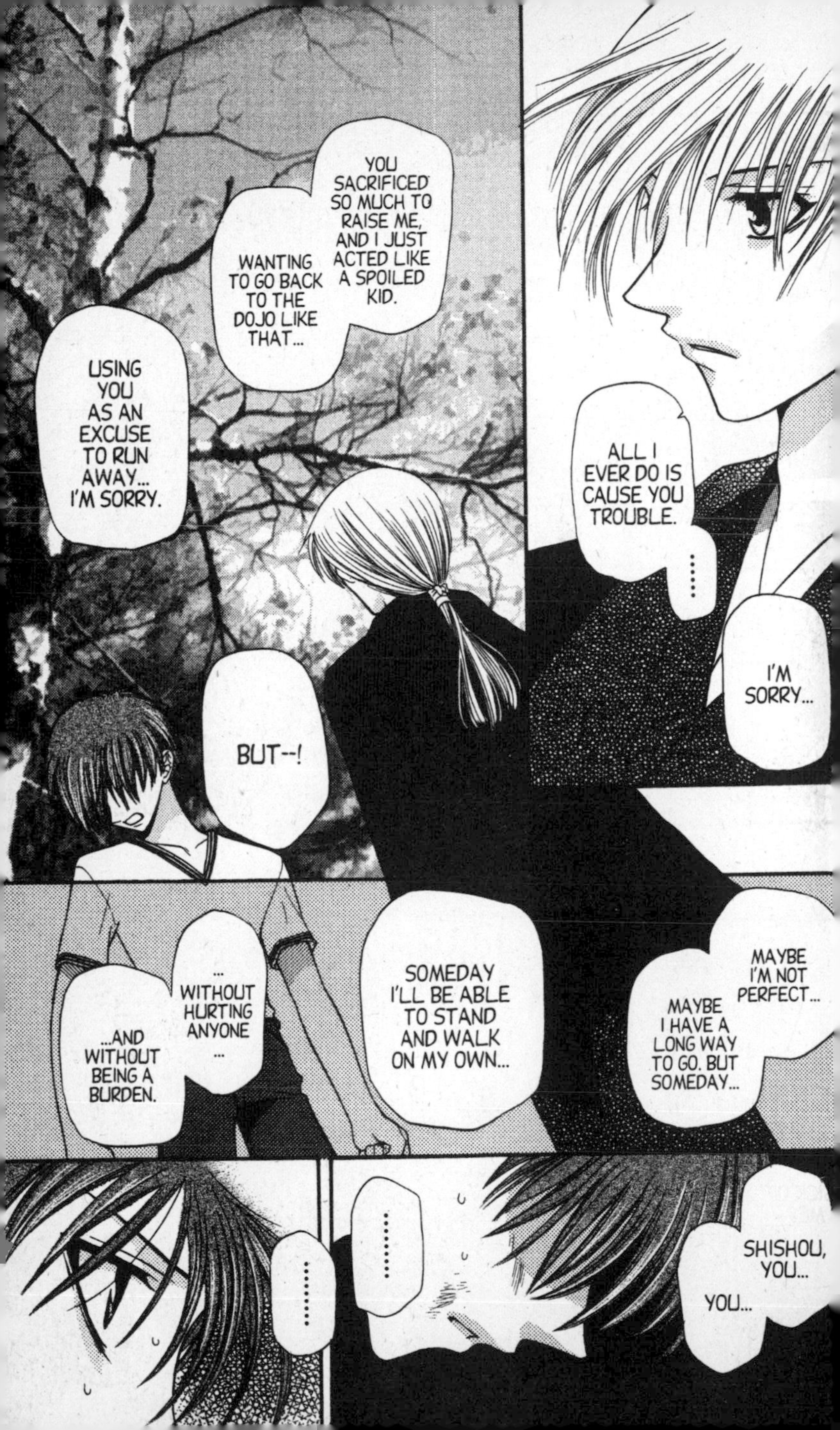
ALL I EVER DO IS CAUSE YOU TROUBLE.
......
I'M SORRY...
YOU SACRIFICED SO MUCH TO RAISE ME, AND I JUST ACTED LIKE A SPOILED KID.
WANTING TO GO BACK TO THE DOJO LIKE THAT...
USING YOU AS AN EXCUSE TO RUN AWAY... I'M SORRY.
BUT--!
MAYBE I'M NOT PERFECT...
MAYBE I HAVE A LONG WAY TO GO. BUT SOMEDAY...
SOMEDAY I'LL BE ABLE TO STAND AND WALK ON MY OWN...
... WITHOUT HURTING ANYONE ...
...AND WITHOUT BEING A BURDEN.
SHISHOU, YOU...
YOU...
......
......

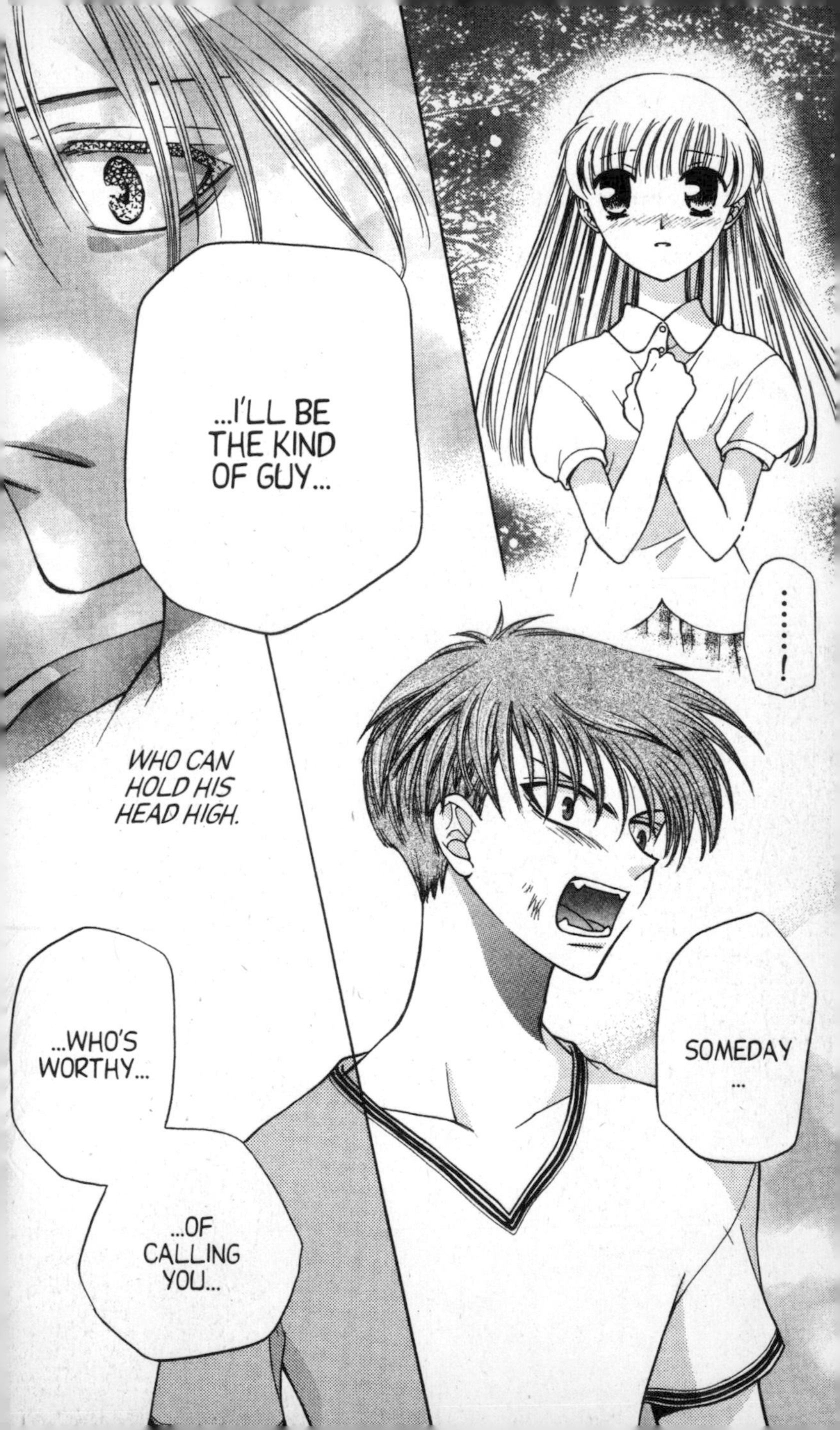
......!
SOMEDAY...
...I'LL BE THE KIND OF GUY...
WHO CAN HOLD HIS HEAD HIGH.
...WHO'S WORTHY...
...OF CALLING YOU...

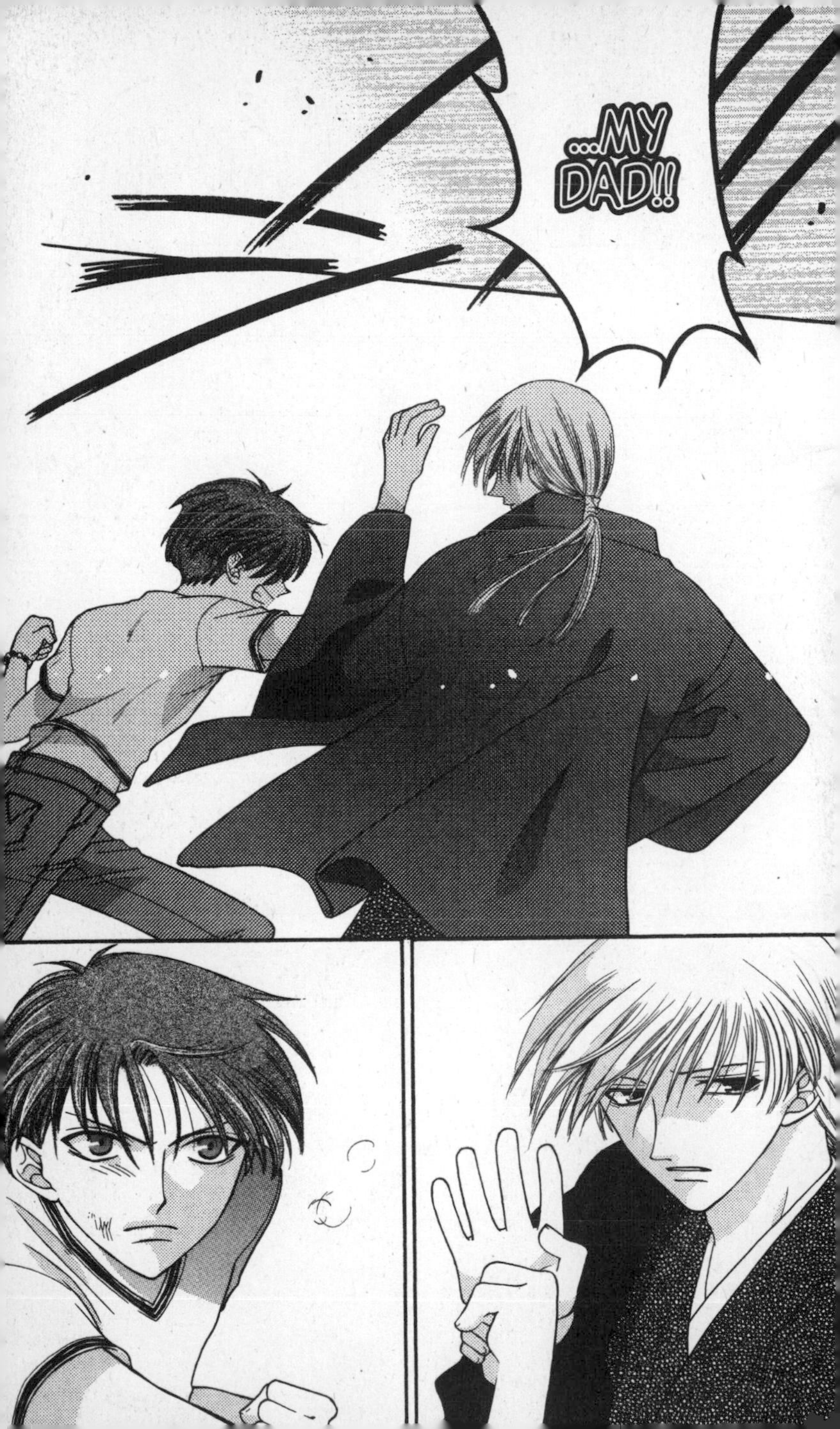
...MY DAD!!

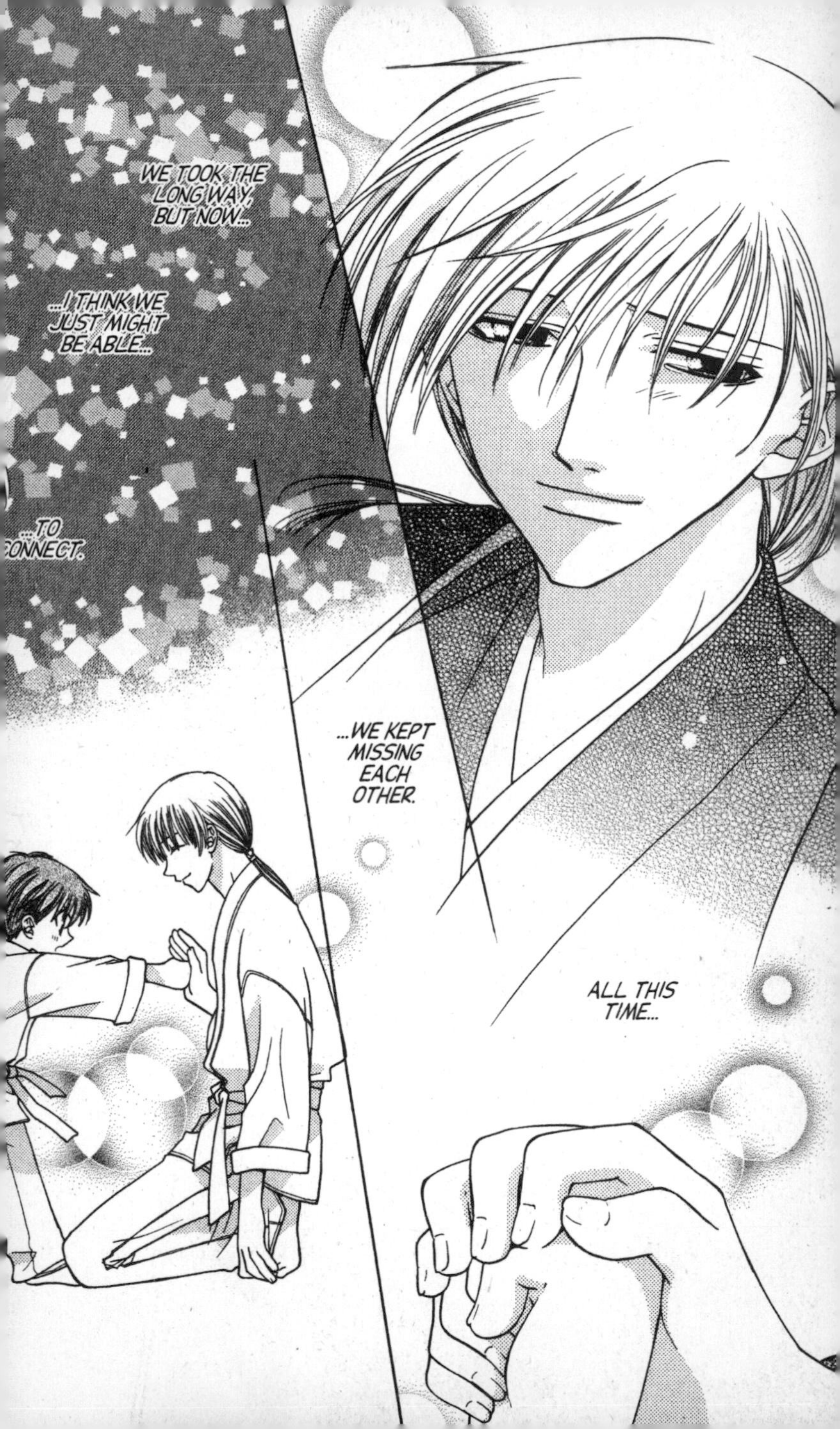
ALL THIS TIME...
...WE KEPT MISSING EACH OTHER.
WE TOOK THE LONG WAY, BUT NOW...
...I THINK WE JUST MIGHT BE ABLE...
...TO CONNECT.

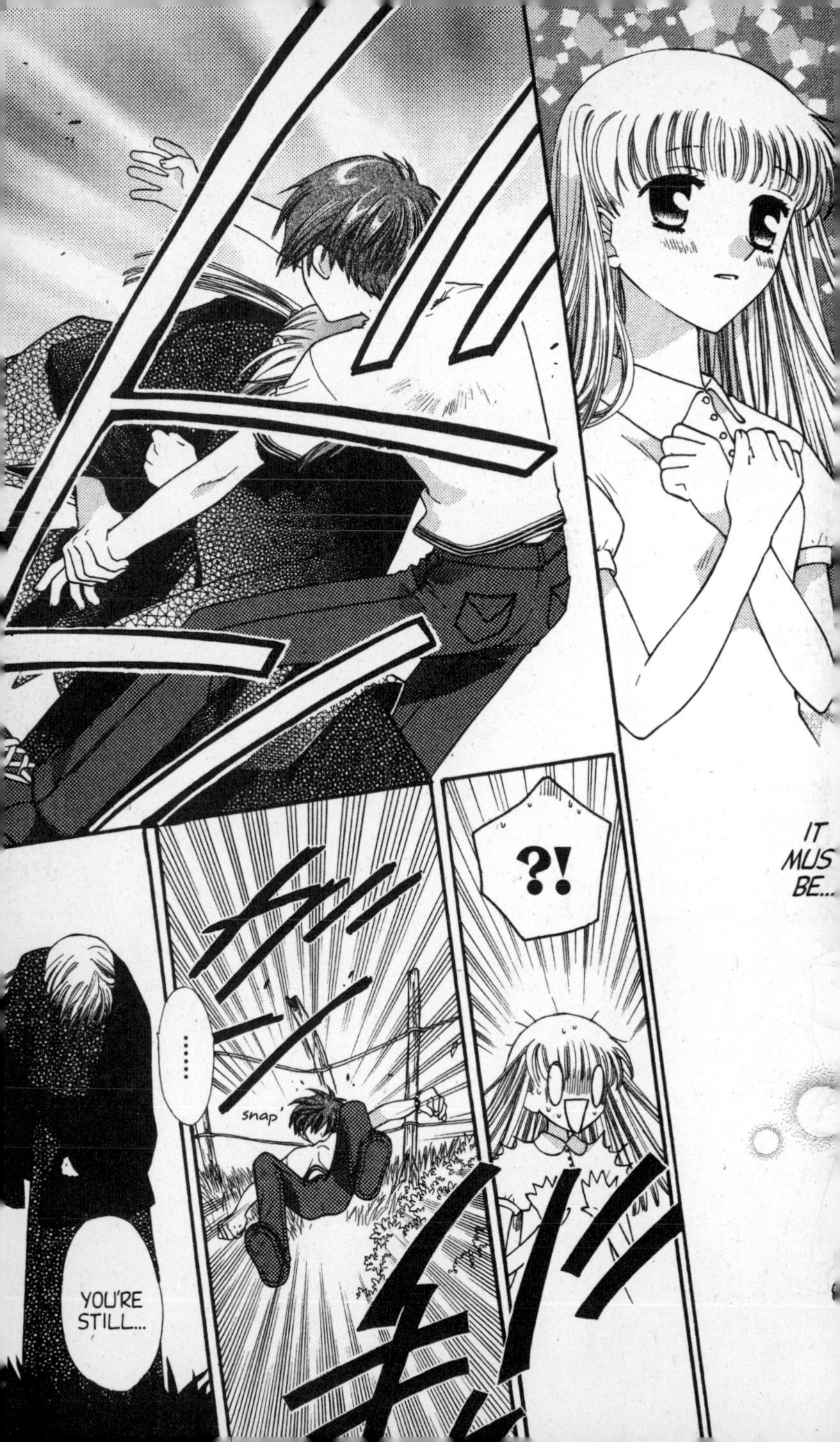
IT MUS BE...
?!
snap
......
YOU'RE STILL...

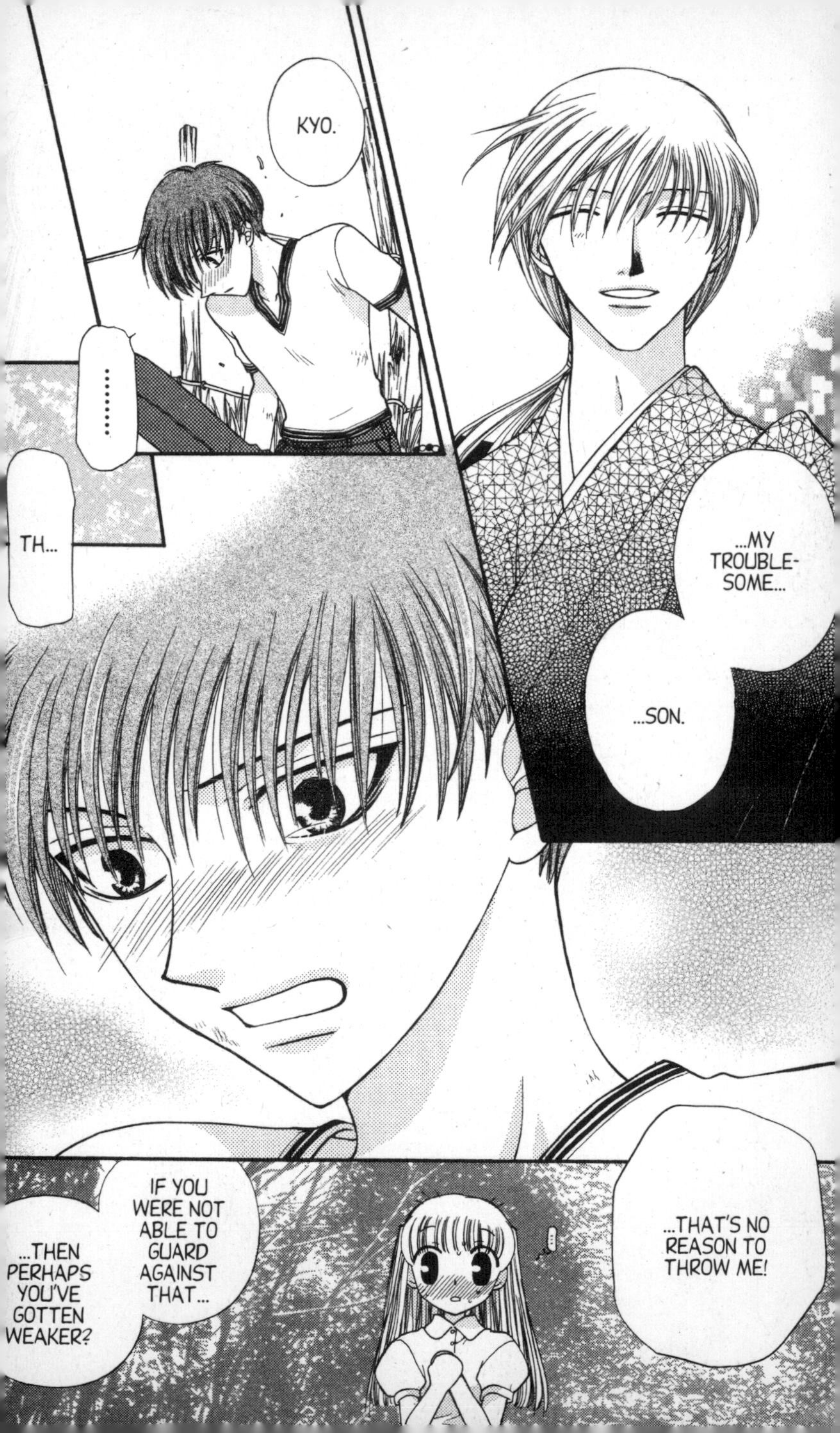
...MY TROUBLE-SOME...
...SON.
KYO.
....
TH...
...THAT'S NO REASON TO THROW ME!
IF YOU WERE NOT ABLE TO GUARD AGAINST THAT...
...THEN PERHAPS YOU'VE GOTTEN WEAKER?
...

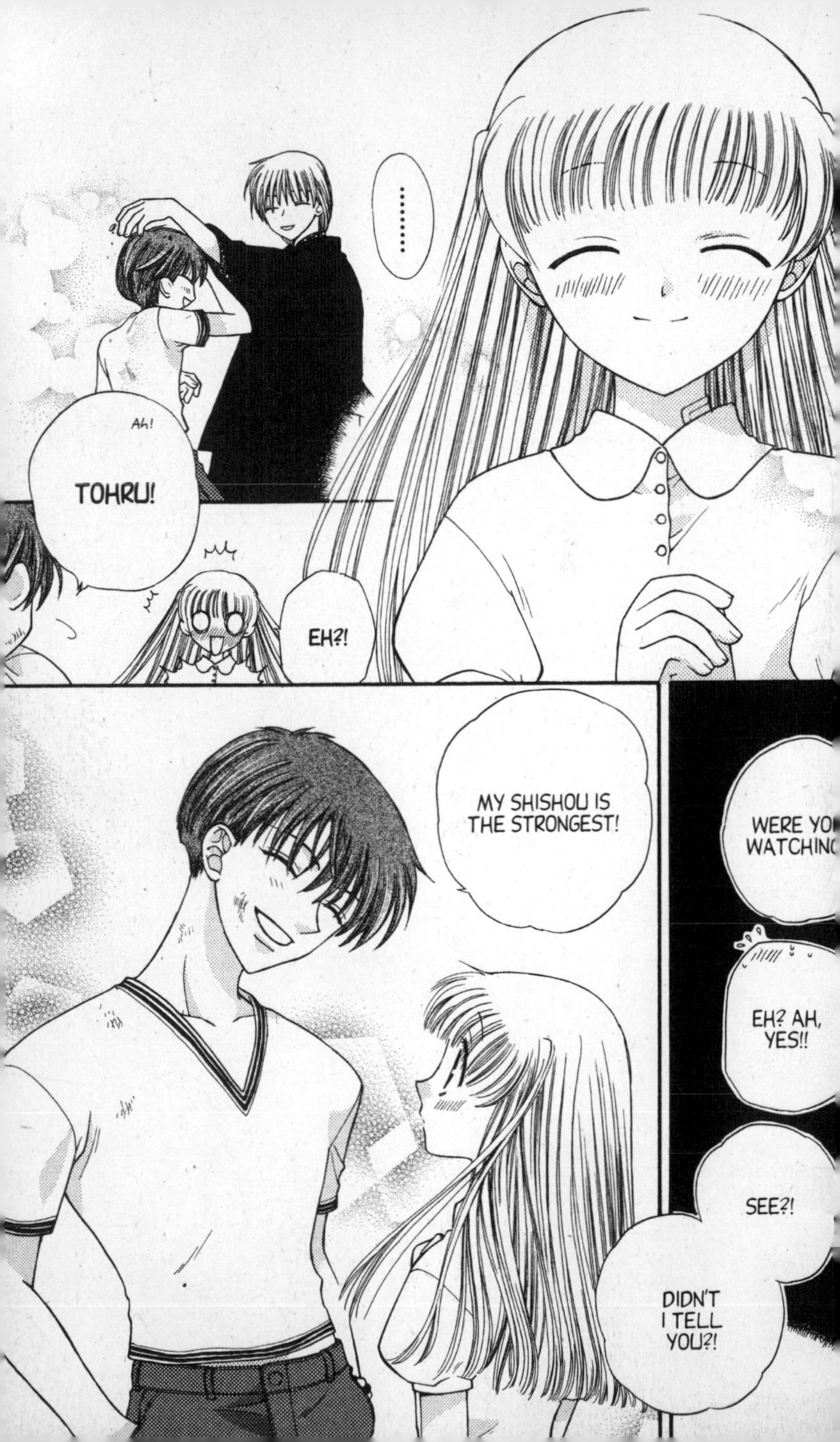
......
Ah!
TOHRU!
EH?!
WERE YO
WATCHIN
EH? AH, YES!!
SEE?!
DIDN'T I TELL YOU?!
MY SHISHOU IS THE STRONGEST!

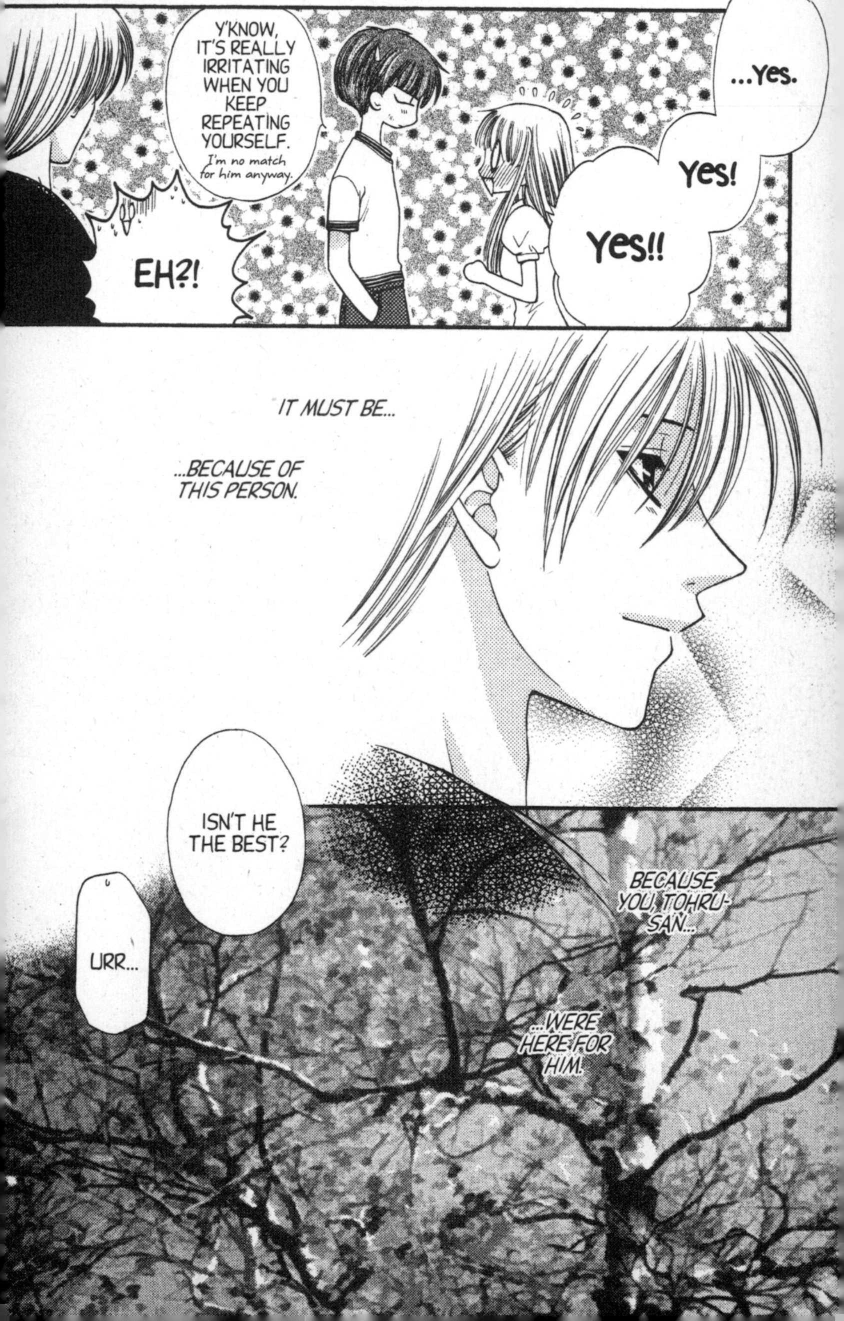
...Yes.
Yes!
Yes!!
Y'KNOW, IT'S REALLY IRRITATING WHEN YOU KEEP REPEATING YOURSELF.
I'm no match for him anyway.
EH?!
IT MUST BE...
...BECAUSE OF THIS PERSON.
BECAUSE YOU, TOHRU-SAN...
...WERE HERE FOR HIM.
ISN'T HE THE BEST?
URR...

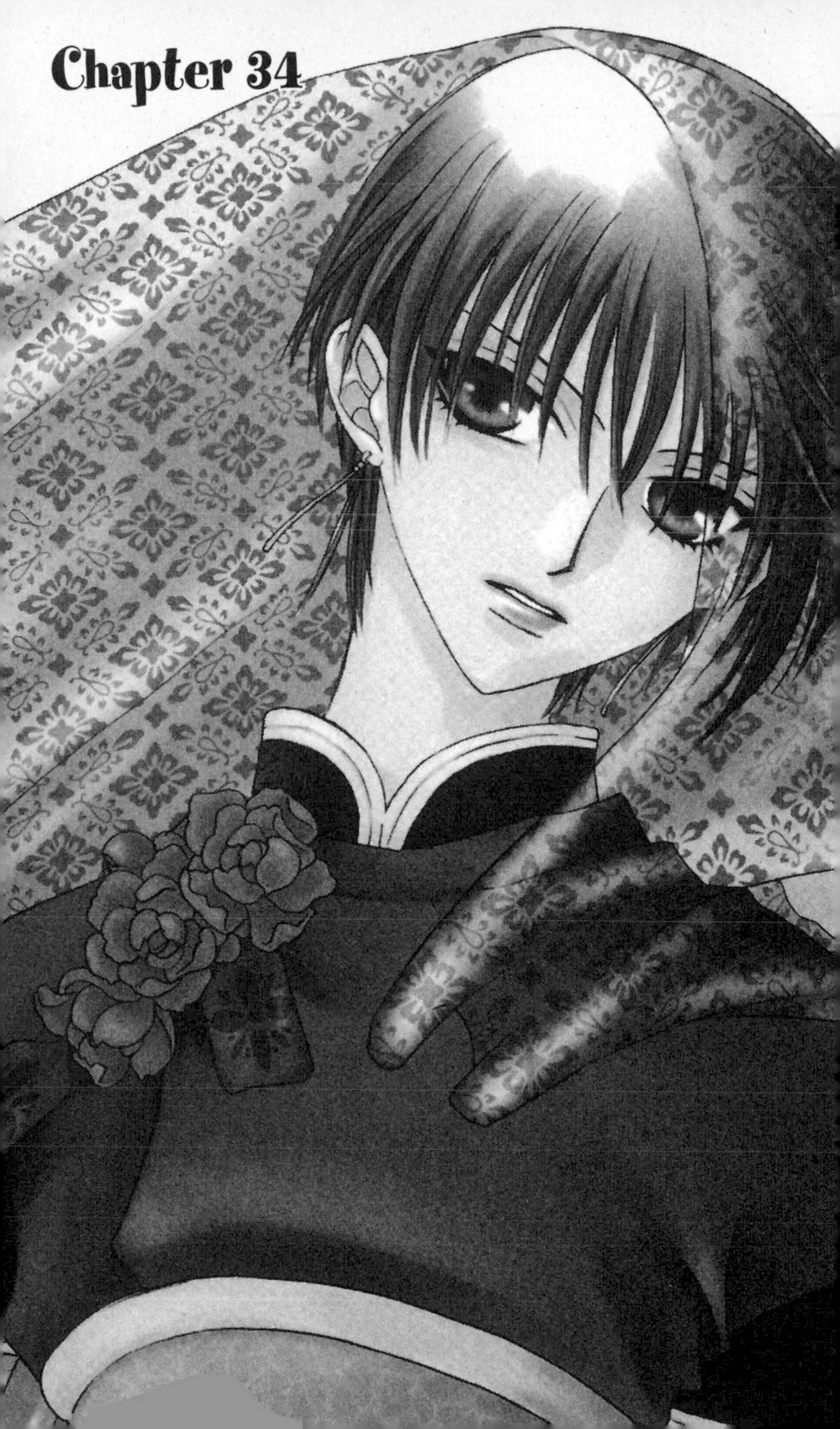
Chapter 34

ople say...

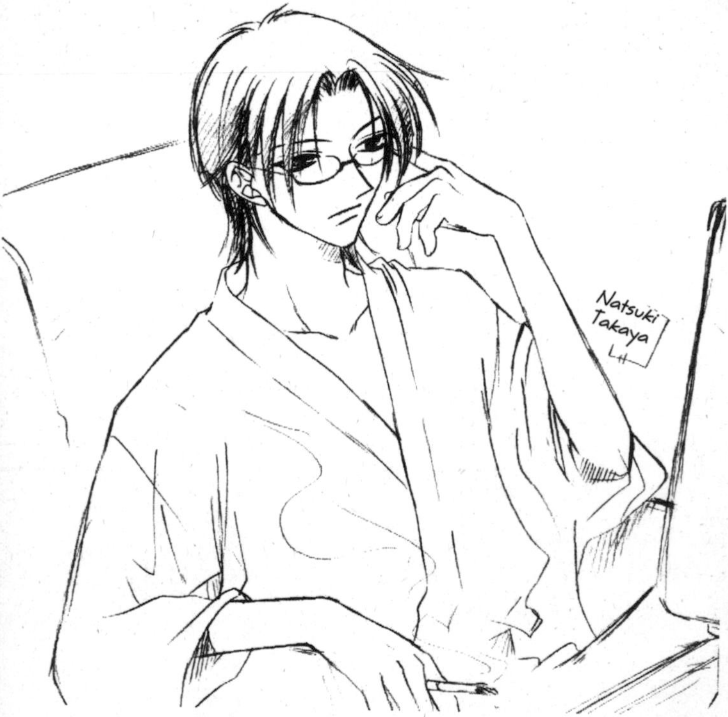
Natsuki Takaya

Shigure—he looks like he's worrying, but Shigure never worries. I look forward to drawing him more deeply. (With this and that...) No, but I like to draw all the characters. I might want to draw that soon! (laugh)

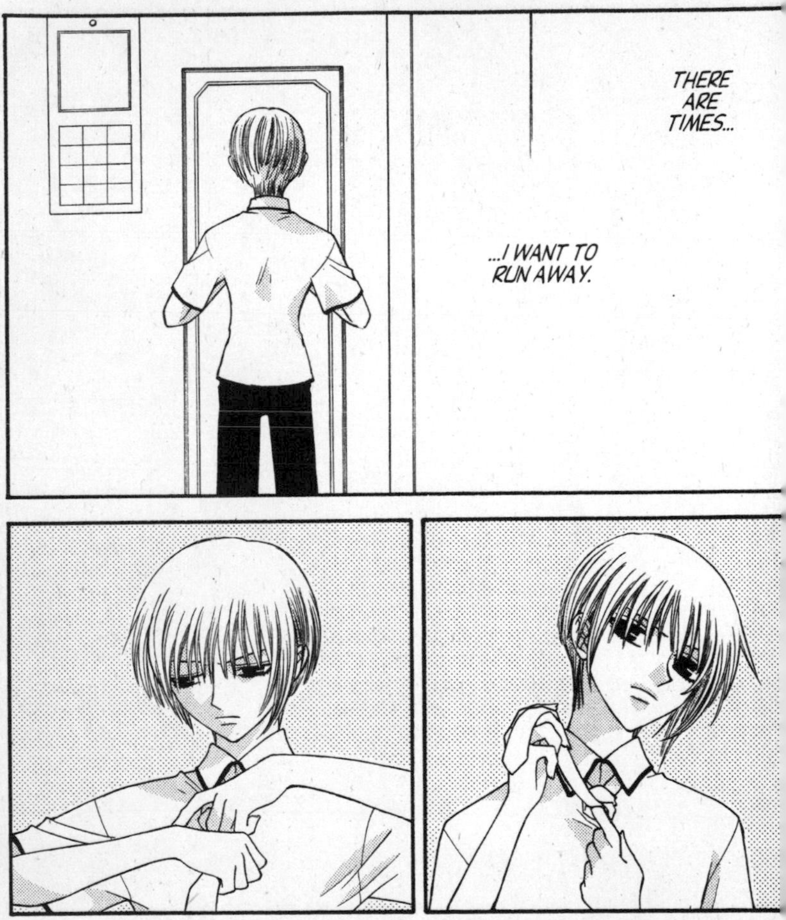
THERE ARE TIMES...
...I WANT TO RUN AWAY.

ULTRA SPECIAL BLAH BLAH BLAH 3

Aaya is worrying about his brother in his own special way (laugh). holding a crab claw... By the way, the colors are all secretly unified. There's no really deep meaning in it.

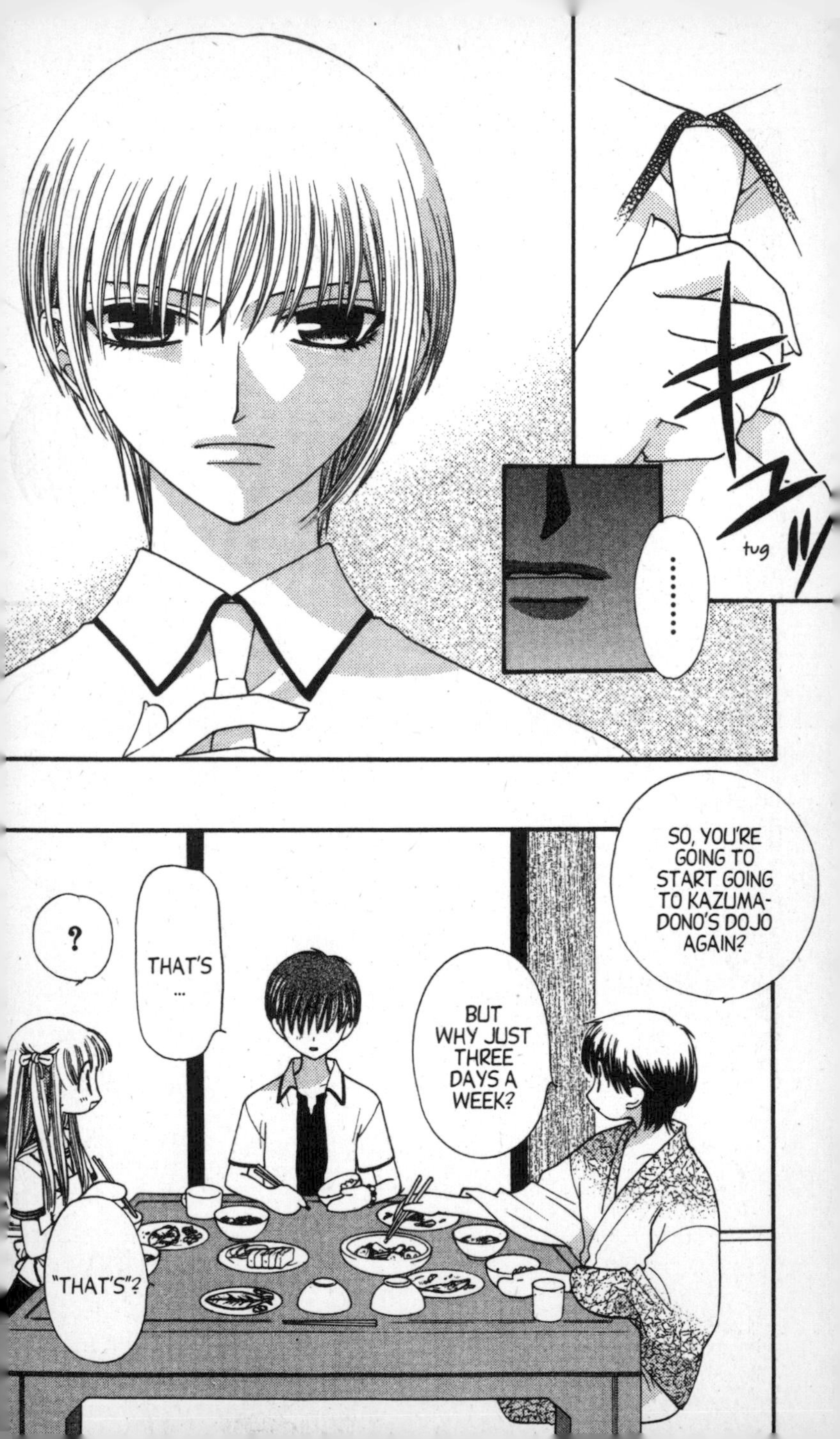
キュッ
tug
....
SO, YOU'RE GOING TO START GOING TO KAZUMA-DONO'S DOJO AGAIN?
BUT WHY JUST THREE DAYS A WEEK?
THAT'S ...
?
"THAT'S"?

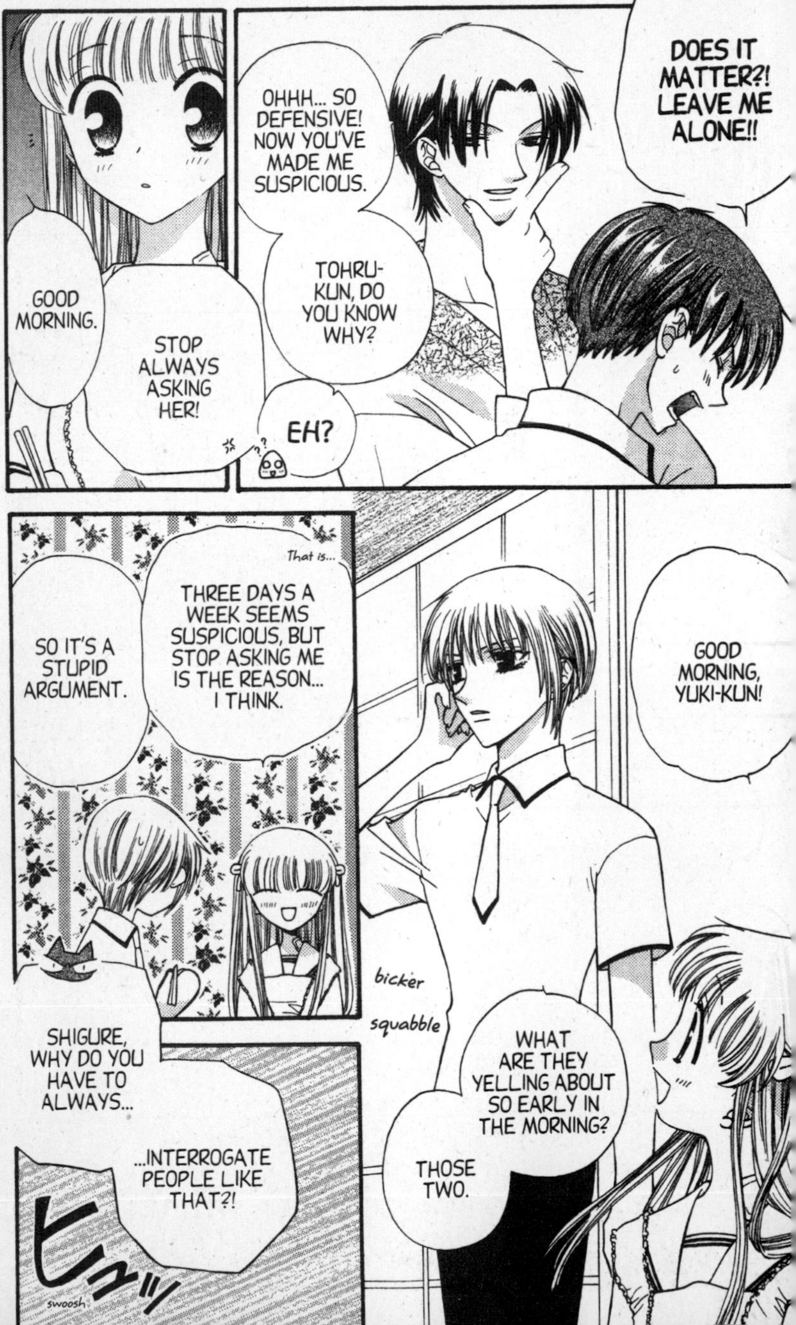
DOES IT MATTER?! LEAVE ME ALONE!!
OHHH... SO DEFENSIVE! NOW YOU'VE MADE ME SUSPICIOUS.
TOHRU-KUN, DO YOU KNOW WHY?
EH?
STOP ALWAYS ASKING HER!
GOOD MORNING.
GOOD MORNING, YUKI-KUN!
bicker
squabble
WHAT ARE THEY YELLING ABOUT SO EARLY IN THE MORNING?
THOSE TWO.
That is...
THREE DAYS A WEEK SEEMS SUSPICIOUS, BUT STOP ASKING ME IS THE REASON... I THINK.
SO IT'S A STUPID ARGUMENT.
SHIGURE, WHY DO YOU HAVE TO ALWAYS...
...INTERROGATE PEOPLE LIKE THAT?!
swoosh

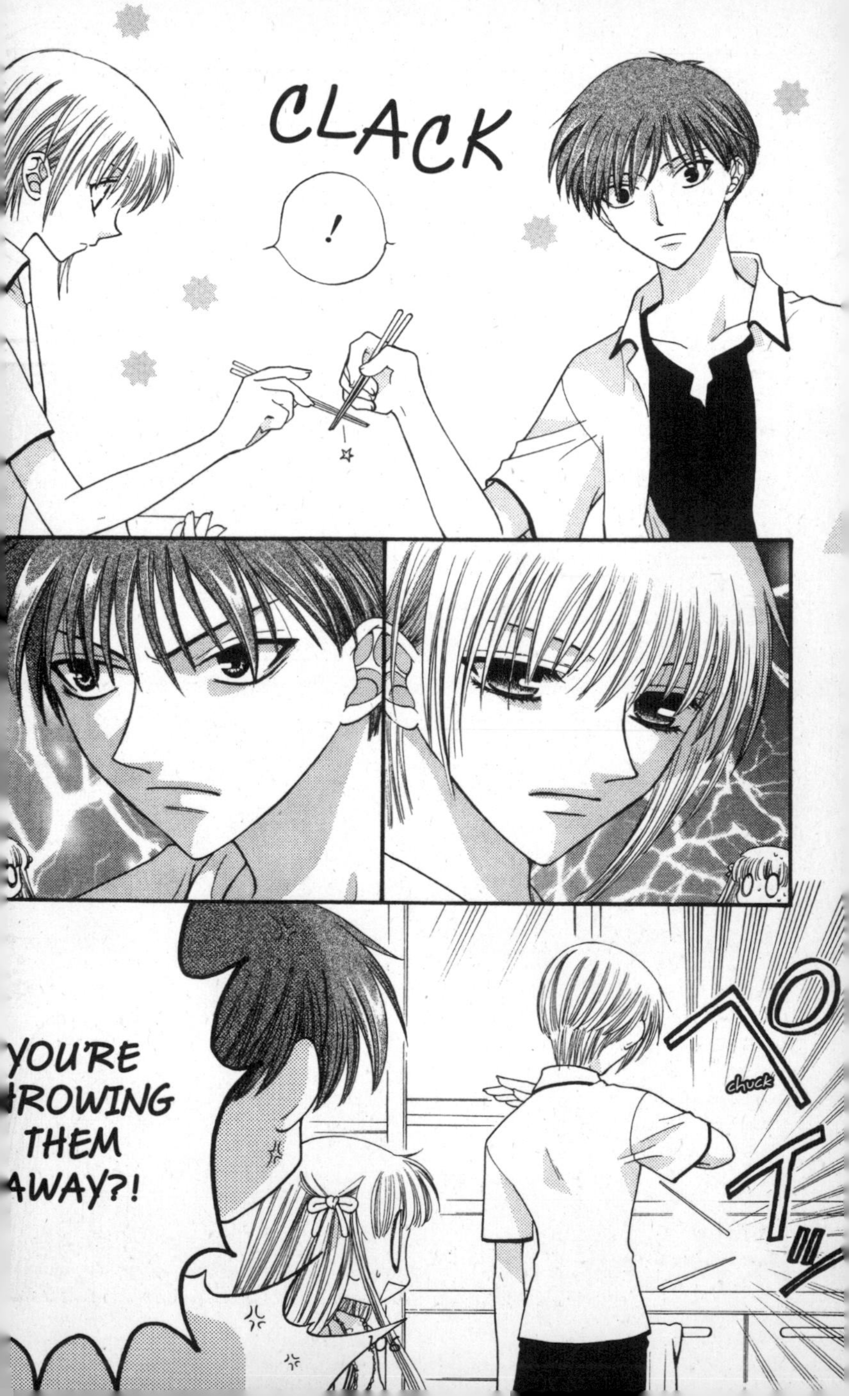
CLACK
!
chuck
YOU'RE ROWING THEM AWAY?!

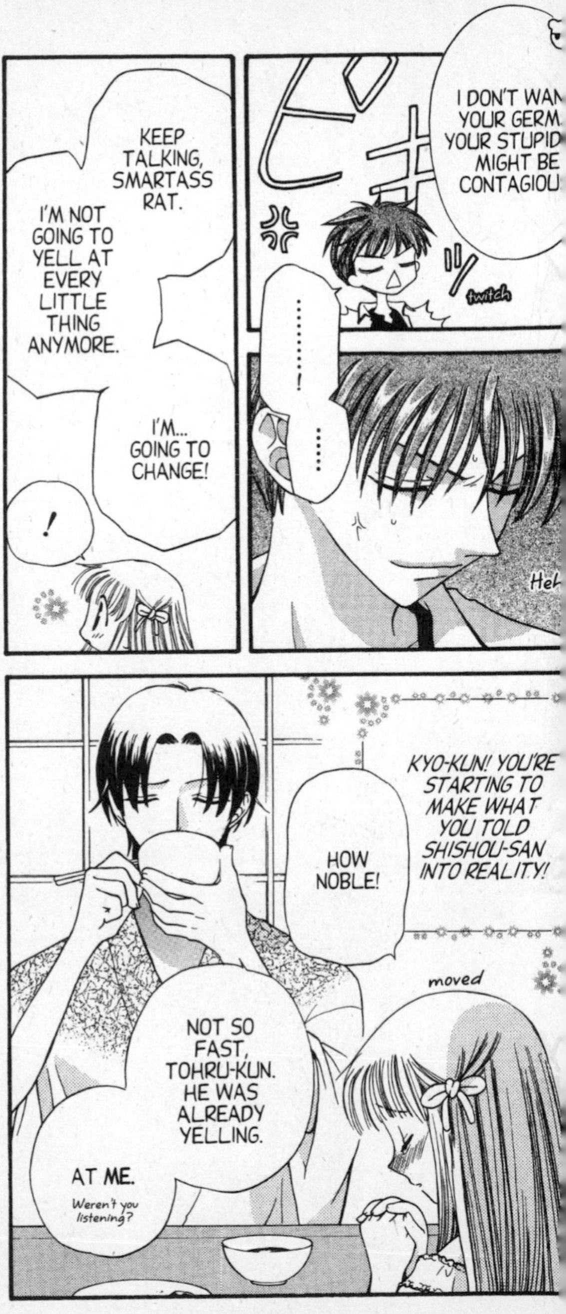
I DON'T WAN YOUR GERM YOUR STUPID MIGHT BE CONTAGIOU
twitch
......!
......
Heh
KEEP TALKING, SMARTASS RAT.
I'M NOT GOING TO YELL AT EVERY LITTLE THING ANYMORE.
I'M... GOING TO CHANGE!
!
KYO-KUN! YOU'RE STARTING TO MAKE WHAT YOU TOLD SHISHOU-SAN INTO REALITY!
HOW NOBLE!
moved
NOT SO FAST, TOHRU-KUN. HE WAS ALREADY YELLING.
AT ME.
Weren't you listening?

Fruits Basket 6 Part 5:

Ahh, I can't move my hand anymore... I have to go to the doctor. *VALKYRIE PROFILE* is a wonderful game, isn't it?" I thought. No, oh how do I explain it, the system and everything... come to think of it, I don't really have anything to say about it. When Lucian dropped a broken crystal (it ended up broken), I got chills. That may not have anything to do with it, though. (laugh) Now that I think of it, I keep all the games I've beaten. All those jewel cases and cartridges, you know? They're taking up so much space it's not even funny! I don't know what to do with them. I just can't throw them away. It's a conundrum.

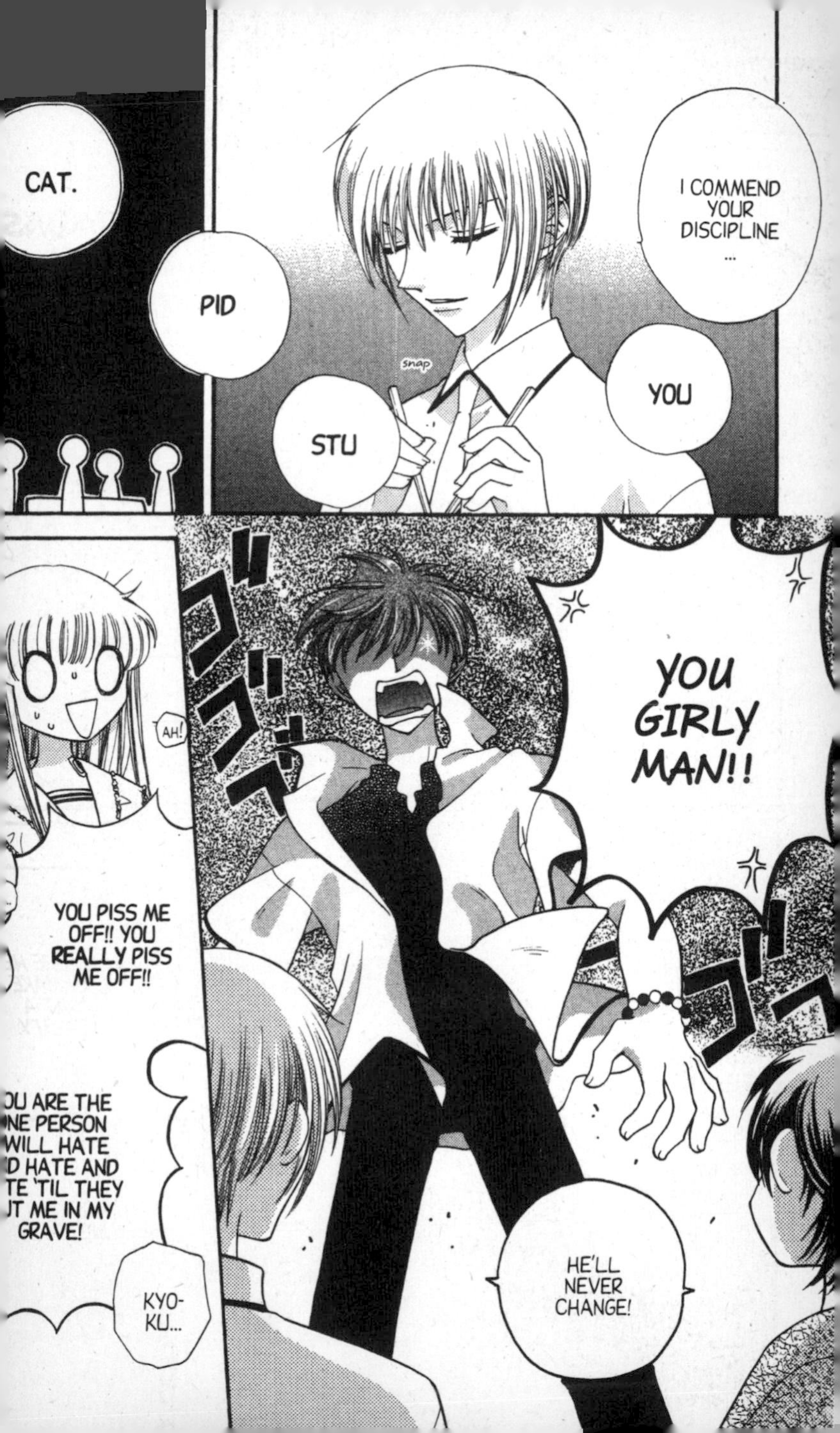
I COMMEND YOUR DISCIPLINE ...
YOU
STU
snap
PID
CAT.
YOU GIRLY MAN!!
HE'LL NEVER CHANGE!
AH!
YOU PISS ME OFF!! YOU REALLY PISS ME OFF!!
OU ARE THE
NE PERSON
WILL HATE
D HATE AND
TE 'TIL THEY
JT ME IN MY
GRAVE!
KYO-KU...

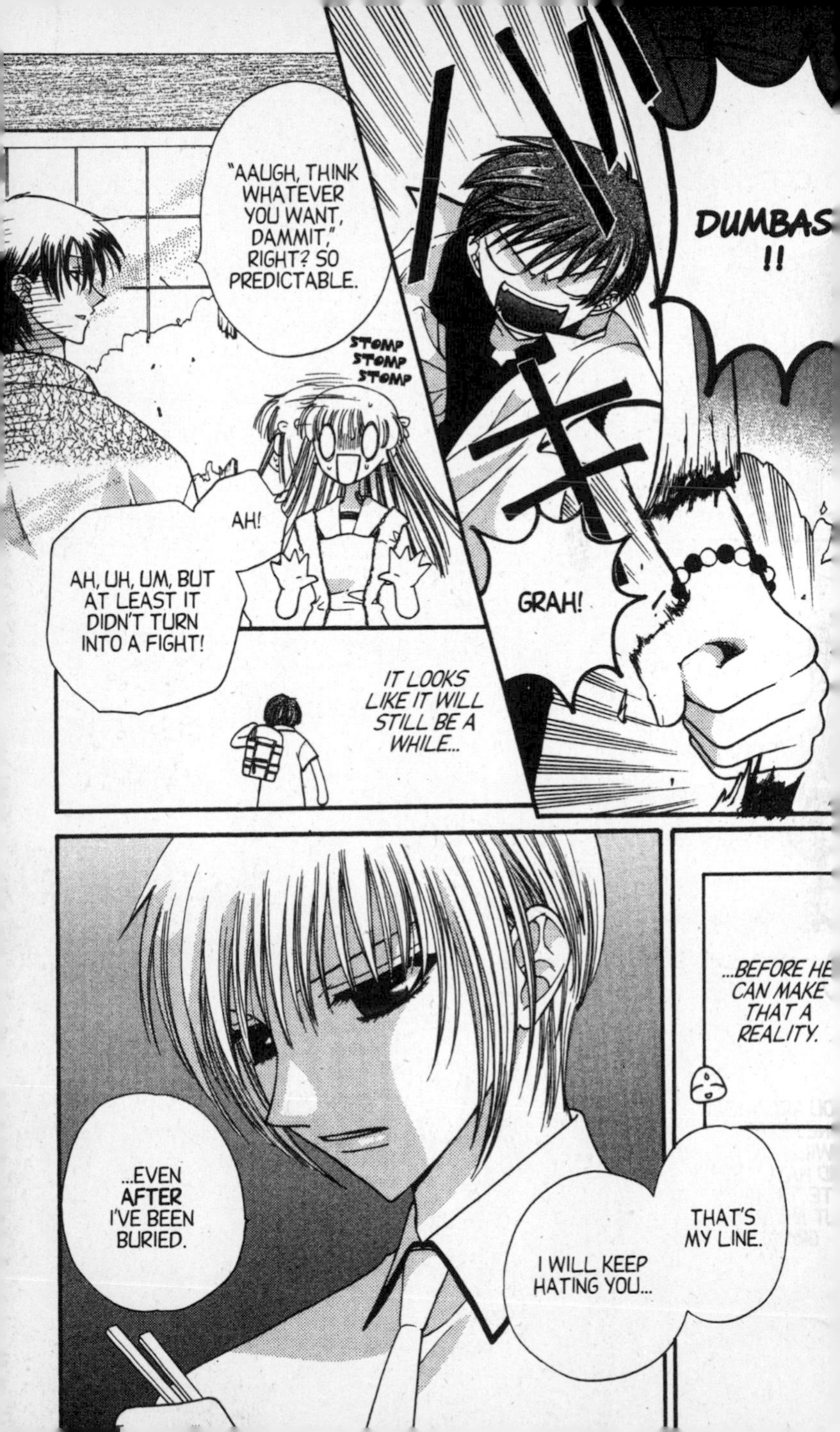
DUMBAS !!
GRAH!
"AAUGH, THINK WHATEVER YOU WANT, DAMMIT," RIGHT? SO PREDICTABLE.
STOMP STOMP STOMP
AH!
AH, UH, UM, BUT AT LEAST IT DIDN'T TURN INTO A FIGHT!
IT LOOKS LIKE IT WILL STILL BE A WHILE...
...BEFORE HE CAN MAKE THAT A REALITY.
THAT'S MY LINE.
I WILL KEEP HATING YOU...
...EVEN AFTER I'VE BEEN BURIED.

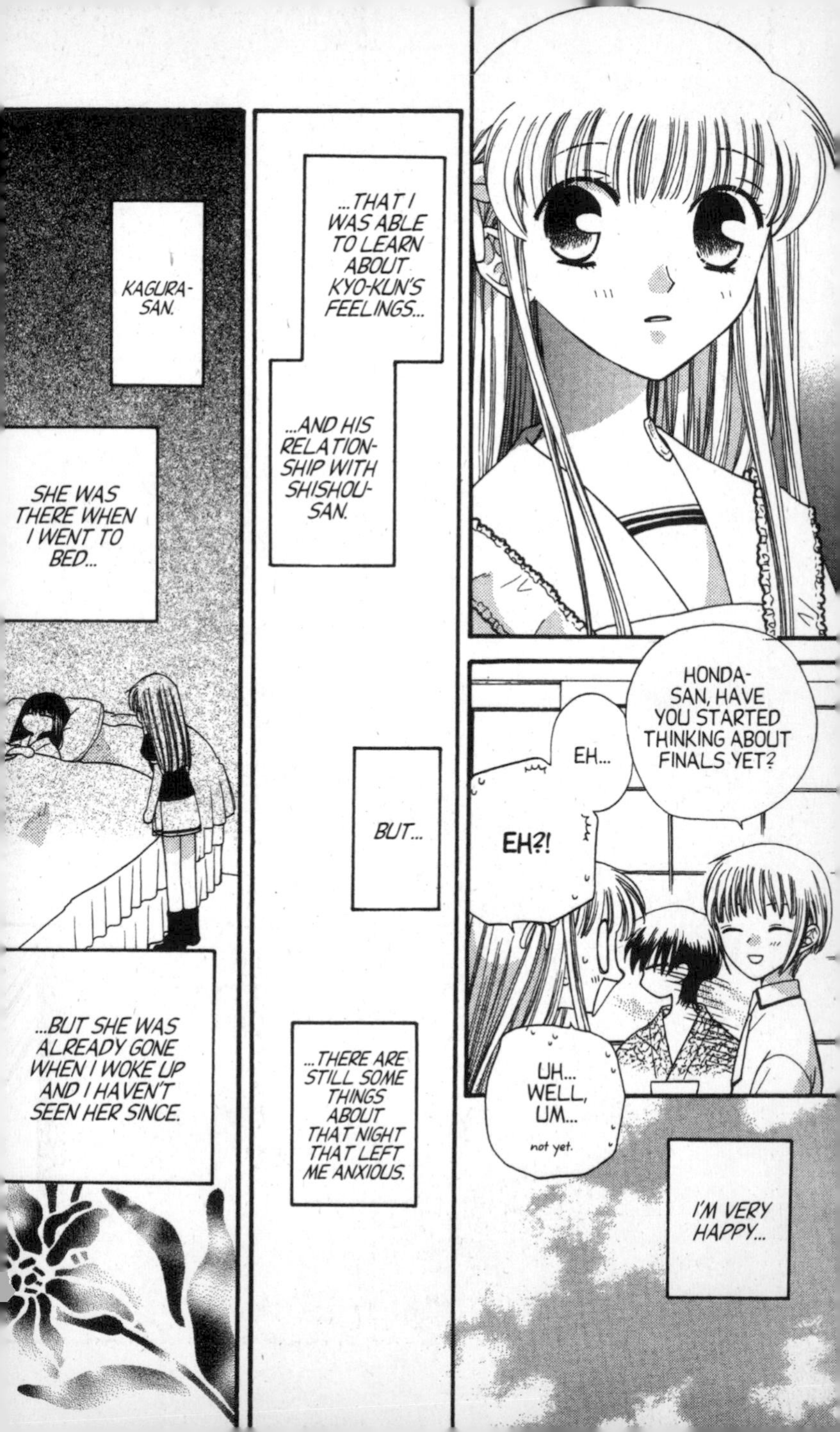
HONDA-SAN, HAVE YOU STARTED THINKING ABOUT FINALS YET?
EH...
EH?!
UH... WELL, UM...
not yet.
I'M VERY HAPPY...
...THAT I WAS ABLE TO LEARN ABOUT KYO-KUN'S FEELINGS...
...AND HIS RELATIONSHIP WITH SHISHOU-SAN.
BUT...
...THERE ARE STILL SOME THINGS ABOUT THAT NIGHT THAT LEFT ME ANXIOUS.
KAGURA-SAN.
SHE WAS THERE WHEN I WENT TO BED...
...BUT SHE WAS ALREADY GONE WHEN I WOKE UP AND I HAVEN'T SEEN HER SINCE.

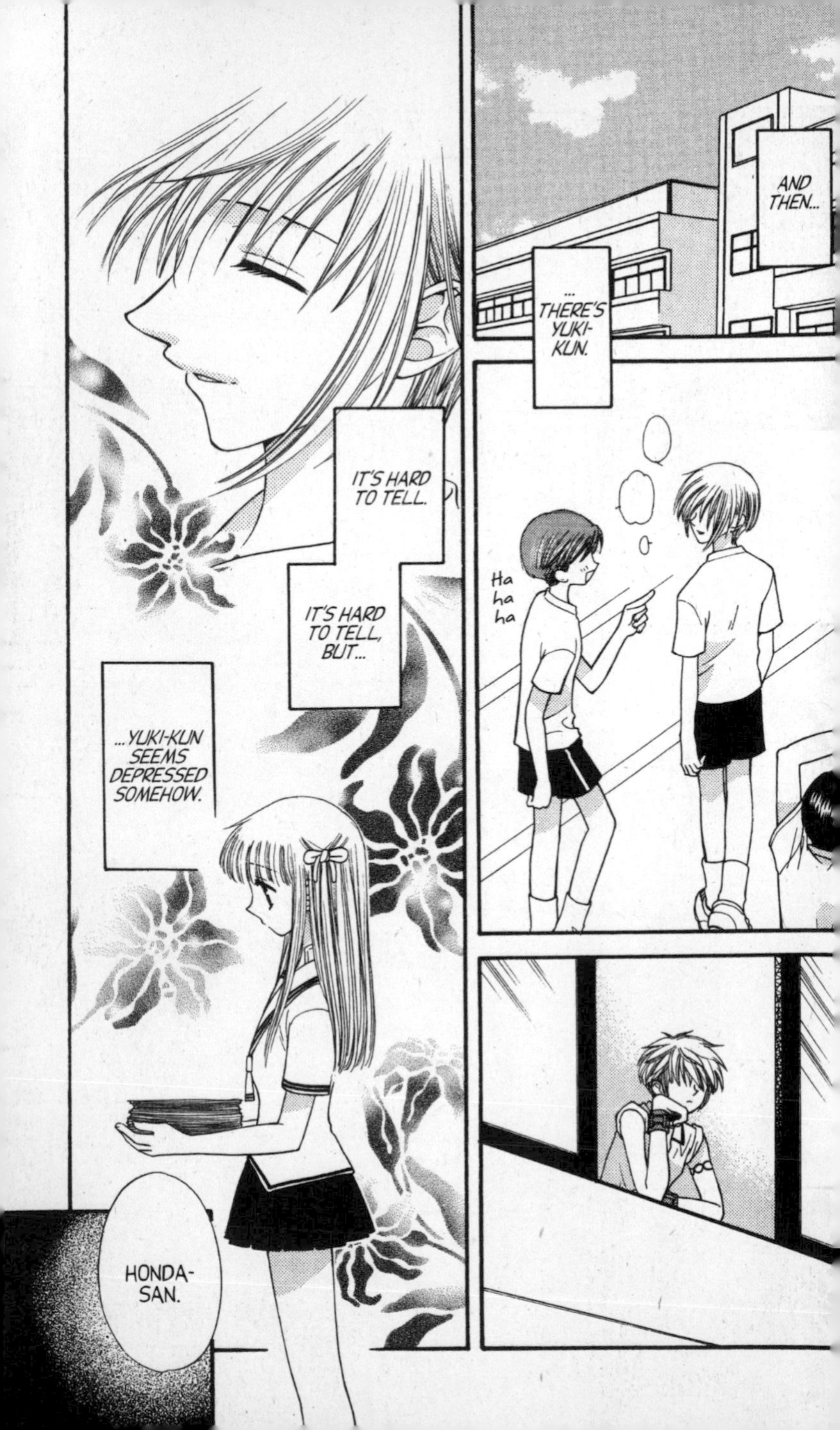
AND THEN...
...THERE'S YUKI-KUN.
Ha ha ha
IT'S HARD TO TELL.
IT'S HARD TO TELL, BUT...
...YUKI-KUN SEEMS DEPRESSED SOMEHOW.
HONDA-SAN.

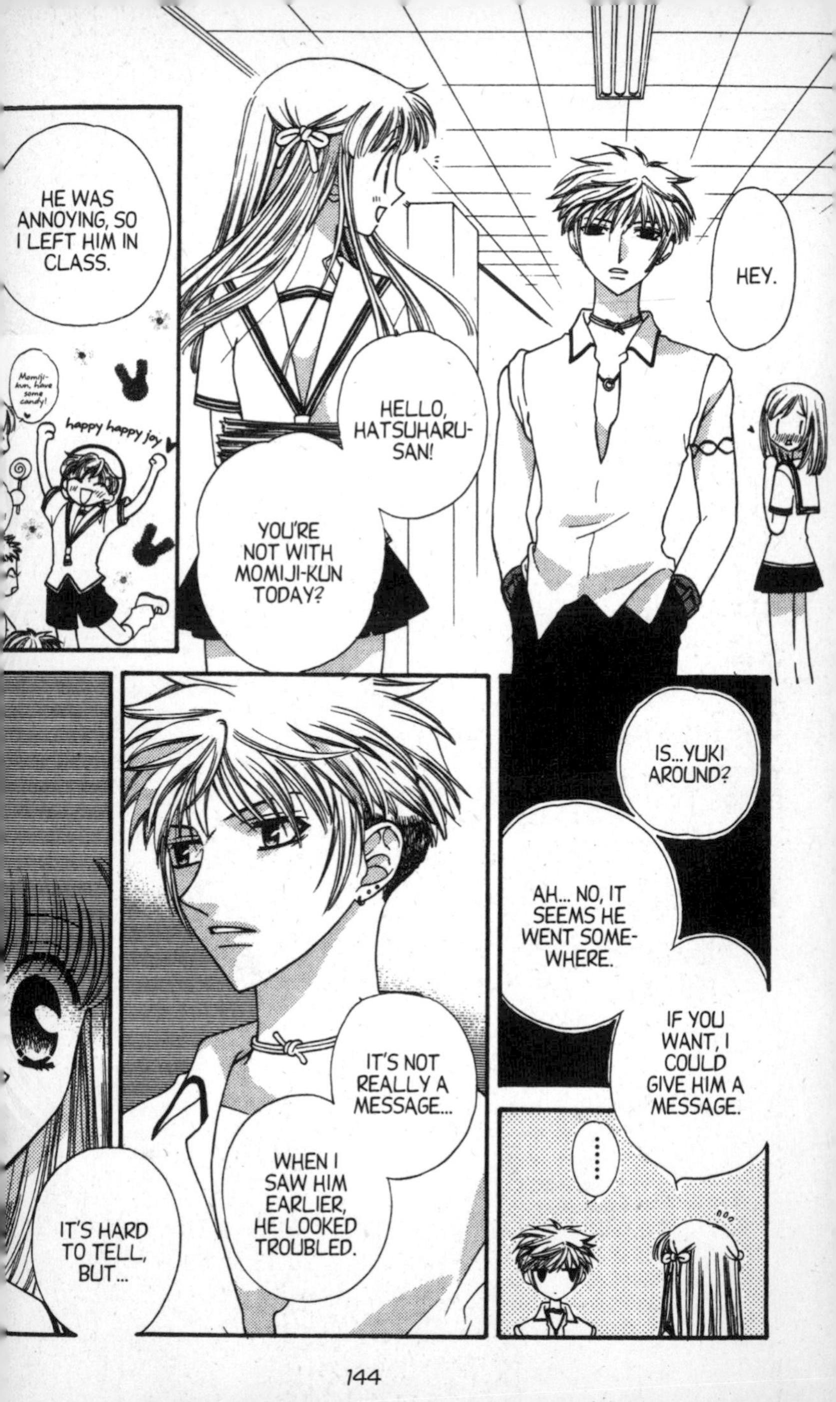
HEY.
HELLO, HATSUHARU-SAN!
YOU'RE NOT WITH MOMIJI-KUN TODAY?
HE WAS ANNOYING, SO I LEFT HIM IN CLASS.
Momiji-kun, have some candy!
happy happy joy
IS...YUKI AROUND?
AH... NO, IT SEEMS HE WENT SOMEWHERE.
IF YOU WANT, I COULD GIVE HIM A MESSAGE.
......
IT'S NOT REALLY A MESSAGE...
WHEN I SAW HIM EARLIER, HE LOOKED TROUBLED.
IT'S HARD TO TELL, BUT...

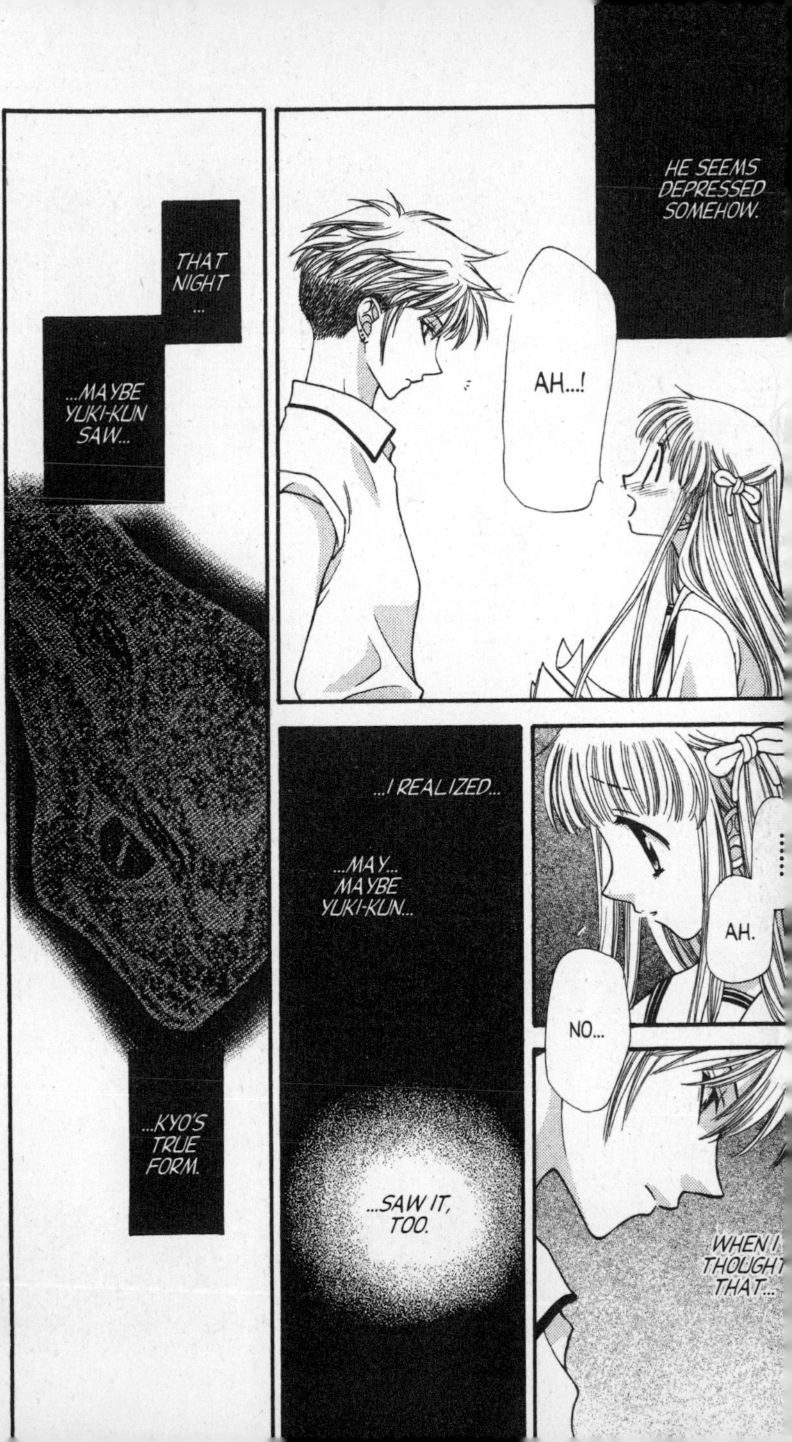
HE SEEMS DEPRESSED SOMEHOW.
AH...!
AH.
NO...
WHEN I THOUGHT THAT...
...I REALIZED...
...MAY... MAYBE YUKI-KUN...
...SAW IT, TOO.
THAT NIGHT...
...MAYBE YUKI-KUN SAW...
...KYO'S TRUE FORM.

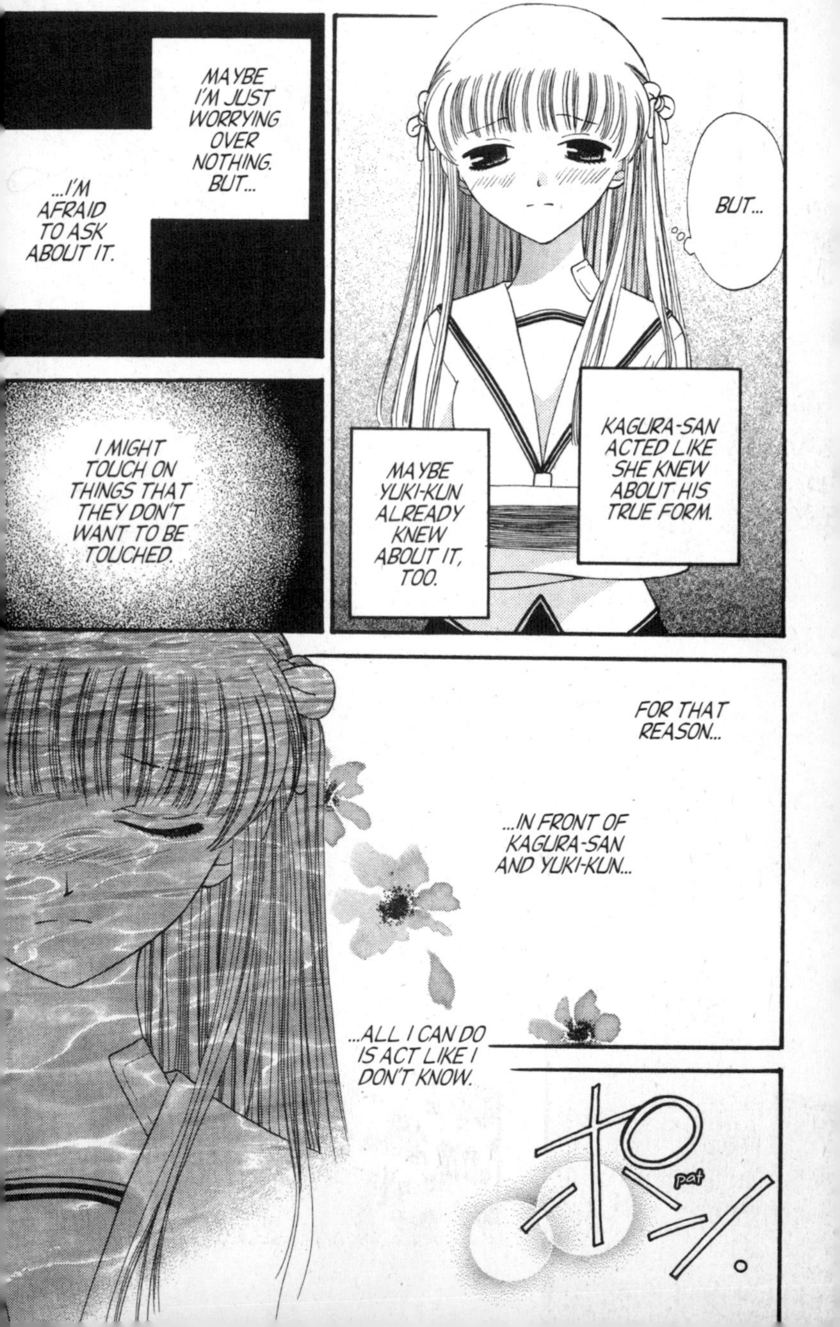
BUT...
KAGURA-SAN ACTED LIKE SHE KNEW ABOUT HIS TRUE FORM.
MAYBE YUKI-KUN ALREADY KNEW ABOUT IT, TOO.
MAYBE I'M JUST WORRYING OVER NOTHING. BUT...
...I'M AFRAID TO ASK ABOUT IT.
I MIGHT TOUCH ON THINGS THAT THEY DON'T WANT TO BE TOUCHED.
FOR THAT REASON...
...IN FRONT OF KAGURA-SAN AND YUKI-KUN...
...ALL I CAN DO IS ACT LIKE I DON'T KNOW.
pat

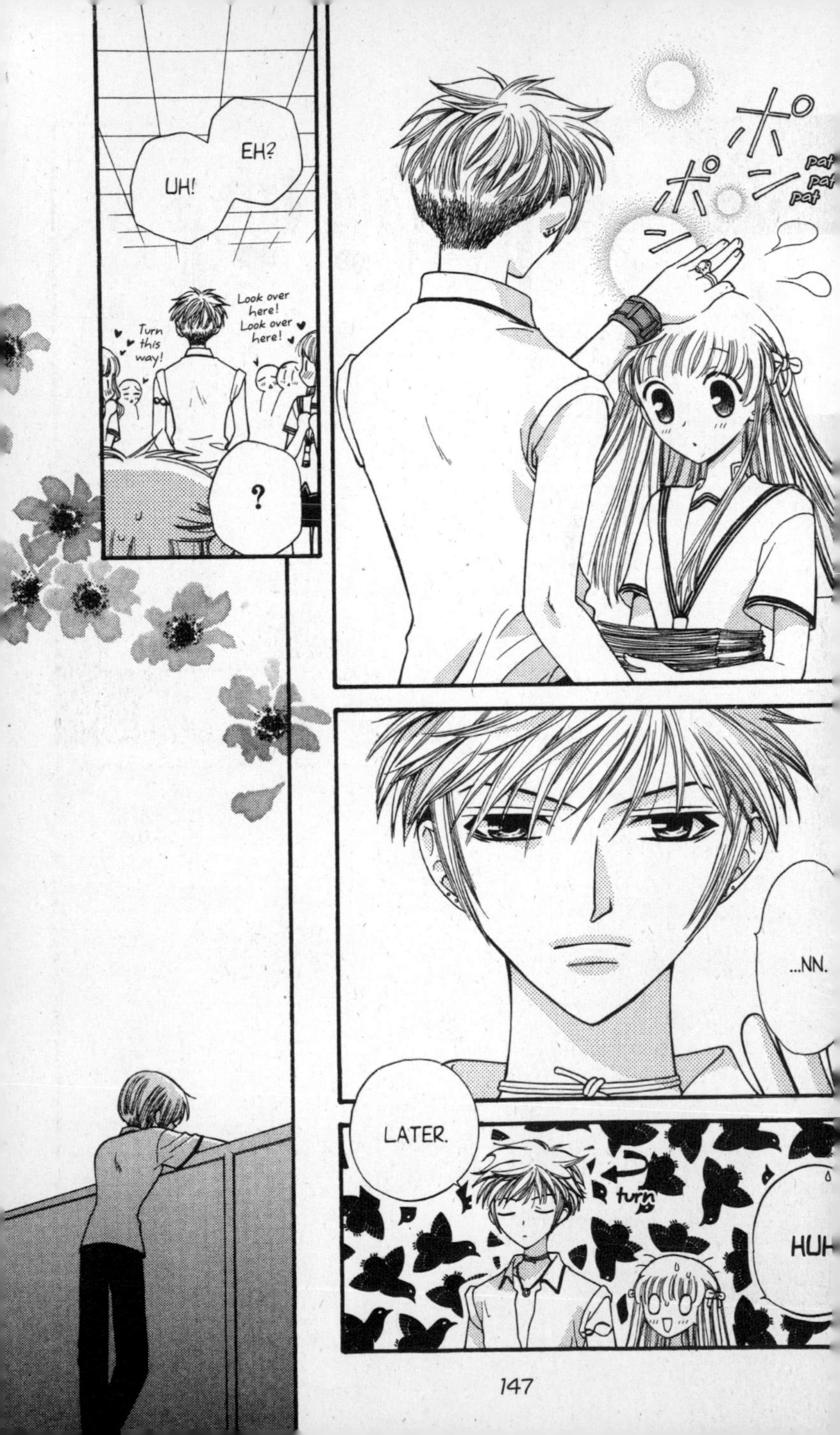
ポンポン
pat pat pat
EH?
UH!
Look over here! Look over here!
Turn this way!
?
...NN.
LATER.
turn
HUH

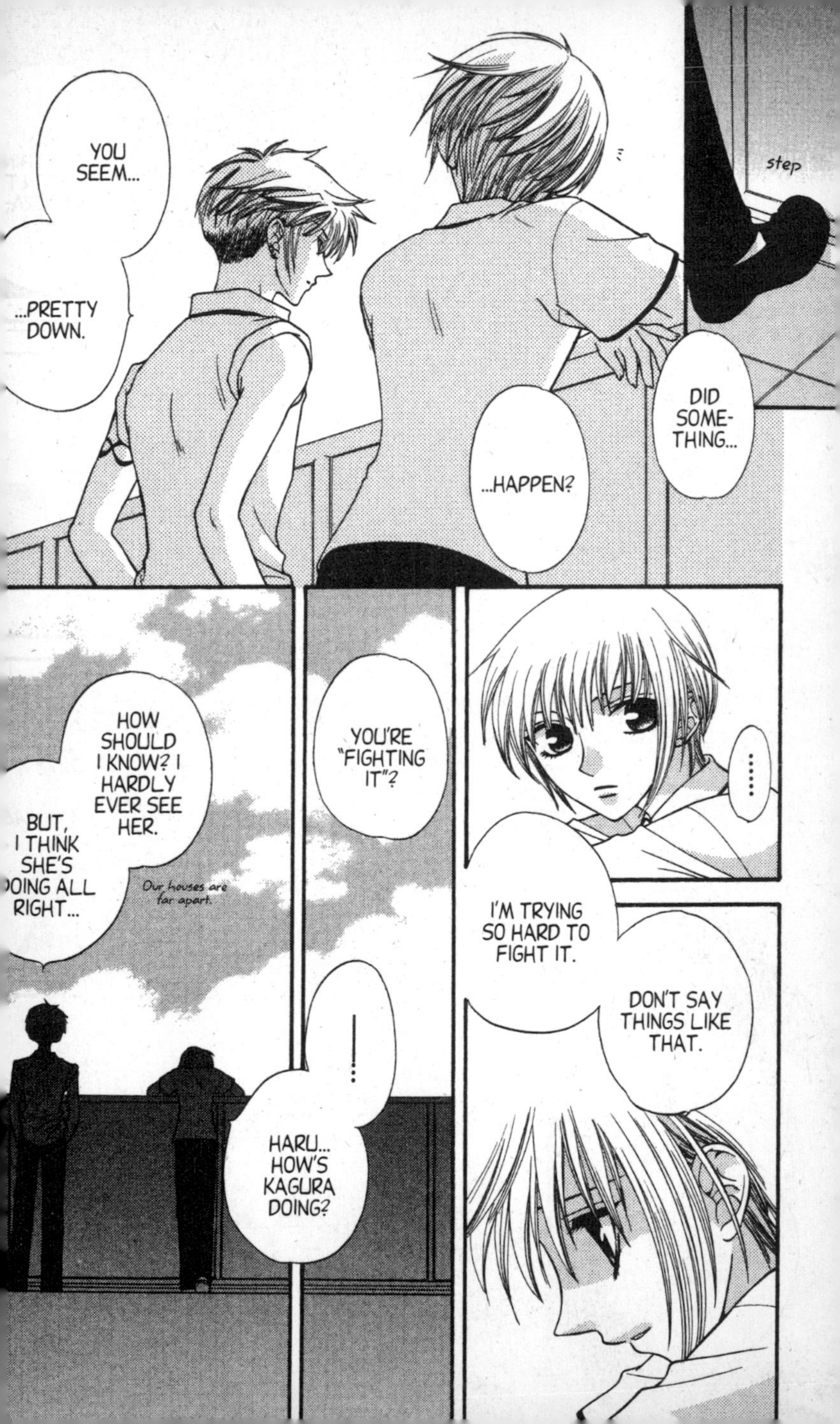
step
DID SOME-THING...
...HAPPEN?
YOU SEEM...
...PRETTY DOWN.
......
I'M TRYING SO HARD TO FIGHT IT.
DON'T SAY THINGS LIKE THAT.
YOU'RE "FIGHTING IT"?
......!
HARU... HOW'S KAGURA DOING?
HOW SHOULD I KNOW? I HARDLY EVER SEE HER.
BUT, I THINK SHE'S DOING ALL RIGHT...
Our houses are far apart.

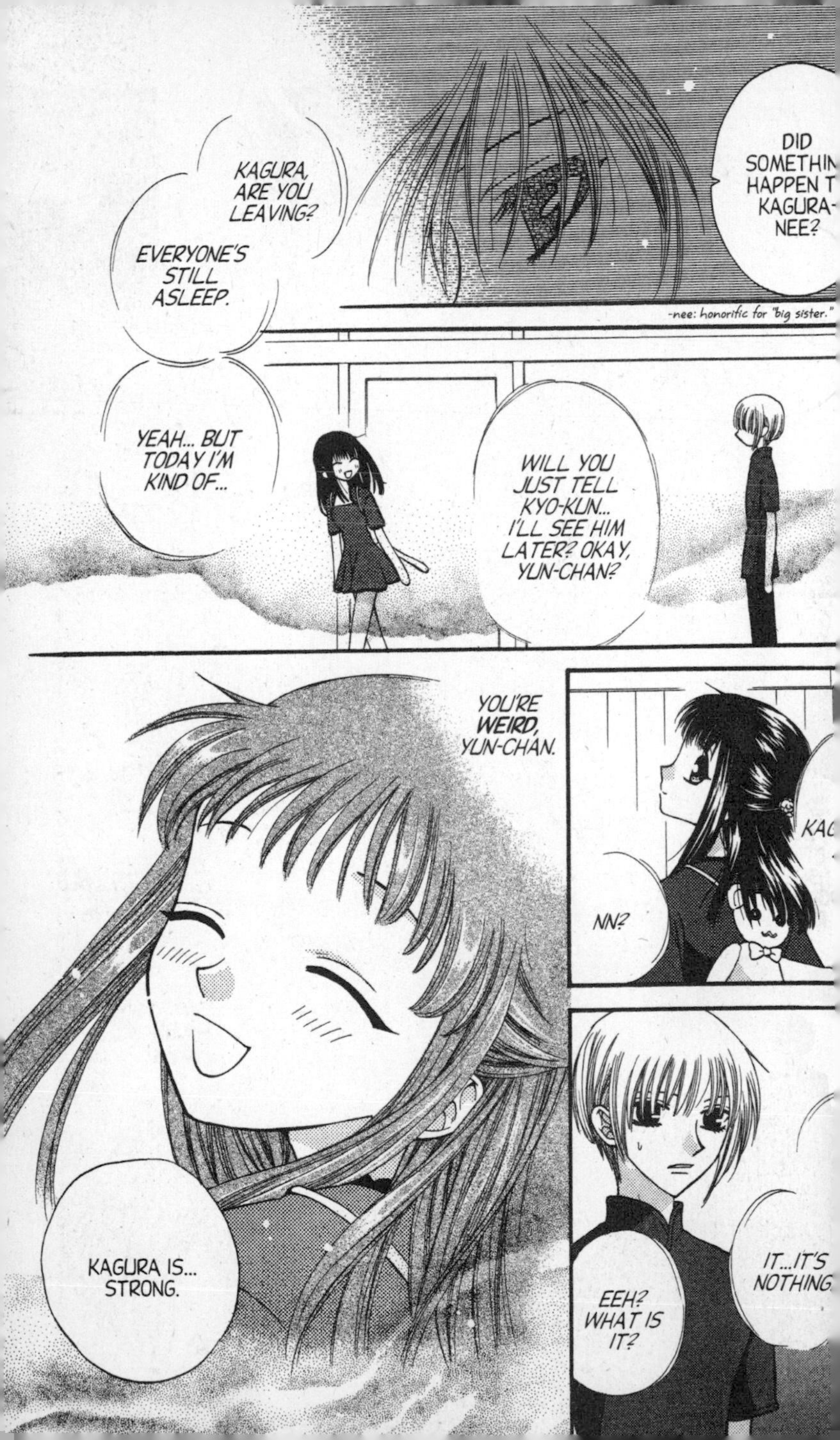
DID SOMETHIN HAPPEN T KAGURA-NEE?
KAGURA, ARE YOU LEAVING?
EVERYONE'S STILL ASLEEP.
-nee: honorific for "big sister."
YEAH... BUT TODAY I'M KIND OF...
WILL YOU JUST TELL KYO-KUN... I'LL SEE HIM LATER? OKAY, YUN-CHAN?
KA
NN?
IT...IT'S NOTHING.
EEH? WHAT IS IT?
YOU'RE WEIRD, YUN-CHAN.
KAGURA IS... STRONG.

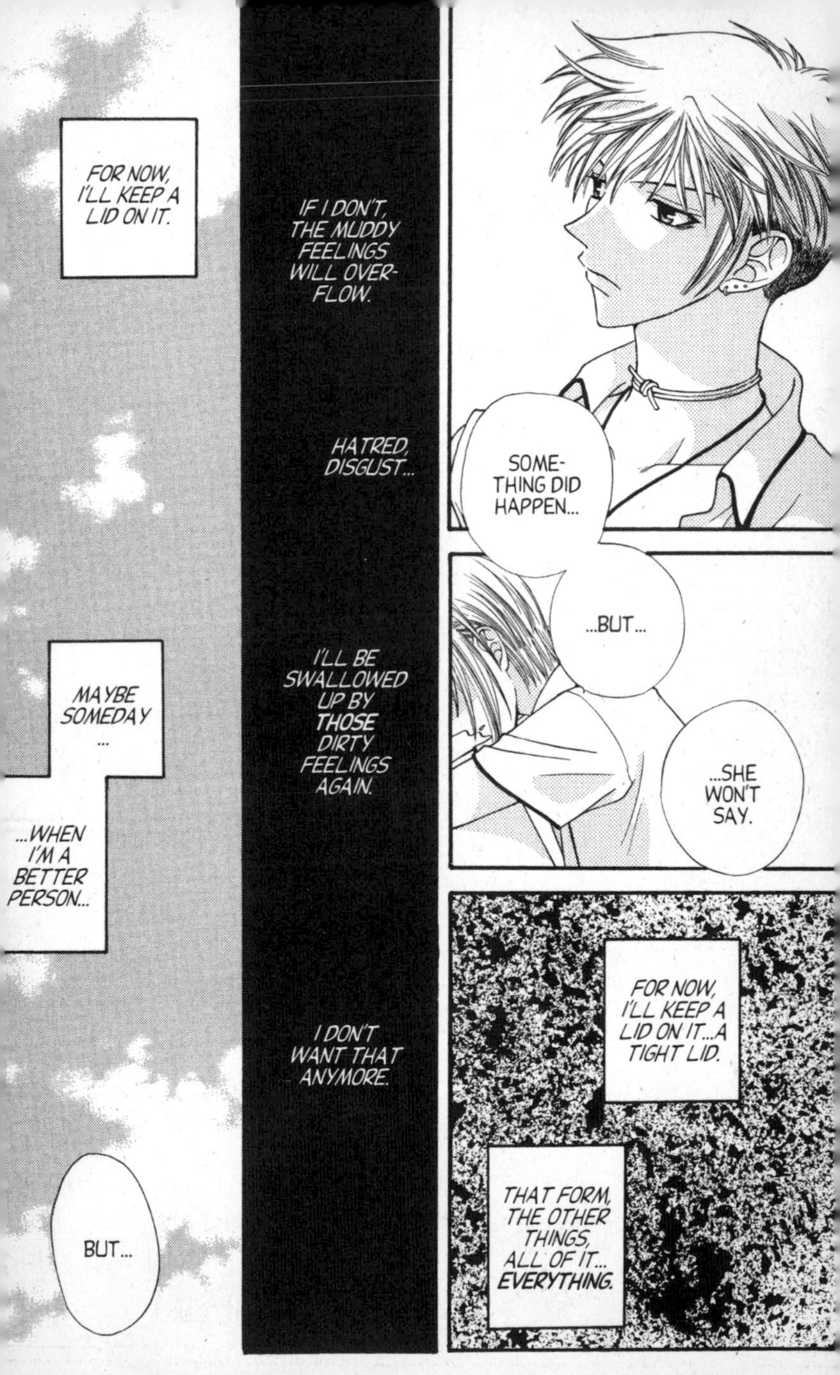
SOME-THING DID HAPPEN...
...BUT...
...SHE WON'T SAY.
FOR NOW, I'LL KEEP A LID ON IT...A TIGHT LID.
THAT FORM, THE OTHER THINGS, ALL OF IT... EVERYTHING.
IF I DON'T, THE MUDDY FEELINGS WILL OVER-FLOW.
HATRED, DISGUST...
I'LL BE SWALLOWED UP BY THOSE DIRTY FEELINGS AGAIN.
I DON'T WANT THAT ANYMORE.
FOR NOW, I'LL KEEP A LID ON IT.
MAYBE SOMEDAY ...
...WHEN I'M A BETTER PERSON...
BUT...

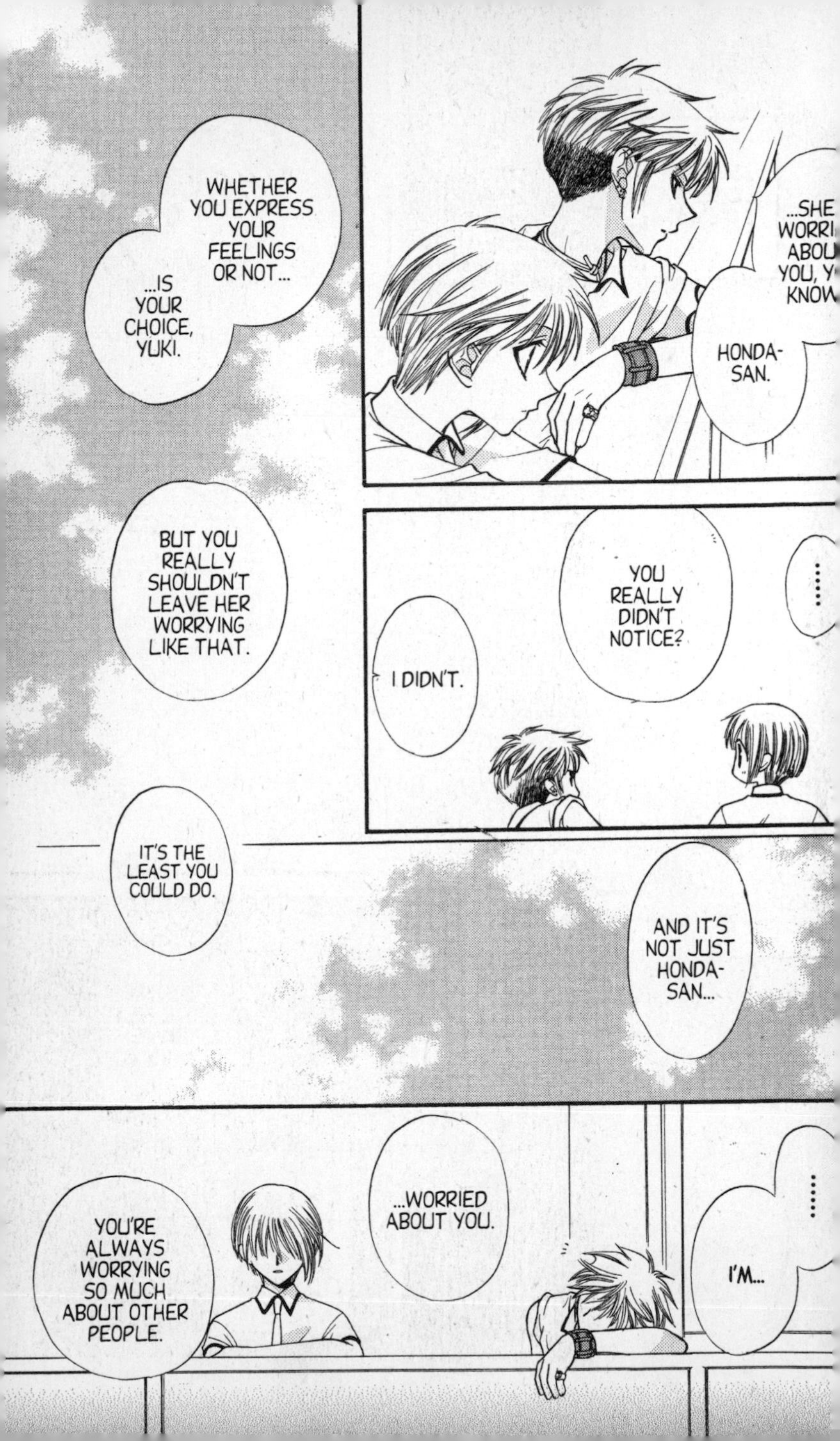
...SHE WORRI ABOU YOU, Y KNOW
HONDA-SAN.
WHETHER YOU EXPRESS YOUR FEELINGS OR NOT...
...IS YOUR CHOICE, YUKI.
......
YOU REALLY DIDN'T NOTICE?
I DIDN'T.
BUT YOU REALLY SHOULDN'T LEAVE HER WORRYING LIKE THAT.
IT'S THE LEAST YOU COULD DO.
AND IT'S NOT JUST HONDA-SAN...
......
I'M...
...WORRIED ABOUT YOU.
YOU'RE ALWAYS WORRYING SO MUCH ABOUT OTHER PEOPLE.

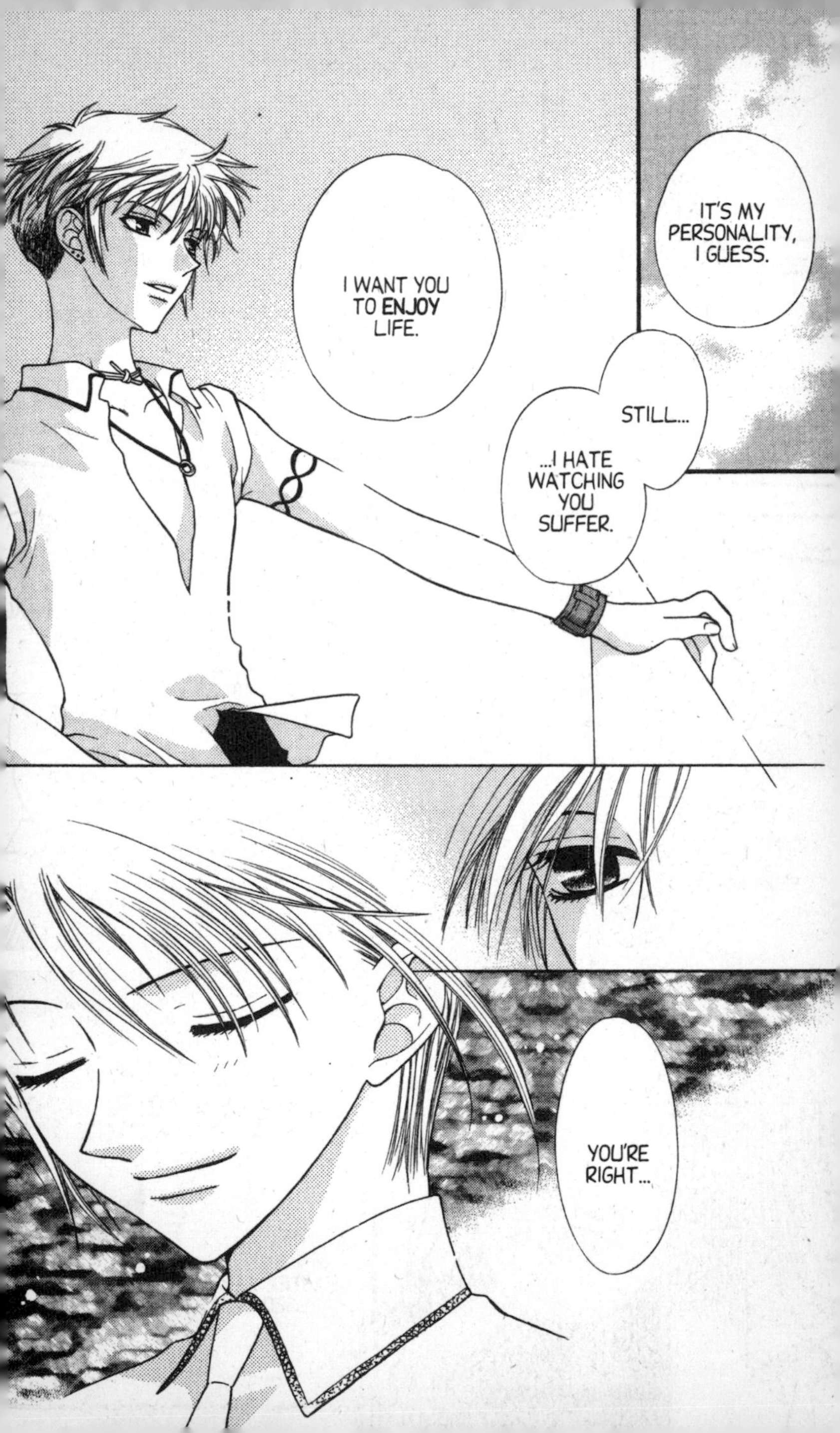
IT'S MY PERSONALITY, I GUESS.
STILL...
...I HATE WATCHING YOU SUFFER.
I WANT YOU TO ENJOY LIFE.
YOU'RE RIGHT...

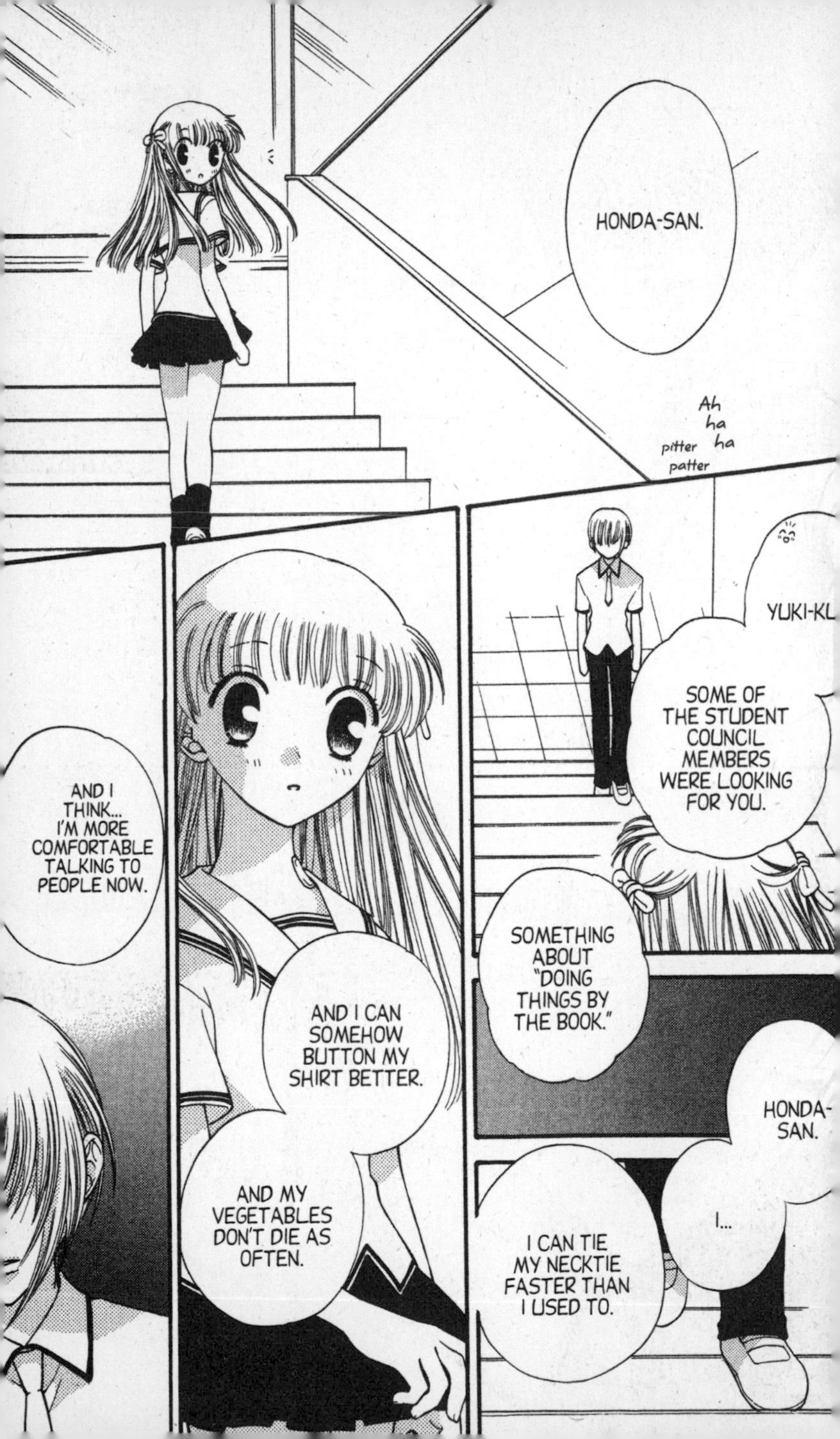
HONDA-SAN.
Ah ha ha
pitter patter
YUKI-KU
SOME OF THE STUDENT COUNCIL MEMBERS WERE LOOKING FOR YOU.
SOMETHING ABOUT "DOING THINGS BY THE BOOK."
HONDA-SAN.
I...
I CAN TIE MY NECKTIE FASTER THAN I USED TO.
AND I CAN SOMEHOW BUTTON MY SHIRT BETTER.
AND MY VEGETABLES DON'T DIE AS OFTEN.
AND I THINK... I'M MORE COMFORTABLE TALKING TO PEOPLE NOW.

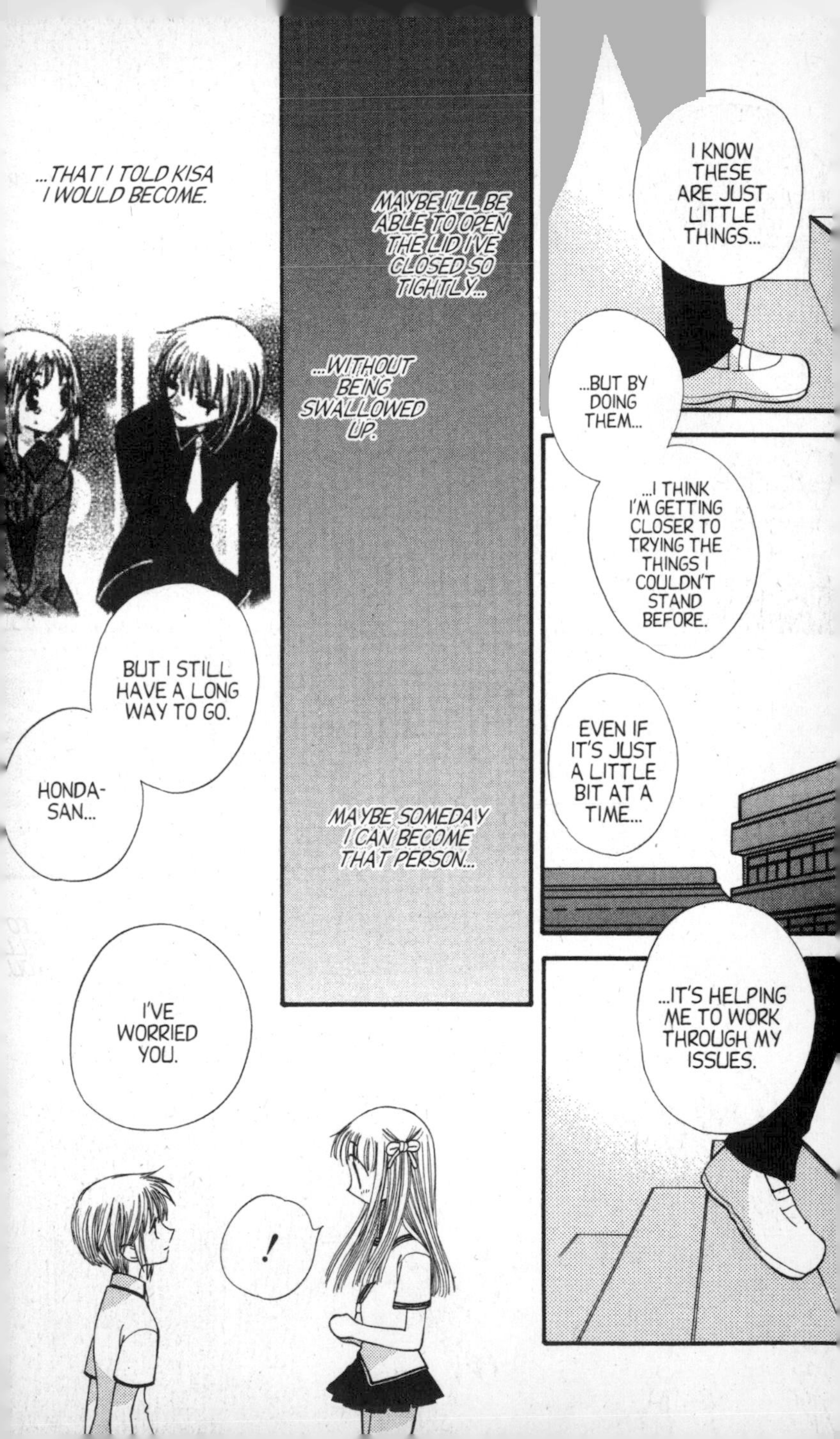
I KNOW THESE ARE JUST LITTLE THINGS...
...BUT BY DOING THEM...
...I THINK I'M GETTING CLOSER TO TRYING THE THINGS I COULDN'T STAND BEFORE.
EVEN IF IT'S JUST A LITTLE BIT AT A TIME...
...IT'S HELPING ME TO WORK THROUGH MY ISSUES.
MAYBE I'LL BE ABLE TO OPEN THE LID I'VE CLOSED SO TIGHTLY...
...WITHOUT BEING SWALLOWED UP.
MAYBE SOMEDAY I CAN BECOME THAT PERSON...
...THAT I TOLD KISA I WOULD BECOME.
BUT I STILL HAVE A LONG WAY TO GO.
HONDA-SAN...
I'VE WORRIED YOU.
!

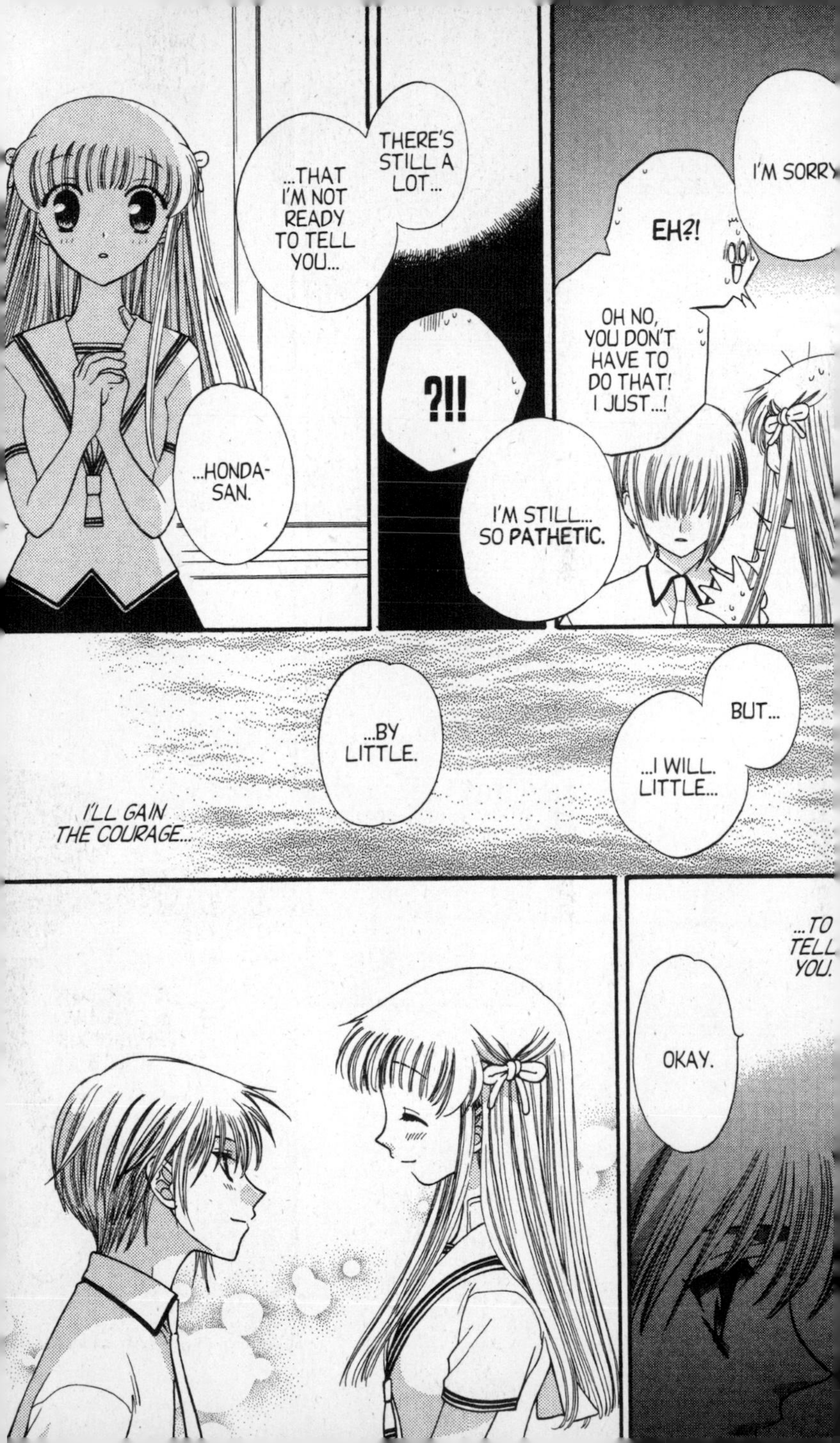
I'M SORRY
EH?!
OH NO, YOU DON'T HAVE TO DO THAT! I JUST...!
I'M STILL... SO **PATHETIC.**
?!!
THERE'S STILL A LOT...
...THAT I'M NOT READY TO TELL YOU...
...HONDA-SAN.
BUT...
...I WILL. LITTLE...
...BY LITTLE.
I'LL GAIN THE COURAGE...
...TO TELL YOU.
OKAY.

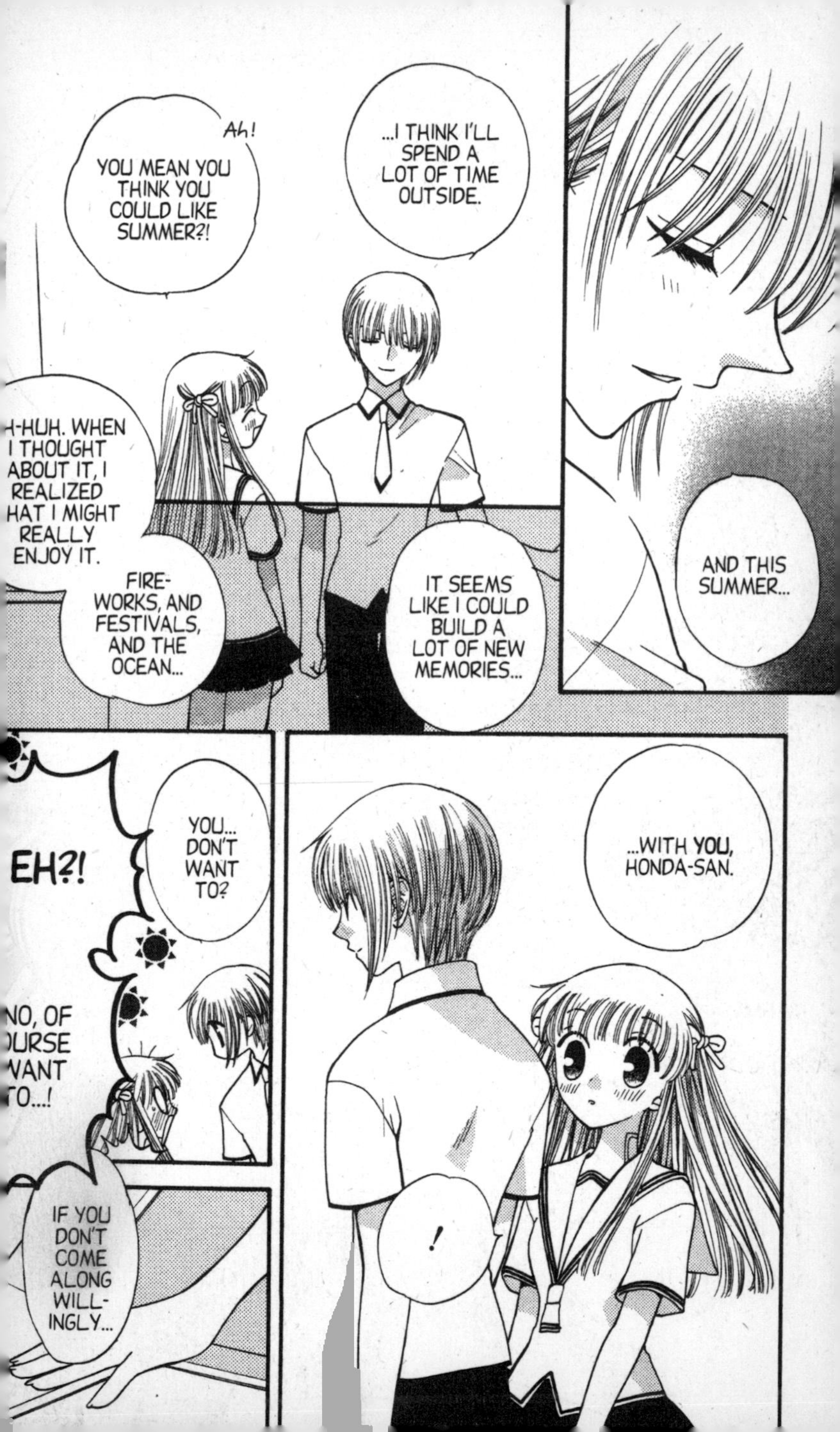
...I THINK I'LL SPEND A LOT OF TIME OUTSIDE.
Ah!
YOU MEAN YOU THINK YOU COULD LIKE SUMMER?!
AND THIS SUMMER...
IT SEEMS LIKE I COULD BUILD A LOT OF NEW MEMORIES...
H-HUH. WHEN I THOUGHT ABOUT IT, I REALIZED HAT I MIGHT REALLY ENJOY IT.
FIRE-WORKS, AND FESTIVALS, AND THE OCEAN...
...WITH YOU, HONDA-SAN.
!
YOU... DON'T WANT TO?
EH?!
NO, OF URSE WANT TO...!
IF YOU DON'T COME ALONG WILL-INGLY...

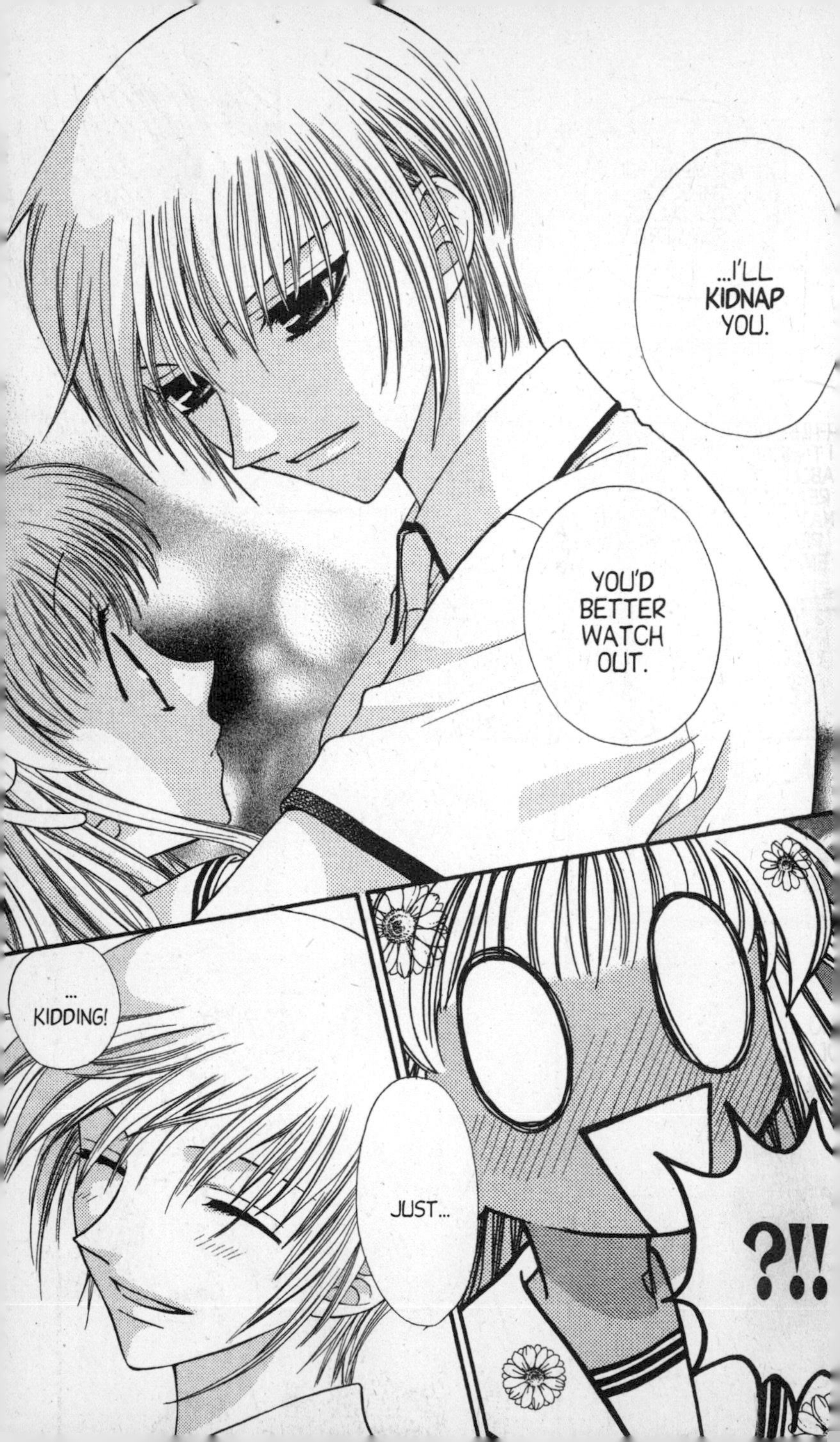
...I'LL KIDNAP YOU.
YOU'D BETTER WATCH OUT.
?!!
JUST...
... KIDDING!

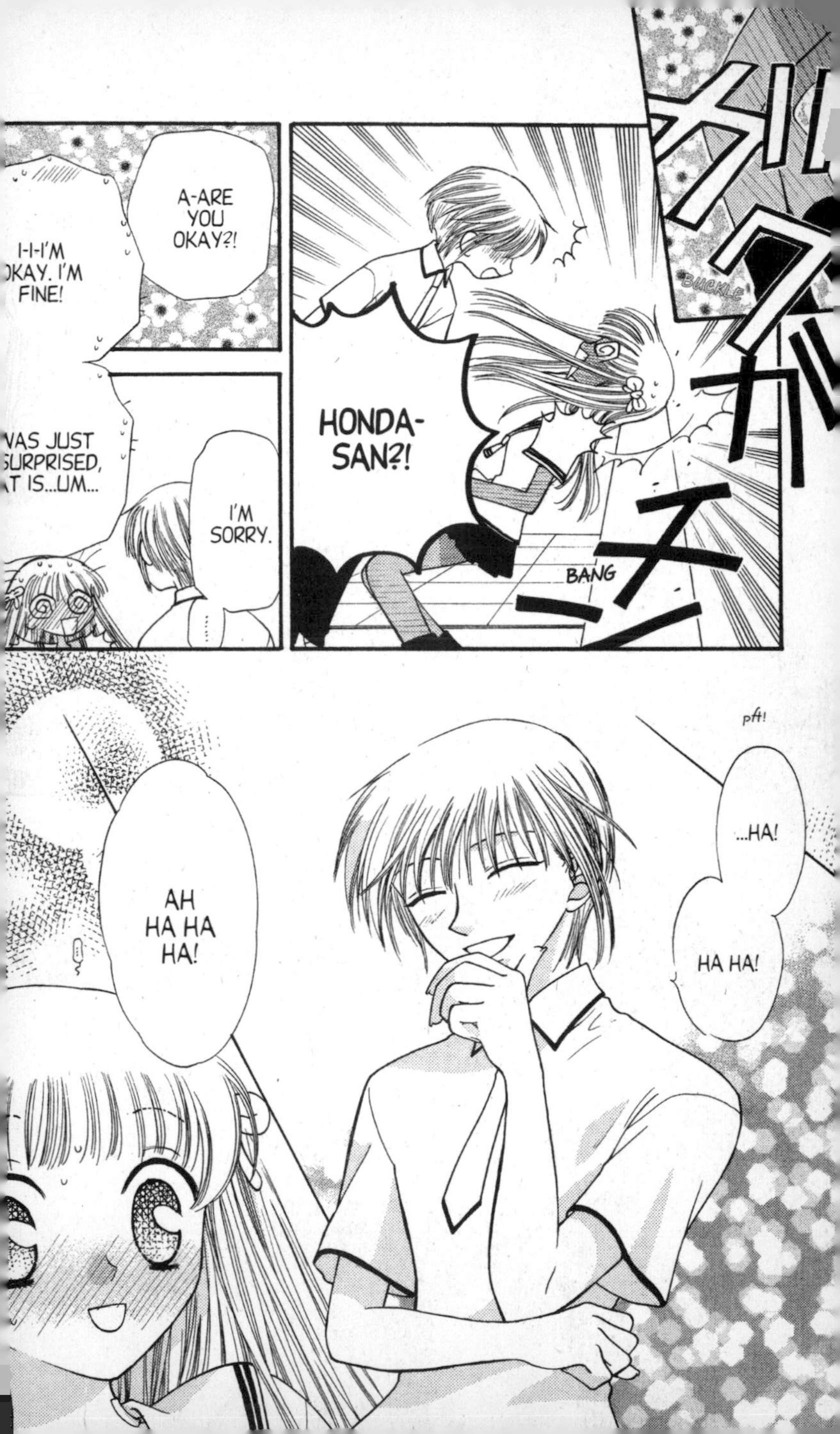
BUCKLE
HONDA-SAN?!
BANG
A-ARE YOU OKAY?!
I-I-I'M OKAY. I'M FINE!
I'M SORRY.
WAS JUST SURPRISED, AT IS...UM...
pft!
...HA!
HA HA!
AH HA HA HA!

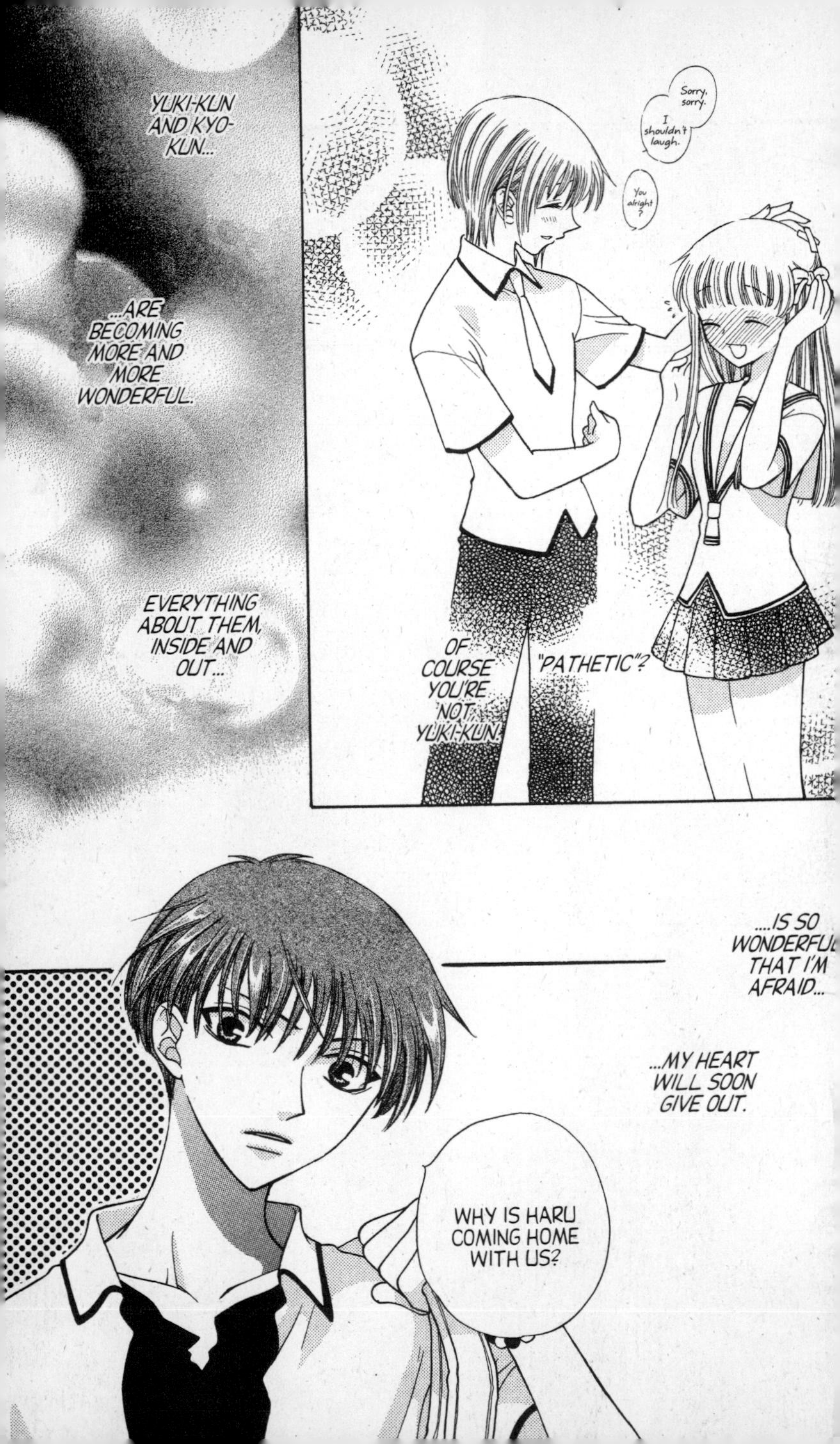
Sorry, sorry. I shouldn't laugh.
You alright?
"PATHETIC"?
OF COURSE YOU'RE NOT YUKI-KUN.
YUKI-KUN AND KYO-KUN...
...ARE BECOMING MORE AND MORE WONDERFUL.
EVERYTHING ABOUT THEM, INSIDE AND OUT...
....IS SO WONDERFUL THAT I'M AFRAID...
...MY HEART WILL SOON GIVE OUT.
WHY IS HARU COMING HOME WITH US?

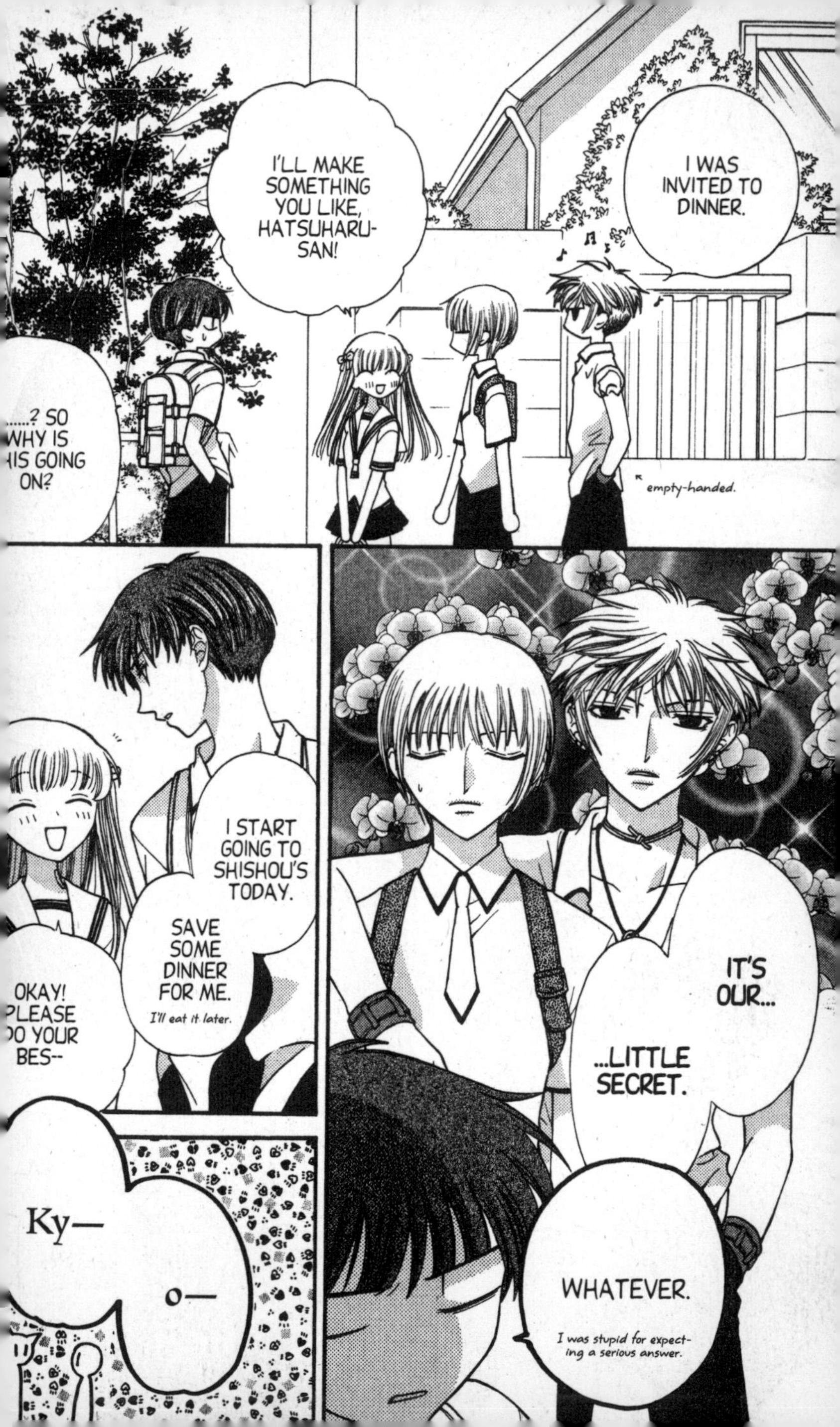
I WAS INVITED TO DINNER.
empty-handed.
I'LL MAKE SOMETHING YOU LIKE, HATSUHARU-SAN!
......? SO WHY IS HIS GOING ON?
IT'S OUR...
...LITTLE SECRET.
WHATEVER.
I was stupid for expecting a serious answer.
I START GOING TO SHISHOU'S TODAY.
SAVE SOME DINNER FOR ME.
I'll eat it later.
OKAY! PLEASE DO YOUR BES--
Ky—
o—

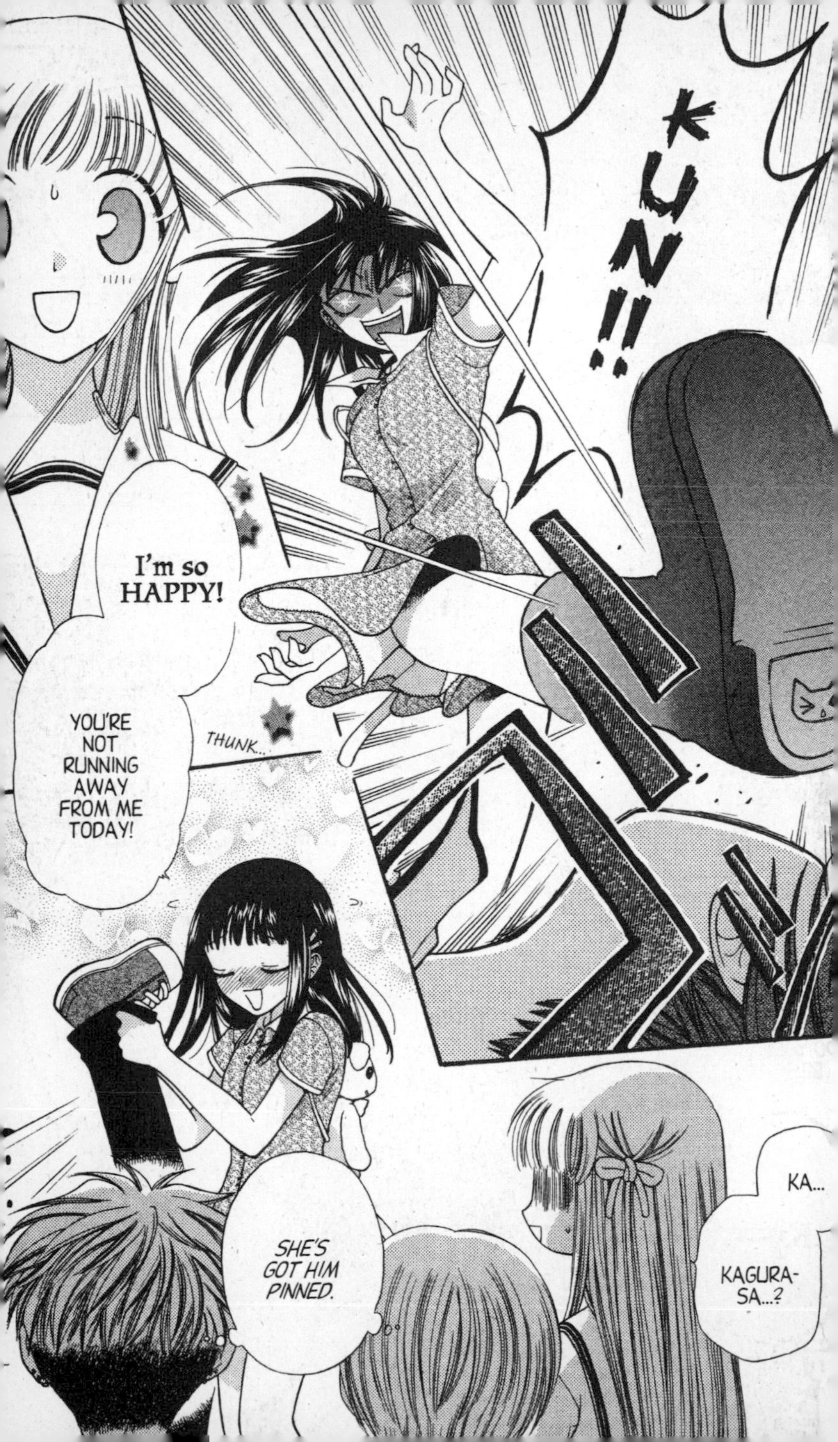
KUN!!
I'm so HAPPY!
THUNK...
YOU'RE NOT RUNNING AWAY FROM ME TODAY!
KA...
KAGURA-SA...?
SHE'S GOT HIM PINNED.

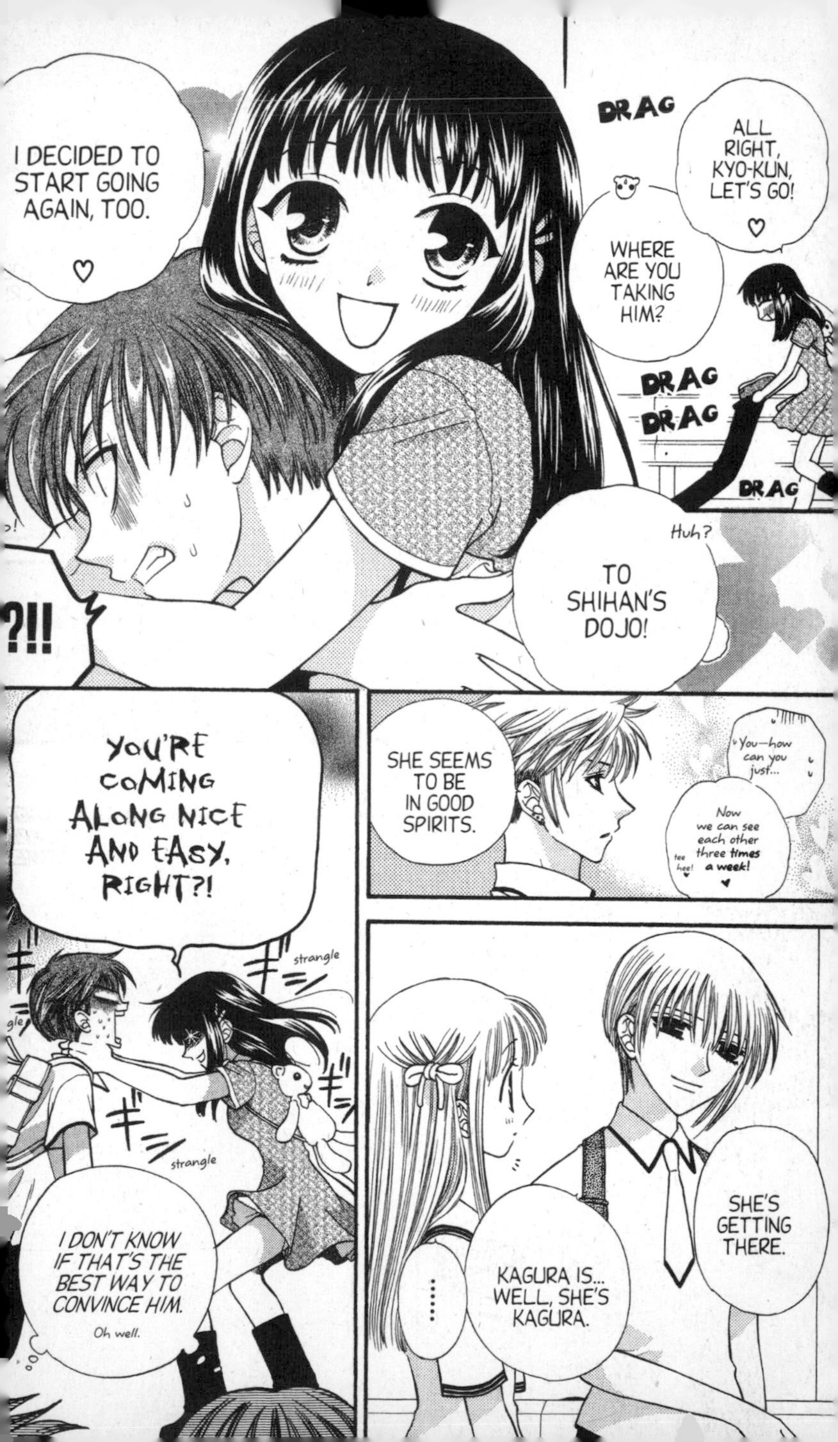
DRAG
ALL RIGHT, KYO-KUN, LET'S GO! ♡
WHERE ARE YOU TAKING HIM?
DRAG
DRAG
DRAG
Huh?
TO SHIHAN'S DOJO!
I DECIDED TO START GOING AGAIN, TOO. ♡
?!!
You—how can you just...
Now we can see each other three times a week!
tee hee!
SHE SEEMS TO BE IN GOOD SPIRITS.
SHE'S GETTING THERE.
KAGURA IS... WELL, SHE'S KAGURA.
......
YOU'RE COMING ALONG NICE AND EASY, RIGHT?!
strangle
strangle
I DON'T KNOW IF THAT'S THE BEST WAY TO CONVINCE HIM.
Oh well.

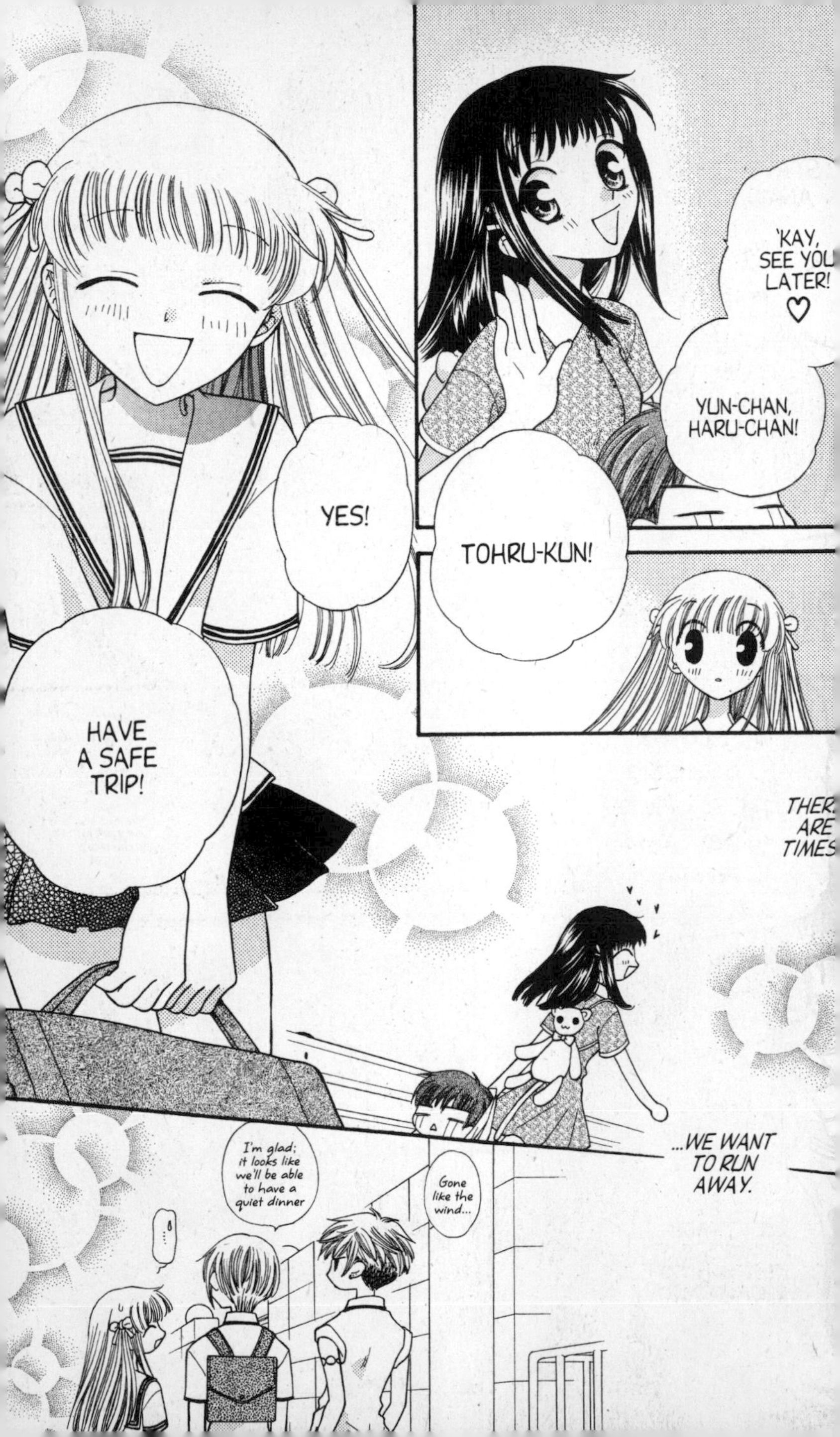
'KAY, SEE YOU LATER! ♡
YUN-CHAN, HARU-CHAN!
TOHRU-KUN!
YES!
HAVE A SAFE TRIP!
THER ARE TIMES
...WE WANT TO RUN AWAY.
Gone like the wind...
I'm glad; it looks like we'll be able to have a quiet dinner
...

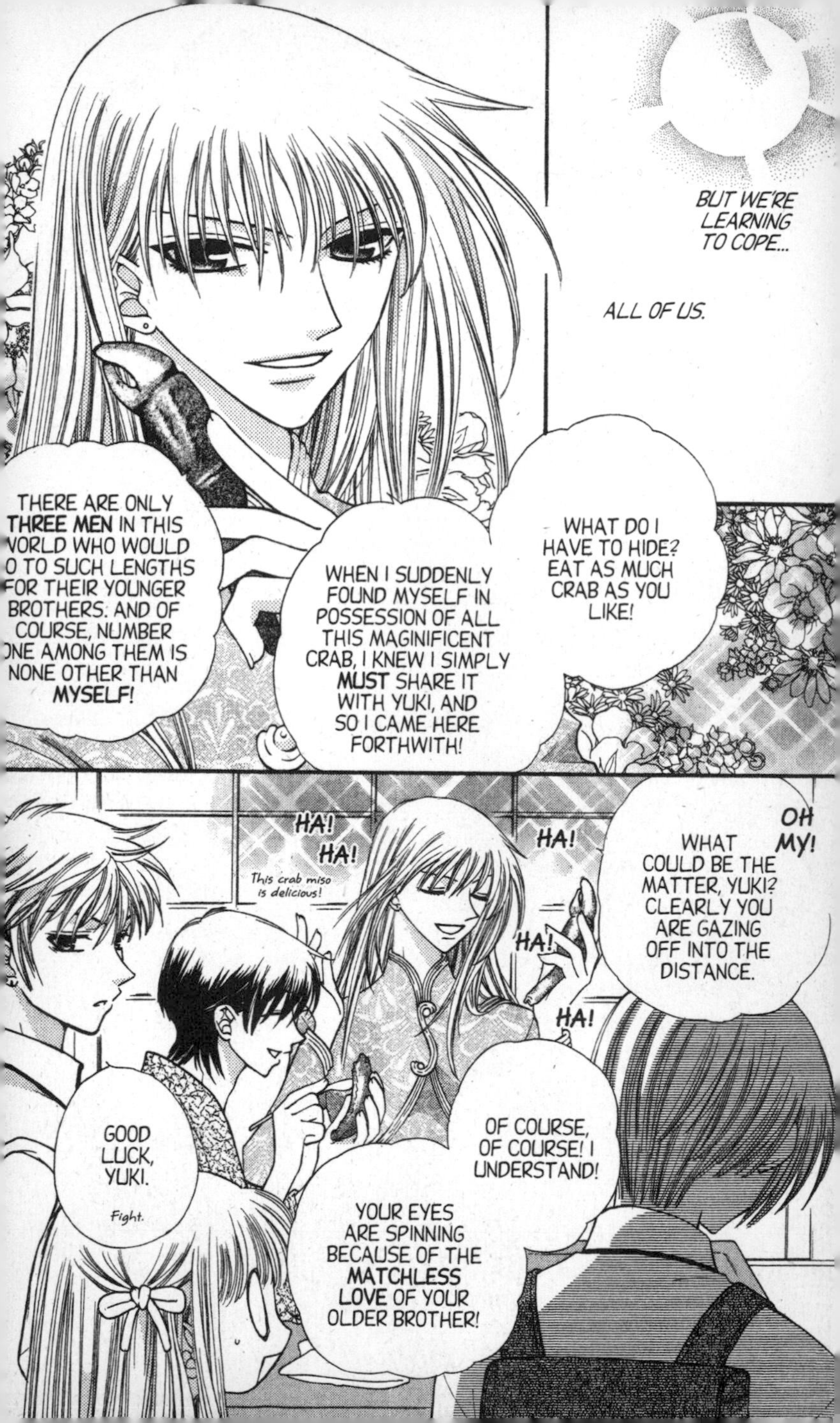
BUT WE'RE LEARNING TO COPE...
ALL OF US.
WHAT DO I HAVE TO HIDE? EAT AS MUCH CRAB AS YOU LIKE!
WHEN I SUDDENLY FOUND MYSELF IN POSSESSION OF ALL THIS MAGINIFICENT CRAB, I KNEW I SIMPLY MUST SHARE IT WITH YUKI, AND SO I CAME HERE FORTHWITH!
THERE ARE ONLY THREE MEN IN THIS VORLD WHO WOULD O TO SUCH LENGTHS FOR THEIR YOUNGER BROTHERS. AND OF COURSE, NUMBER ONE AMONG THEM IS NONE OTHER THAN MYSELF!
OH MY!
WHAT COULD BE THE MATTER, YUKI? CLEARLY YOU ARE GAZING OFF INTO THE DISTANCE.
HA! HA! HA! HA! HA! HA!
OF COURSE, OF COURSE! I UNDERSTAND!
YOUR EYES ARE SPINNING BECAUSE OF THE MATCHLESS LOVE OF YOUR OLDER BROTHER!
This crab miso is delicious!
GOOD LUCK, YUKI.
Fight.

Chapter 36

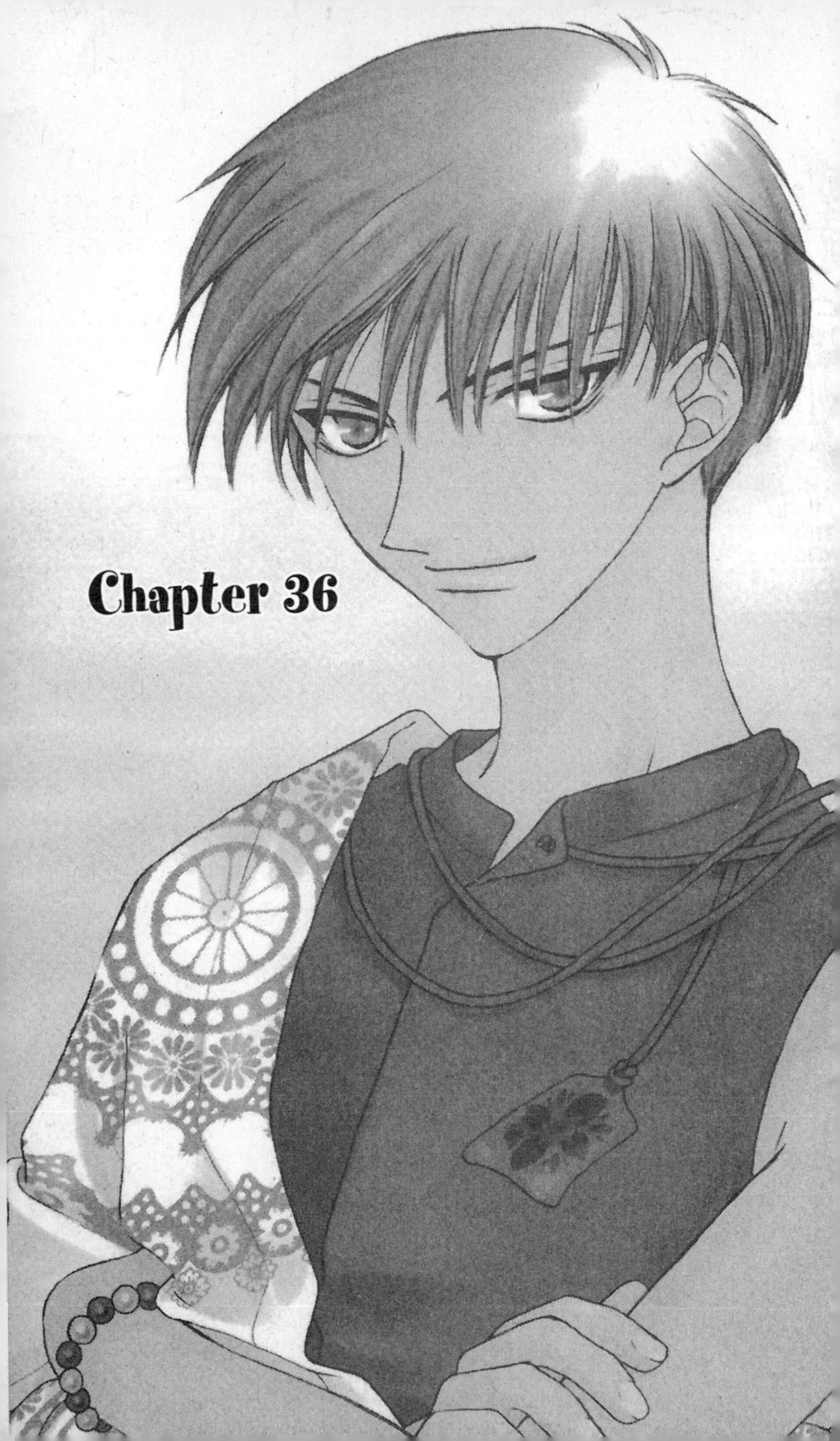

I feel so grateful!

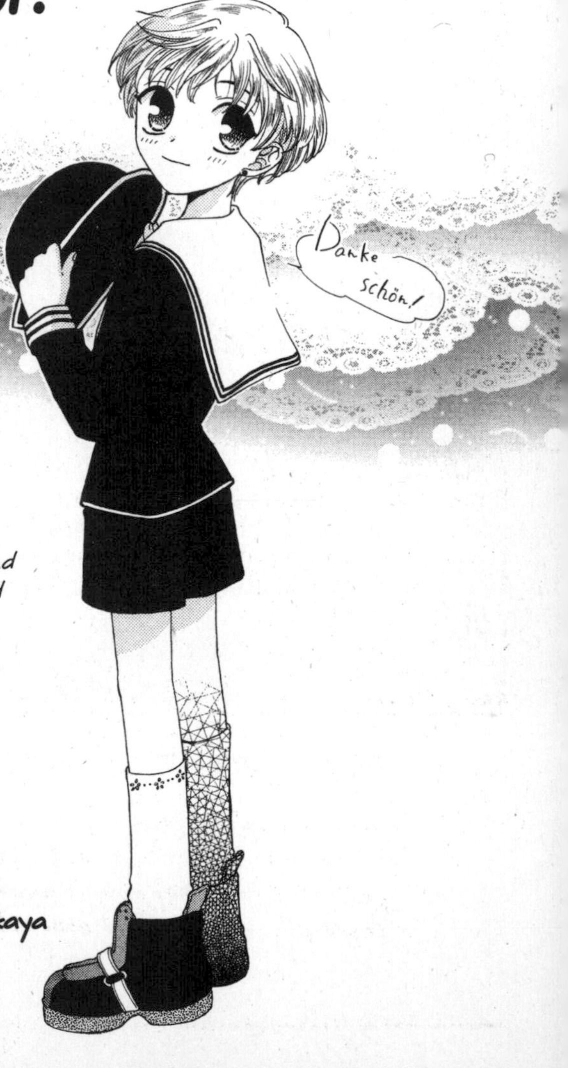

Danke schön!

ırada-sama, Araki-sama,
wai-sama, mom, dad, and
ıryone who reads this and
ports me, I couldn't have
ıe it without you!

ıatori, you're up next!

has been Natsuki Takaya

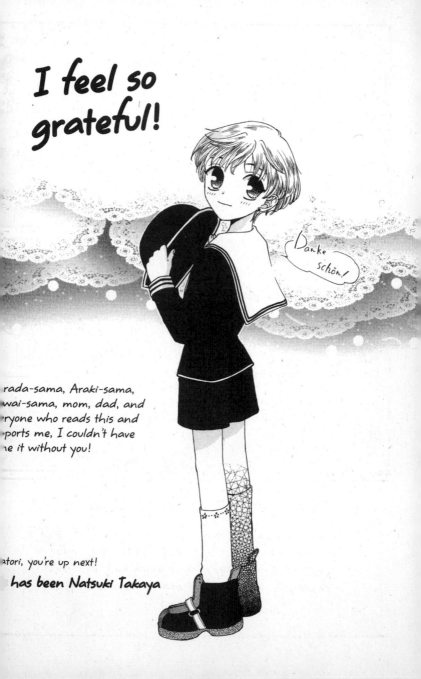

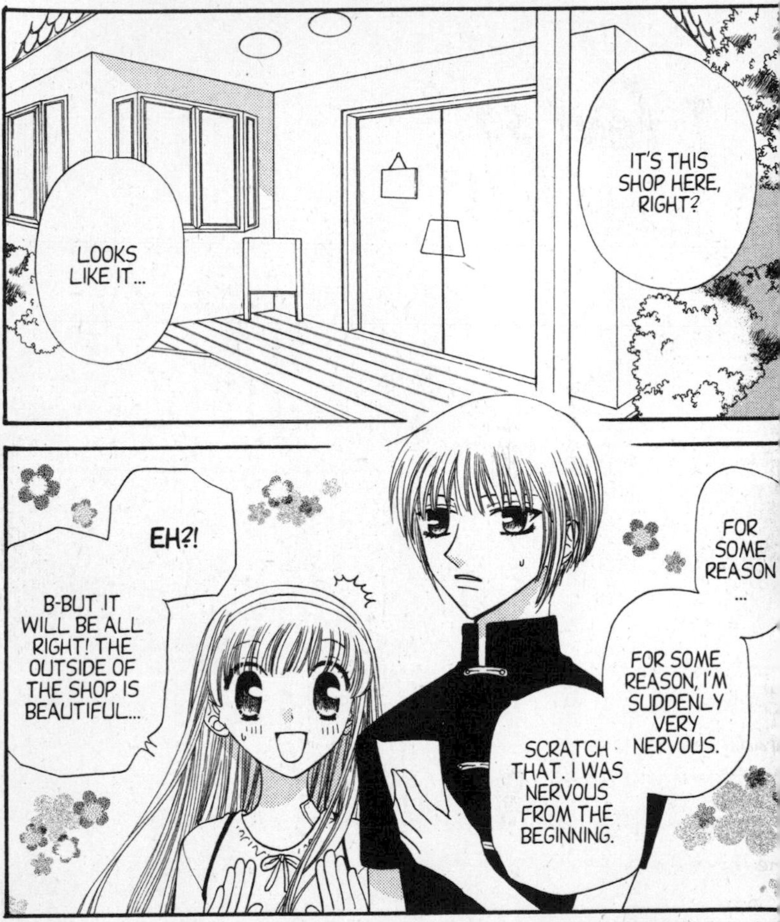
IT'S THIS SHOP HERE, RIGHT?
LOOKS LIKE IT...
FOR SOME REASON ...
FOR SOME REASON, I'M SUDDENLY VERY NERVOUS.
SCRATCH THAT. I WAS NERVOUS FROM THE BEGINNING.
EH?!
B-BUT IT WILL BE ALL RIGHT! THE OUTSIDE OF THE SHOP IS BEAUTIFUL...

ULTRA SPECIAL BLAH BLAH BLAH. 4

Ever since I started drawing this manga, I thought, "I want to draw a color picture of Kyo smiling!" And so, his first smile. That doesn't mean he'll always be smiling though. This boy really is hopeless. (laugh)

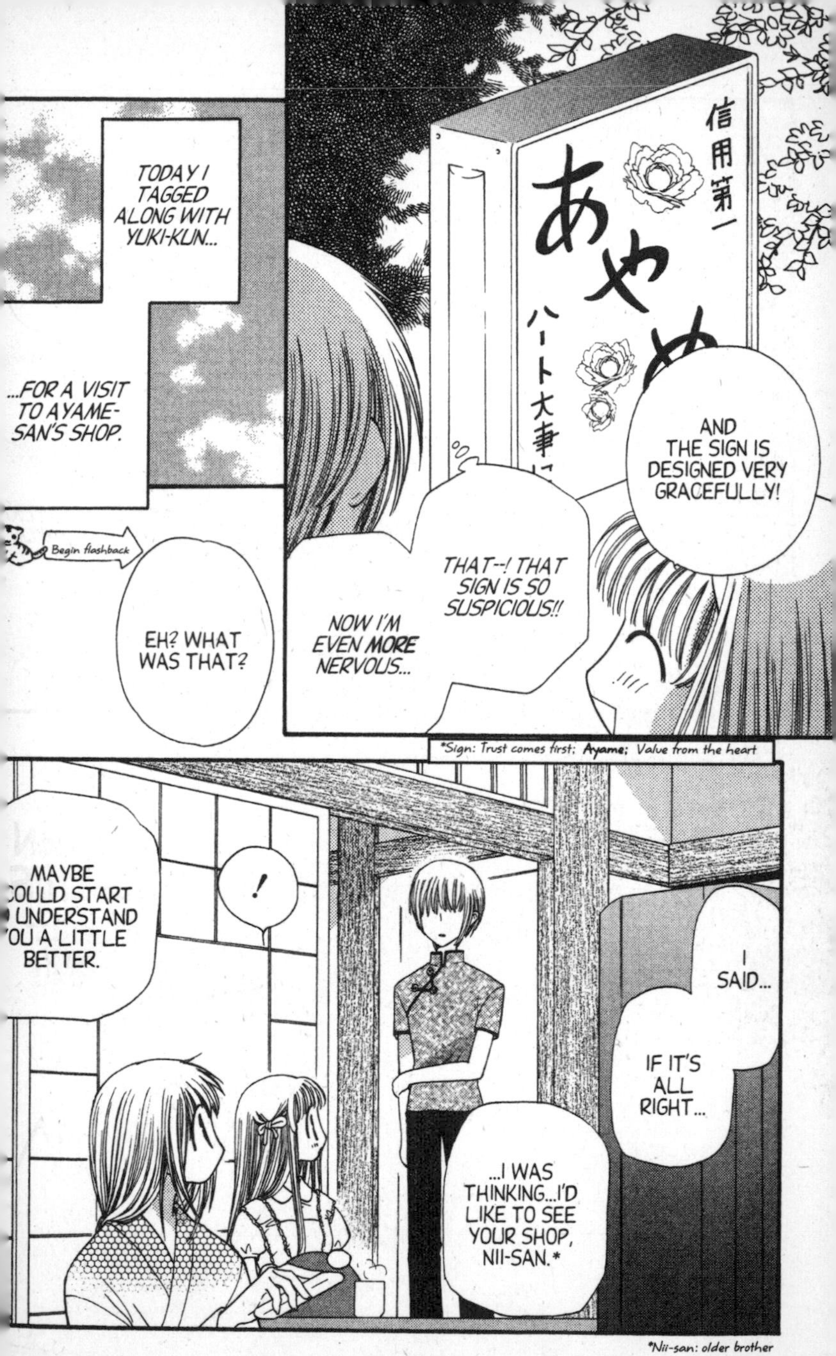

信用第一
あやめ
ハート大事
AND THE SIGN IS DESIGNED VERY GRACEFULLY!
THAT--! THAT SIGN IS SO SUSPICIOUS!!
NOW I'M EVEN MORE NERVOUS...
TODAY I TAGGED ALONG WITH YUKI-KUN...
...FOR A VISIT TO AYAME-SAN'S SHOP.
Begin flashback
EH? WHAT WAS THAT?
I SAID...
IF IT'S ALL RIGHT...
...I WAS THINKING...I'D LIKE TO SEE YOUR SHOP, NII-SAN.*
!
MAYBE COULD START O UNDERSTAND OU A LITTLE BETTER.

*Sign: Trust comes first; **Ayame**; Value from the heart

*Nii-san: older brother

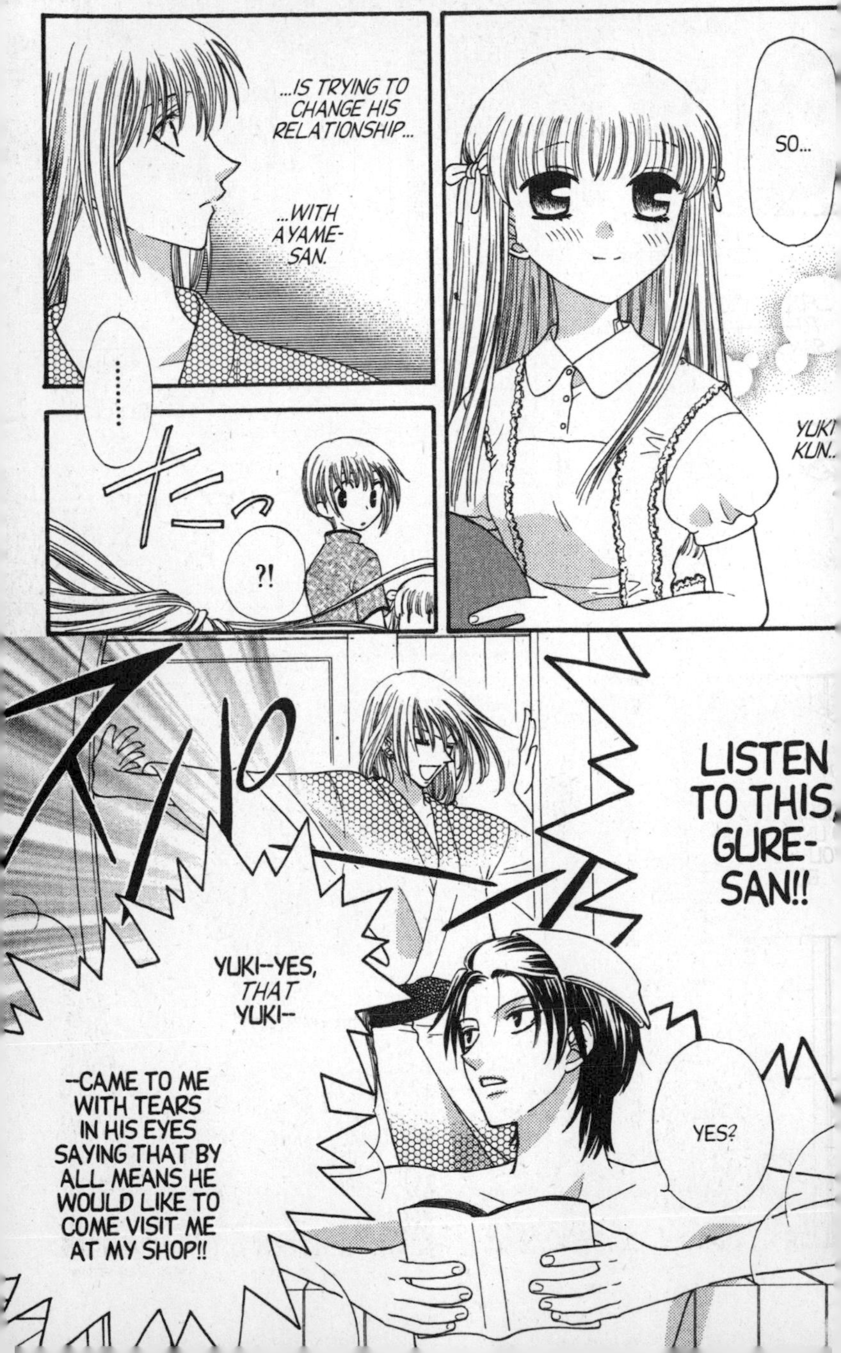
SO...
YUKI-KUN...
...IS TRYING TO CHANGE HIS RELATIONSHIP...
...WITH AYAME-SAN.
......
?!
LISTEN TO THIS, GURE-SAN!!
YES?
YUKI--YES, *THAT* YUKI--
--CAME TO ME WITH TEARS IN HIS EYES SAYING THAT BY ALL MEANS HE WOULD LIKE TO COME VISIT ME AT MY SHOP!!

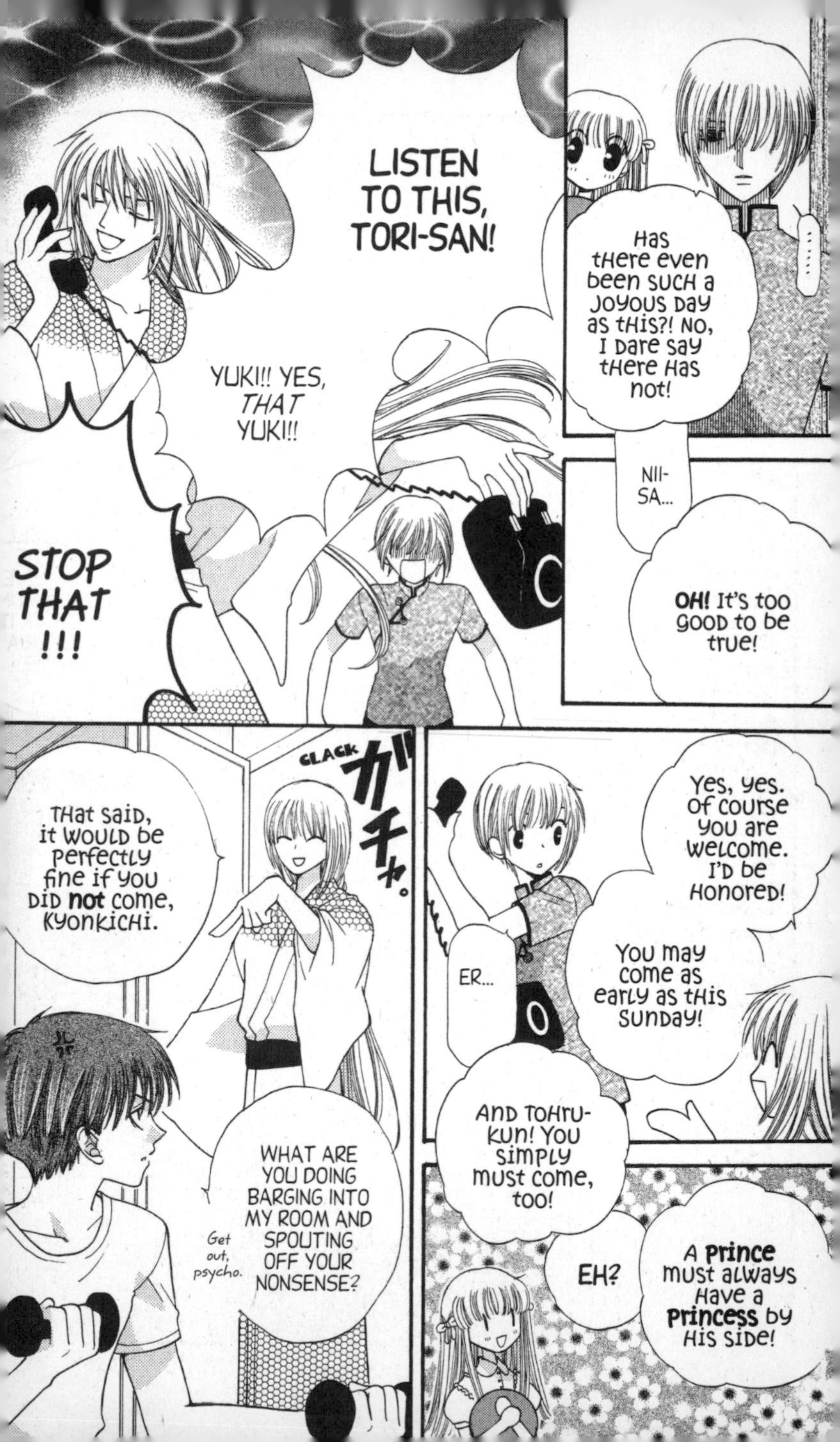
.....
Has there even been such a joyous day as this?! No, I dare say there has not!
NII-SA...
OH! It's too good to be true!
LISTEN TO THIS, TORI-SAN!
YUKI!! YES, *THAT* YUKI!!
STOP THAT !!!
Yes, yes. Of course you are welcome. I'd be honored!
You may come as early as this Sunday!
ER...
And Tohru-kun! You simply must come, too!
A **Prince** must always have a **Princess** by his side!
EH?
CLACK
ガチャ。
That said, it would be perfectly fine if you did **not** come, Kyonkichi.
WHAT ARE YOU DOING BARGING INTO MY ROOM AND SPOUTING OFF YOUR NONSENSE?
Get out, psycho.

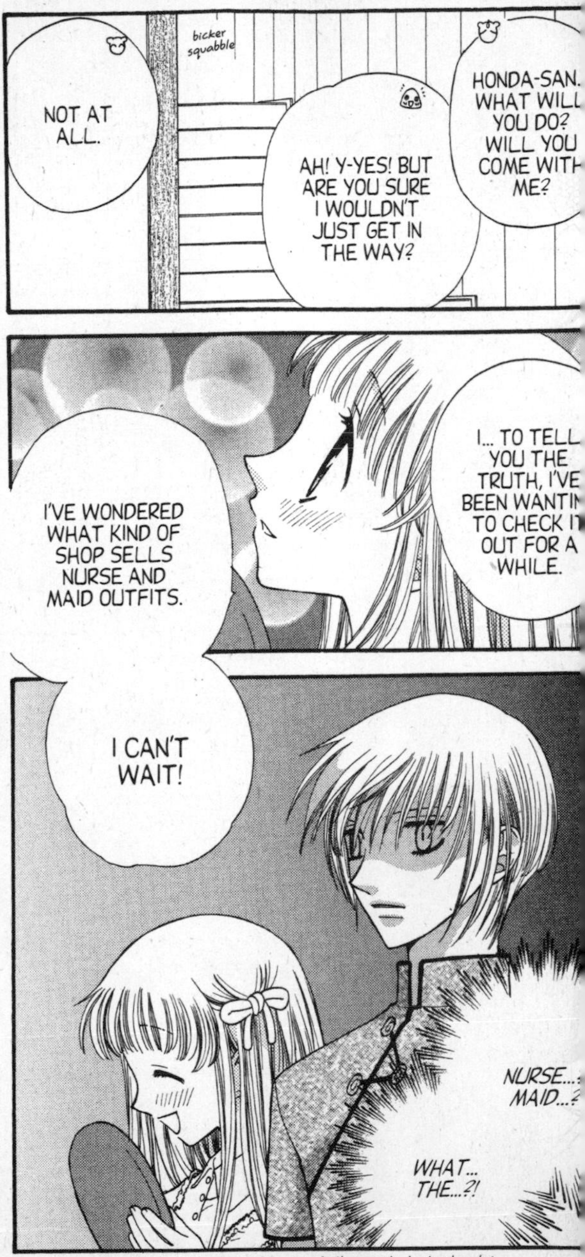
HONDA-SAN. WHAT WILL YOU DO? WILL YOU COME WITH ME?
AH! Y-YES! BUT ARE YOU SURE I WOULDN'T JUST GET IN THE WAY?
bicker squabble
NOT AT ALL.
I... TO TELL YOU THE TRUTH, I'VE BEEN WANTIN TO CHECK IT OUT FOR A WHILE.
I'VE WONDERED WHAT KIND OF SHOP SELLS NURSE AND MAID OUTFITS.
I CAN'T WAIT!
NURSE...? MAID...?
WHAT... THE...?!

↑ He knew he had a shop, but he had no idea what it sold.

Fruits Basket 6 Part 6:

In the last volume, I talked about what kind of snacks I liked at the time, but since then I've moved from "fugashi" to "egg booro" and now it's Choco-Balls (with caramel!). What toy did it come with...? Since I was a kid, it made me wonder. I was one of those kids who thinks, "I wanna hurry and grow up!" There were a lot of reasons, and one of them was, "So I'll be able to eat as many 'cucumber shrimp sen' as I want!" In hindsight, that's a pretty petty reason to want to grow up (laugh). But now that I can buy things with money I earned myself, that dream has come true. It was a very happy revelation.

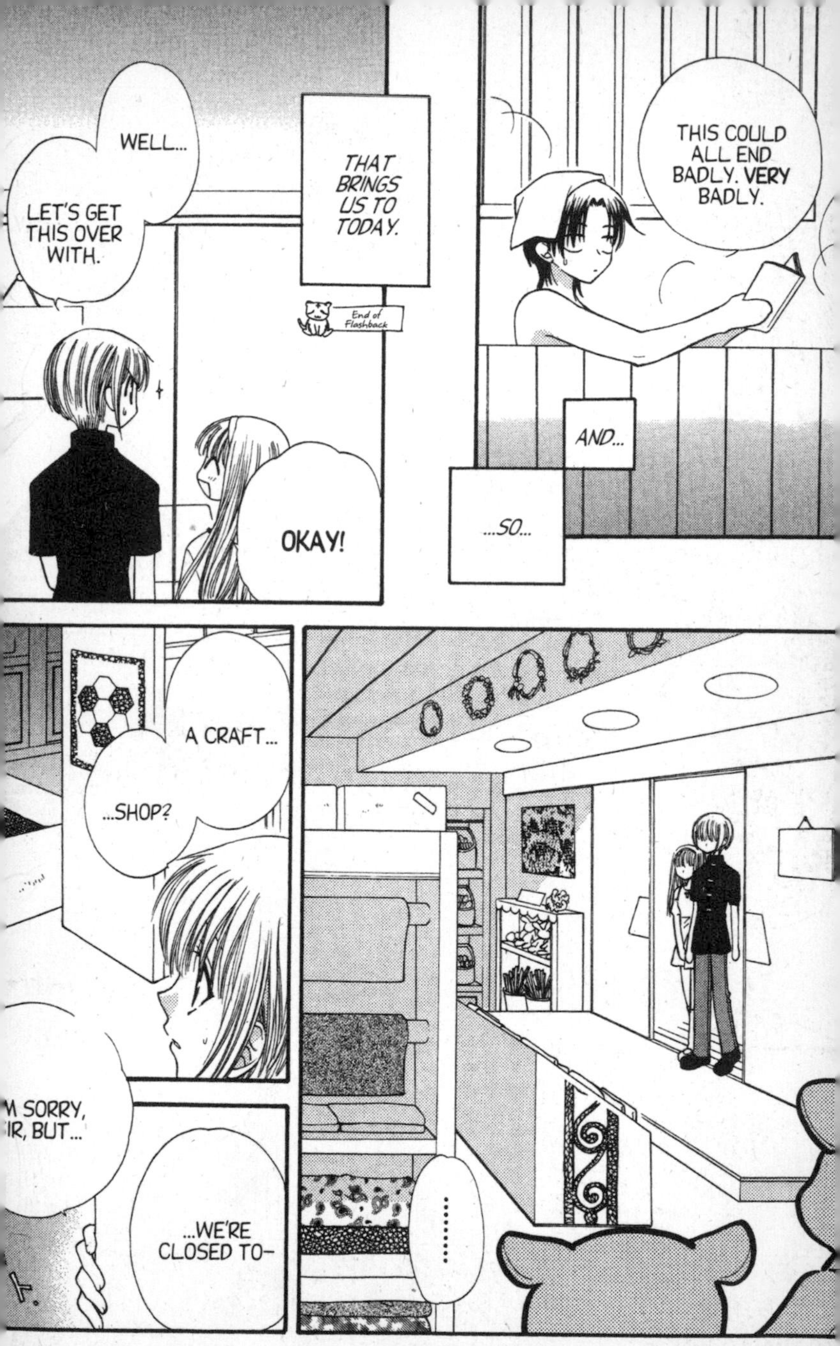
THIS COULD ALL END BADLY. **VERY** BADLY.
AND...
...SO...
THAT BRINGS US TO TODAY.
End of Flashback
WELL...
LET'S GET THIS OVER WITH.
OKAY!
....
A CRAFT...
...SHOP?
M SORRY, IR, BUT...
...WE'RE CLOSED TO-

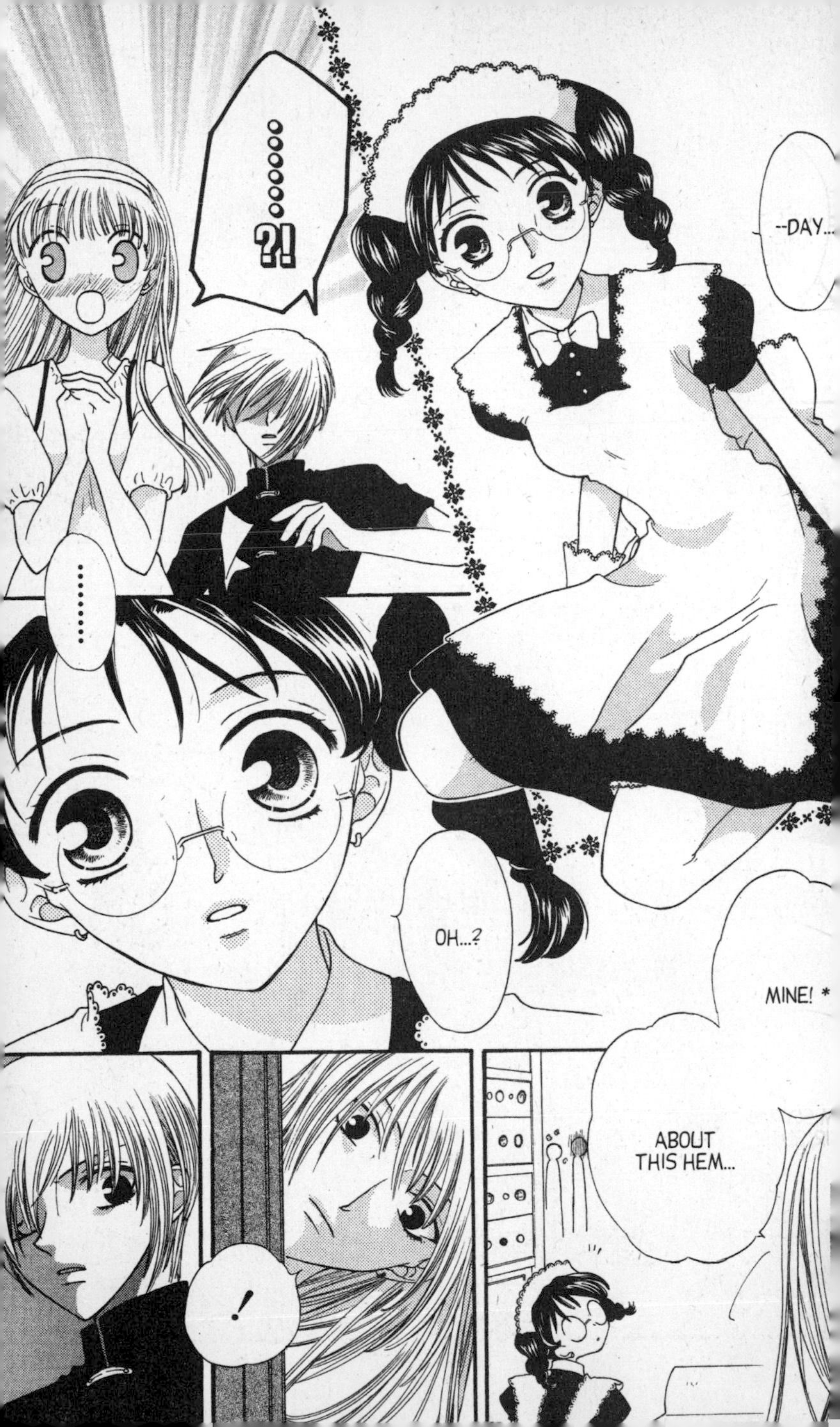
--DAY...
MINE! *
OOOOOO
?!
......
OH...?
ABOUT THIS HEM...
!

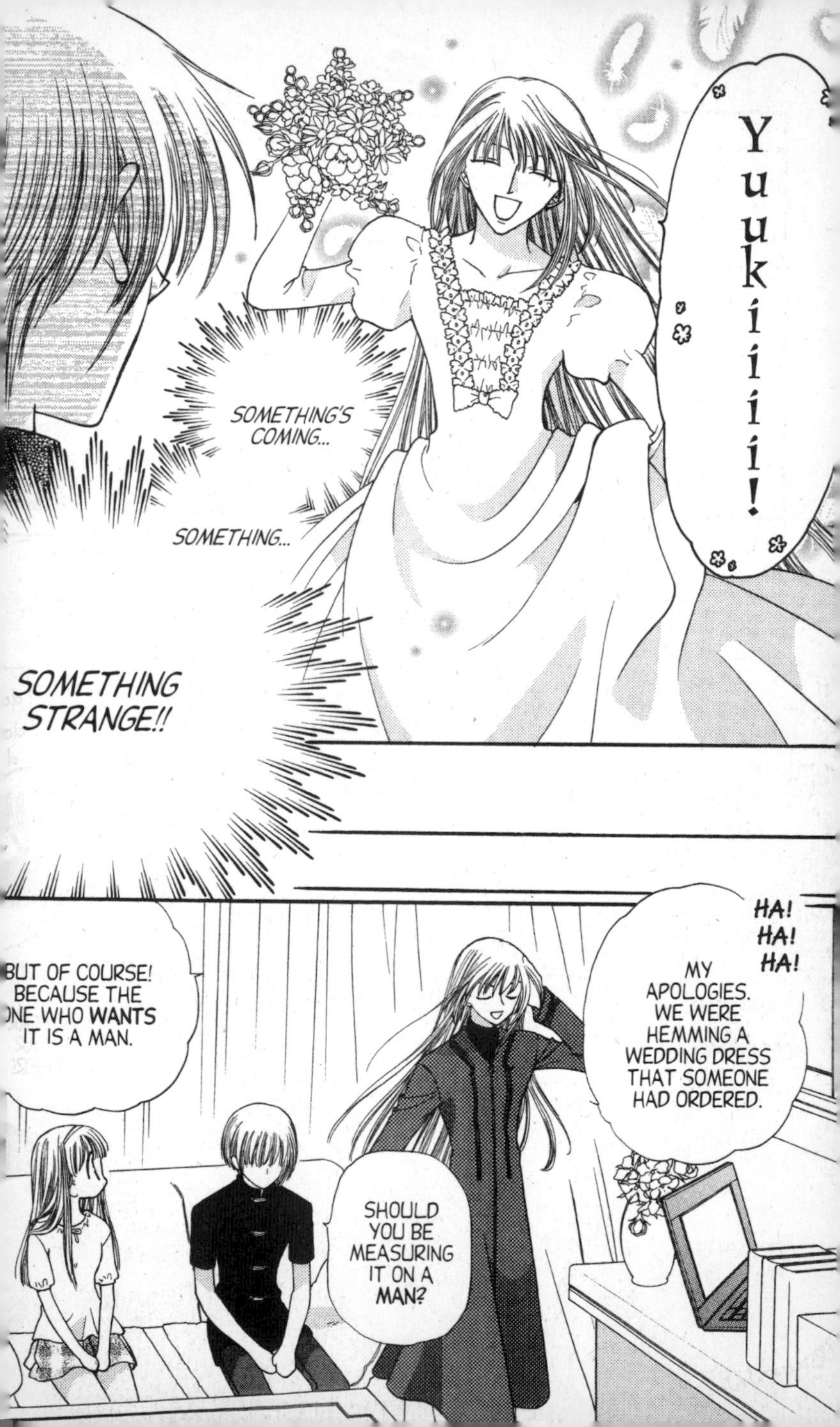

Yuukiiii!
SOMETHING'S COMING...
SOMETHING...
SOMETHING STRANGE!!
HA! HA! HA!
MY APOLOGIES. WE WERE HEMMING A WEDDING DRESS THAT SOMEONE HAD ORDERED.
SHOULD YOU BE MEASURING IT ON A MAN?
BUT OF COURSE! BECAUSE THE ONE WHO WANTS IT IS A MAN.

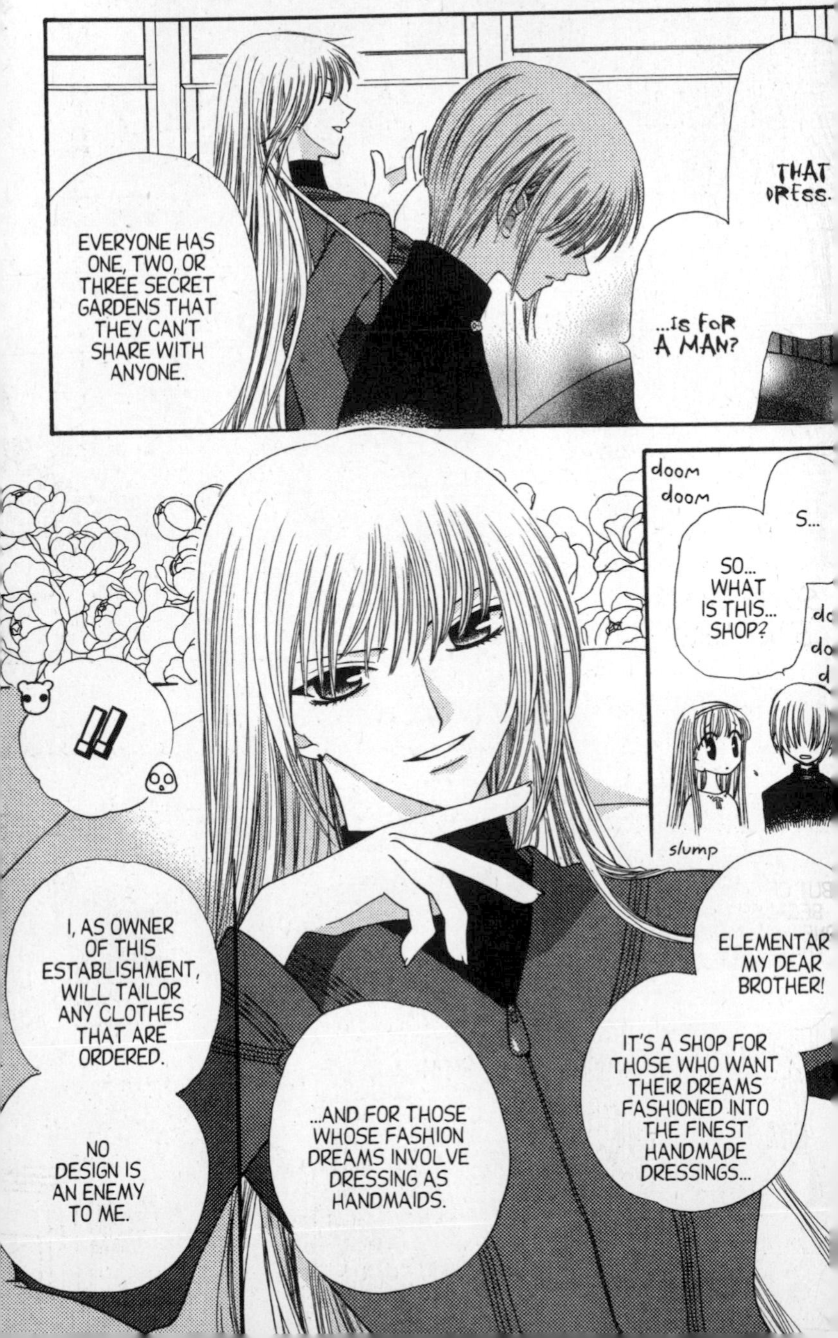
THAT dress.
...is for A MAN?
EVERYONE HAS ONE, TWO, OR THREE SECRET GARDENS THAT THEY CAN'T SHARE WITH ANYONE.
doom doom
S...
SO... WHAT IS THIS... SHOP?
slump
!!
ELEMENTAR MY DEAR BROTHER!
IT'S A SHOP FOR THOSE WHO WANT THEIR DREAMS FASHIONED INTO THE FINEST HANDMADE DRESSINGS...
...AND FOR THOSE WHOSE FASHION DREAMS INVOLVE DRESSING AS HANDMAIDS.
I, AS OWNER OF THIS ESTABLISHMENT, WILL TAILOR ANY CLOTHES THAT ARE ORDERED.
NO DESIGN IS AN ENEMY TO ME.

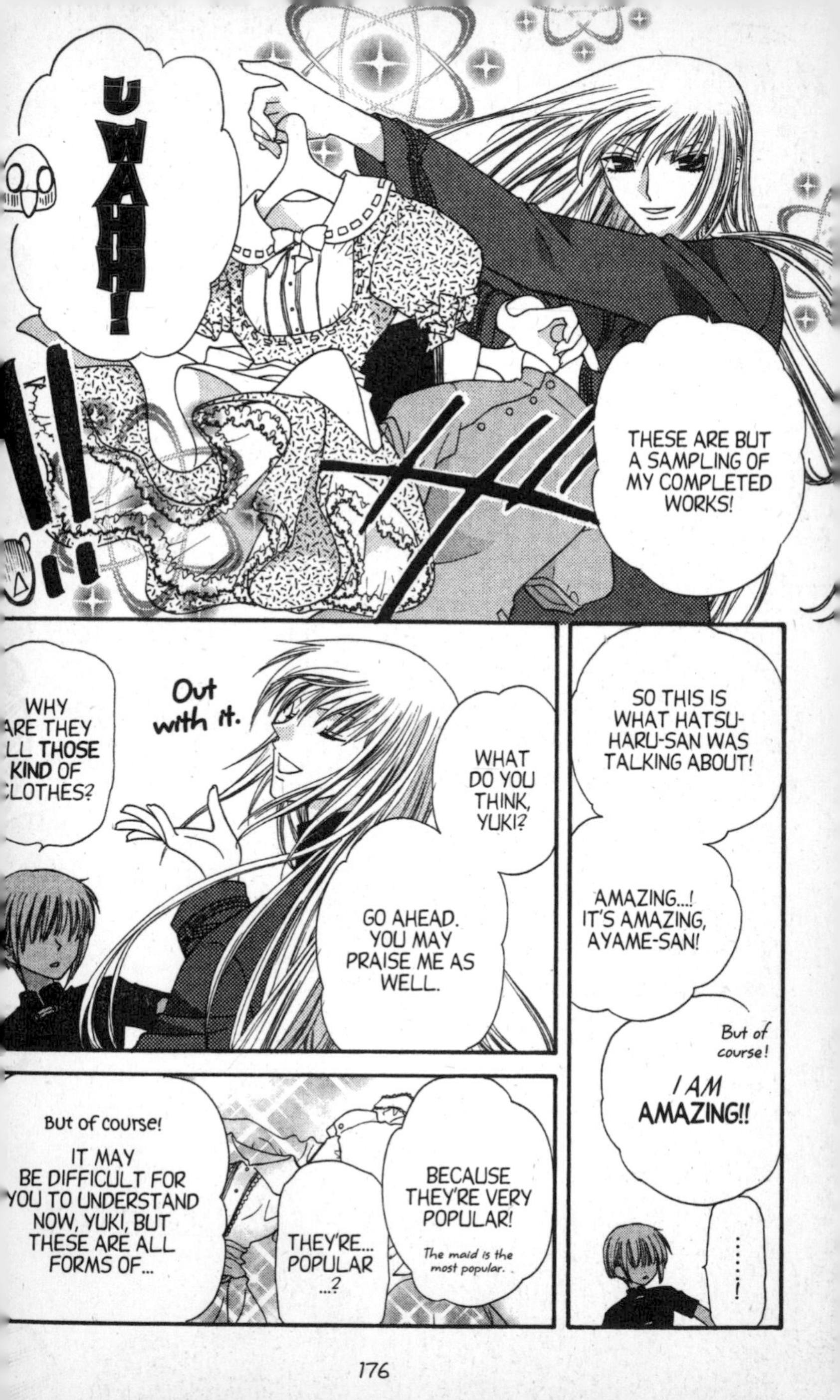
THESE ARE BUT A SAMPLING OF MY COMPLETED WORKS!
UWAHH!!
!!
SO THIS IS WHAT HATSUHARU-SAN WAS TALKING ABOUT!
AMAZING...! IT'S AMAZING, AYAME-SAN!
But of course!
I AM AMAZING!!
......!
WHAT DO YOU THINK, YUKI?
GO AHEAD. YOU MAY PRAISE ME AS WELL.
Out with it.
WHY ARE THEY LL THOSE KIND OF LOTHES?
BECAUSE THEY'RE VERY POPULAR!
The maid is the most popular.
THEY'RE... POPULAR ...?
But of course!
IT MAY BE DIFFICULT FOR YOU TO UNDERSTAND NOW, YUKI, BUT THESE ARE ALL FORMS OF...

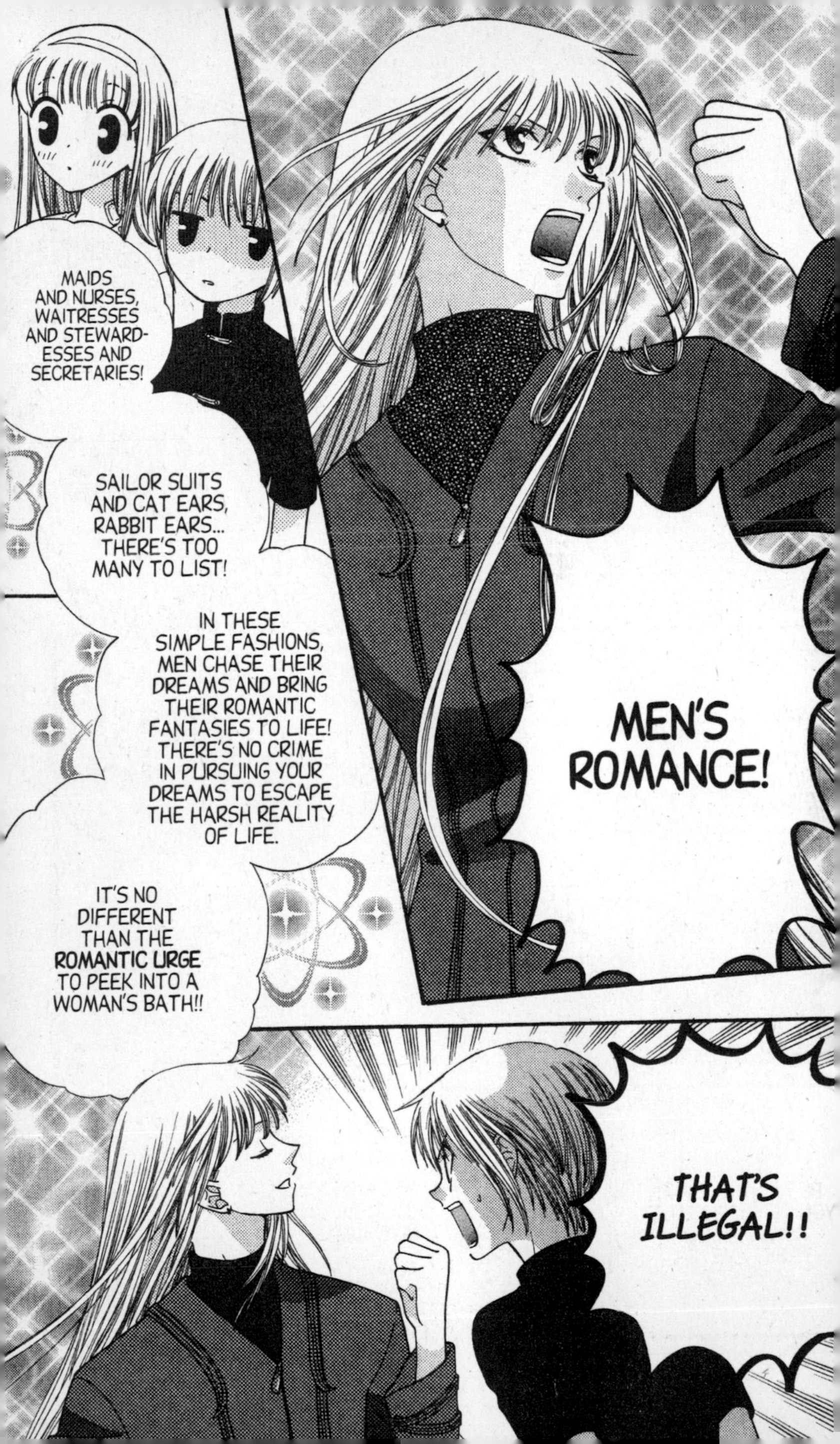
MEN'S ROMANCE!
MAIDS AND NURSES, WAITRESSES AND STEWARD-ESSES AND SECRETARIES!
SAILOR SUITS AND CAT EARS, RABBIT EARS... THERE'S TOO MANY TO LIST!
IN THESE SIMPLE FASHIONS, MEN CHASE THEIR DREAMS AND BRING THEIR ROMANTIC FANTASIES TO LIFE! THERE'S NO CRIME IN PURSUING YOUR DREAMS TO ESCAPE THE HARSH REALITY OF LIFE.
IT'S NO DIFFERENT THAN THE **ROMANTIC URGE** TO PEEK INTO A WOMAN'S BATH!!
THAT'S ILLEGAL!!

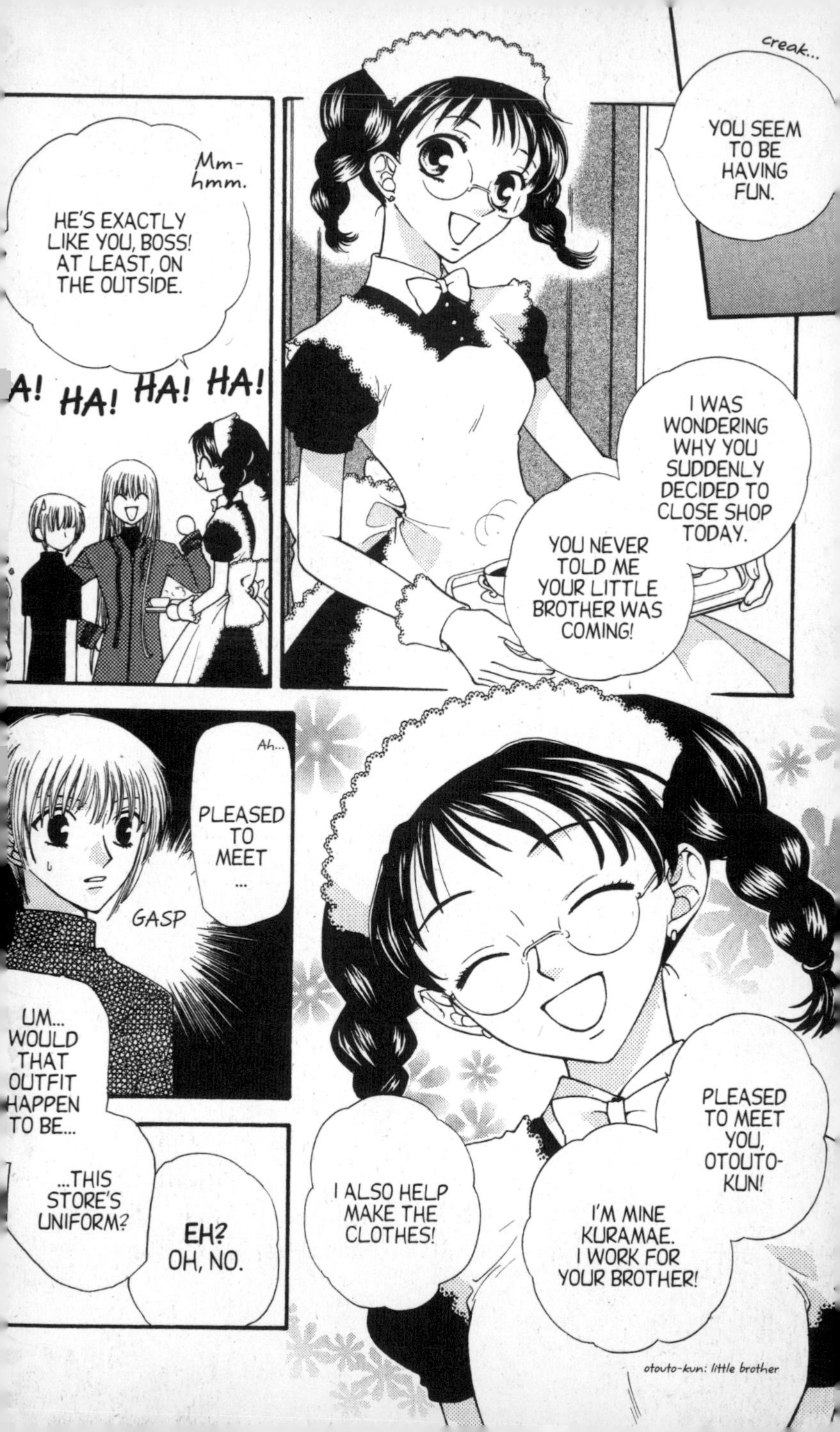
creak...
YOU SEEM TO BE HAVING FUN.
I WAS WONDERING WHY YOU SUDDENLY DECIDED TO CLOSE SHOP TODAY.
YOU NEVER TOLD ME YOUR LITTLE BROTHER WAS COMING!
Mm-hmm.
HE'S EXACTLY LIKE YOU, BOSS! AT LEAST, ON THE OUTSIDE.
A! HA! HA! HA!
PLEASED TO MEET YOU, OTOUTO-KUN!
I'M MINE KURAMAE. I WORK FOR YOUR BROTHER!
I ALSO HELP MAKE THE CLOTHES!
Ah...
PLEASED TO MEET ...
GASP
UM... WOULD THAT OUTFIT HAPPEN TO BE...
...THIS STORE'S UNIFORM?
EH? OH, NO.
otouto-kun: little brother

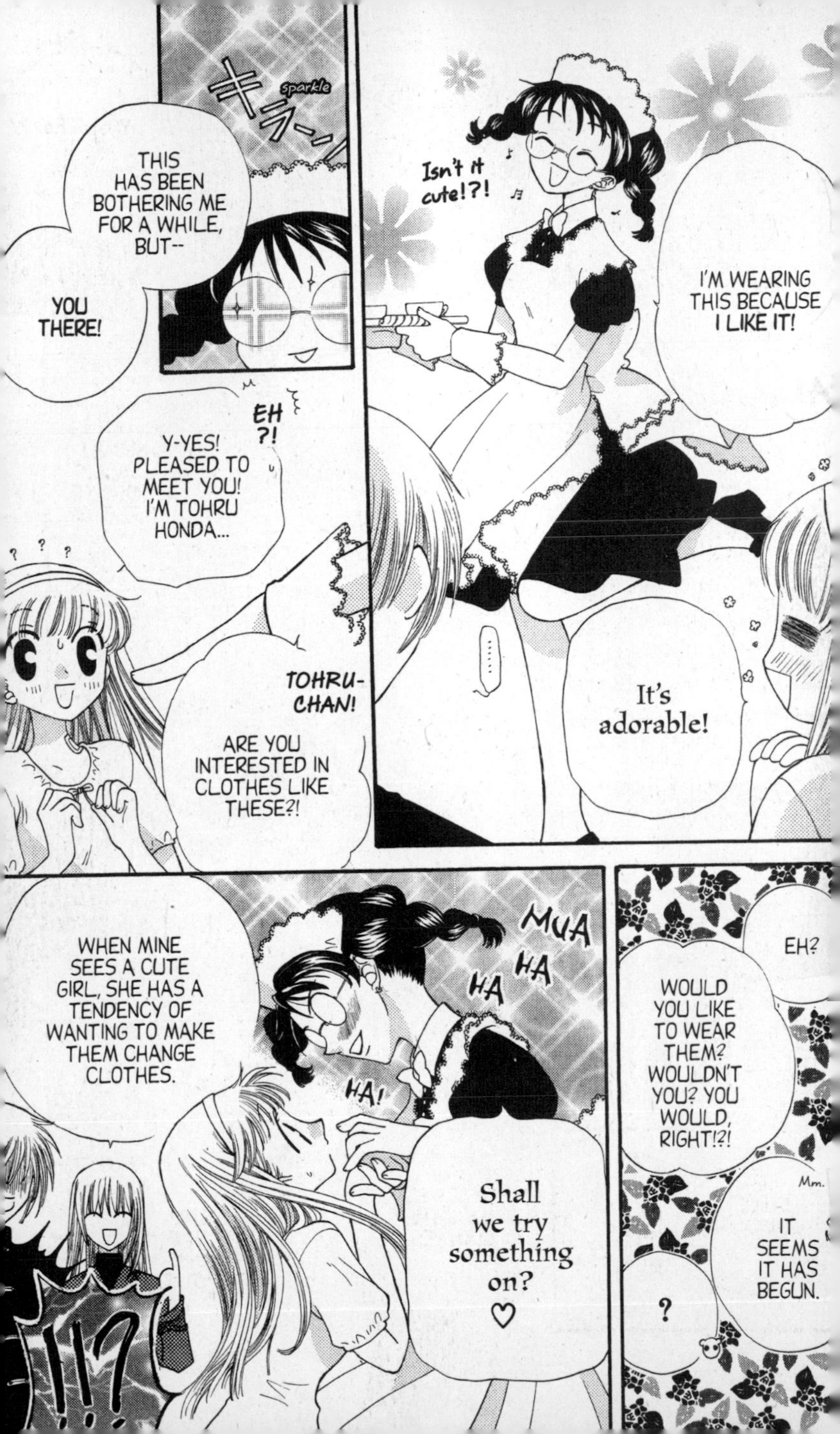
Isn't it cute!?!
I'M WEARING THIS BECAUSE I LIKE IT!
It's adorable!
......
sparkle
THIS HAS BEEN BOTHERING ME FOR A WHILE, BUT--
YOU THERE!
EH?!
Y-YES! PLEASED TO MEET YOU! I'M TOHRU HONDA...
TOHRU-CHAN!
ARE YOU INTERESTED IN CLOTHES LIKE THESE?!
EH?
WOULD YOU LIKE TO WEAR THEM? WOULDN'T YOU? YOU WOULD, RIGHT!?!
Mm.
IT SEEMS IT HAS BEGUN.
?
MUA HA HA HA!
WHEN MINE SEES A CUTE GIRL, SHE HAS A TENDENCY OF WANTING TO MAKE THEM CHANGE CLOTHES.
Shall we try something on? ♡
!!?

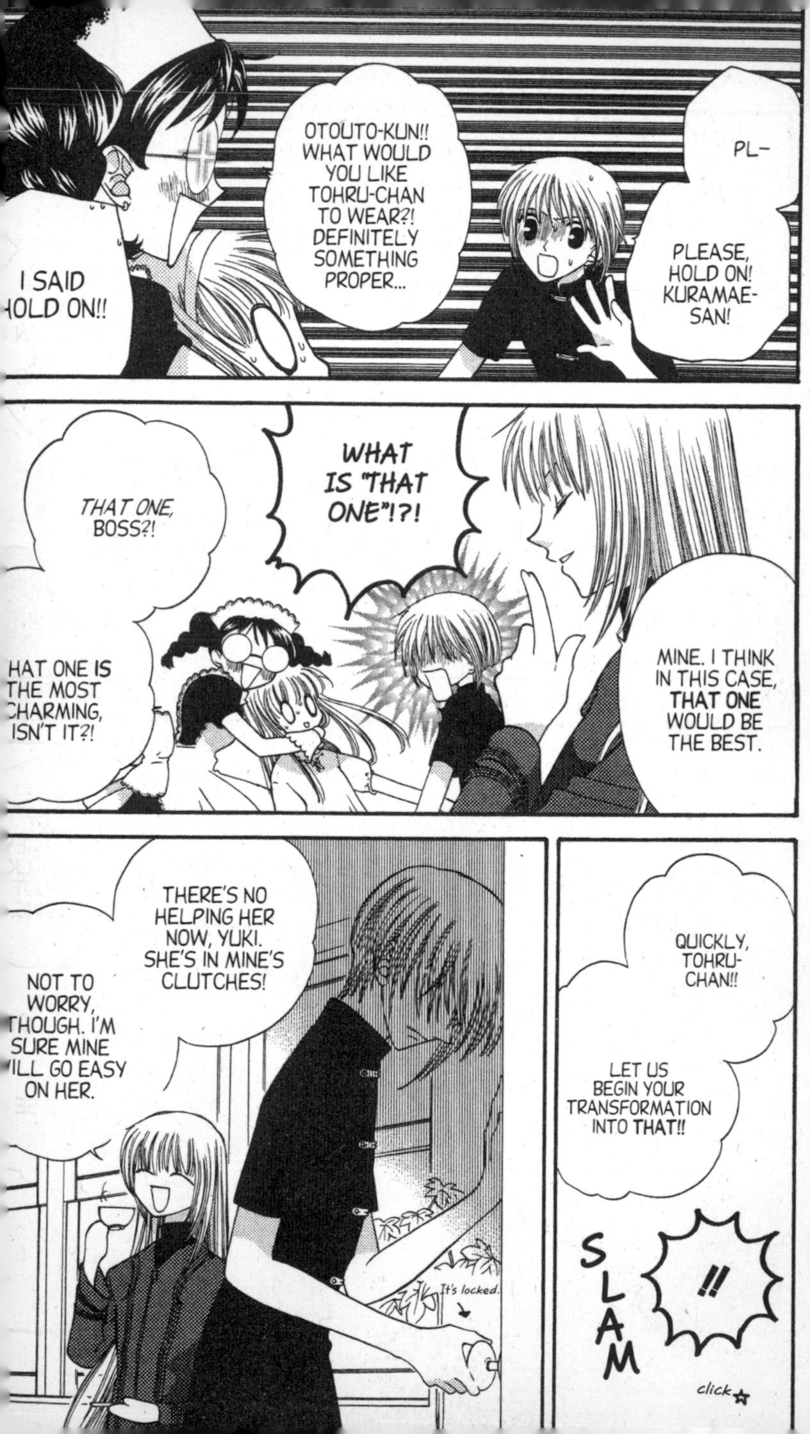
PL–
PLEASE, HOLD ON! KURAMAE-SAN!
OTOUTO-KUN!! WHAT WOULD YOU LIKE TOHRU-CHAN TO WEAR?! DEFINITELY SOMETHING PROPER...
I SAID HOLD ON!!
MINE. I THINK IN THIS CASE, **THAT ONE** WOULD BE THE BEST.
WHAT IS "THAT ONE"!?!
THAT ONE, BOSS?!
THAT ONE **IS** THE MOST CHARMING, ISN'T IT?!
QUICKLY, TOHRU-CHAN!!
LET US BEGIN YOUR TRANSFORMATION INTO **THAT**!!
!!
SLAM
click☆
It's locked.
THERE'S NO HELPING HER NOW, YUKI. SHE'S IN MINE'S CLUTCHES!
NOT TO WORRY, THOUGH. I'M SURE MINE WILL GO EASY ON HER.

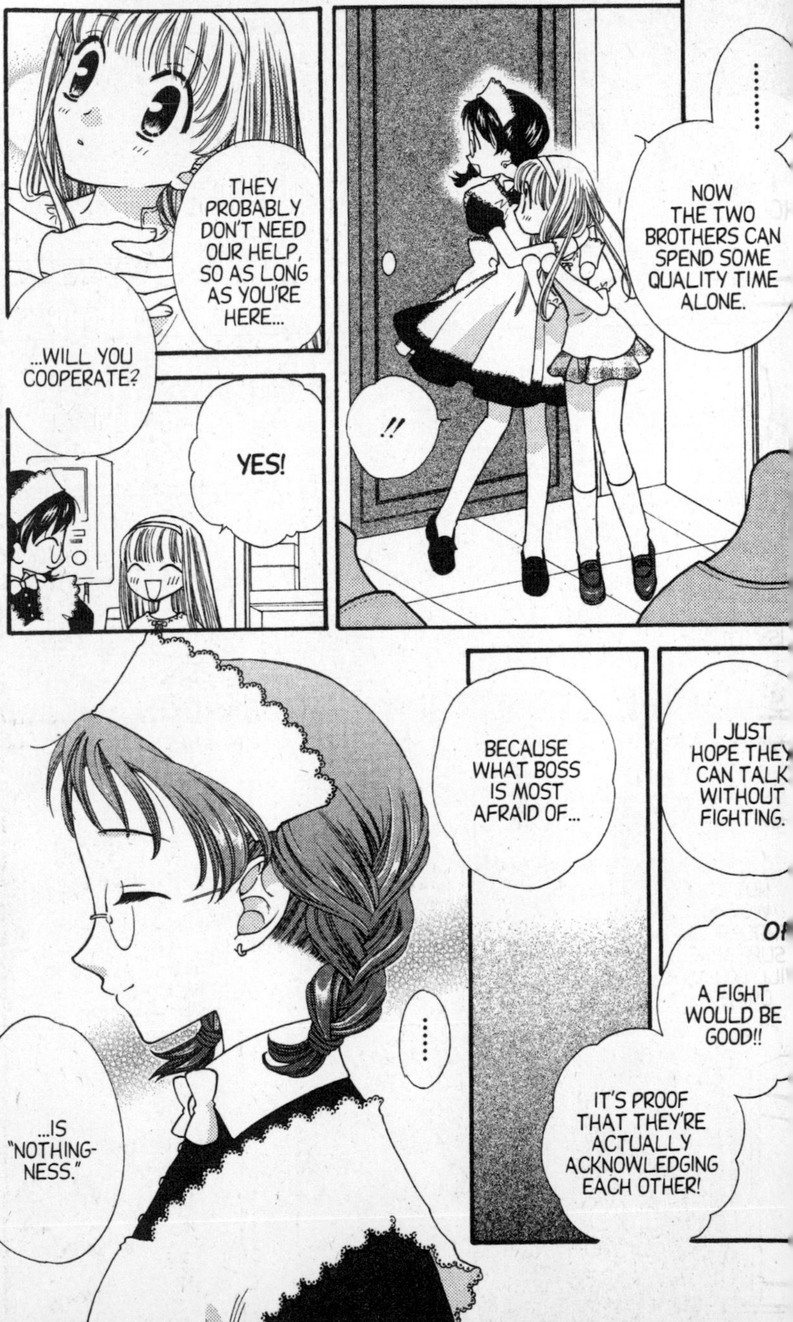
......
NOW THE TWO BROTHERS CAN SPEND SOME QUALITY TIME ALONE.
!!
THEY PROBABLY DON'T NEED OUR HELP, SO AS LONG AS YOU'RE HERE...
...WILL YOU COOPERATE?
YES!
I JUST HOPE THEY CAN TALK WITHOUT FIGHTING.
A FIGHT WOULD BE GOOD!!
IT'S PROOF THAT THEY'RE ACTUALLY ACKNOWLEDGING EACH OTHER!
BECAUSE WHAT BOSS IS MOST AFRAID OF...
......
...IS "NOTHINGNESS."

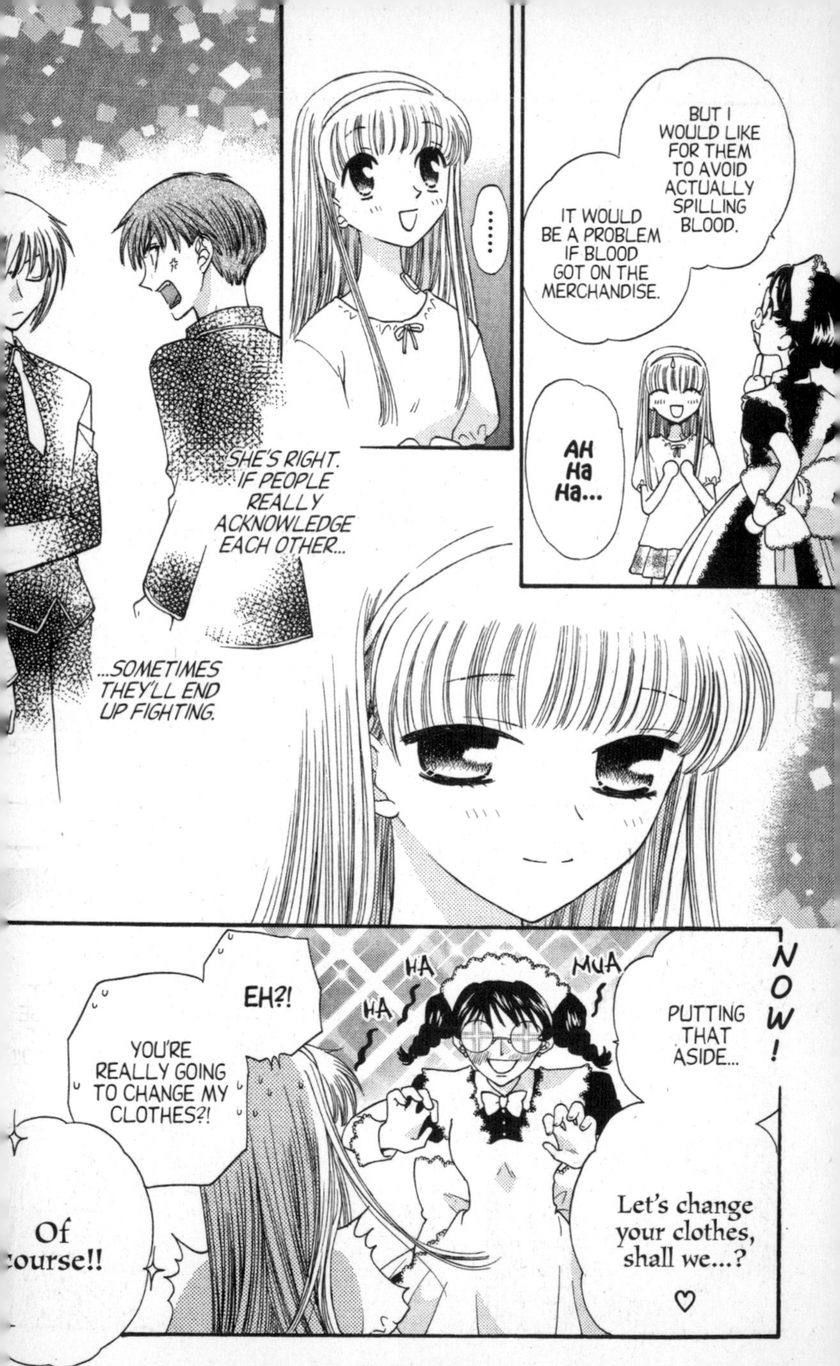
BUT I WOULD LIKE FOR THEM TO AVOID ACTUALLY SPILLING BLOOD.
IT WOULD BE A PROBLEM IF BLOOD GOT ON THE MERCHANDISE.
AH Ha Ha...
......
SHE'S RIGHT. IF PEOPLE REALLY ACKNOWLEDGE EACH OTHER...
...SOMETIMES THEY'LL END UP FIGHTING.
NOW!
PUTTING THAT ASIDE...
Let's change your clothes, shall we...? ♡
MUA HA HA
EH?!
YOU'RE REALLY GOING TO CHANGE MY CLOTHES?!
Of course!!

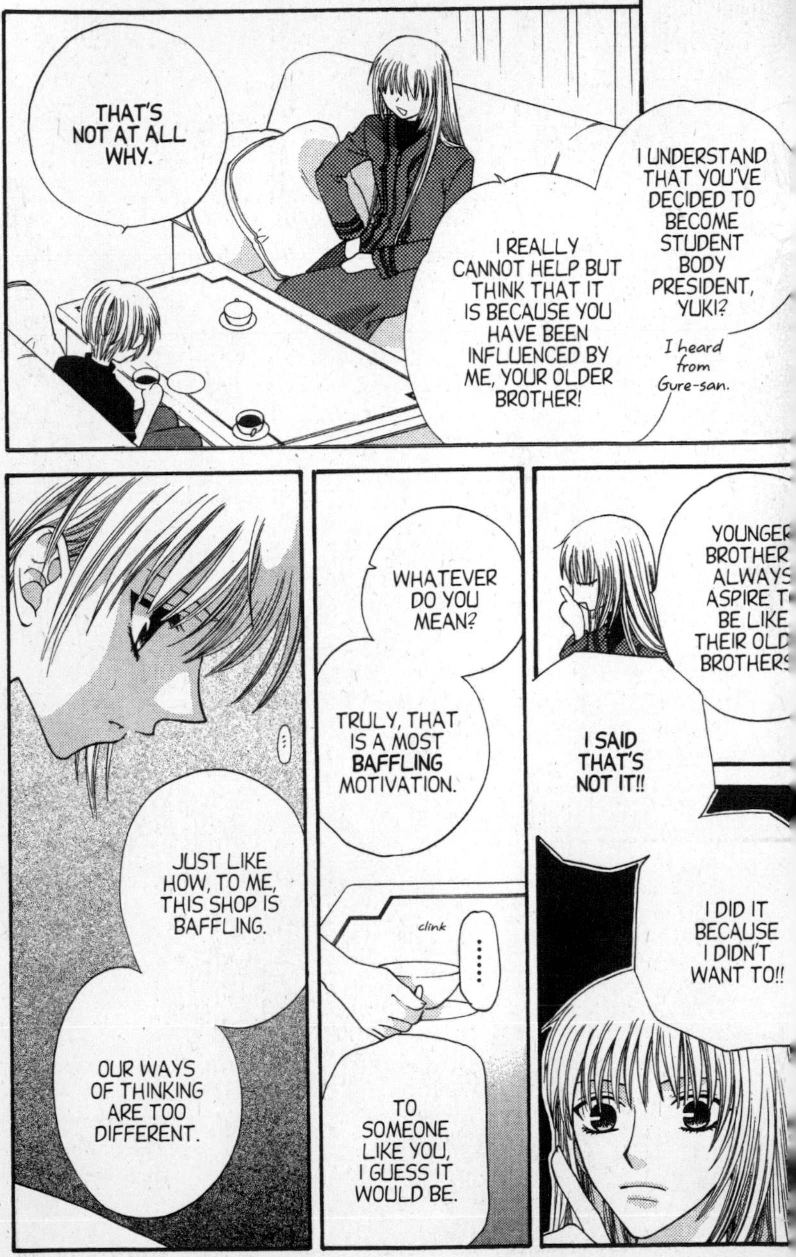
I UNDERSTAND THAT YOU'VE DECIDED TO BECOME STUDENT BODY PRESIDENT, YUKI?
I heard from Gure-san.
I REALLY CANNOT HELP BUT THINK THAT IT IS BECAUSE YOU HAVE BEEN INFLUENCED BY ME, YOUR OLDER BROTHER!
THAT'S NOT AT ALL WHY.
YOUNGER BROTHER ALWAYS ASPIRE T BE LIKE THEIR OLD BROTHERS
I SAID THAT'S NOT IT!!
I DID IT BECAUSE I DIDN'T WANT TO!!
WHATEVER DO YOU MEAN?
TRULY, THAT IS A MOST **BAFFLING** MOTIVATION.
clink
......
TO SOMEONE LIKE YOU, I GUESS IT WOULD BE.
...
JUST LIKE HOW, TO ME, THIS SHOP IS BAFFLING.
OUR WAYS OF THINKING ARE TOO DIFFERENT.

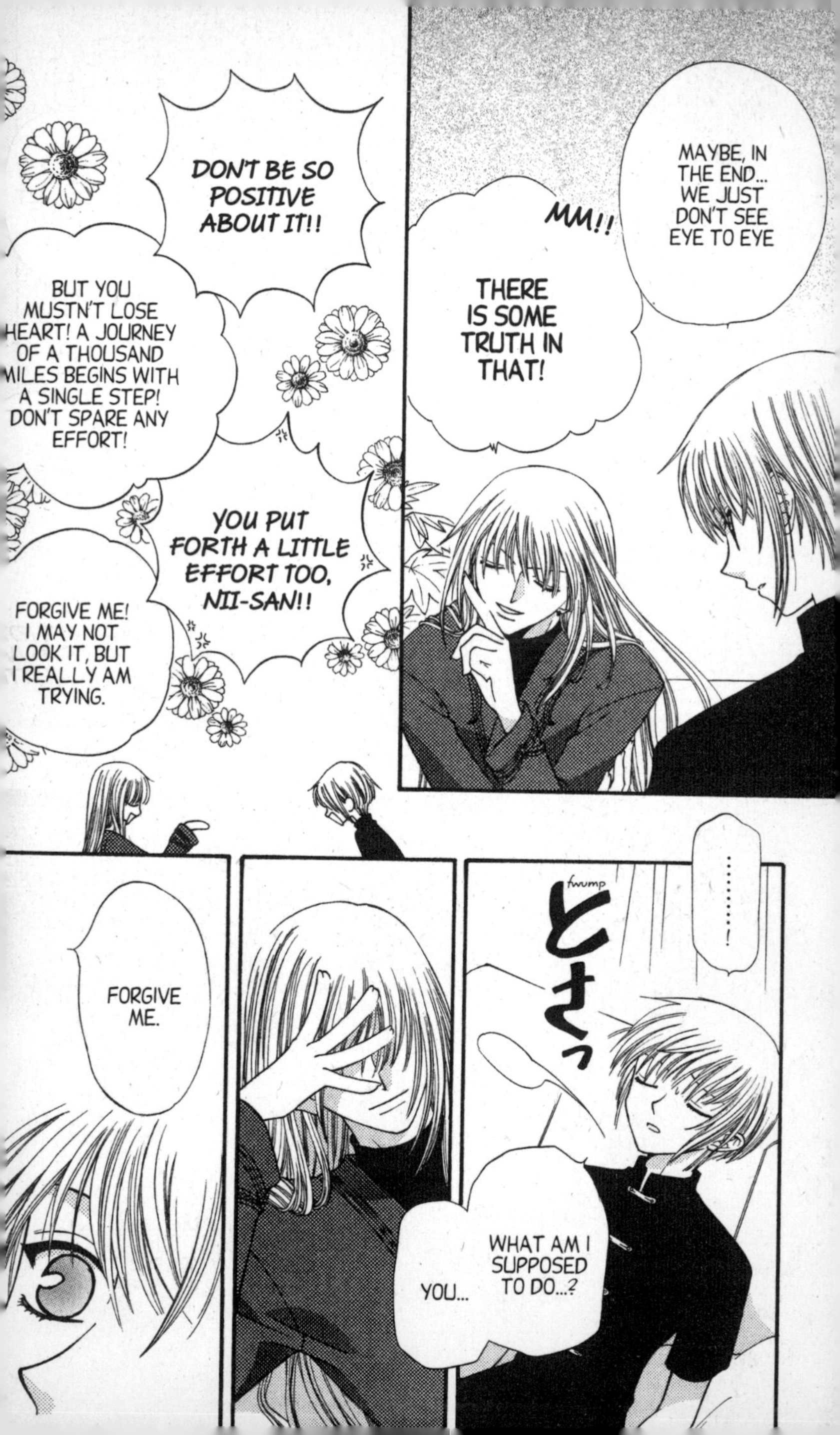
MAYBE, IN THE END... WE JUST DON'T SEE EYE TO EYE
MM!!
THERE IS SOME TRUTH IN THAT!
DON'T BE SO POSITIVE ABOUT IT!!
BUT YOU MUSTN'T LOSE HEART! A JOURNEY OF A THOUSAND MILES BEGINS WITH A SINGLE STEP! DON'T SPARE ANY EFFORT!
YOU PUT FORTH A LITTLE EFFORT TOO, NII-SAN!!
FORGIVE ME! I MAY NOT LOOK IT, BUT I REALLY AM TRYING.
......!
fwump
とさっ
WHAT AM I SUPPOSED TO DO...?
YOU...
FORGIVE ME.

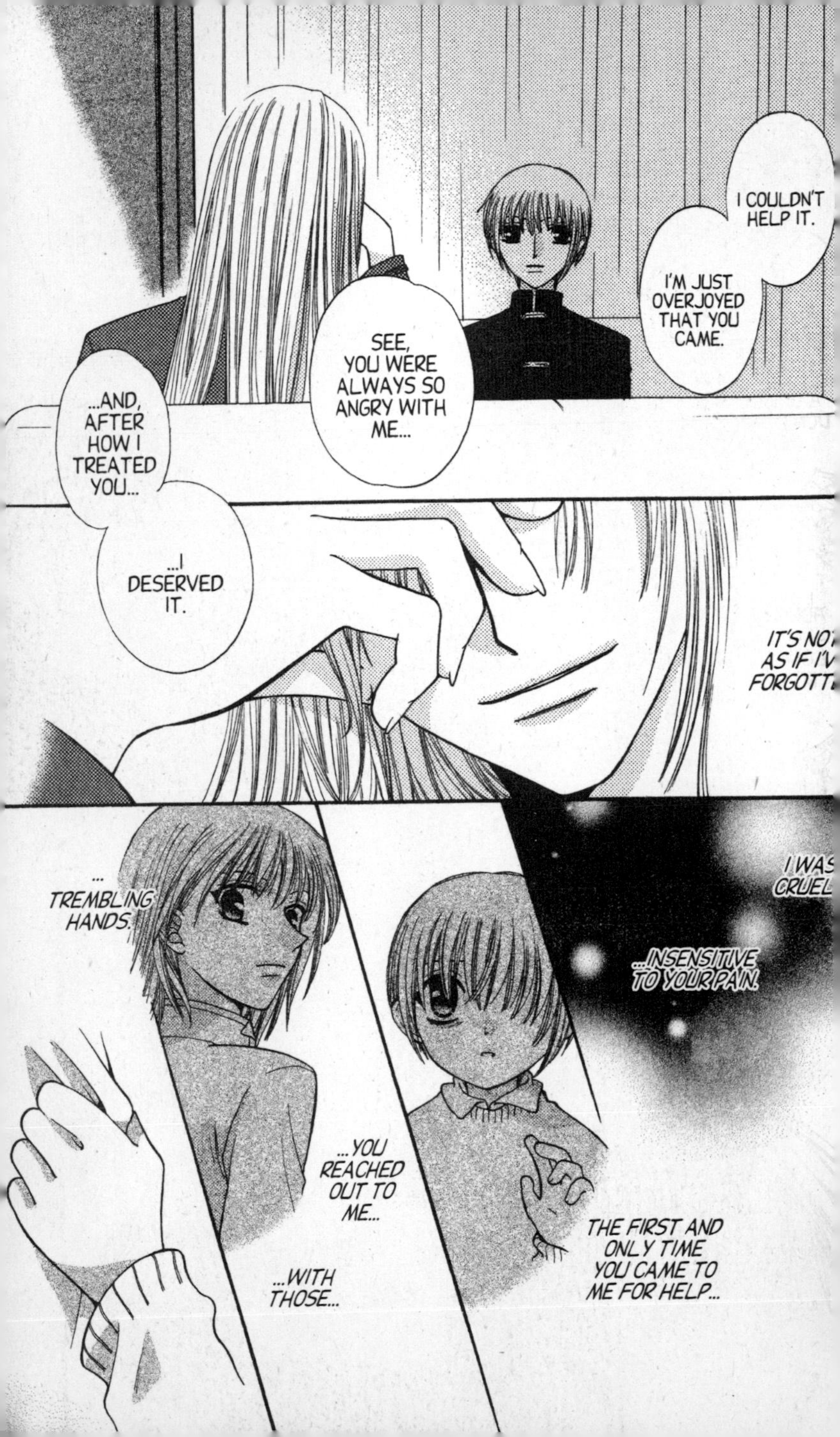
I COULDN'T HELP IT.
I'M JUST OVERJOYED THAT YOU CAME.
SEE, YOU WERE ALWAYS SO ANGRY WITH ME...
...AND, AFTER HOW I TREATED YOU...
...I DESERVED IT.
IT'S NO AS IF I'V FORGOTT
I WAS CRUEL
...INSENSITIVE TO YOUR PAIN.
THE FIRST AND ONLY TIME YOU CAME TO ME FOR HELP...
...YOU REACHED OUT TO ME...
...WITH THOSE...
...TREMBLING HANDS.

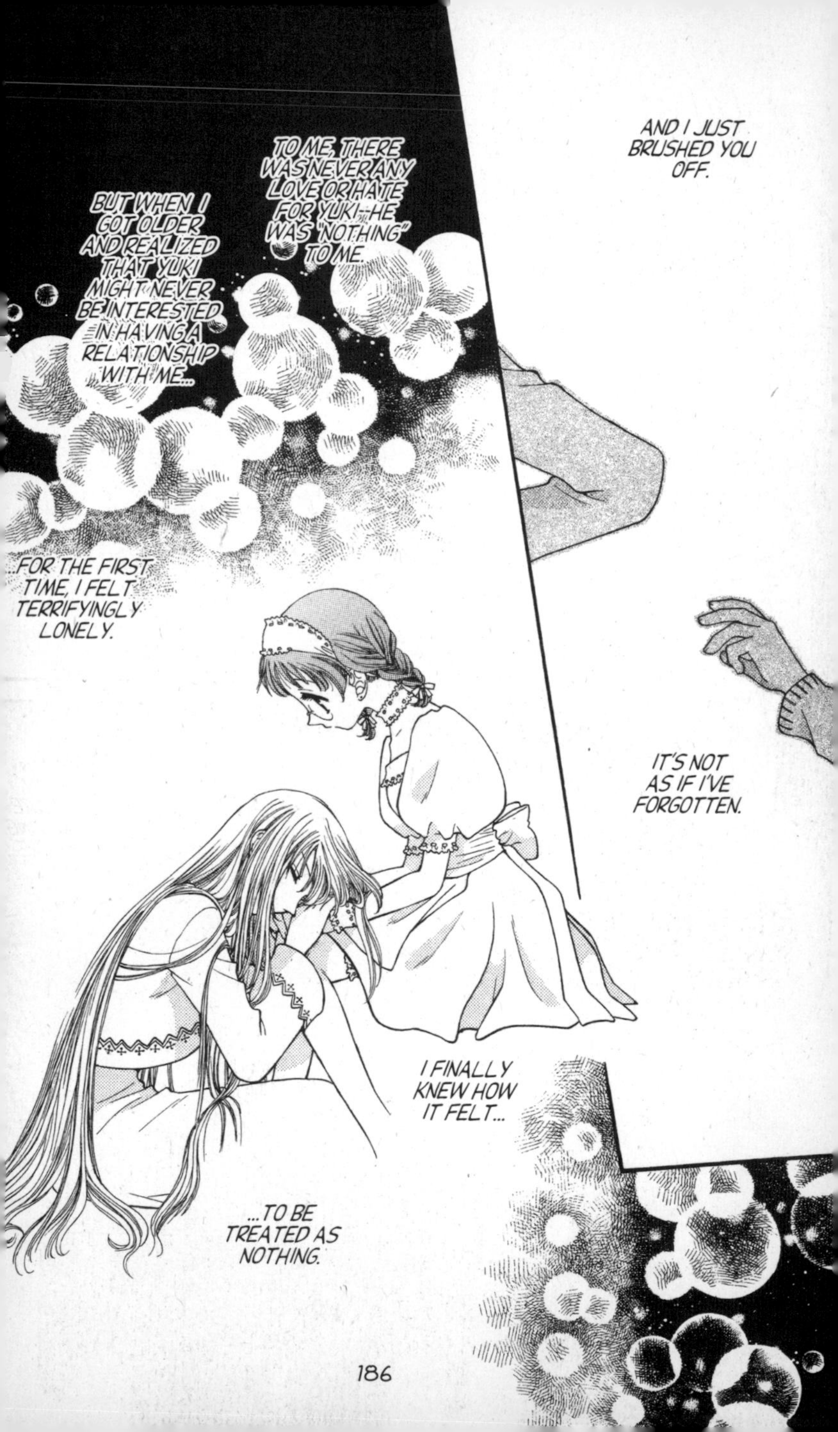
AND I JUST BRUSHED YOU OFF.
IT'S NOT AS IF I'VE FORGOTTEN.
TO ME, THERE WAS NEVER ANY LOVE OR HATE FOR YUKI--HE WAS "NOTHING" TO ME.
BUT WHEN I GOT OLDER AND REALIZED THAT YUKI MIGHT NEVER BE INTERESTED IN HAVING A RELATIONSHIP WITH ME...
...FOR THE FIRST TIME, I FELT TERRIFYINGLY LONELY.
I FINALLY KNEW HOW IT FELT...
...TO BE TREATED AS NOTHING.

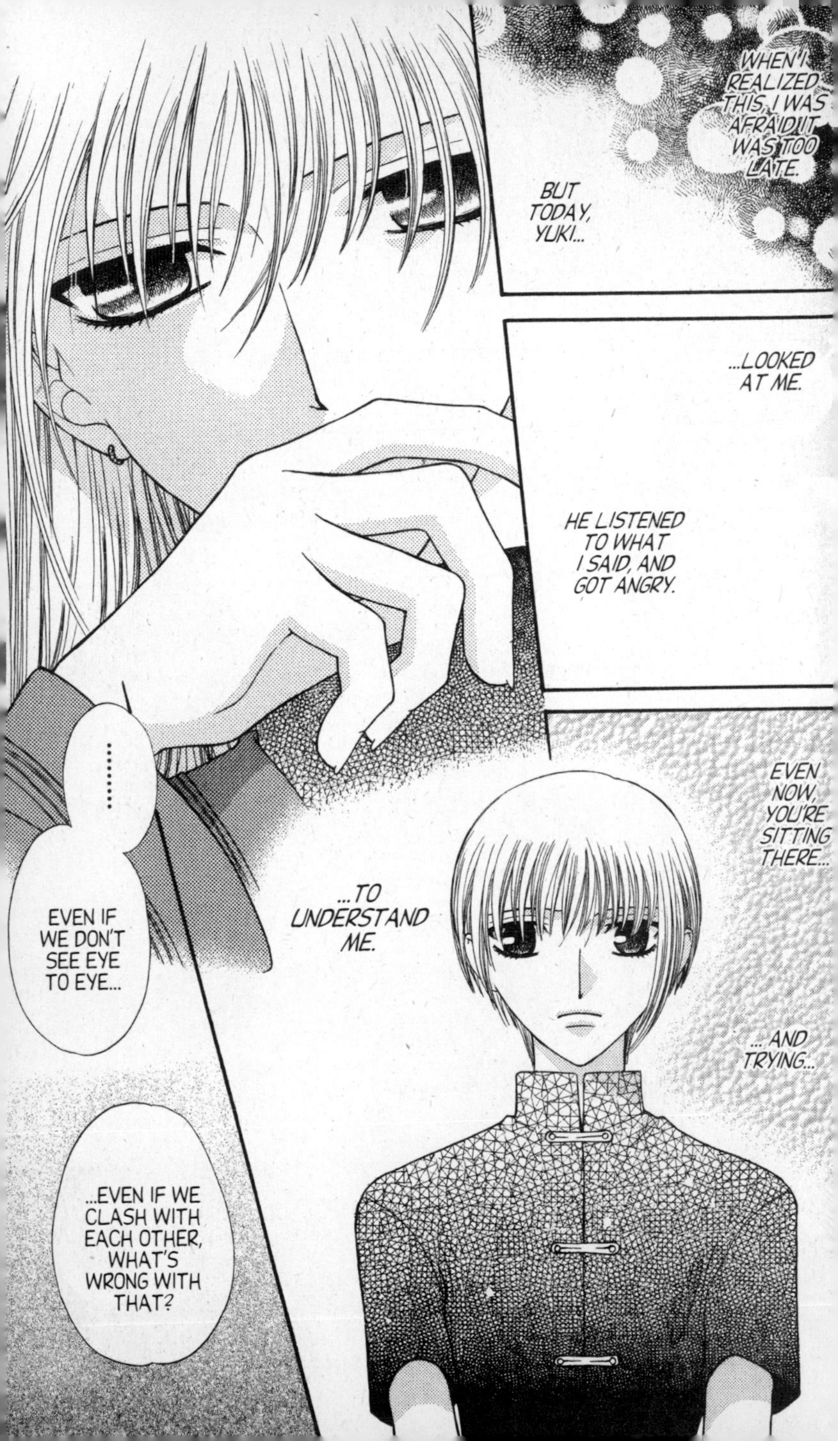
WHEN I REALIZED THIS, I WAS AFRAID IT WAS TOO LATE.
BUT TODAY, YUKI...
...LOOKED AT ME.
HE LISTENED TO WHAT I SAID, AND GOT ANGRY.
EVEN NOW, YOU'RE SITTING THERE...
...AND TRYING...
...TO UNDERSTAND ME.
......
EVEN IF WE DON'T SEE EYE TO EYE...
...EVEN IF WE CLASH WITH EACH OTHER, WHAT'S WRONG WITH THAT?

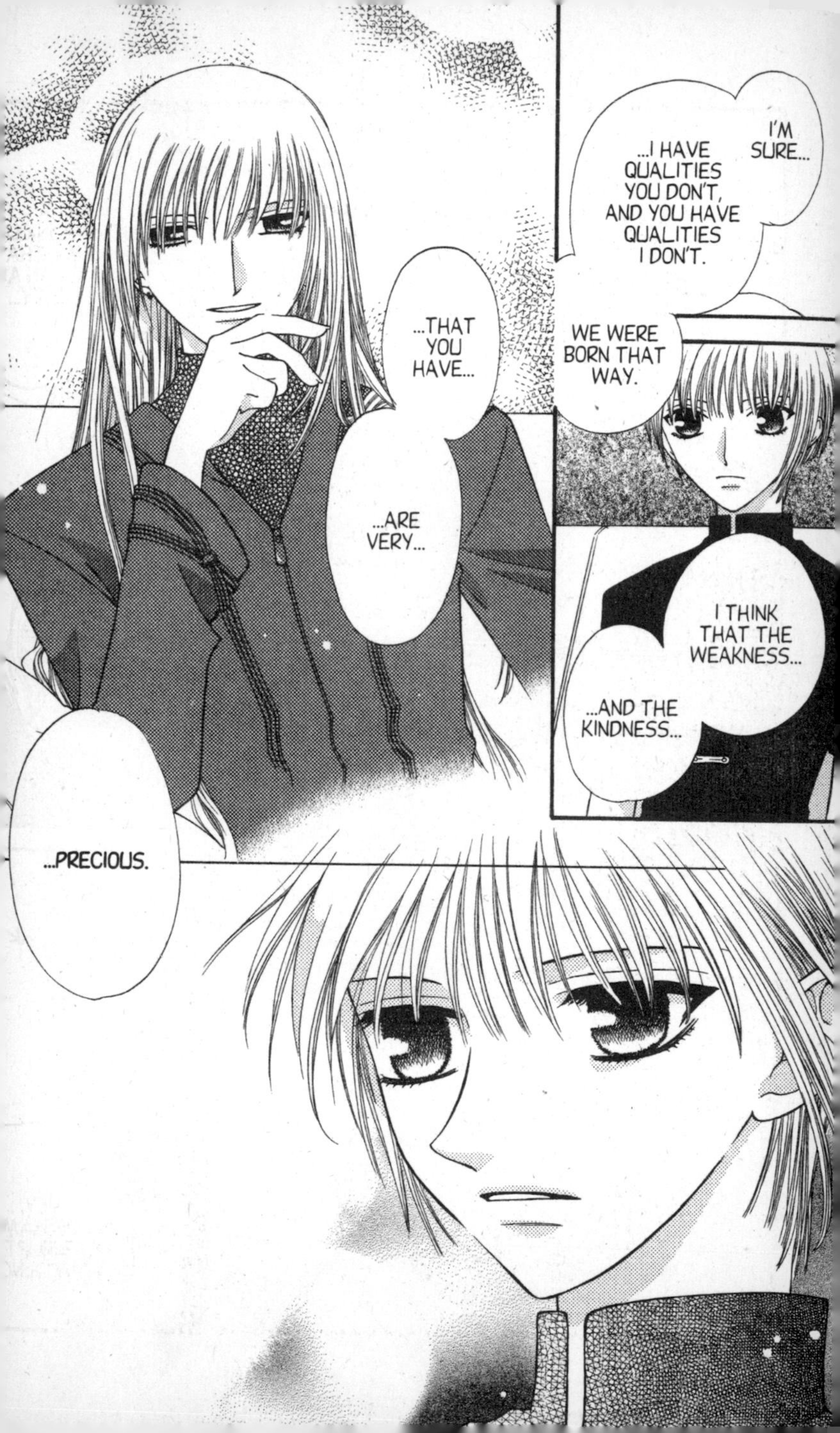
I'M SURE...
...I HAVE QUALITIES YOU DON'T, AND YOU HAVE QUALITIES I DON'T.
WE WERE BORN THAT WAY.
I THINK THAT THE WEAKNESS...
...AND THE KINDNESS...
...THAT YOU HAVE...
...ARE VERY...
...PRECIOUS.

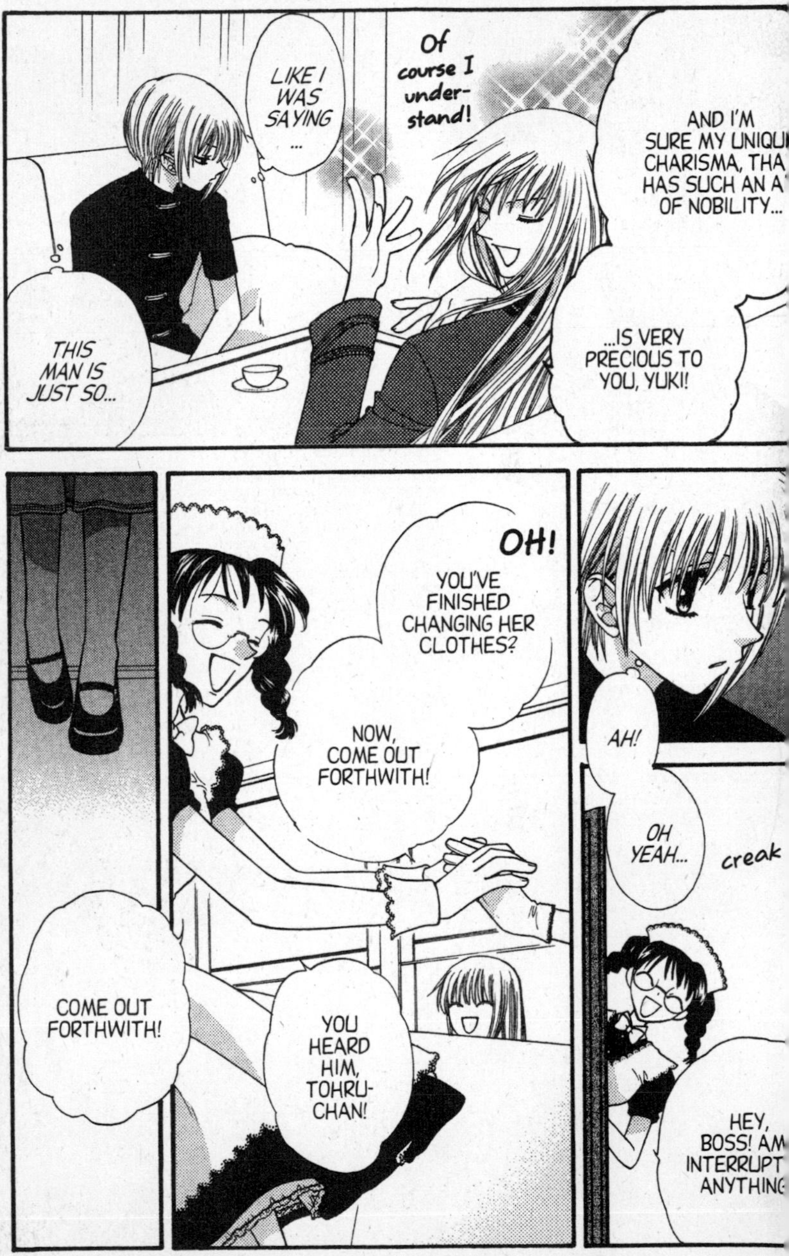
AND I'M SURE MY UNIQU CHARISMA, THA HAS SUCH AN A OF NOBILITY...
...IS VERY PRECIOUS TO YOU, YUKI!
Of course I understand!
LIKE I WAS SAYING ...
THIS MAN IS JUST SO...
AH!
OH YEAH...
creak
HEY, BOSS! AM INTERRUPT ANYTHING
OH!
YOU'VE FINISHED CHANGING HER CLOTHES?
NOW, COME OUT FORTHWITH!
YOU HEARD HIM, TOHRU-CHAN!
COME OUT FORTHWITH!

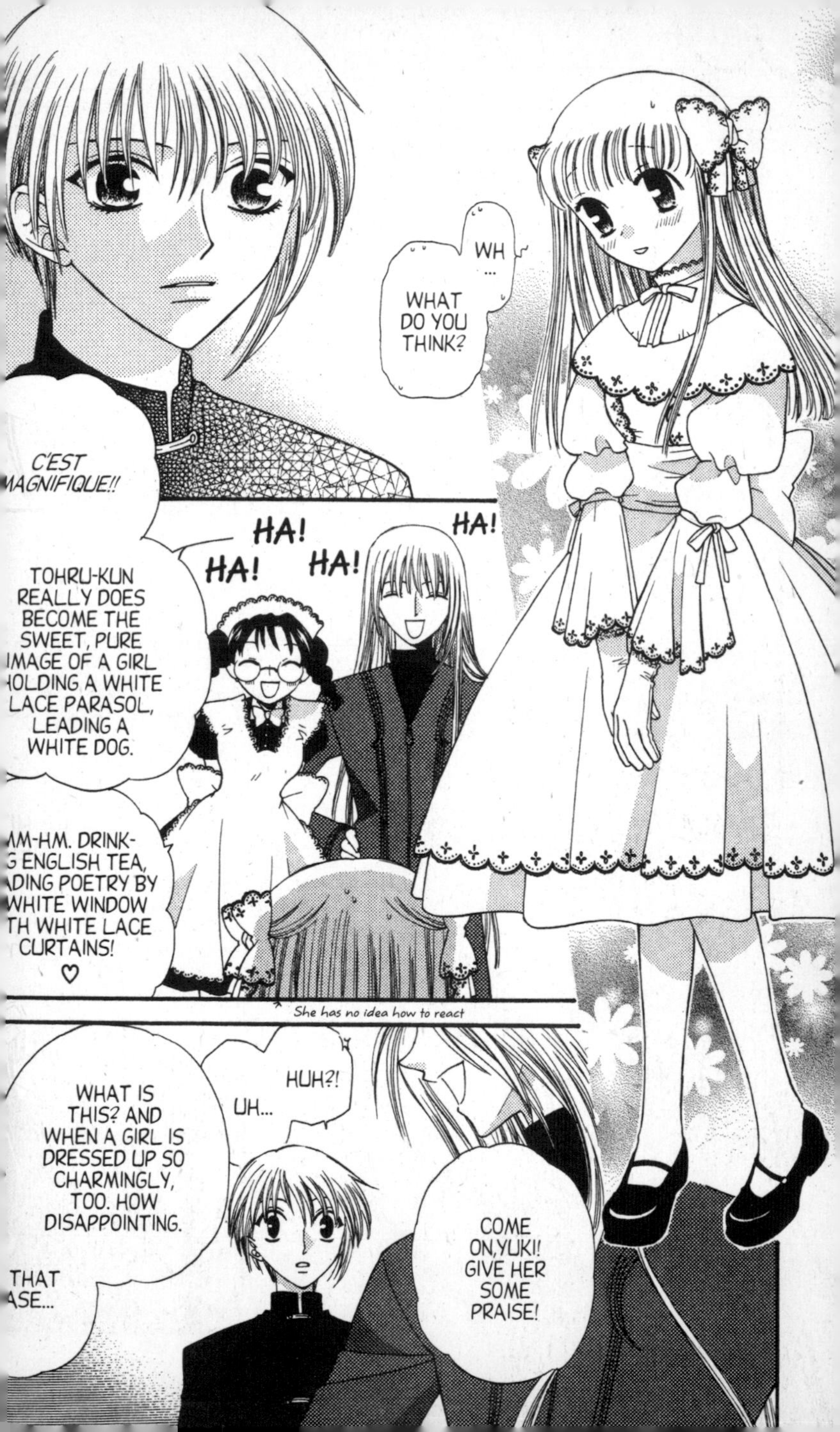
WH...
WHAT DO YOU THINK?
C'EST AGNIFIQUE!!
HA! HA! HA! HA!
TOHRU-KUN REALLY DOES BECOME THE SWEET, PURE IMAGE OF A GIRL HOLDING A WHITE LACE PARASOL, LEADING A WHITE DOG.
MM-HM. DRINK- G ENGLISH TEA, ADING POETRY BY WHITE WINDOW TH WHITE LACE CURTAINS! ♡
She has no idea how to react
COME ON, YUKI! GIVE HER SOME PRAISE!
HUH?!
UH...
WHAT IS THIS? AND WHEN A GIRL IS DRESSED UP SO CHARMINGLY, TOO. HOW DISAPPOINTING.
THAT ASE...

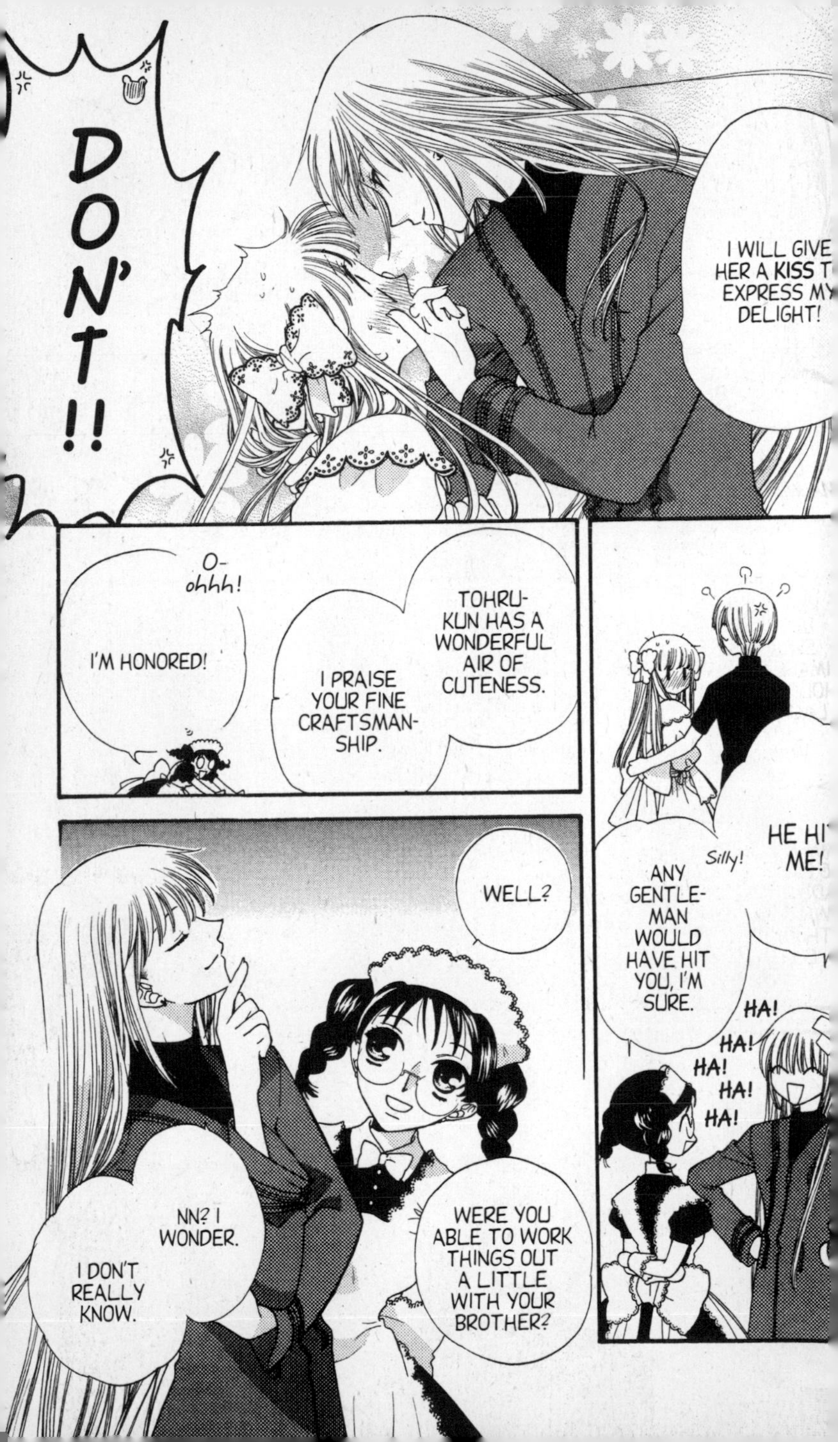
I WILL GIVE HER A KISS T EXPRESS MY DELIGHT!
DON'T!!
HE HI ME!
Silly!
ANY GENTLEMAN WOULD HAVE HIT YOU, I'M SURE.
HA! HA! HA! HA! HA!
TOHRU-KUN HAS A WONDERFUL AIR OF CUTENESS.
I PRAISE YOUR FINE CRAFTSMANSHIP.
O-ohhh!
I'M HONORED!
WELL?
WERE YOU ABLE TO WORK THINGS OUT A LITTLE WITH YOUR BROTHER?
NN? I WONDER.
I DON'T REALLY KNOW.

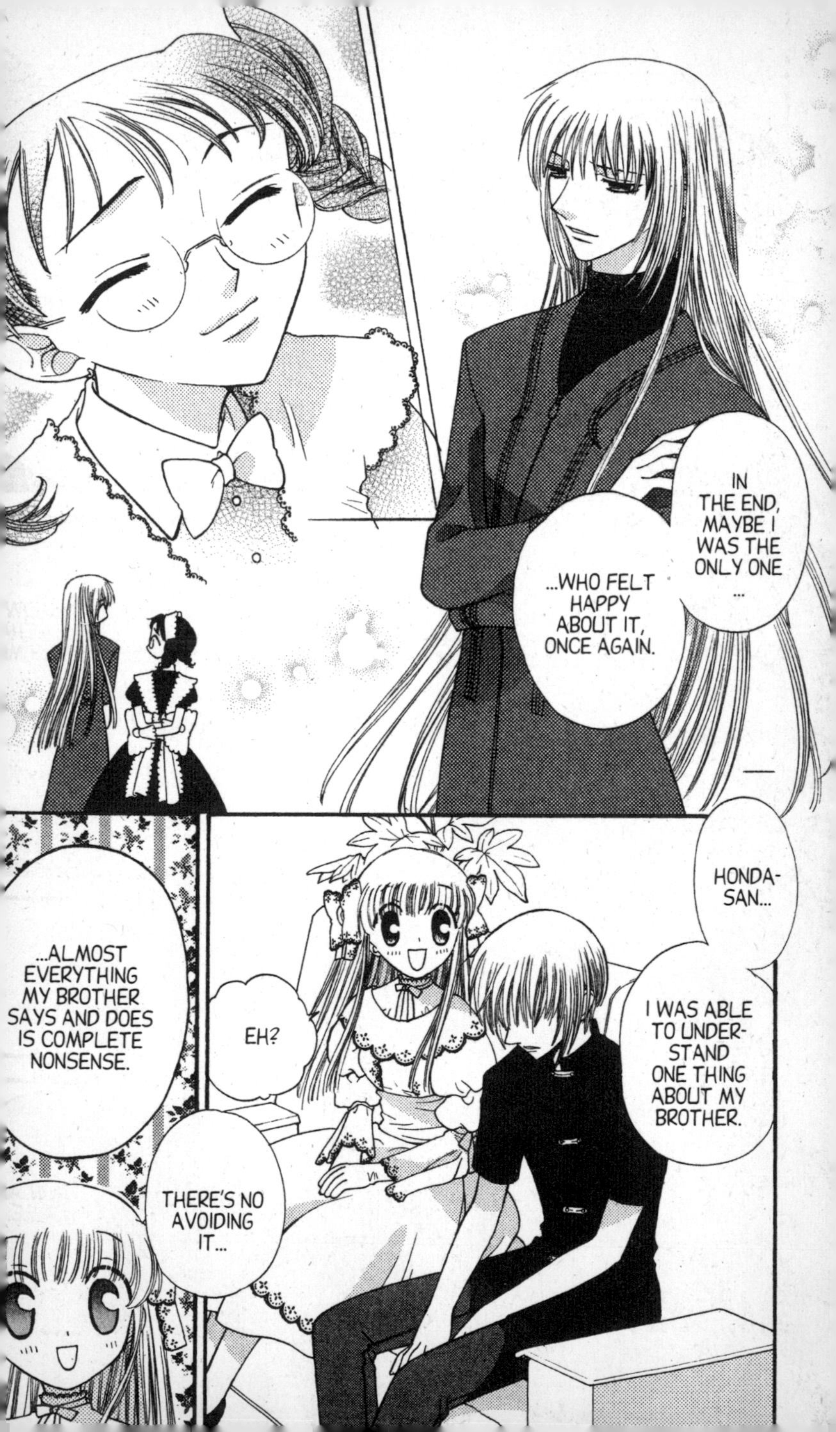
IN THE END, MAYBE I WAS THE ONLY ONE ...
...WHO FELT HAPPY ABOUT IT, ONCE AGAIN.
HONDA-SAN...
I WAS ABLE TO UNDER-STAND ONE THING ABOUT MY BROTHER.
EH?
...ALMOST EVERYTHING MY BROTHER SAYS AND DOES IS COMPLETE NONSENSE.
THERE'S NO AVOIDING IT...

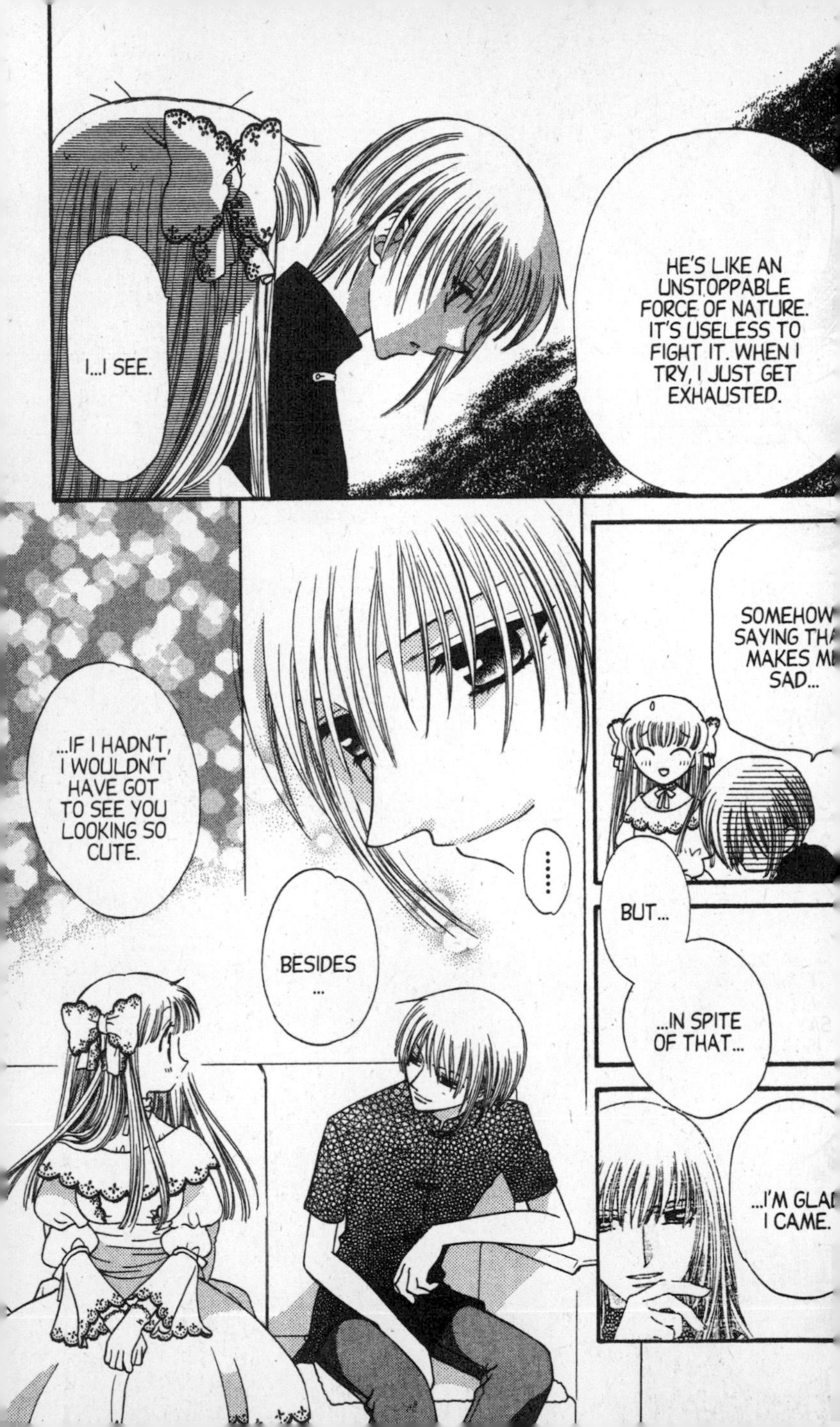
HE'S LIKE AN UNSTOPPABLE FORCE OF NATURE. IT'S USELESS TO FIGHT IT. WHEN I TRY, I JUST GET EXHAUSTED.
I...I SEE.
SOMEHOW SAYING THA MAKES M SAD...
BUT...
...IN SPITE OF THAT...
...I'M GLA I CAME.
......
BESIDES...
...IF I HADN'T, I WOULDN'T HAVE GOT TO SEE YOU LOOKING SO CUTE.

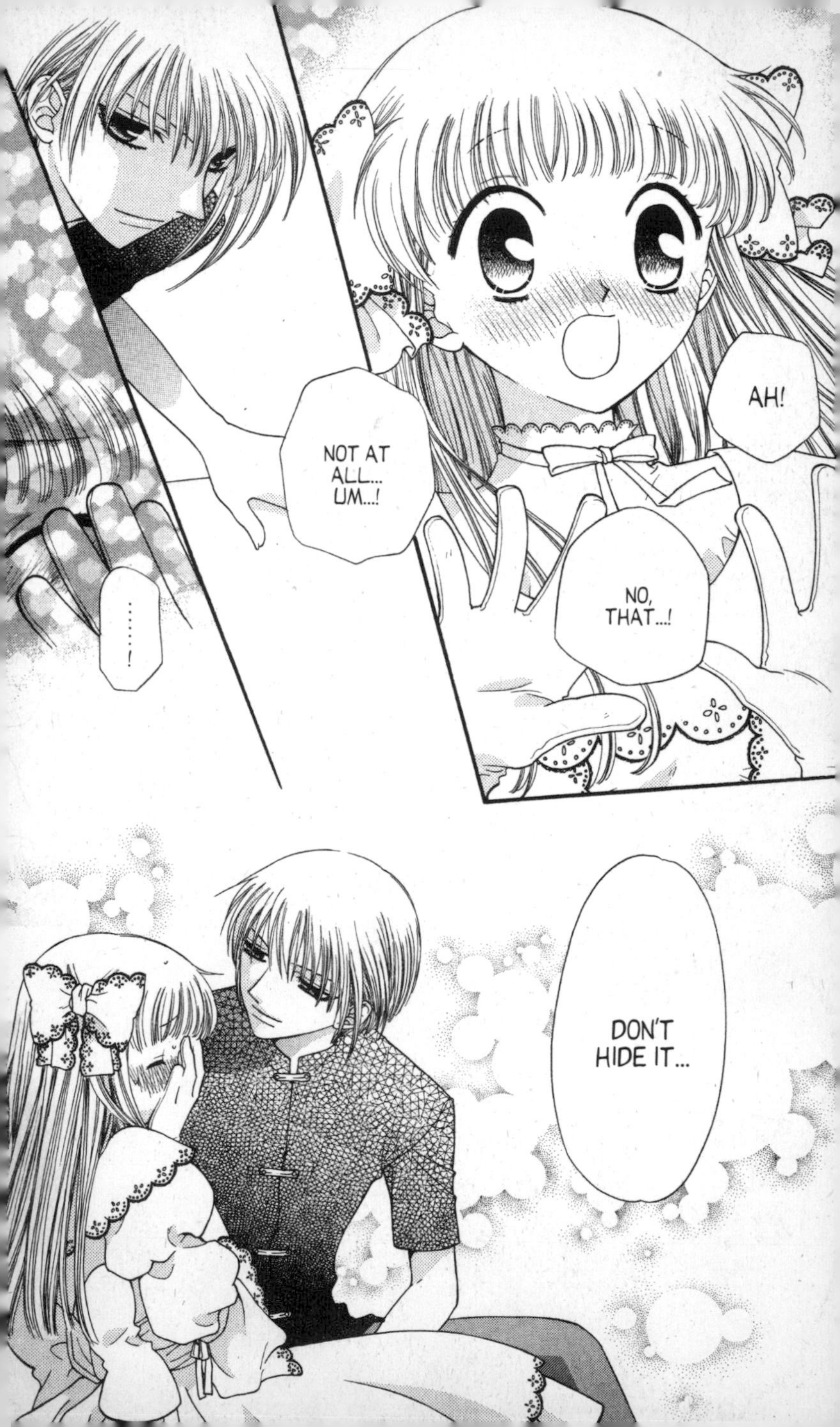
AH!
NOT AT ALL... UM...!
NO, THAT...!
......!
DON'T HIDE IT...

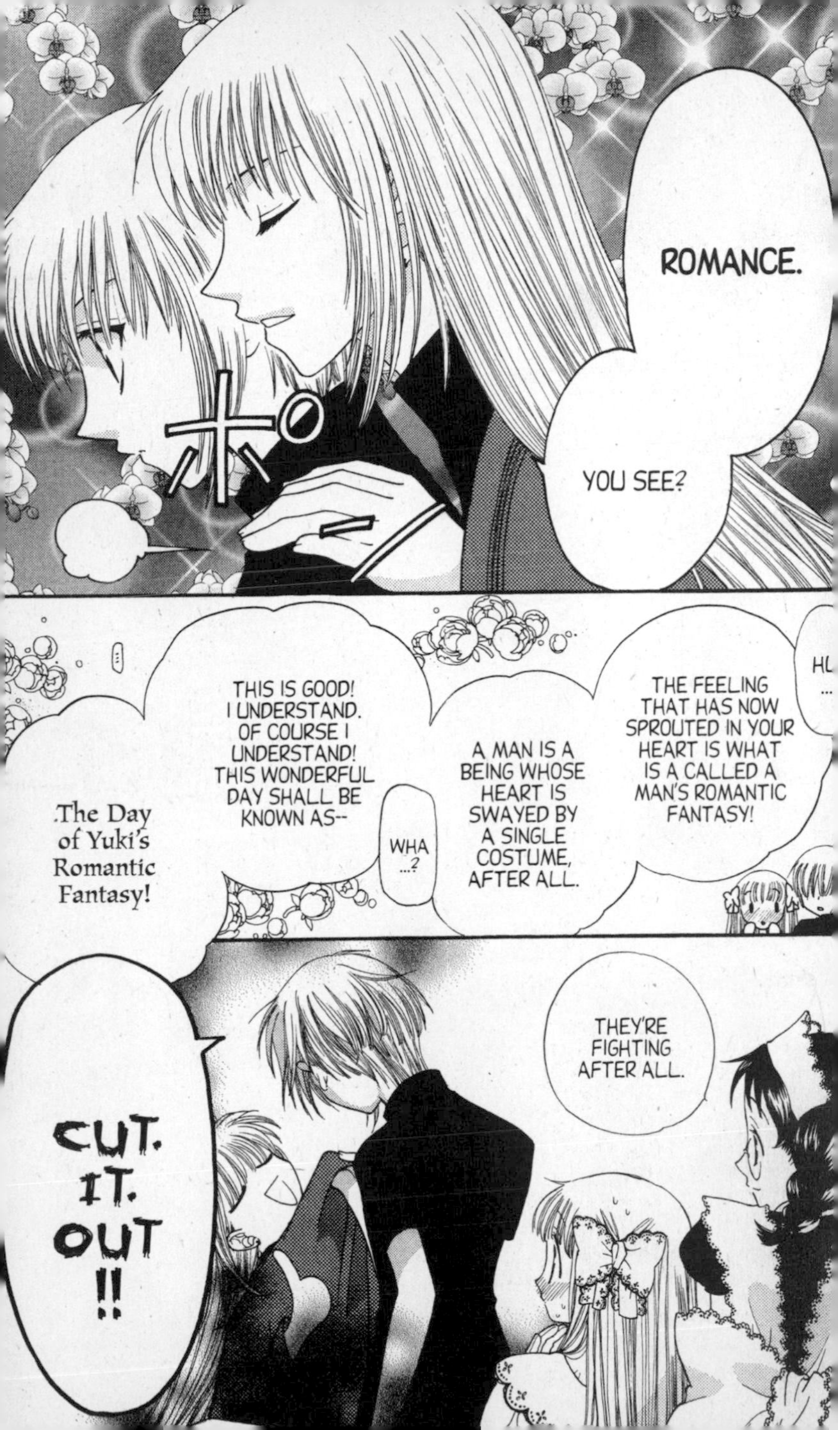

ROMANCE.
YOU SEE?
THE FEELING THAT HAS NOW SPROUTED IN YOUR HEART IS WHAT IS A CALLED A MAN'S ROMANTIC FANTASY!
A MAN IS A BEING WHOSE HEART IS SWAYED BY A SINGLE COSTUME, AFTER ALL.
WHA ...?
THIS IS GOOD! I UNDERSTAND. OF COURSE I UNDERSTAND! THIS WONDERFUL DAY SHALL BE KNOWN AS--
The Day of Yuki's Romantic Fantasy!
THEY'RE FIGHTING AFTER ALL.
CUT. IT. OUT!!

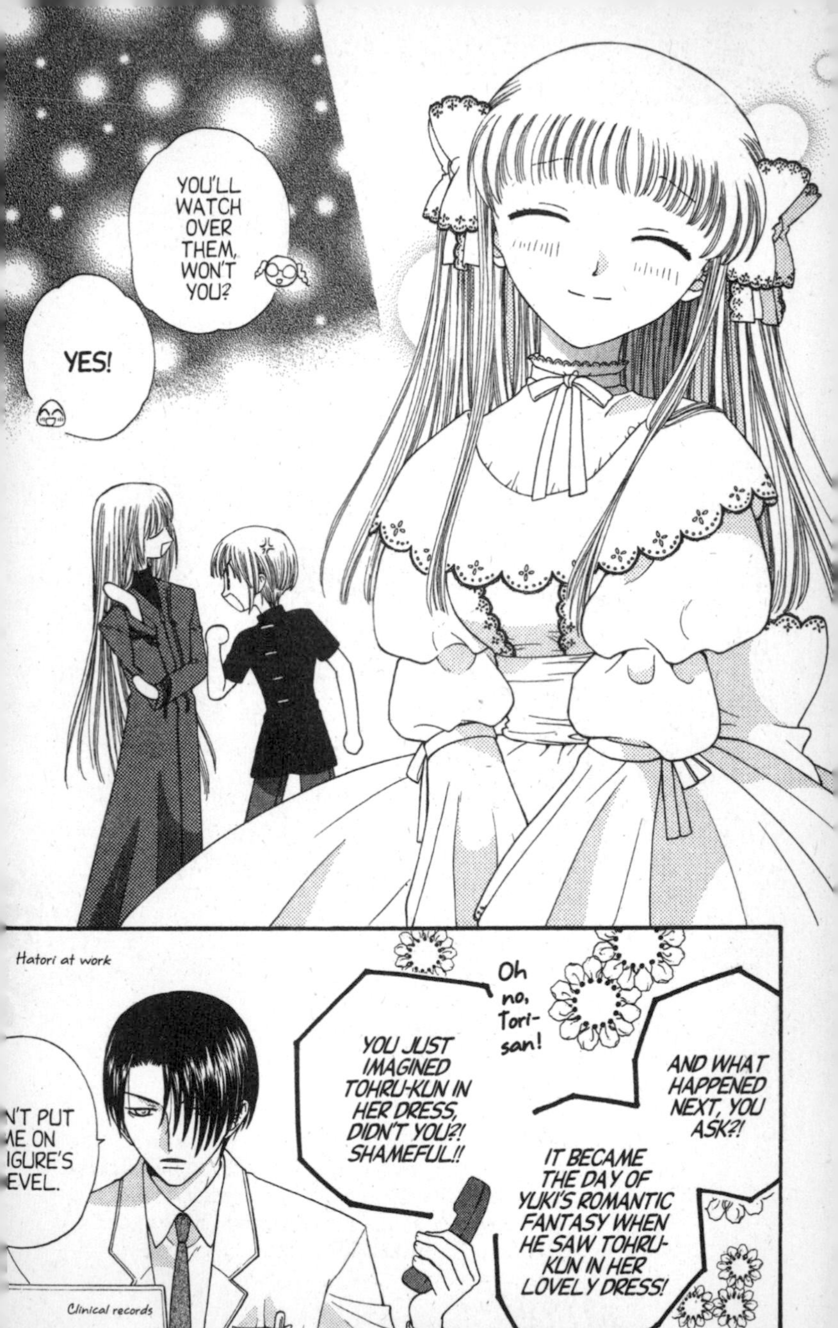
YOU'LL WATCH OVER THEM, WON'T YOU?
YES!
Hatori at work
AND WHAT HAPPENED NEXT, YOU ASK?!
IT BECAME THE DAY OF YUKI'S ROMANTIC FANTASY WHEN HE SAW TOHRU-KUN IN HER LOVELY DRESS!
Oh no, Tori-san!
YOU JUST IMAGINED TOHRU-KUN IN HER DRESS, DIDN'T YOU?! SHAMEFUL!!
N'T PUT ME ON IGURE'S EVEL.
Clinical records

To be continued in volume 7...

Next time in...

Fruits Basket
7
Natsuki Takaya
TOKYOPOP

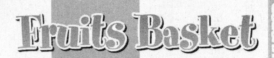

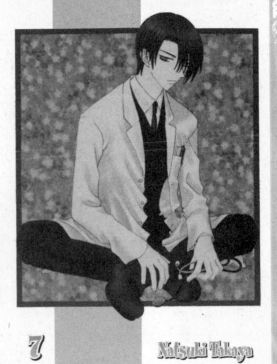

New kid on the block...

Tohru and company have been having a lot more fun ever since Kisa came to visit. Now it's time for Tohru to meet another member of the Zodiac--the skillfully sarcastic grade-school student, Hiro! One way or another, this tyke will have to deal with his resentment of Tohru and his affection for Kisa!

Fruits Basket Volume 7
Available Feburary 2005

Year of the Rabbit: Splitting Hares

Rabbit

Years*: 1939, 1951, 1963, 1975, 1987, 1999, 2011, 2023, 2035
Positive Qualities: sympathetic, affectionate, humble, creative, optimistic
Negative Qualities: too sentimental, avoids conflict
Suitable Jobs: Diplomat, Lawyer, College Professor, Actor
Compatible With: Sheep, Boar and Rat
Must Avoid: Rooster, Tiger and Horse
Ruling Hours: 5 AM to 7 AM
Season: Spring
Ruling Month: March
Sign Direction: East
Fixed Element: Wood
Corresponding Western Sign: Pisces

...n in the year of the Rabbit tend to be
...s and refined and carry themselves
... gentlemen. They are resourceful and
... sought out for their strong advice,
...tend to think quite unrealistically
... a hard time dealing with misfortune.

...abbits tend to be very serious people,
...love company. Among friends, they are
...siderate and caring, however when
...to their taste in men, women rabbits
...e more insecure, dating guys who
...hem with gifts.

...Rabbits:
...s
...rter
...ates
...Houston
...Jolie
...Gwire
...ers
...ny

The year of the Rabbit--a calm year where everyone is more leisurely than normal and where days go by at seemingly carefree pace. For anyone born in this year, luck will surely follow. However, like Momiji Sohma, Rabbits often have are seen to have a frail outward appearance because they are so gentle-natured, but deep within they are strong-minded and very idealistic.

Rabbits make great companions and their marriages are usually free of strife. Rabbits keep a mental record of both a person's good points and their mistakes, but they tend to be very forgiving as long as the mistakes do not have dire consequences. But even as Rabbits are good at offering support and advice, they find it difficult to accept advice or criticism from others. Their desire to avoid conflict can make them come off as overly sentimental or even superficial, making deep emotional connections difficult. But when it happens, the relationships they form are very strong.

...f you were born in January or early February, then chances are you are probably
... of the preceding year. The only way to know for certain is to know on which day
...ew Year's was held. Example: 1987 actually began on January 29, so anyone born
...anuary 1 and January 28 is actually a Tiger.

Fans Basket

Kylie B.
Age 12
Danbury, CT

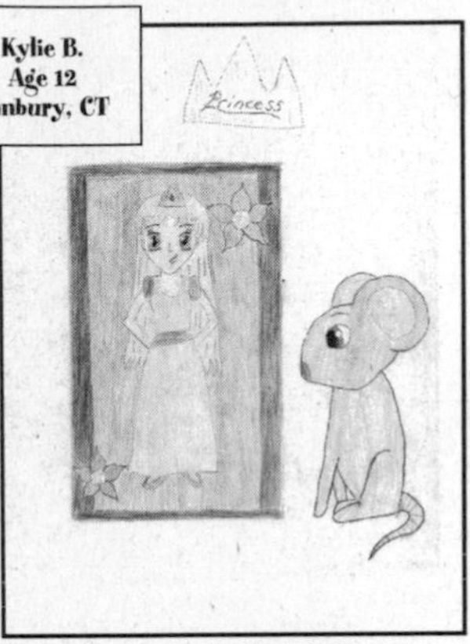
Princess

Princess Tohrua

Tohru Honda is like a princess
To Yuki and Kyo she is truly a bless

Shigure's house was a huge mess
But now it's clean thanks to the princess

Tohru has a terrible past
But like Momiji, she makes memories last

Kyo sometimes calls her stupid
But Arisa says he was hit by Cupid

Akito called her an ugly girl
His head must be in a whirl

For Tohru is pretty inside and out
For Momiji and me that fact is no doubt

Tohru has made family and friends
The Sohmas will stick with her to the end

What a lovely poem. And a matching picture, too!
Thanks so much!

LaDonna L.
AZ

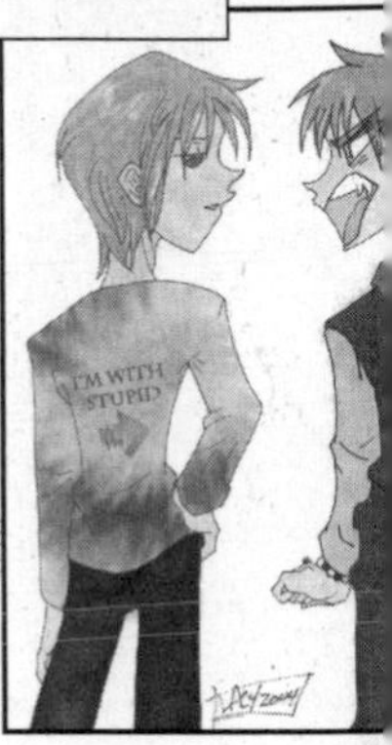
I'M WITH STUPID

This picture is a lot of fun. Lov
But I have a hard time imaginin
Tie-Dye...

KT SHY
Age 20
Ontario, Canada

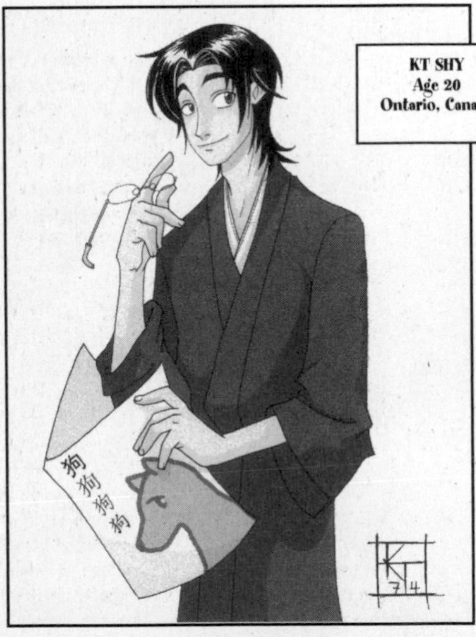
狗狗狗狗

Shigure has been Disneyfied! He's adorable! Thanks so much KT. (I loved your Peach Girl fan art, too!)

LaDonna L.
AZ

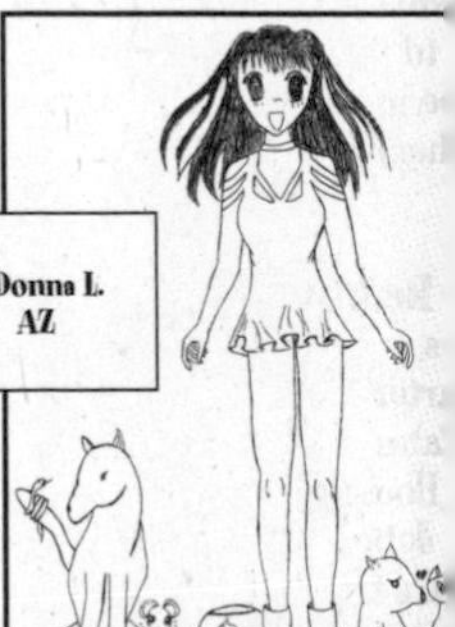

Tohru Honda had a farm, E-I
Thank goodness there isn't a year of th
wise the Sohma household would l

X

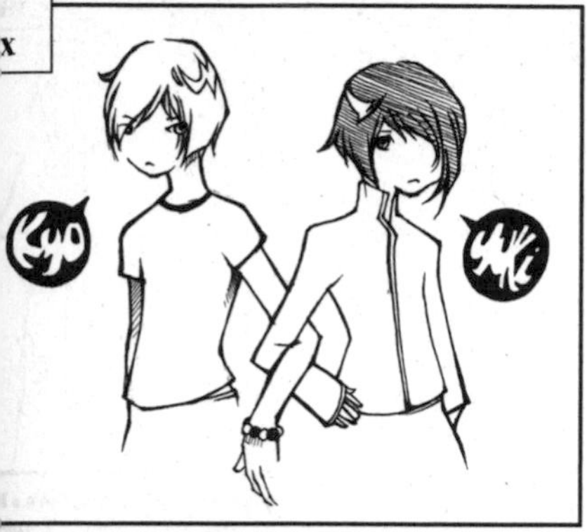
Kyo
Yuki

Yuki and Kyo linking arms?! I love it!
Your style is so unique. Thank you so much.

I.
NY

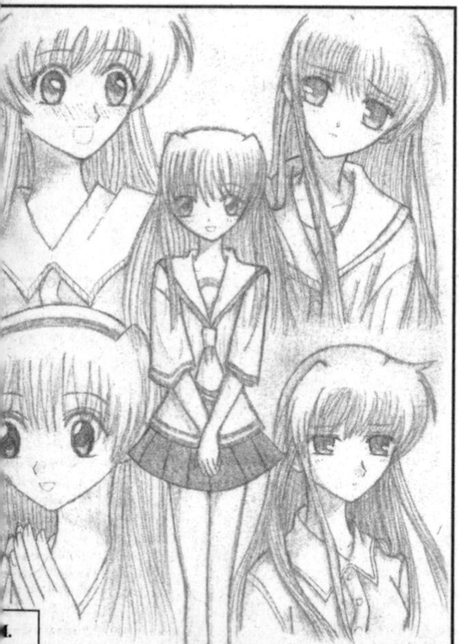

The many faces of Tohru Honda.
Your drawings are so expressive. Very cute! I like them all.

Christy S.
Age 27
Gainesville, FL

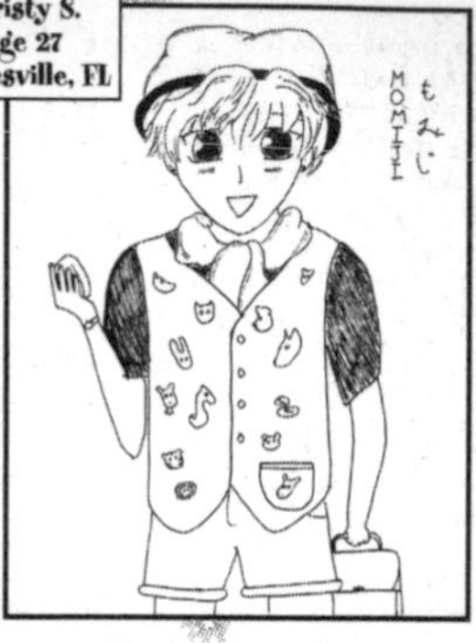
MOMIJI
もみじ

Momiji! Our cover boy.
Look at all those pins–the entire juunishi!
And an onigiri in his hand. Great idea!

"Sora"
Age 14
Sierra Vista, AZ

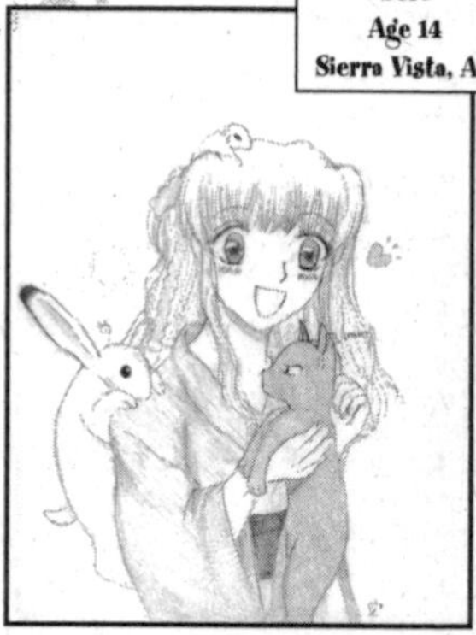

Tohru in a Yukata. And she's wearing Yuki's ribbon! I wonder if we'll get to see the onsen again?

Erin B.
Age 12
Oakdale, NY

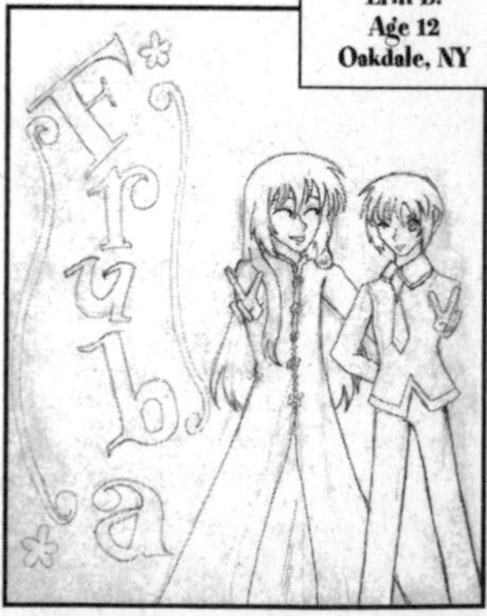
Fruba

The two brothers. They're finally getting closer!
Wasn't Ayame's shop great?

Do you want to share your love for *Fruits Basket* with fans around the world? "Fans Basket" is taking submissions of fan art, poetry, cosplay photos, or any other Furuba fun you'd like to share!

How to submit:

1) Send your work via regular mail (NOT e-mail) to:

"Fans Basket"
c/o TOKYOPOP
5900 Wilshire Blvd.
Suite 2000
Los Angeles, CA 90036

2) All work should be in black-and-white and no larger than 8.5" x 11". (And try not to fold it too many times!)

3) Anything you send will not be returned. If you want to keep your original, it's fine to send us a copy.

4) Please include your full name, age, city and state for us to print with your work. If you'd rather us use a pen name, please include that, too.

5) IMPORTANT: If you're under the age of 18, you must have your parent's permission in order for us to print your work. Any submissions without a signed note of parental consent cannot be used.

6) For full details, please check out our website: http://www.tokyopop.com/aboutus/fanart.php

Disclaimer: Anything you send to us becomes the exclusive property of TOKYOPOP Inc. and, as we said before, will not be returned to you. We will have the right to print, reproduce, distribute, or modify the artwork for use in future volumes of Fruits Basket or on the web royalty-free.

Courtney R.
Age 13
New Smyrna
Beach, FL

Yuki Sohma by way of Kaori Yuki!
What a great concept! And the chain on Kyo's collar...
Daisuki desu!

"
Wo

Shigure in cargo pants! Now that's a l
ably never see in the pages of Furub
Very cool.

Malie-chan
Age 16
Cimarron, KA

Not just a picture, but a fan fiction story, too!
Thanks for a wonderful read, Malie-chan. I'm sorry
we didn't have room to print your story, too.

Look at those snugs
Such a peaceful
I wonder what they're

Theodore W.
Age 16
Brooklyn, NY

Haru and his accessories. "W
exactly is the pendant on the
Theodore asks—"a blade or a
son?" Good question! Theo
also asks how Haru and Mo
can both be the same age if th
different Zodiac years. Well
truth is that the cursed Soh
weren't necessarily born on
same year as their Zodiac si
Just like Momiji and Haru ar
same age, the Mabudachi Tri
also the same age. I guess th
lucky 13 members are the o
people in the world immun
the character dictating qualit
their birthday year! Oh, and a
nice Hatsuharu pie, Theodo
Thanks for representing th
chromosome in this very g
month. Boy power!

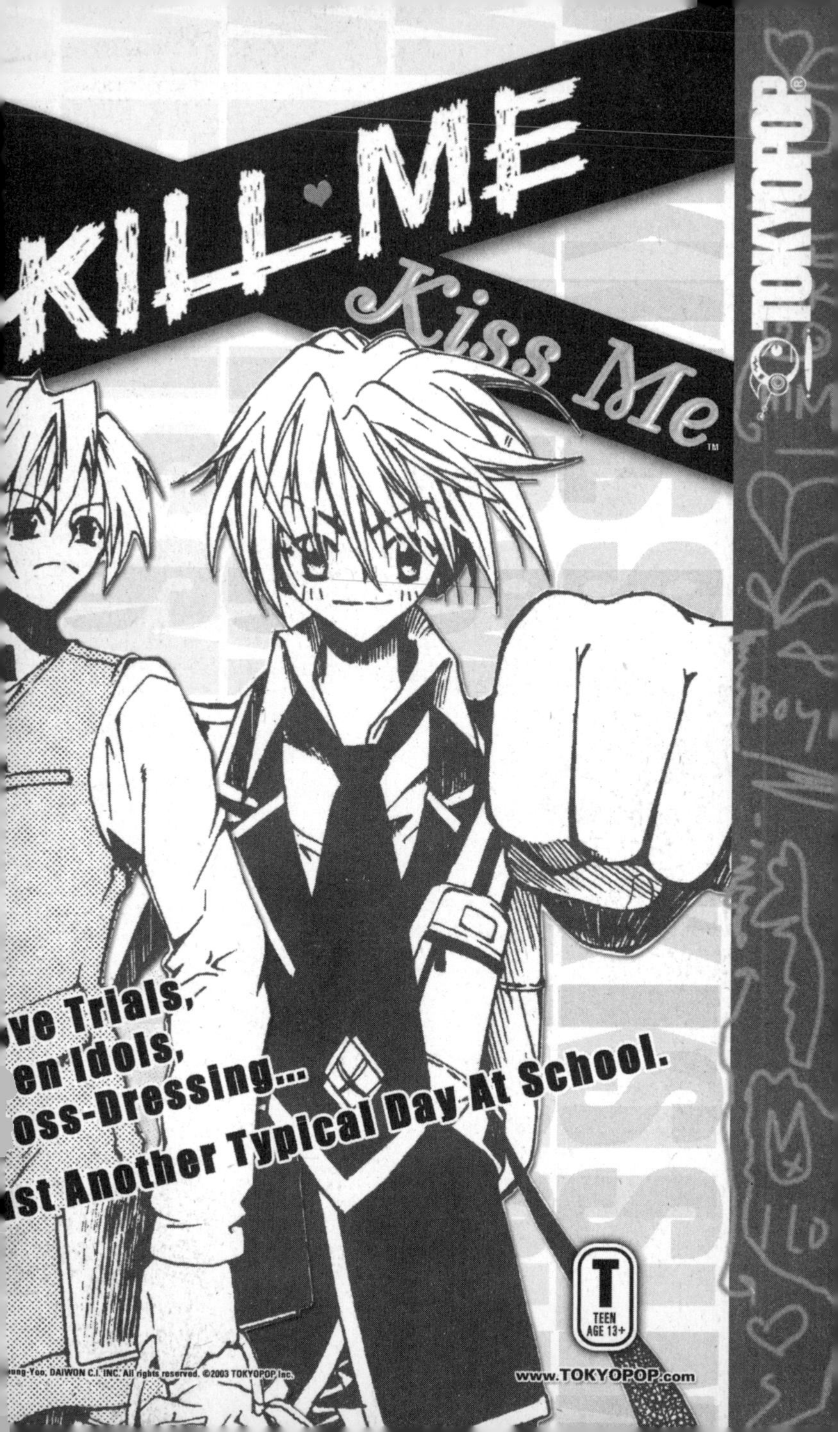
KILL ♥ ME
Kiss Me™
TOKYOPOP
ve Trials,
en Idols,
oss-Dressing...
st Another Typical Day At School.
T
TEEN
AGE 13+
ung-Yoo, DAIWON C.I. INC. All rights reserved. ©2003 TOKYOPOP Inc.
www.TOKYOPOP.com

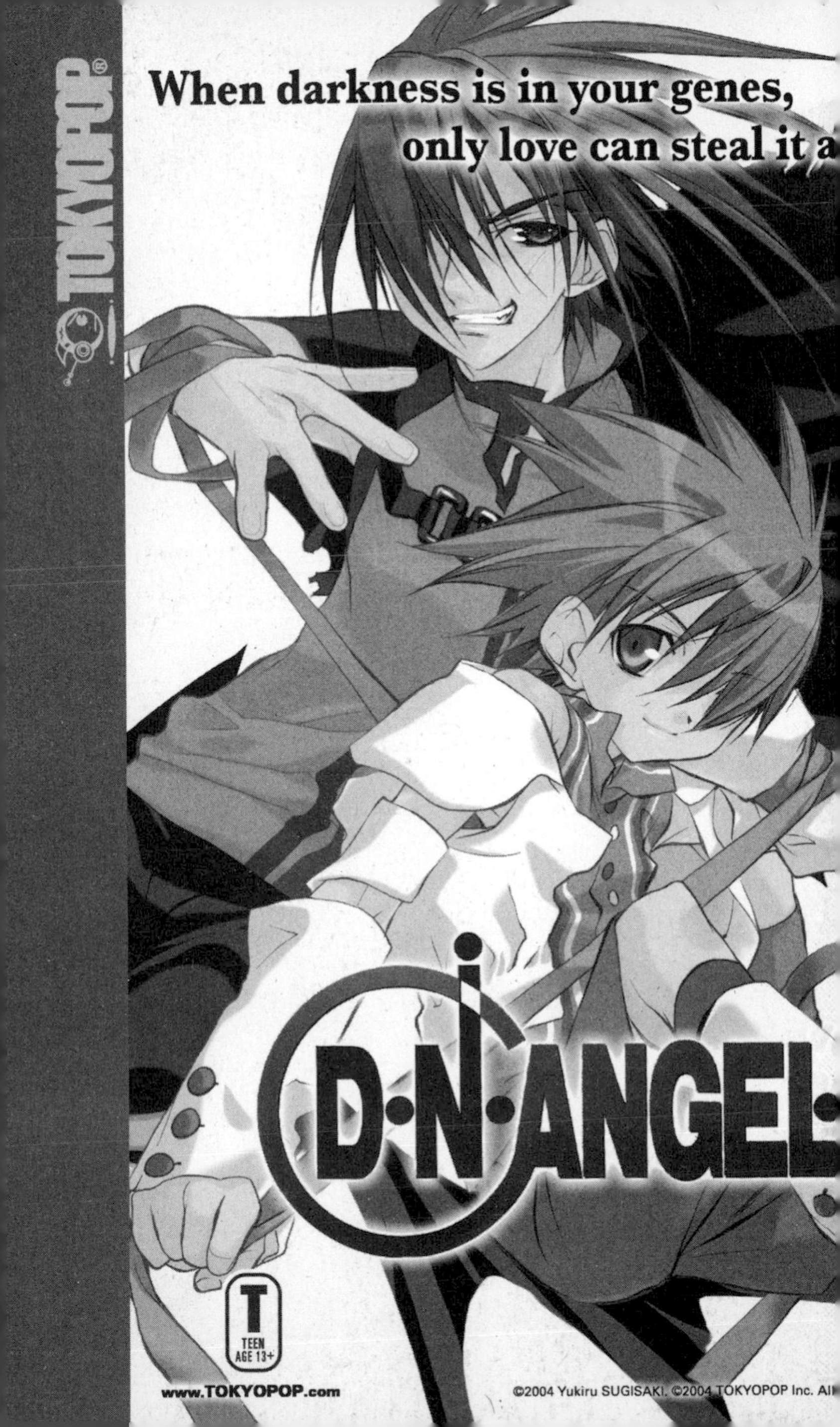
TOKYOPOP
When darkness is in your genes,
only love can steal it a
D·N·ANGEL
T TEEN AGE 13+
www.TOKYOPOP.com
©2004 Yukiru SUGISAKI. ©2004 TOKYOPOP Inc. All

AVAILABLE FROM TOKYOPOP.

ANIME GUIDES

COWBOY BEBOP
GUNDAM TECHNICAL MANUALS
SAILOR MOON SCOUT GUIDES

TOKYOPOP KIDS

STRAY SHEEP

CINE-MANGA™

ALADDIN
CARDCAPTORS
DUEL MASTERS
FAIRLY ODDPARENTS, THE
FAMILY GUY
FINDING NEMO
G.I. JOE SPY TROOPS
GREATEST STARS OF THE NBA: SHAQUILLE O'NEAL
GREATEST STARS OF THE NBA: TIM DUNCAN
JACKIE CHAN ADVENTURES
JIMMY NEUTRON: BOY GENIUS, THE ADVENTURES OF
KIM POSSIBLE
LILO & STITCH: THE SERIES
LIZZIE MCGUIRE
LIZZIE MCGUIRE MOVIE, THE
MALCOLM IN THE MIDDLE
POWER RANGERS: DINO THUNDER
POWER RANGERS: NINJA STORM
PRINCESS DIARIES 2
RAVE MASTER
SHREK 2
SIMPLE LIFE, THE
SPONGEBOB SQUAREPANTS
SPY KIDS 2
SPY KIDS 3-D: GAME OVER
TEENAGE MUTANT NINJA TURTLES
THAT'S SO RAVEN
TOTALLY SPIES
TRANSFORMERS: ARMADA
TRANSFORMERS: ENERGON

08.20.04T

MANGA

.HACK//LEGEND OF THE TWILIGHT
@LARGE
ABENOBASHI: MAGICAL SHOPPING ARCADE
A.I. LOVE YOU
AI YORI AOSHI
ALICHINO
ANGELIC LAYER
ARM OF KANNON
BABY BIRTH
BATTLE ROYALE
BATTLE VIXENS
BOYS BE...
BRAIN POWERED
BRIGADOON
B'TX
CANDIDATE FOR GODDESS, THE
CARDCAPTOR SAKURA
CARDCAPTOR SAKURA - MASTER OF THE CLOW
CHOBITS
CHRONICLES OF THE CURSED SWORD
CLAMP SCHOOL DETECTIVES
CLOVER
COMIC PARTY
CONFIDENTIAL CONFESSIONS
CORRECTOR YUI
COWBOY BEBOP
COWBOY BEBOP: SHOOTING STAR
CRAZY LOVE STORY
CRESCENT MOON
CROSS
CULDCEPT
CYBORG 009
D•N•ANGEL
DEARS
DEMON DIARY
DEMON ORORON, THE
DEUS VITAE
DIGIMON
DIGIMON TAMERS
DIGIMON ZERO TWO
DOLL
DRAGON HUNTER
DRAGON KNIGHTS
DRAGON VOICE
DREAM SAGA
DUKLYON: CLAMP SCHOOL DEFENDERS
EERIE QUEERIE!
ERICA SAKURAZAWA: COLLECTED WORKS
ET CETERA
ETERNITY
EVIL'S RETURN
FAERIES' LANDING
FAKE
FLCL
FLOWER OF THE DEEP SLEEP, THE
FORBIDDEN DANCE
FRUITS BASKET

G GUNDAM
GATEKEEPERS
GETBACKERS
GIRL GOT GAME
GRAVITATION
GTO
GUNDAM SEED ASTRAY
GUNDAM WING
GUNDAM WING: BATTLEFIELD OF PACIFISTS
GUNDAM WING: ENDLESS WALTZ
GUNDAM WING: THE LAST OUTPOST (G-UNIT)
HANDS OFF!
HAPPY MANIA
HARLEM BEAT
HYPER RUNE
I.N.V.U.
IMMORTAL RAIN
INITIAL D
INSTANT TEEN: JUST ADD NUTS
ISLAND
JING: KING OF BANDITS
JING: KING OF BANDITS - TWILIGHT TALES
JULINE
KARE KANO
KILL ME, KISS ME
KINDAICHI CASE FILES, THE
KING OF HELL
KODOCHA: SANA'S STAGE
LAMENT OF THE LAMB
LEGAL DRUG
LEGEND OF CHUN HYANG, THE
LES BIJOUX
LOVE HINA
LOVE OR MONEY
LUPIN III
LUPIN III: WORLD'S MOST WANTED
MAGIC KNIGHT RAYEARTH I
MAGIC KNIGHT RAYEARTH II
MAHOROMATIC: AUTOMATIC MAIDEN
MAN OF MANY FACES
MARMALADE BOY
MARS
MARS: HORSE WITH NO NAME
MINK
MIRACLE GIRLS
MIYUKI-CHAN IN WONDERLAND
MODEL
MOURYOU KIDEN: LEGEND OF THE NYMPHS
NECK AND NECK
ONE
ONE I LOVE, THE
PARADISE KISS
PARASYTE
PASSION FRUIT
PEACH GIRL
PEACH GIRL: CHANGE OF HEART
PET SHOP OF HORRORS
PITA-TEN
PLANET LADDER

STOP!

This is the back of the book.
wouldn't want to spoil a great ending!

ok is printed "manga-style," in the authentic Japanese right-to-left
Since none of the artwork has been flipped or altered, readers
xperience the story just as the creator intended. You've been
for it, so TOKYOPOP® delivered: authentic, hot-off-the-press,
more fun!

DIRECTIONS

If this is your first time
reading manga-style, here's a
quick guide to help you
understand how it works.

It's easy... just start in the top
right panel and follow the
numbers. Have fun, and look for
more 100% authentic manga
from TOKYOPOP®!